SCREWED

PROJECT FRANKENSTEIN

zenescope
WWW.ZENESCOPE.COM
FACEBOOK.COM/ZENESCOPE

SCREWED
PROJECT FRANKENSTEIN

CREATOR
TYLER KIRKHAM

STORY
TYLER KIRKHAM
KEITH THOMAS

WRITER
KEITH THOMAS

ARTWORK
DAVID MILLER

COLORS
ORACLE

LETTERS
JIM CAMPBELL

ART DIRECTOR
ANTHONY SPAY

TRADE DESIGN
STEPHEN SCHAFFER
CHRISTOPHER COTE

EDITOR
PAT SHAND

THIS VOLUME REPRINTS
THE COMIC SERIES SCREWED #1-6
PUBLISHED BY ZENESCOPE
ENTERTAINMENT.

WWW.ZENESCOPE.COM

FIRST EDITION, JANUARY 2014
ISBN: 978-1-939683-47-2

zenescope
WWW.ZENESCOPE.COM
FACEBOOK.COM/ZENESCOPE

ZENESCOPE ENTERTAINMENT, INC.
Joe Brusha • President & Chief Creative Officer
Ralph Tedesco • Editor-in-Chief
Jennifer Bermel • Director of Licensing & Business Development
Raven Gregory • Executive Editor
Anthony Spay • Art Director
Christopher Cote • Senior Designer & Production Manager
Dave Franchini • Direct Market Sales & Customer Service

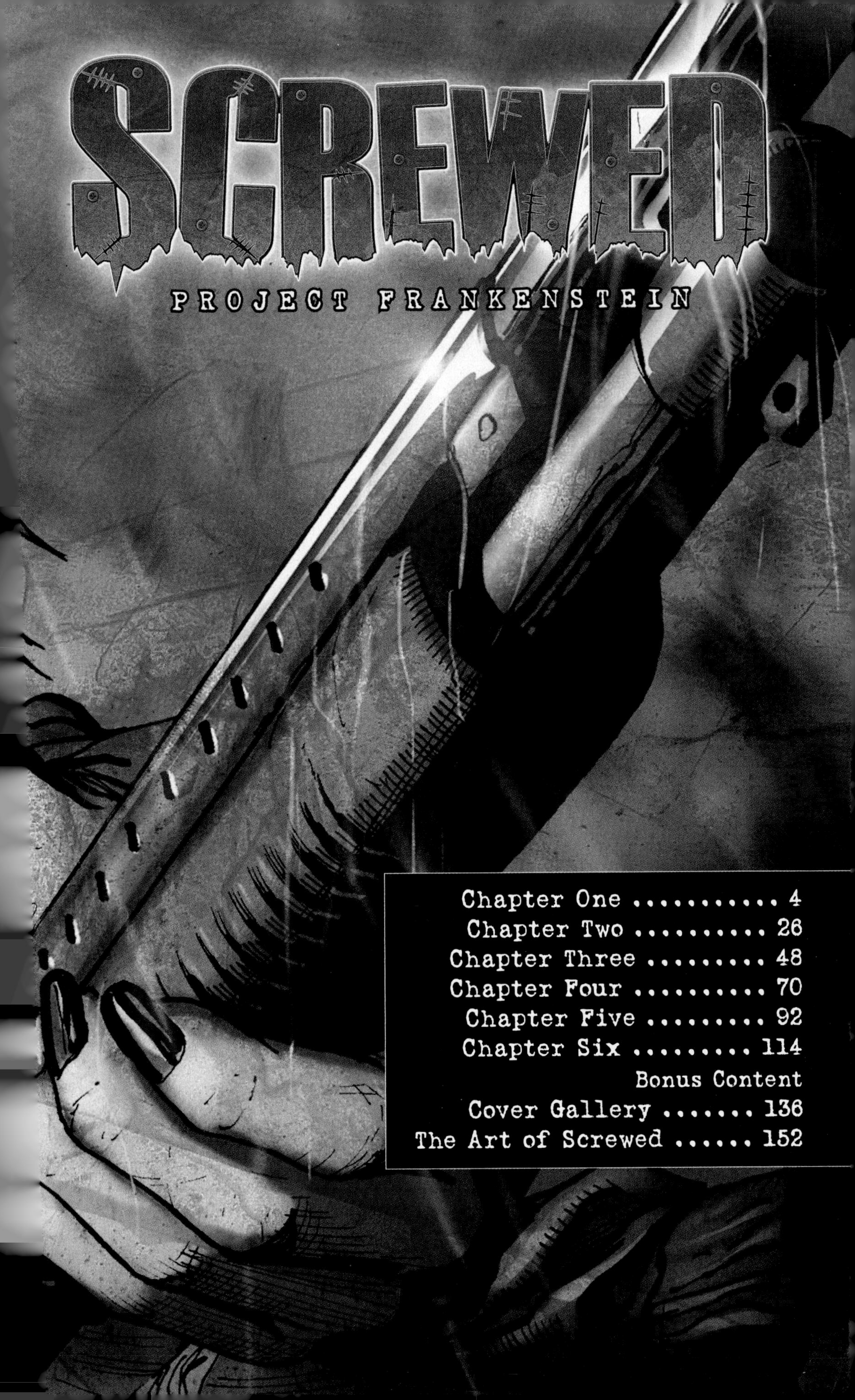

SCREWED

PROJECT FRANKENSTEIN

CHAPTER ONE

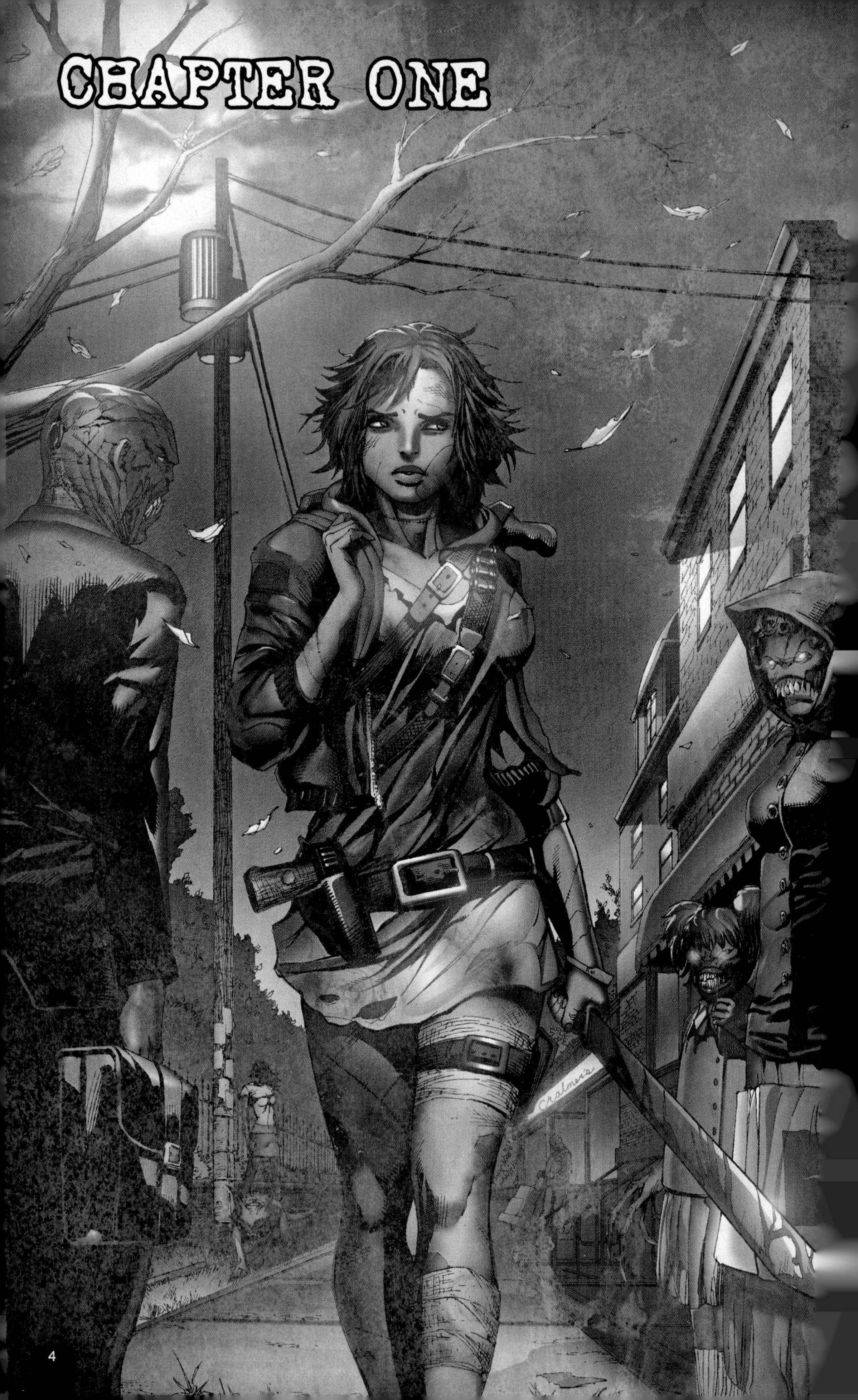
Chalmers

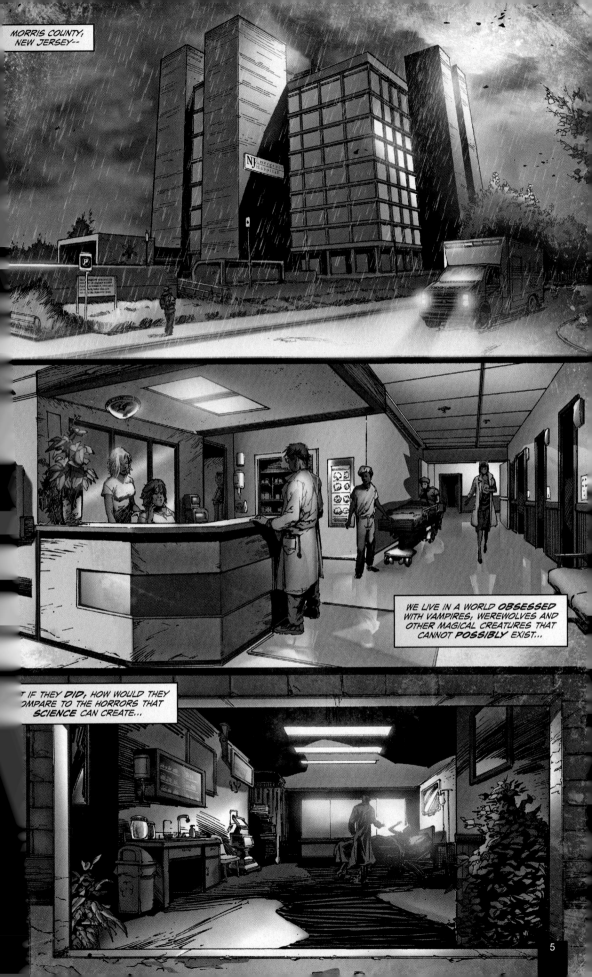

MORRIS COUNTY, NEW JERSEY--

WE LIVE IN A WORLD *OBSESSED* WITH VAMPIRES, WEREWOLVES AND OTHER MAGICAL CREATURES THAT CANNOT *POSSIBLY* EXIST...

T IF THEY *DID*, HOW WOULD THEY OMPARE TO THE HORRORS THAT *SCIENCE* CAN CREATE...

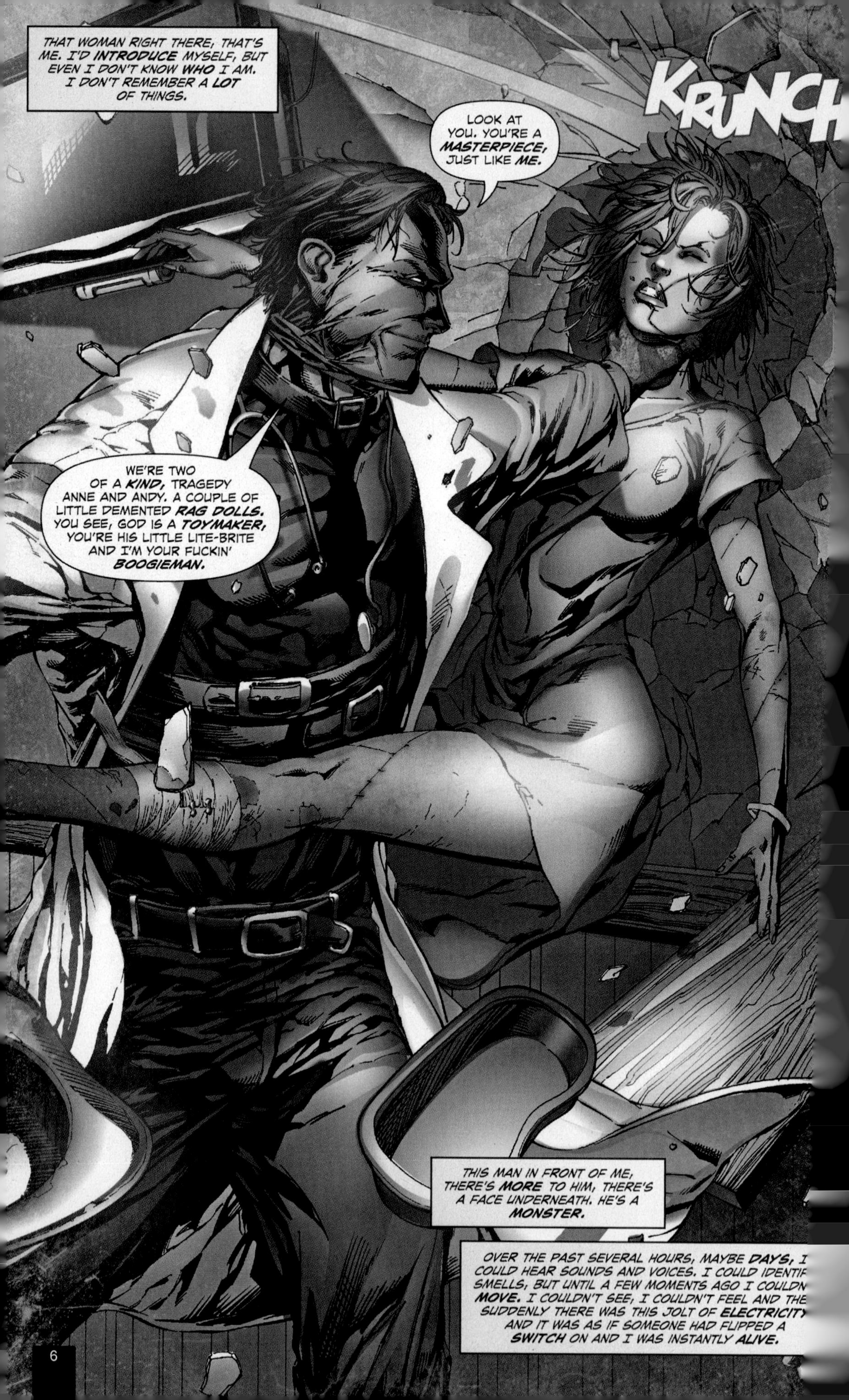
THAT WOMAN RIGHT THERE; THAT'S ME. I'D INTRODUCE MYSELF, BUT EVEN I DON'T KNOW WHO I AM. I DON'T REMEMBER A LOT OF THINGS.
KRUNCH
LOOK AT YOU. YOU'RE A MASTERPIECE; JUST LIKE ME.
WE'RE TWO OF A KIND, TRAGEDY ANNE AND ANDY. A COUPLE OF LITTLE DEMENTED RAG DOLLS. YOU SEE, GOD IS A TOYMAKER, YOU'RE HIS LITTLE LITE-BRITE AND I'M YOUR FUCKIN' BOOGIEMAN.
THIS MAN IN FRONT OF ME; THERE'S MORE TO HIM, THERE'S A FACE UNDERNEATH. HE'S A MONSTER.
OVER THE PAST SEVERAL HOURS, MAYBE DAYS, I COULD HEAR SOUNDS AND VOICES. I COULD IDENTIF SMELLS, BUT UNTIL A FEW MOMENTS AGO I COULDN MOVE. I COULDN'T SEE, I COULDN'T FEEL AND THE SUDDENLY THERE WAS THIS JOLT OF ELECTRICITY AND IT WAS AS IF SOMEONE HAD FLIPPED A SWITCH ON AND I WAS INSTANTLY ALIVE.

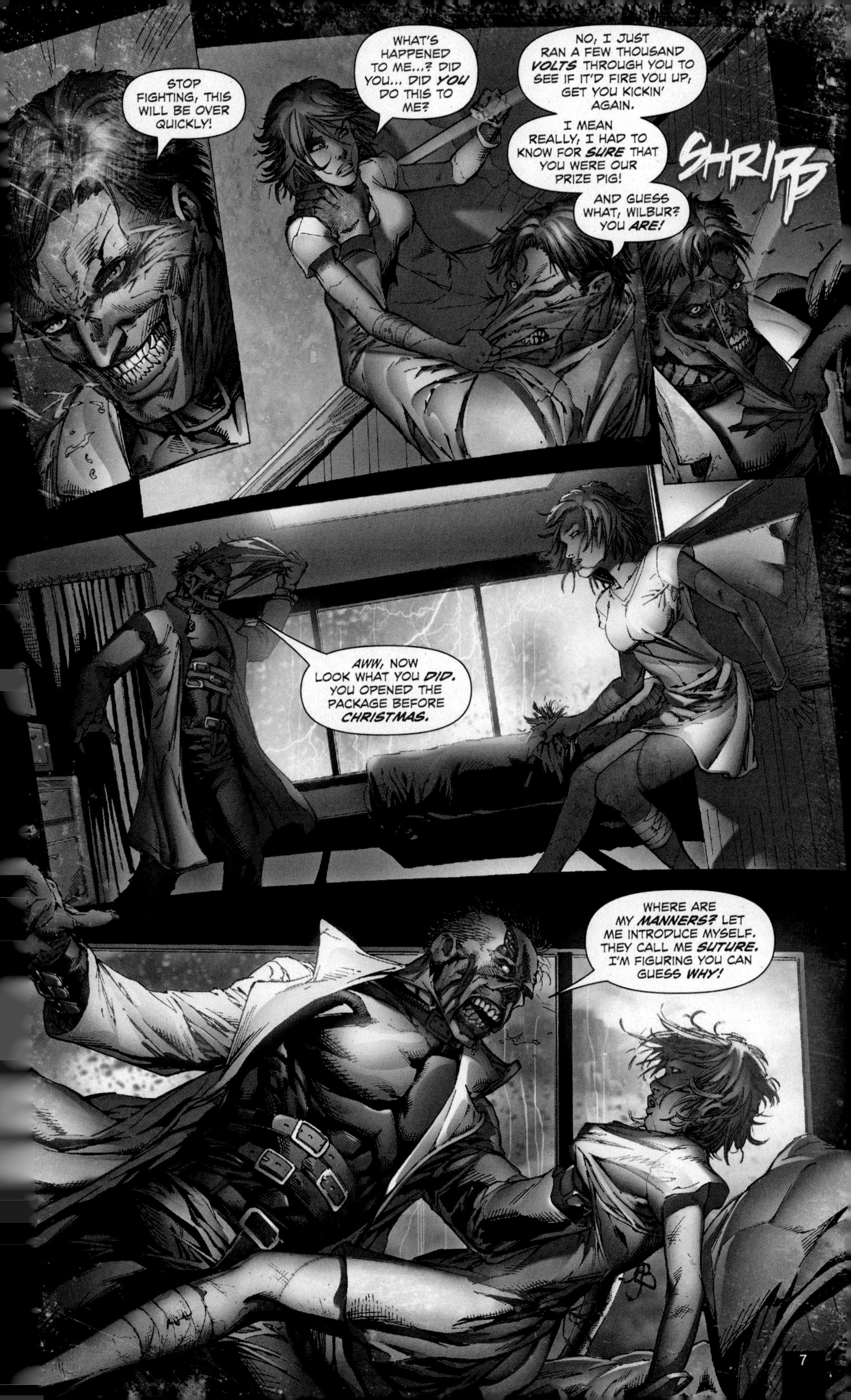
STOP FIGHTING, THIS WILL BE OVER QUICKLY!
WHAT'S HAPPENED TO ME...? DID YOU... DID YOU DO THIS TO ME?
NO, I JUST RAN A FEW THOUSAND VOLTS THROUGH YOU TO SEE IF IT'D FIRE YOU UP, GET YOU KICKIN' AGAIN.
I MEAN REALLY, I HAD TO KNOW FOR SURE THAT YOU WERE OUR PRIZE PIG!
AND GUESS WHAT, WILBUR? YOU ARE!
SHRIPP
AWW, NOW LOOK WHAT YOU DID. YOU OPENED THE PACKAGE BEFORE CHRISTMAS.
WHERE ARE MY MANNERS? LET ME INTRODUCE MYSELF. THEY CALL ME SUTURE. I'M FIGURING YOU CAN GUESS WHY!

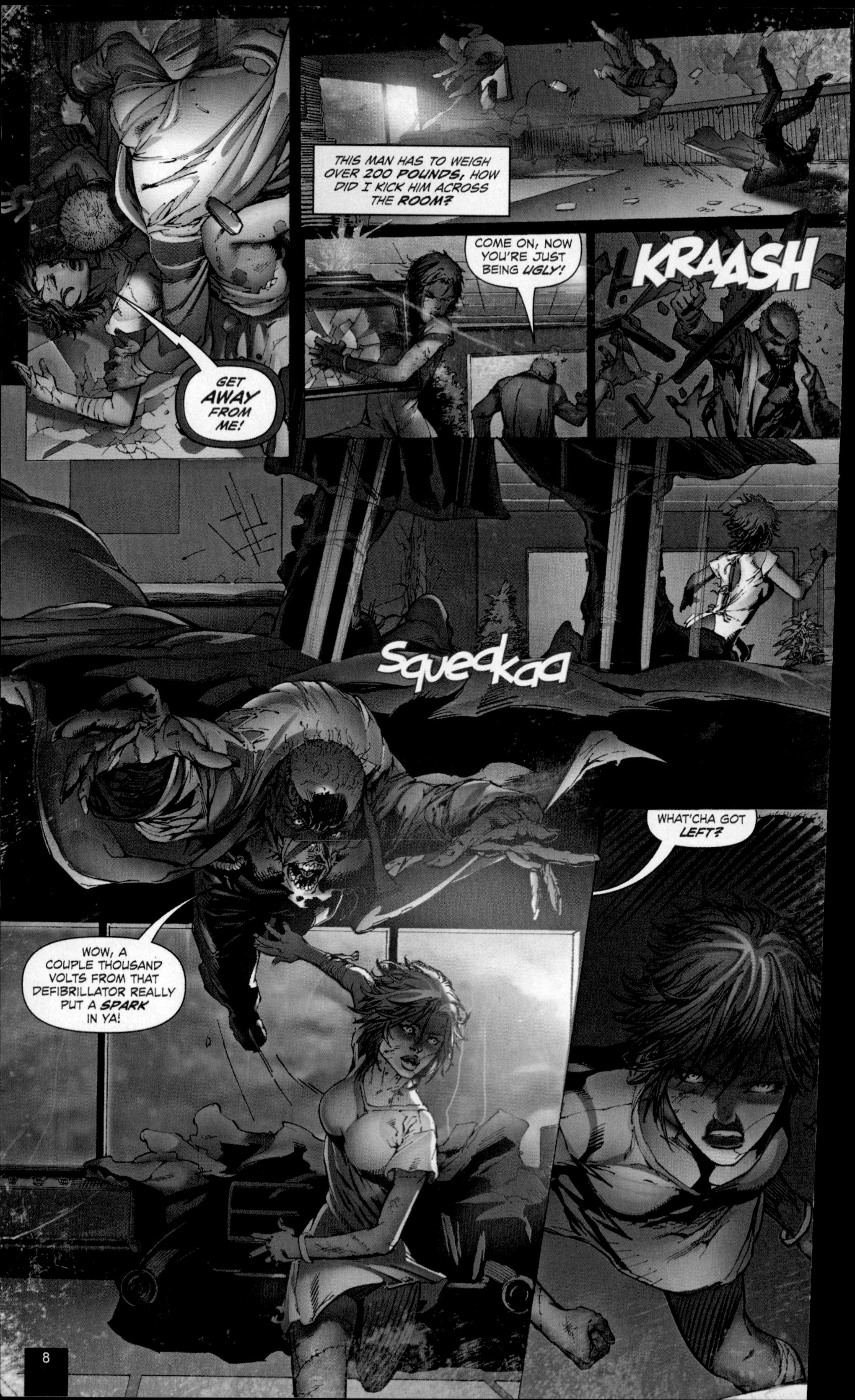

THIS MAN HAS TO WEIGH OVER 200 POUNDS, HOW DID I KICK HIM ACROSS THE ROOM?
GET AWAY FROM ME!
COME ON, NOW YOU'RE JUST BEING UGLY!
KRAASH
SQUEAKAA
WHAT'CHA GOT LEFT?
WOW, A COUPLE THOUSAND VOLTS FROM THAT DEFIBRILLATOR REALLY PUT A SPARK IN YA!

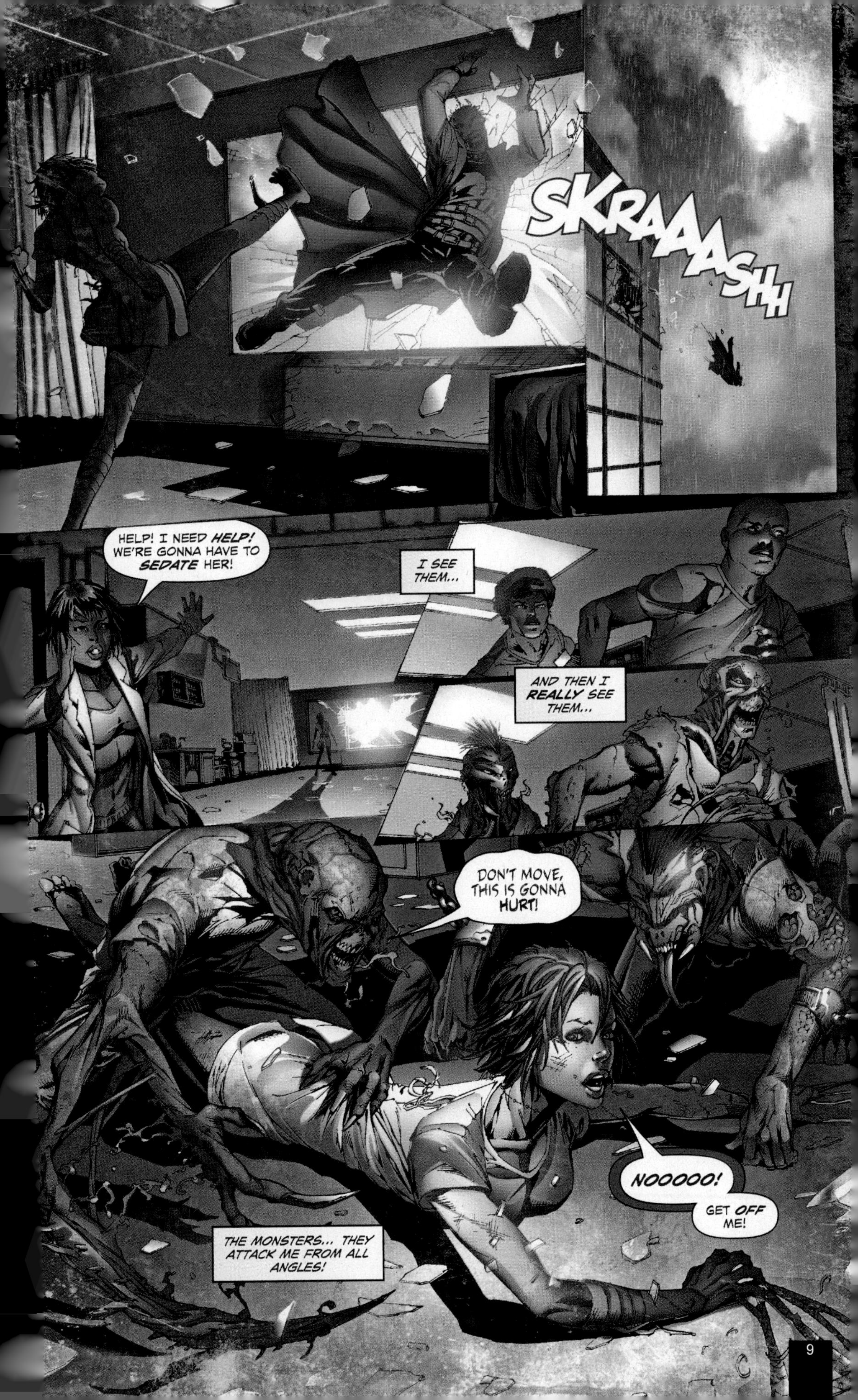
SKRAAAASHH
HELP! I NEED HELP! WE'RE GONNA HAVE TO SEDATE HER!
I SEE THEM...
AND THEN I REALLY SEE THEM...
DON'T MOVE, THIS IS GONNA HURT!
THE MONSTERS... THEY ATTACK ME FROM ALL ANGLES!
NOOOOO!
GET OFF ME!

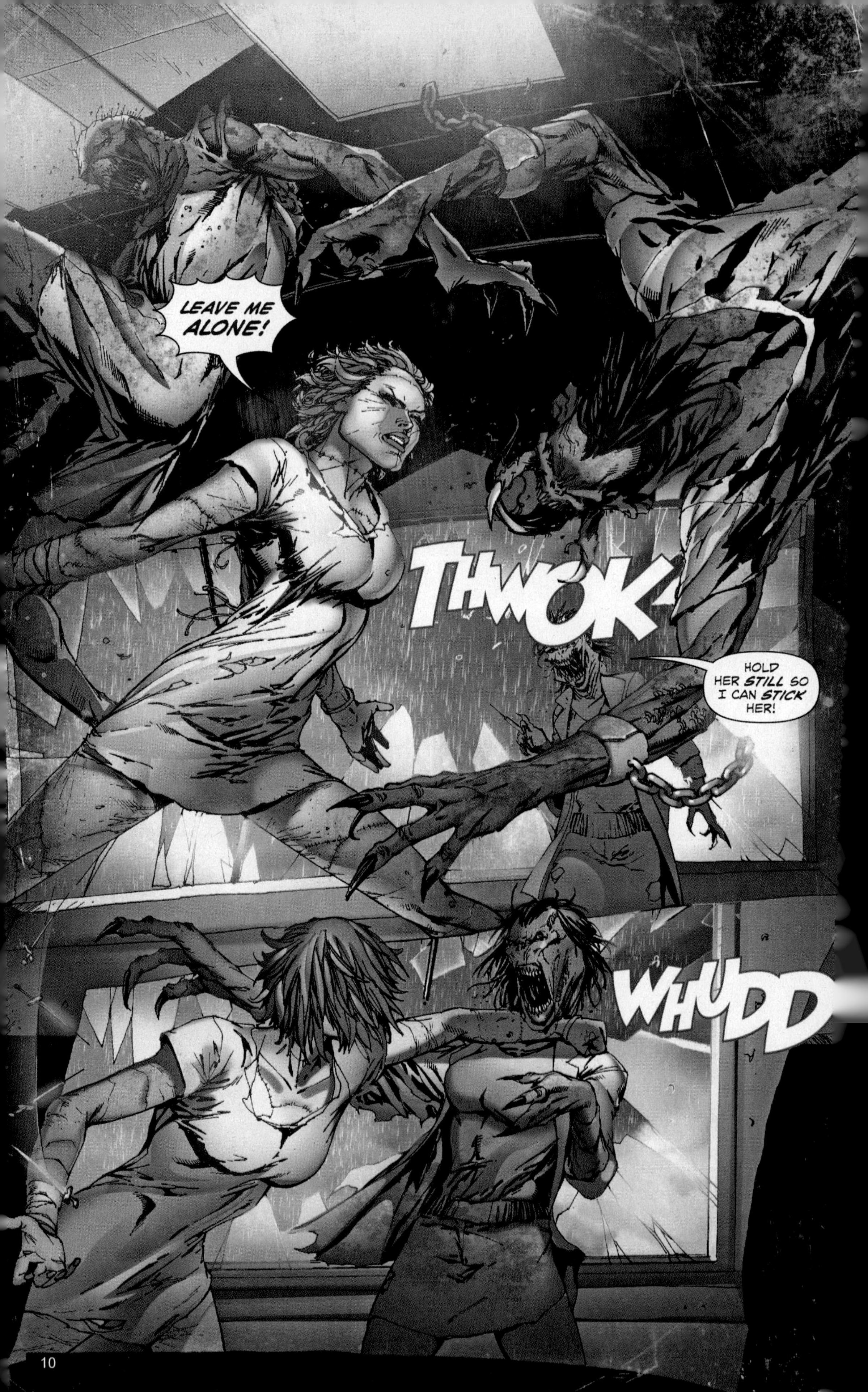
LEAVE ME ALONE!
THWOK
HOLD HER STILL SO I CAN STICK HER!
WHUDD

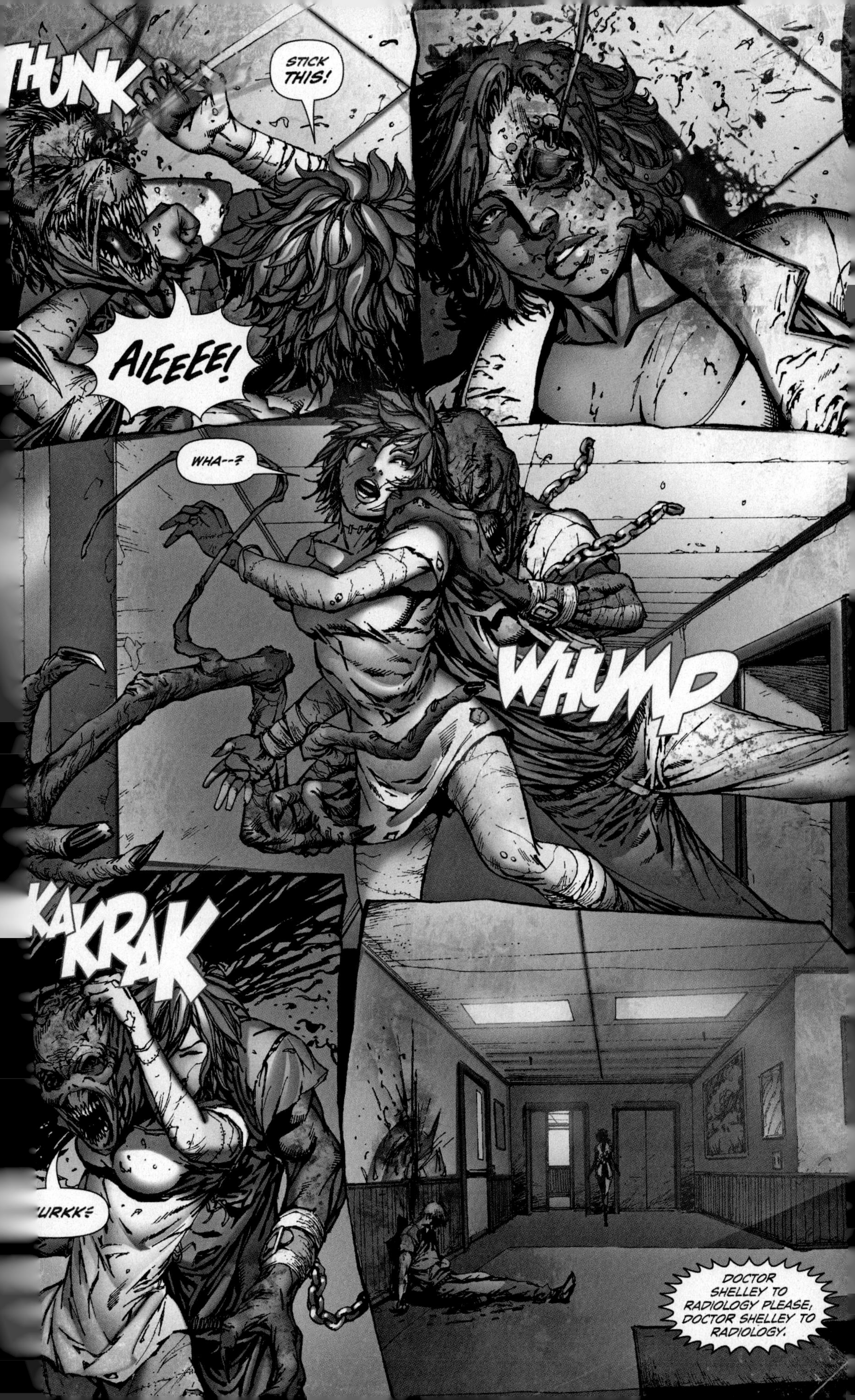
THUNK
STICK THIS!
AIEEEEE!
WHA--?
WHUMP
KAKRAK
URKK
DOCTOR SHELLEY TO RADIOLOGY PLEASE, DOCTOR SHELLEY TO RADIOLOGY.

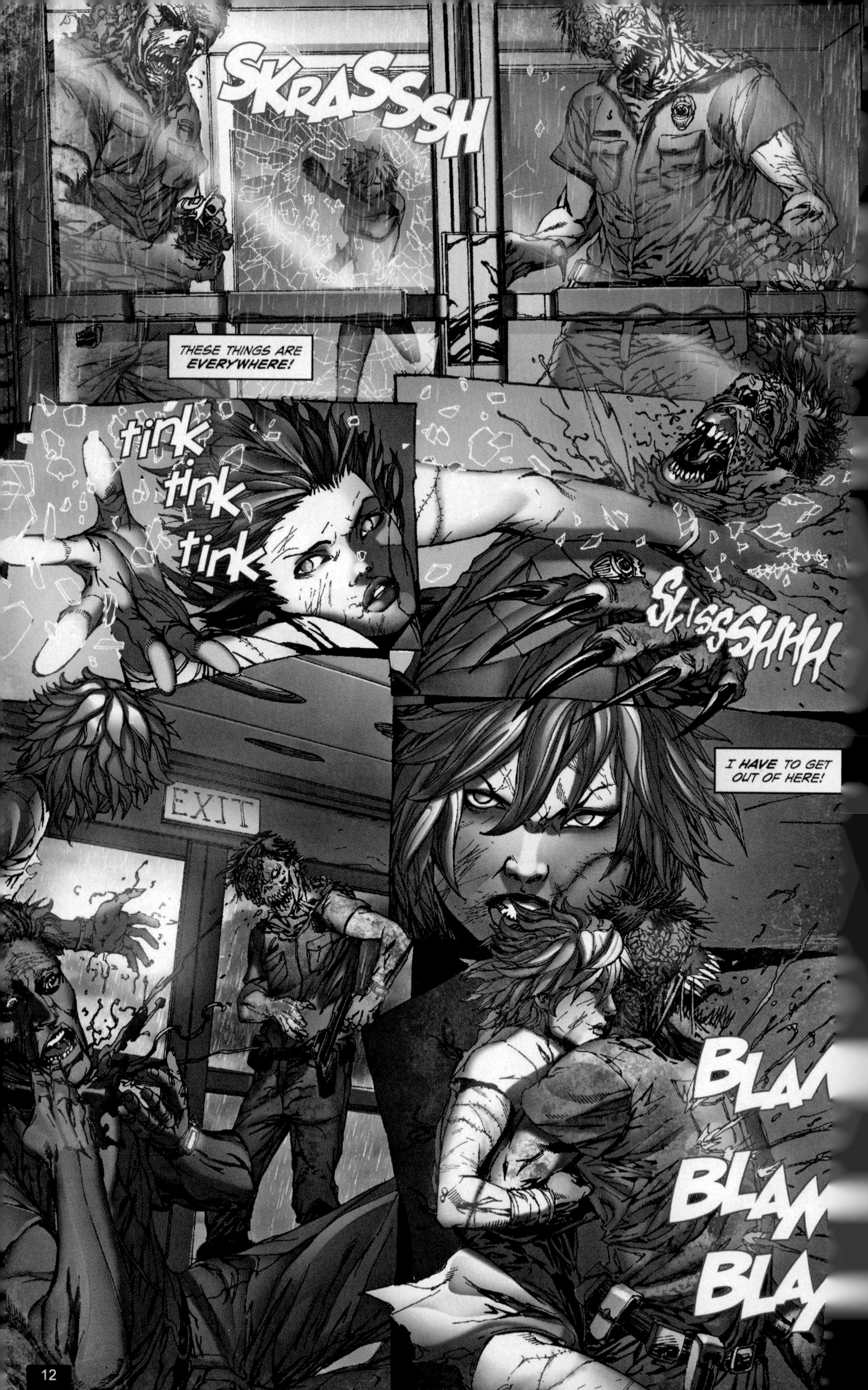
SKRASSSH
THESE THINGS ARE EVERYWHERE!
tink tink tink
SLISSSHHH
I HAVE TO GET OUT OF HERE!
BLAM
BLAM
BLAM

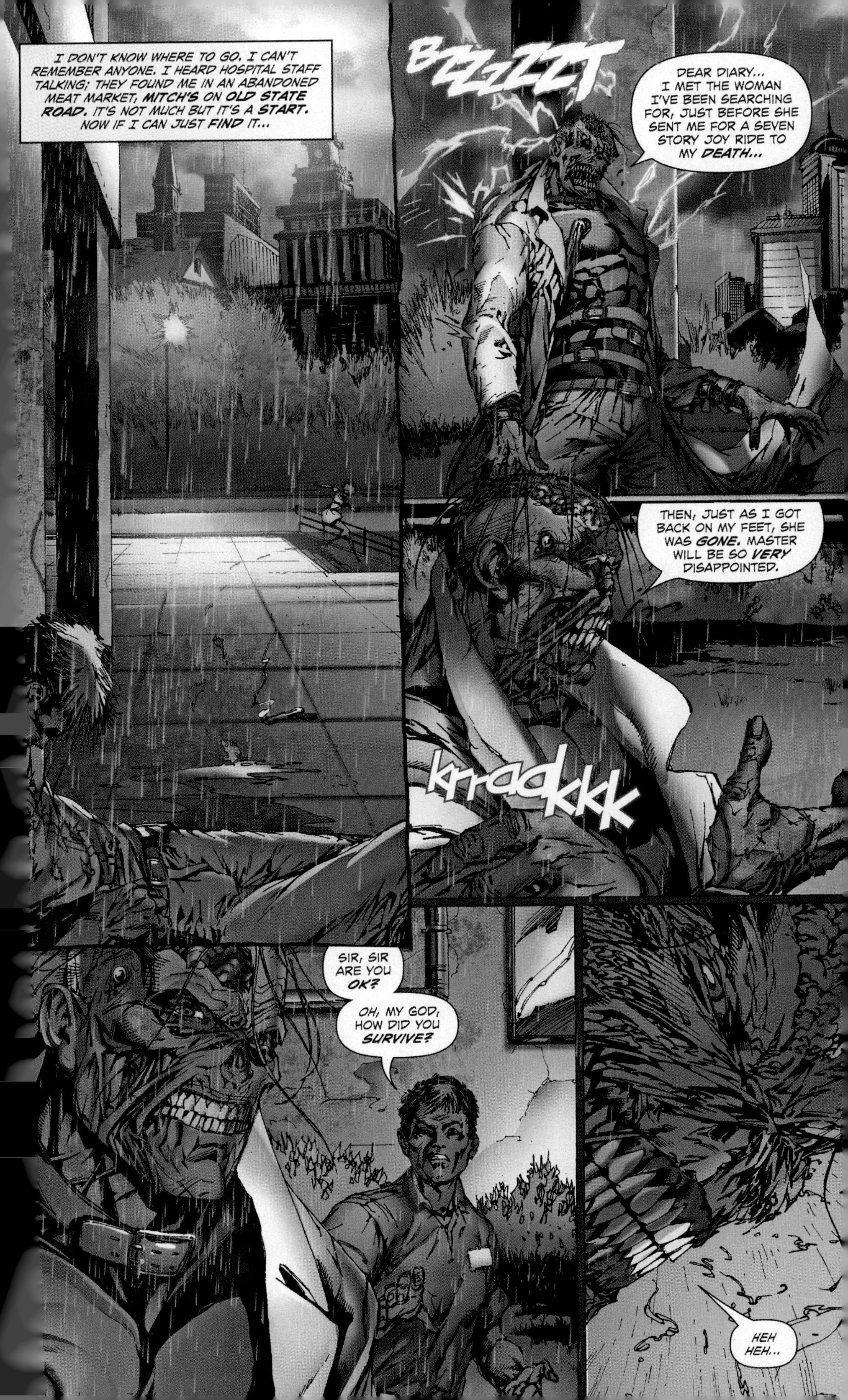

I DON'T KNOW WHERE TO GO. I CAN'T REMEMBER ANYONE. I HEARD HOSPITAL STAFF TALKING; THEY FOUND ME IN AN ABANDONED MEAT MARKET, MITCH'S ON OLD STATE ROAD. IT'S NOT MUCH BUT IT'S A START. NOW IF I CAN JUST FIND IT...
BZZZZZT
DEAR DIARY... I MET THE WOMAN I'VE BEEN SEARCHING FOR, JUST BEFORE SHE SENT ME FOR A SEVEN STORY JOY RIDE TO MY DEATH...
THEN, JUST AS I GOT BACK ON MY FEET, SHE WAS GONE. MASTER WILL BE SO VERY DISAPPOINTED.
krrackkk
SIR, SIR ARE YOU OK?
OH, MY GOD, HOW DID YOU SURVIVE?
HEH HEH...

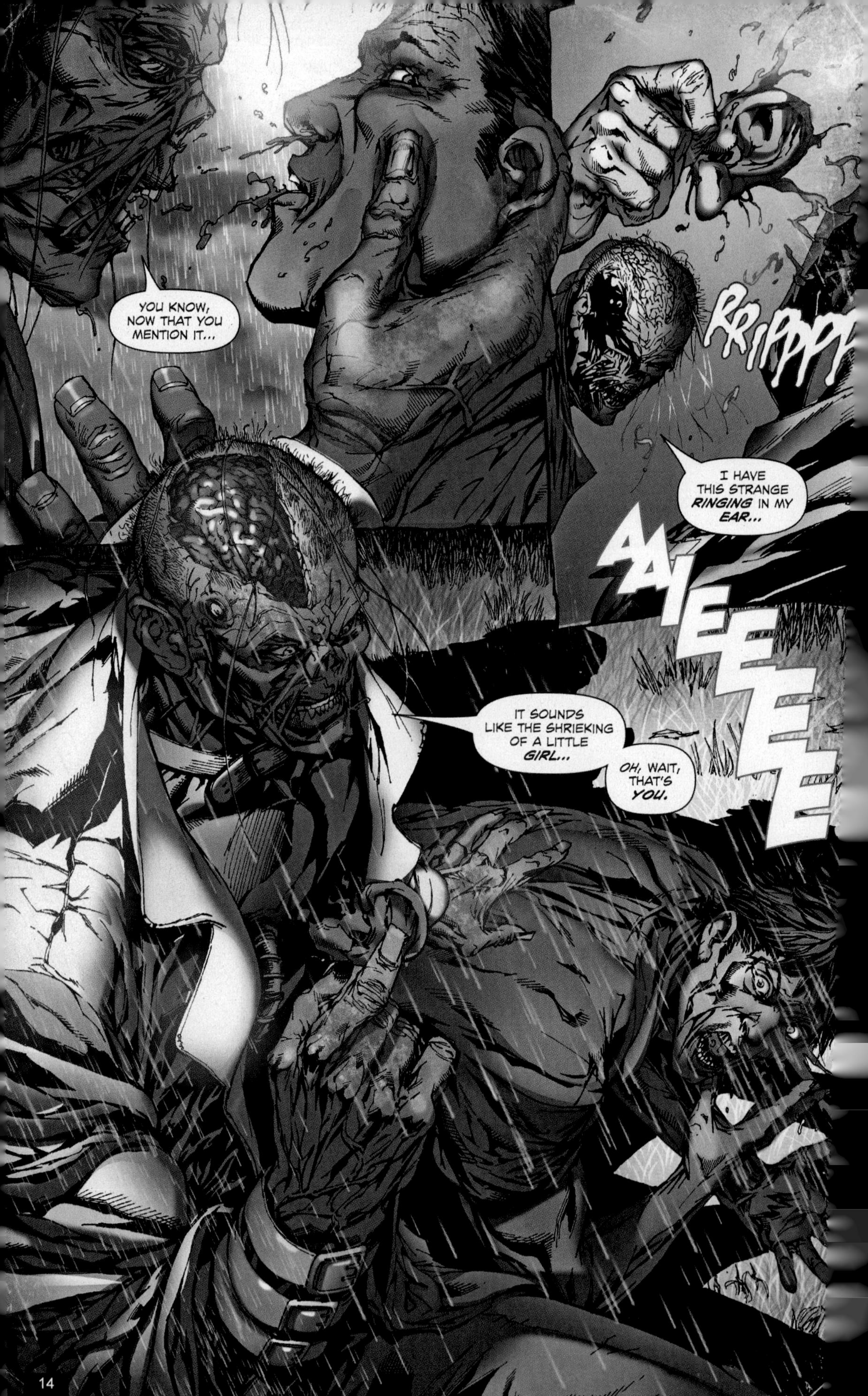
YOU KNOW, NOW THAT YOU MENTION IT...
RRIPPP
I HAVE THIS STRANGE *RINGING* IN MY *EAR*...
AAIEEEEE
IT SOUNDS LIKE THE SHRIEKING OF A LITTLE *GIRL*...
OH, WAIT, THAT'S *YOU*.

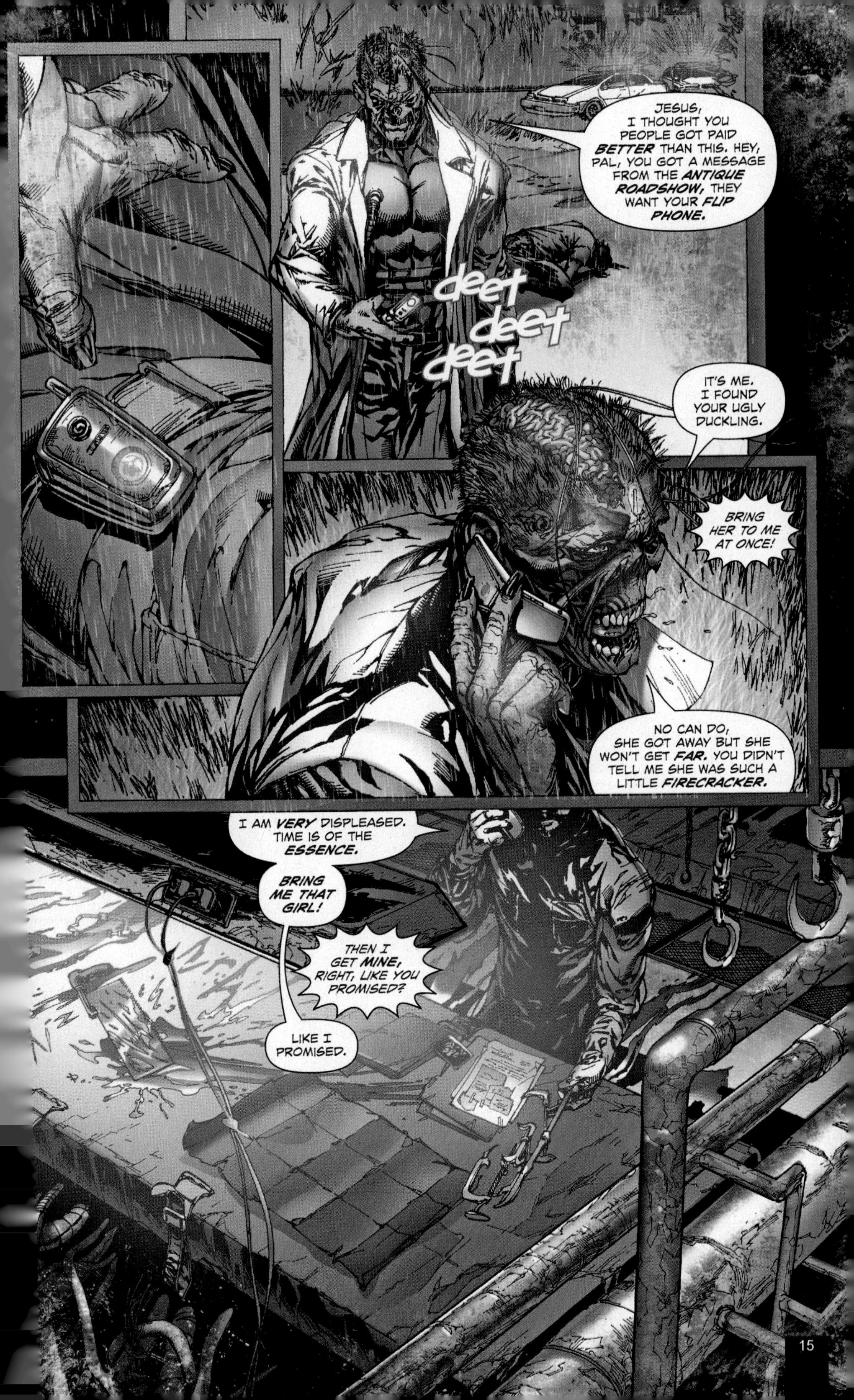
JESUS, I THOUGHT YOU PEOPLE GOT PAID BETTER THAN THIS. HEY, PAL, YOU GOT A MESSAGE FROM THE ANTIQUE ROADSHOW, THEY WANT YOUR FLIP PHONE.
deet deet deet
IT'S ME. I FOUND YOUR UGLY DUCKLING.
BRING HER TO ME AT ONCE!
NO CAN DO, SHE GOT AWAY BUT SHE WON'T GET FAR. YOU DIDN'T TELL ME SHE WAS SUCH A LITTLE FIRECRACKER.
I AM VERY DISPLEASED. TIME IS OF THE ESSENCE.
BRING ME THAT GIRL!
THEN I GET MINE, RIGHT, LIKE YOU PROMISED?
LIKE I PROMISED.

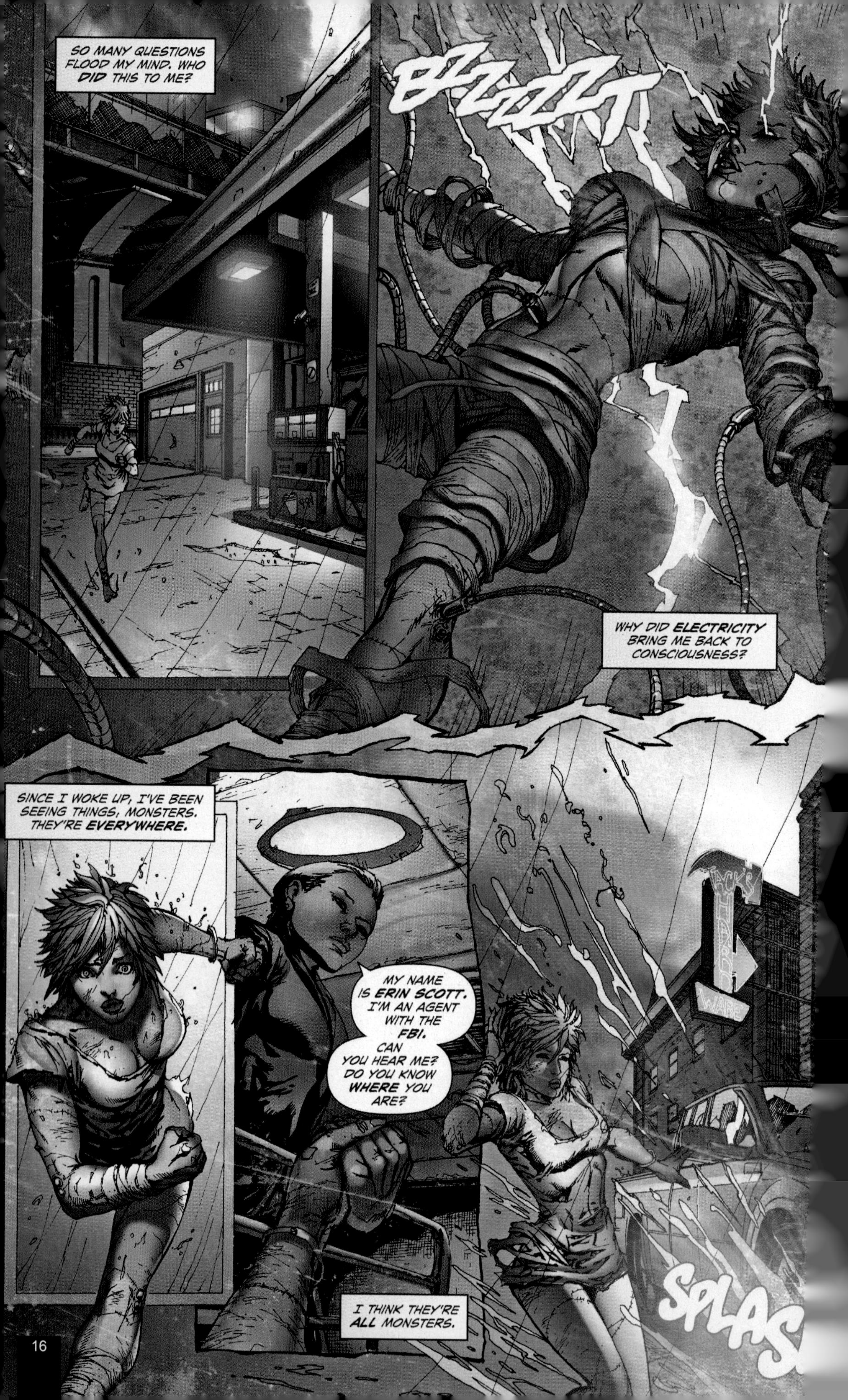

SO MANY QUESTIONS FLOOD MY MIND. WHO DID THIS TO ME?
BZZZZT!
WHY DID ELECTRICITY BRING ME BACK TO CONSCIOUSNESS?
SINCE I WOKE UP, I'VE BEEN SEEING THINGS; MONSTERS. THEY'RE EVERYWHERE.
MY NAME IS ERIN SCOTT. I'M AN AGENT WITH THE FBI. CAN YOU HEAR ME? DO YOU KNOW WHERE YOU ARE?
I THINK THEY'RE ALL MONSTERS.
SPLAS

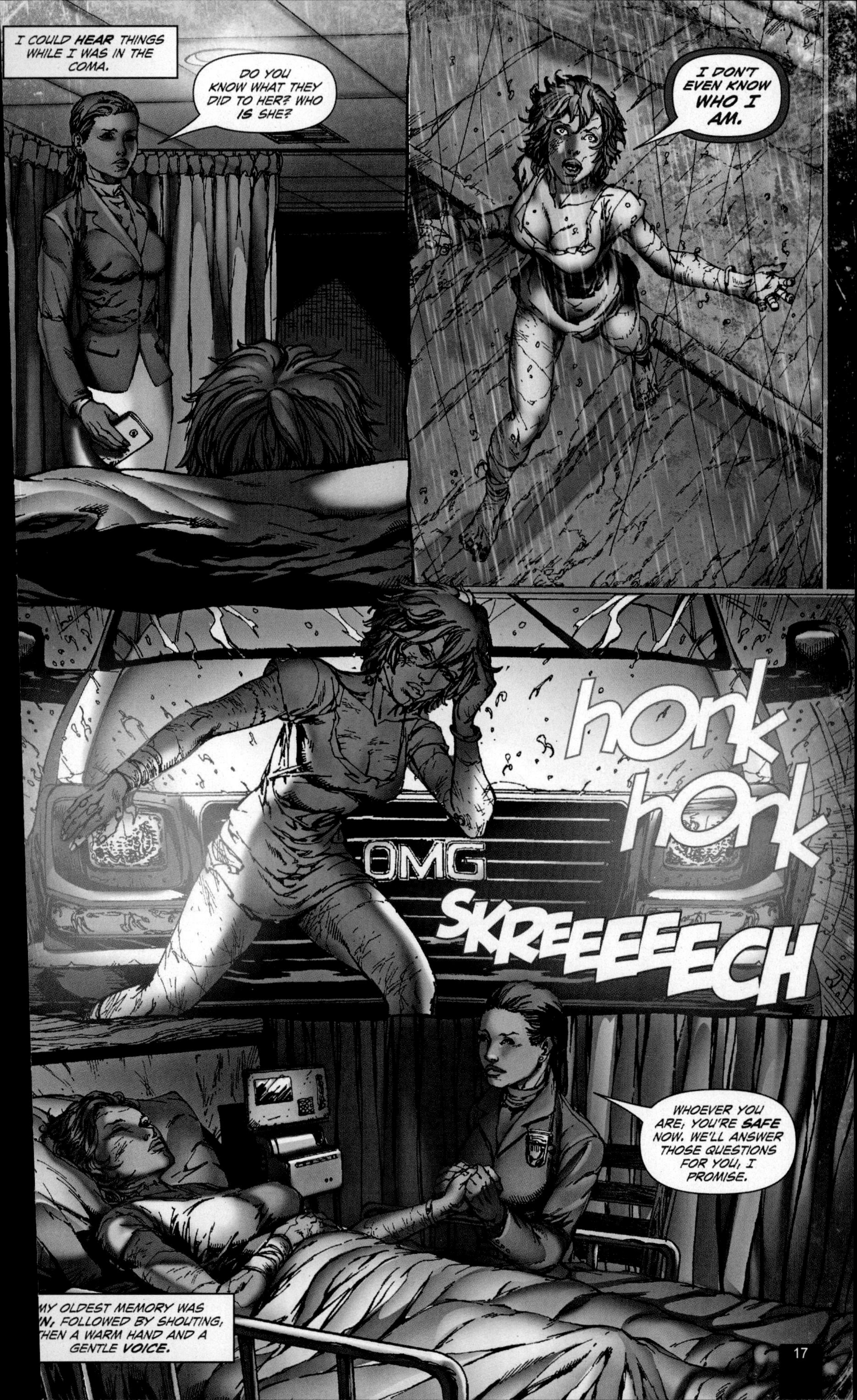
I COULD HEAR THINGS WHILE I WAS IN THE COMA.
DO YOU KNOW WHAT THEY DID TO HER? WHO IS SHE?
I DON'T EVEN KNOW WHO I AM.
honk honk
OMG
SKREEEEEECH
WHOEVER YOU ARE, YOU'RE SAFE NOW. WE'LL ANSWER THOSE QUESTIONS FOR YOU, I PROMISE.
MY OLDEST MEMORY WAS N, FOLLOWED BY SHOUTING, THEN A WARM HAND AND A GENTLE VOICE.

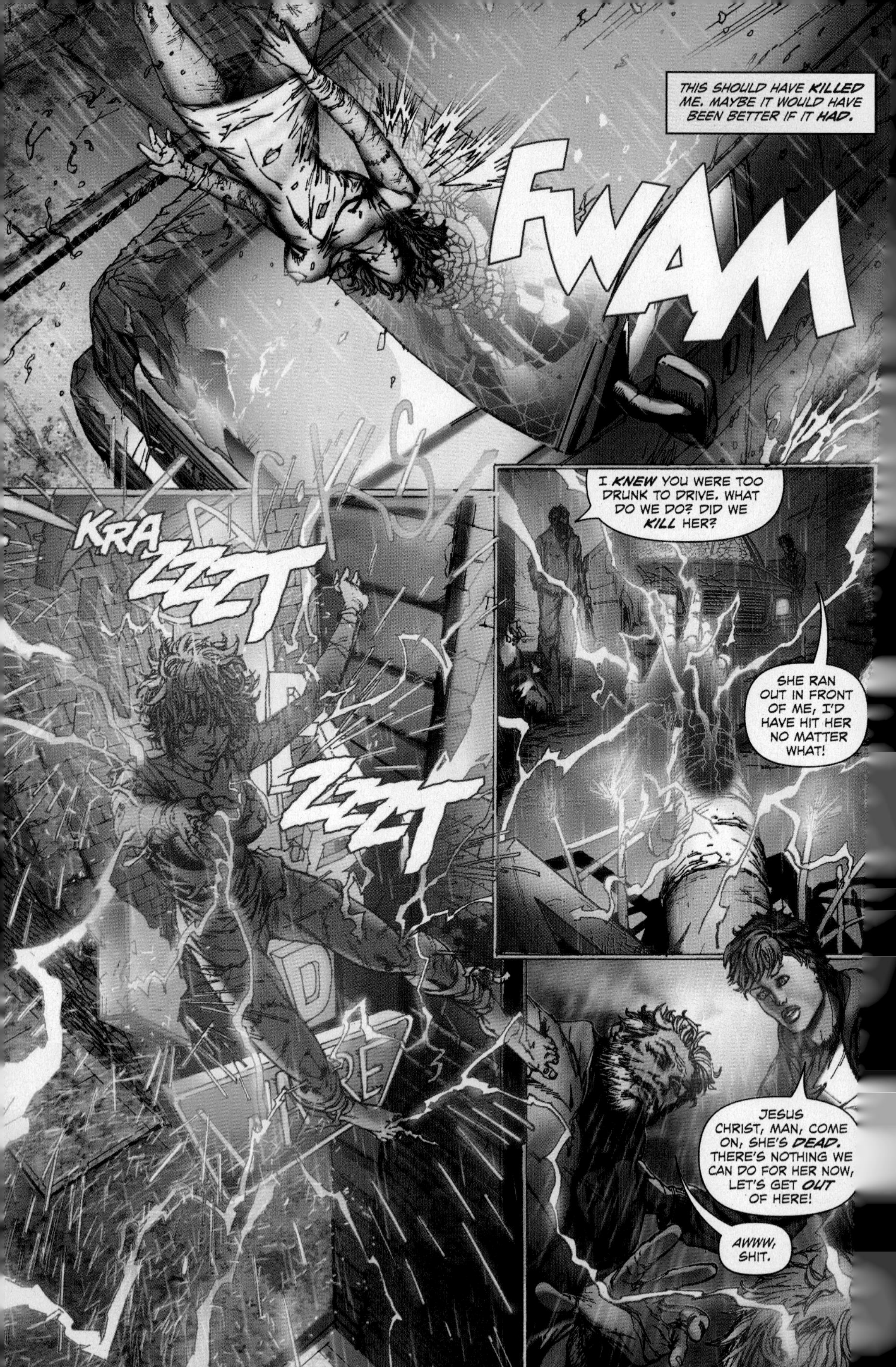
THIS SHOULD HAVE KILLED ME. MAYBE IT WOULD HAVE BEEN BETTER IF IT HAD.
FWAM
KRAZZZT
ZZZT
I KNEW YOU WERE TOO DRUNK TO DRIVE. WHAT DO WE DO? DID WE KILL HER?
SHE RAN OUT IN FRONT OF ME, I'D HAVE HIT HER NO MATTER WHAT!
JESUS CHRIST, MAN, COME ON, SHE'S DEAD. THERE'S NOTHING WE CAN DO FOR HER NOW, LET'S GET OUT OF HERE!
AWWW, SHIT.

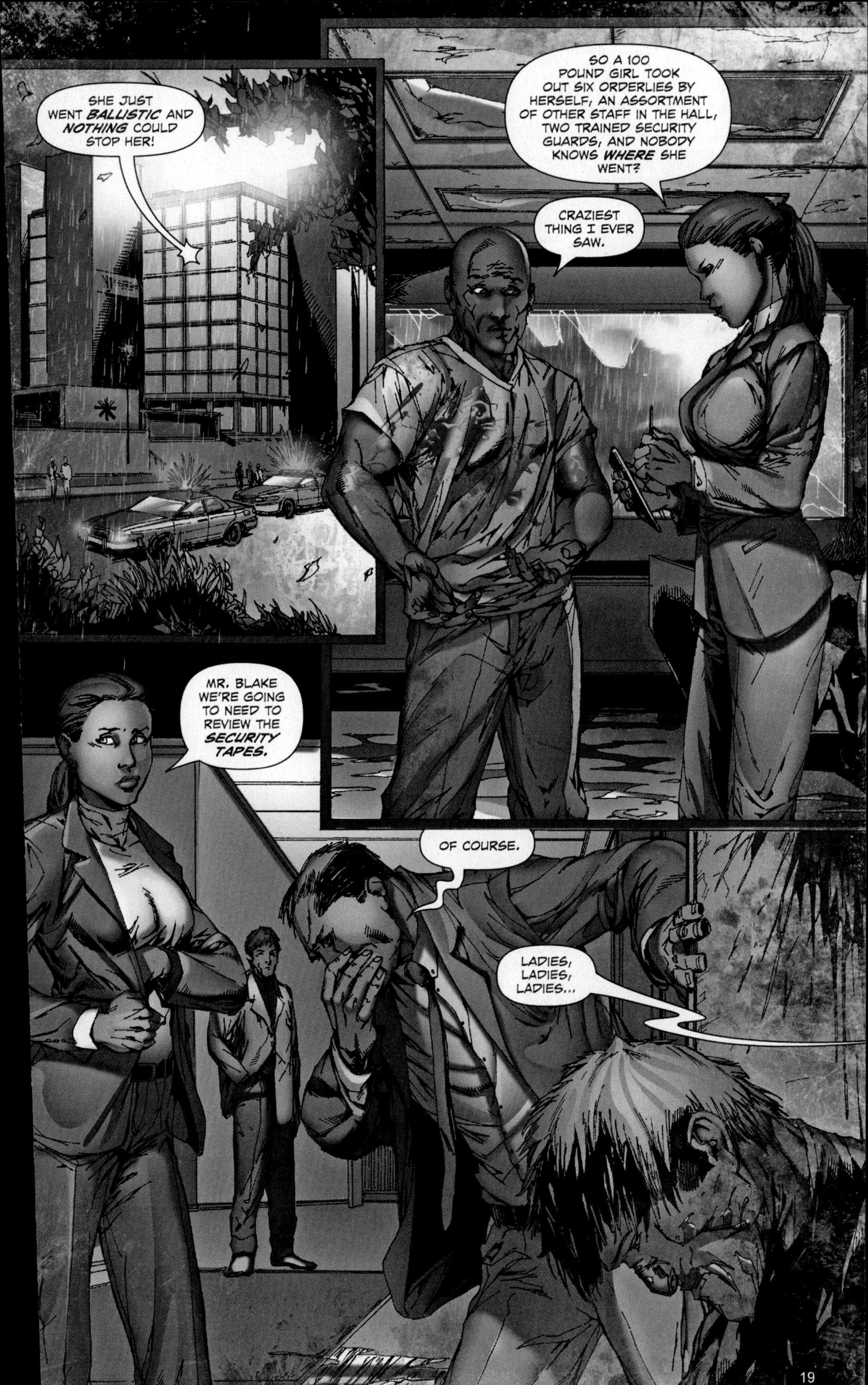
SHE JUST WENT BALLISTIC AND NOTHING COULD STOP HER!
SO A 100 POUND GIRL TOOK OUT SIX ORDERLIES BY HERSELF, AN ASSORTMENT OF OTHER STAFF IN THE HALL, TWO TRAINED SECURITY GUARDS, AND NOBODY KNOWS WHERE SHE WENT?
CRAZIEST THING I EVER SAW.
MR. BLAKE WE'RE GOING TO NEED TO REVIEW THE SECURITY TAPES.
OF COURSE.
LADIES, LADIES, LADIES...

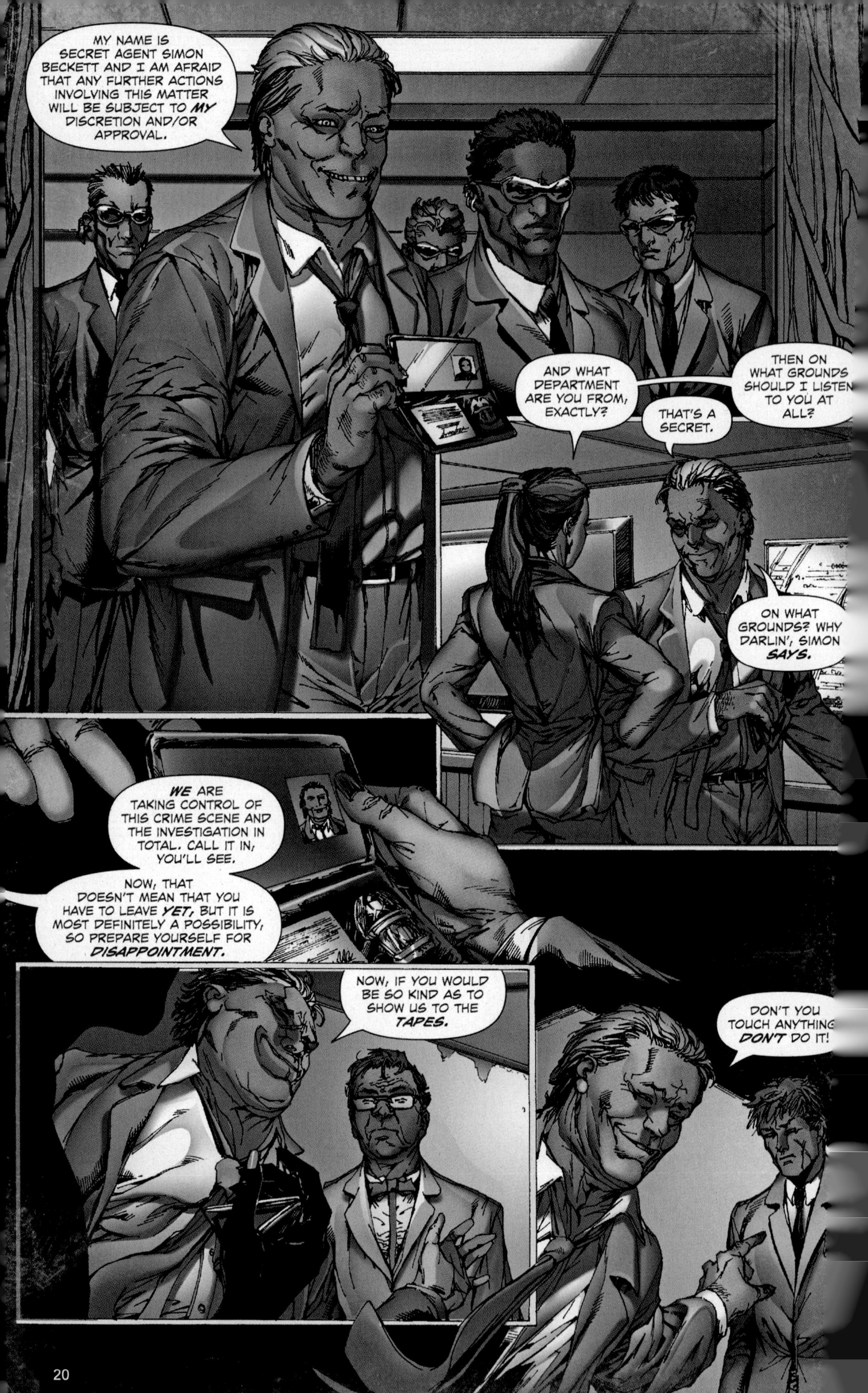
MY NAME IS SECRET AGENT SIMON BECKETT AND I AM AFRAID THAT ANY FURTHER ACTIONS INVOLVING THIS MATTER WILL BE SUBJECT TO *MY* DISCRETION AND/OR APPROVAL.
AND WHAT DEPARTMENT ARE YOU FROM, EXACTLY?
THAT'S A SECRET.
THEN ON WHAT GROUNDS SHOULD I LISTEN TO YOU AT ALL?
ON WHAT GROUNDS? WHY DARLIN', SIMON *SAYS.*
WE ARE TAKING CONTROL OF THIS CRIME SCENE AND THE INVESTIGATION IN TOTAL. CALL IT IN, YOU'LL SEE.
NOW, THAT DOESN'T MEAN THAT YOU HAVE TO LEAVE *YET,* BUT IT IS MOST DEFINITELY A POSSIBILITY, SO PREPARE YOURSELF FOR *DISAPPOINTMENT.*
NOW, IF YOU WOULD BE SO KIND AS TO SHOW US TO THE *TAPES.*
DON'T YOU TOUCH ANYTHING *DON'T* DO IT!

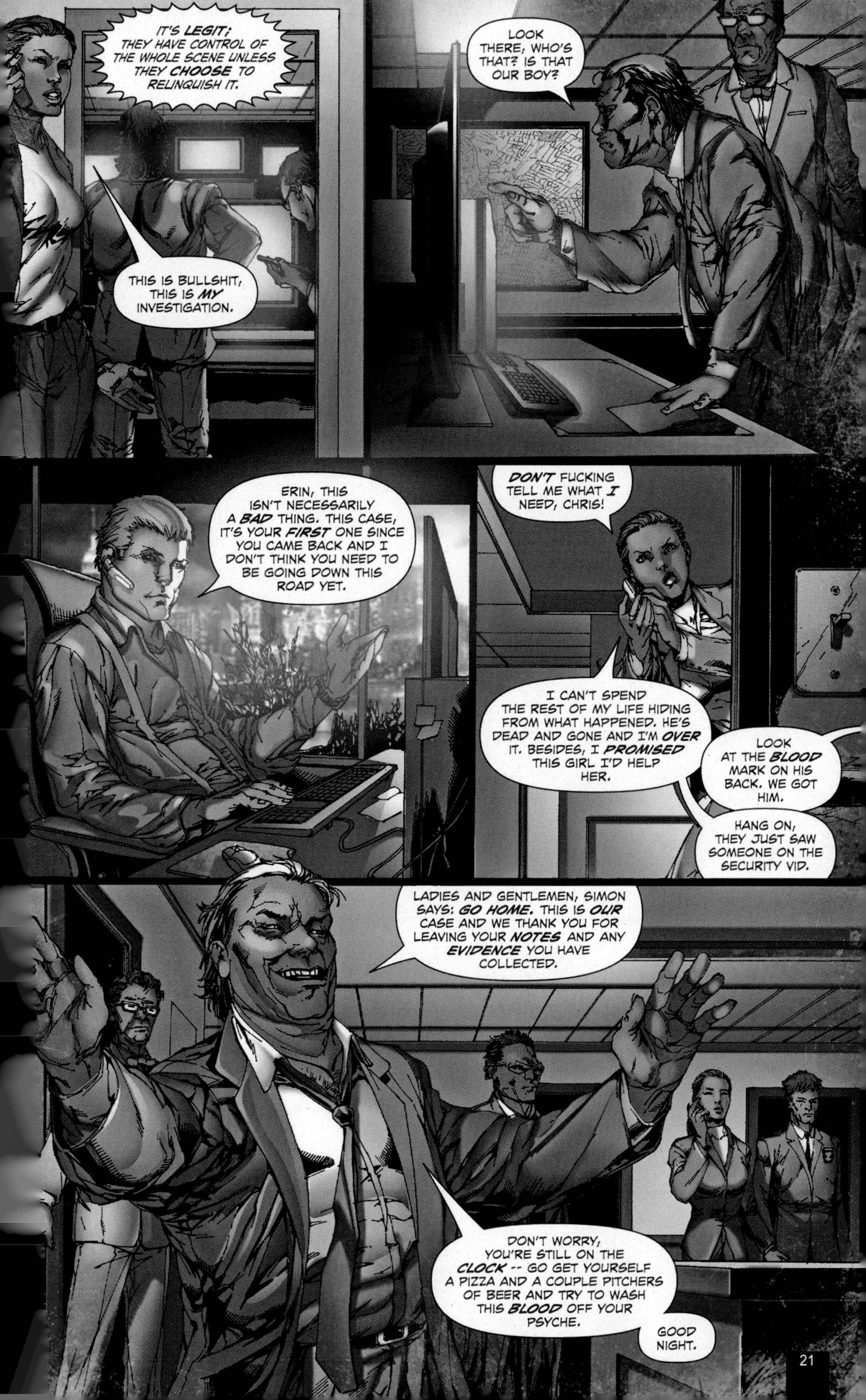
IT'S LEGIT: THEY HAVE CONTROL OF THE WHOLE SCENE UNLESS THEY CHOOSE TO RELINQUISH IT.
THIS IS BULLSHIT, THIS IS MY INVESTIGATION.
LOOK THERE, WHO'S THAT? IS THAT OUR BOY?
ERIN, THIS ISN'T NECESSARILY A BAD THING. THIS CASE, IT'S YOUR FIRST ONE SINCE YOU CAME BACK AND I DON'T THINK YOU NEED TO BE GOING DOWN THIS ROAD YET.
DON'T FUCKING TELL ME WHAT I NEED, CHRIS!
I CAN'T SPEND THE REST OF MY LIFE HIDING FROM WHAT HAPPENED. HE'S DEAD AND GONE AND I'M OVER IT. BESIDES, I PROMISED THIS GIRL I'D HELP HER.
LOOK AT THE BLOOD MARK ON HIS BACK. WE GOT HIM.
HANG ON, THEY JUST SAW SOMEONE ON THE SECURITY VID.
LADIES AND GENTLEMEN, SIMON SAYS: GO HOME. THIS IS OUR CASE AND WE THANK YOU FOR LEAVING YOUR NOTES AND ANY EVIDENCE YOU HAVE COLLECTED.
DON'T WORRY, YOU'RE STILL ON THE CLOCK -- GO GET YOURSELF A PIZZA AND A COUPLE PITCHERS OF BEER AND TRY TO WASH THIS BLOOD OFF YOUR PSYCHE.
GOOD NIGHT.

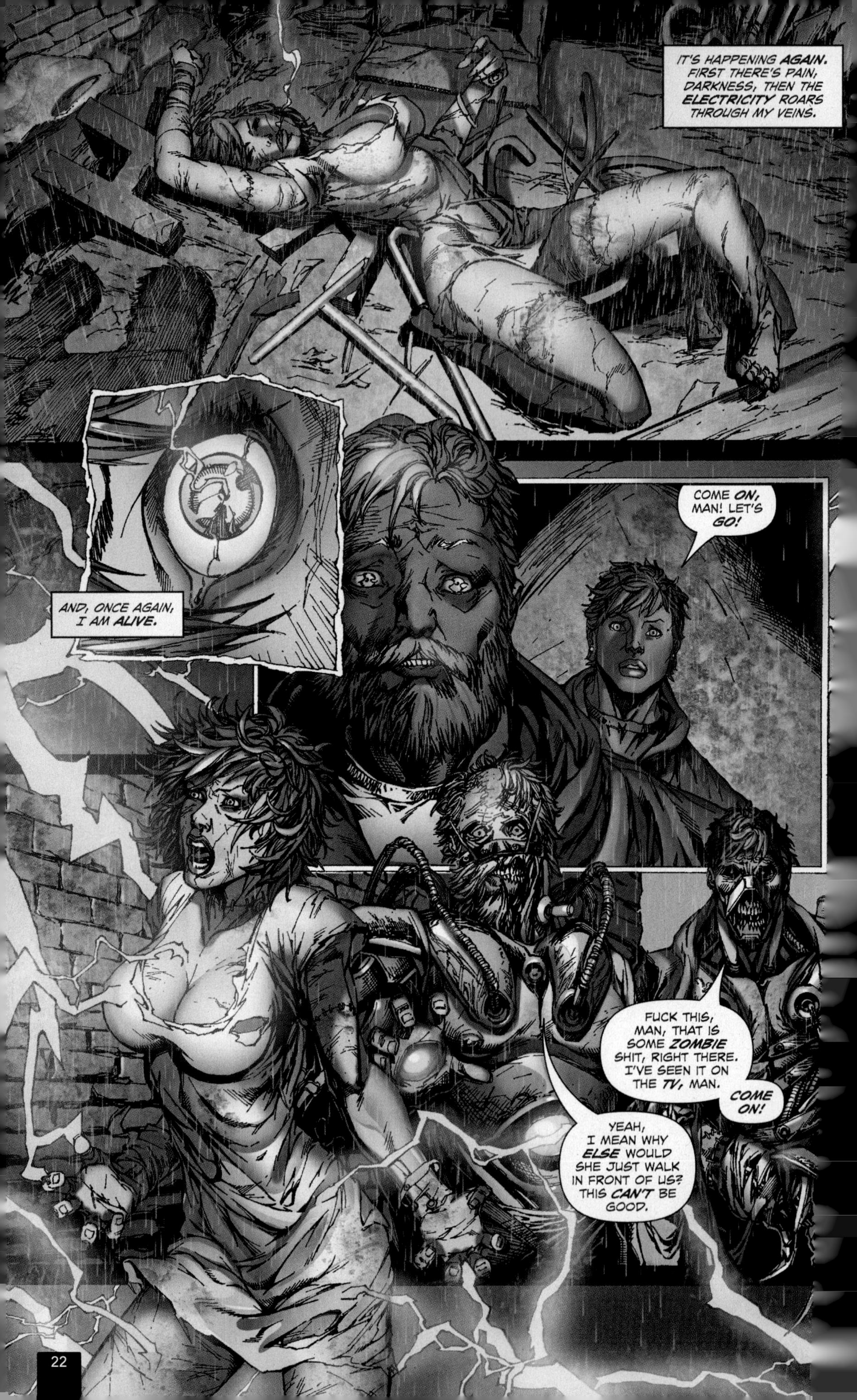

IT'S HAPPENING AGAIN. FIRST THERE'S PAIN, DARKNESS, THEN THE ELECTRICITY ROARS THROUGH MY VEINS.
AND, ONCE AGAIN, I AM ALIVE.
COME ON, MAN! LET'S GO!
FUCK THIS, MAN, THAT IS SOME ZOMBIE SHIT, RIGHT THERE. I'VE SEEN IT ON THE TV, MAN.
COME ON!
YEAH, I MEAN WHY ELSE WOULD SHE JUST WALK IN FRONT OF US? THIS CAN'T BE GOOD.

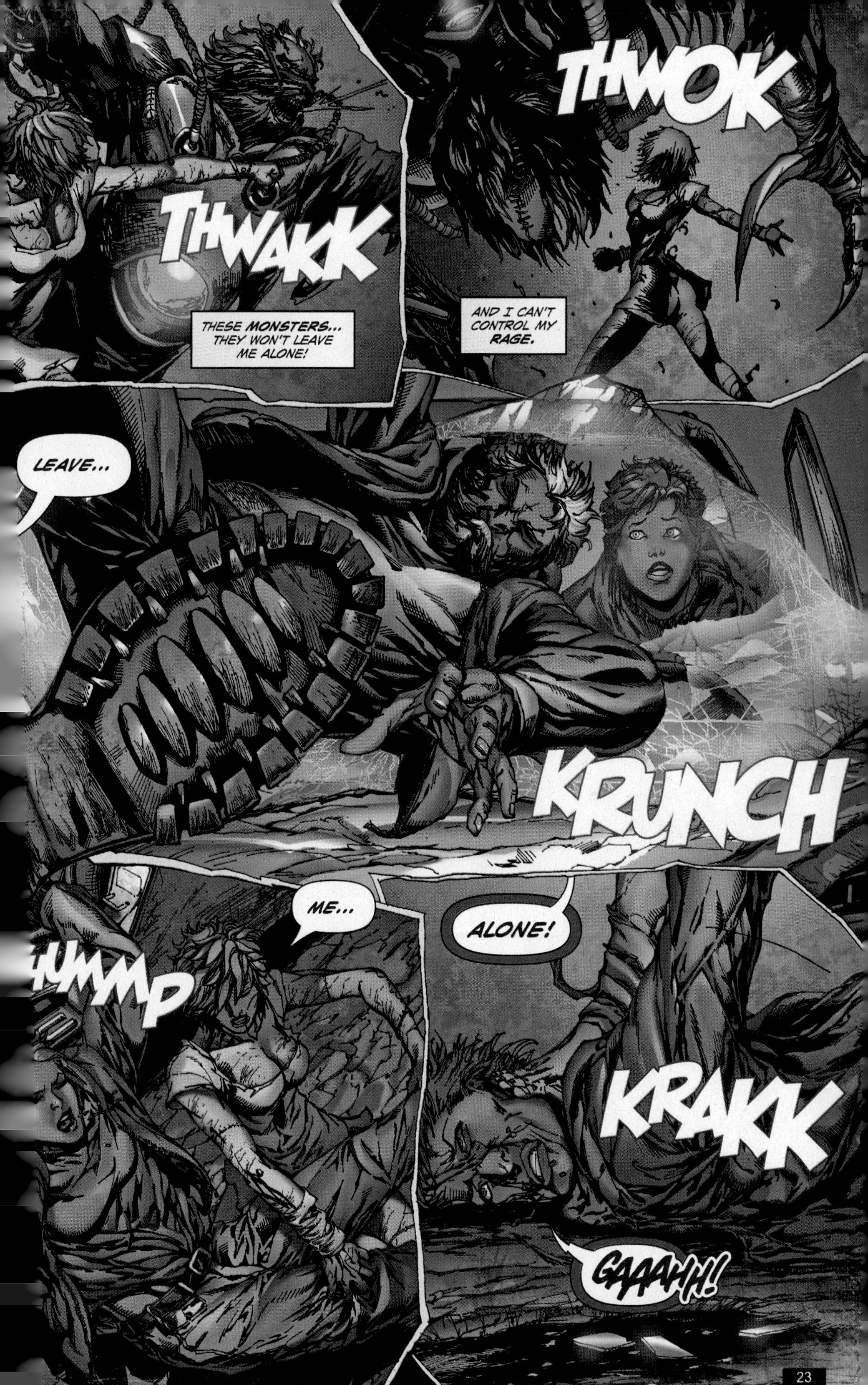
THWAKK
THESE MONSTERS... THEY WON'T LEAVE ME ALONE!
THWOK
AND I CAN'T CONTROL MY RAGE.
LEAVE...
KRUNCH
ME...
ALONE!
HUMMP
KRAKK
GAAAHH!

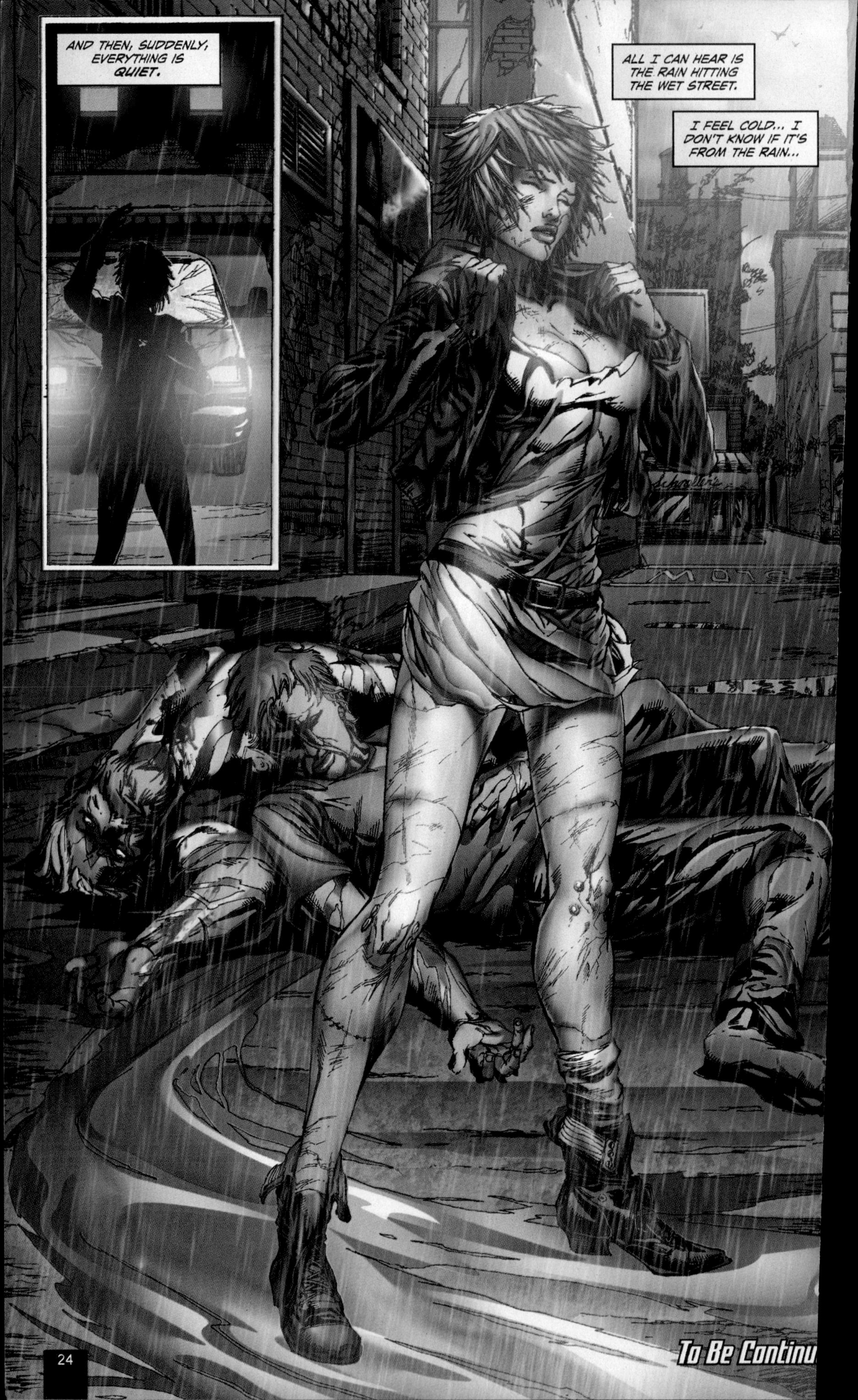
AND THEN, SUDDENLY, EVERYTHING IS QUIET.
ALL I CAN HEAR IS THE RAIN HITTING THE WET STREET.
I FEEL COLD... I DON'T KNOW IF IT'S FROM THE RAIN...
To Be Continu

SCREWED

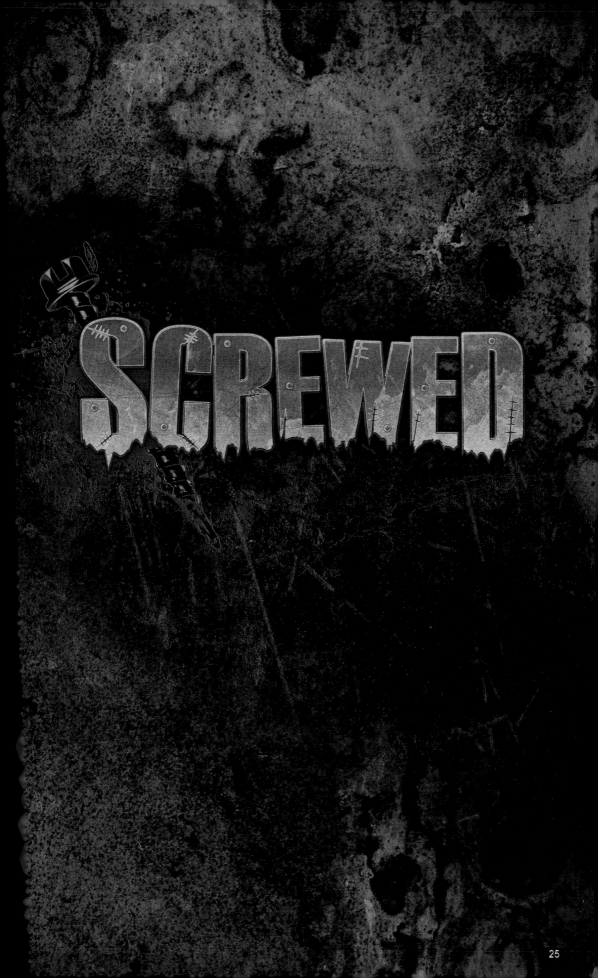

CHAPTER TWO

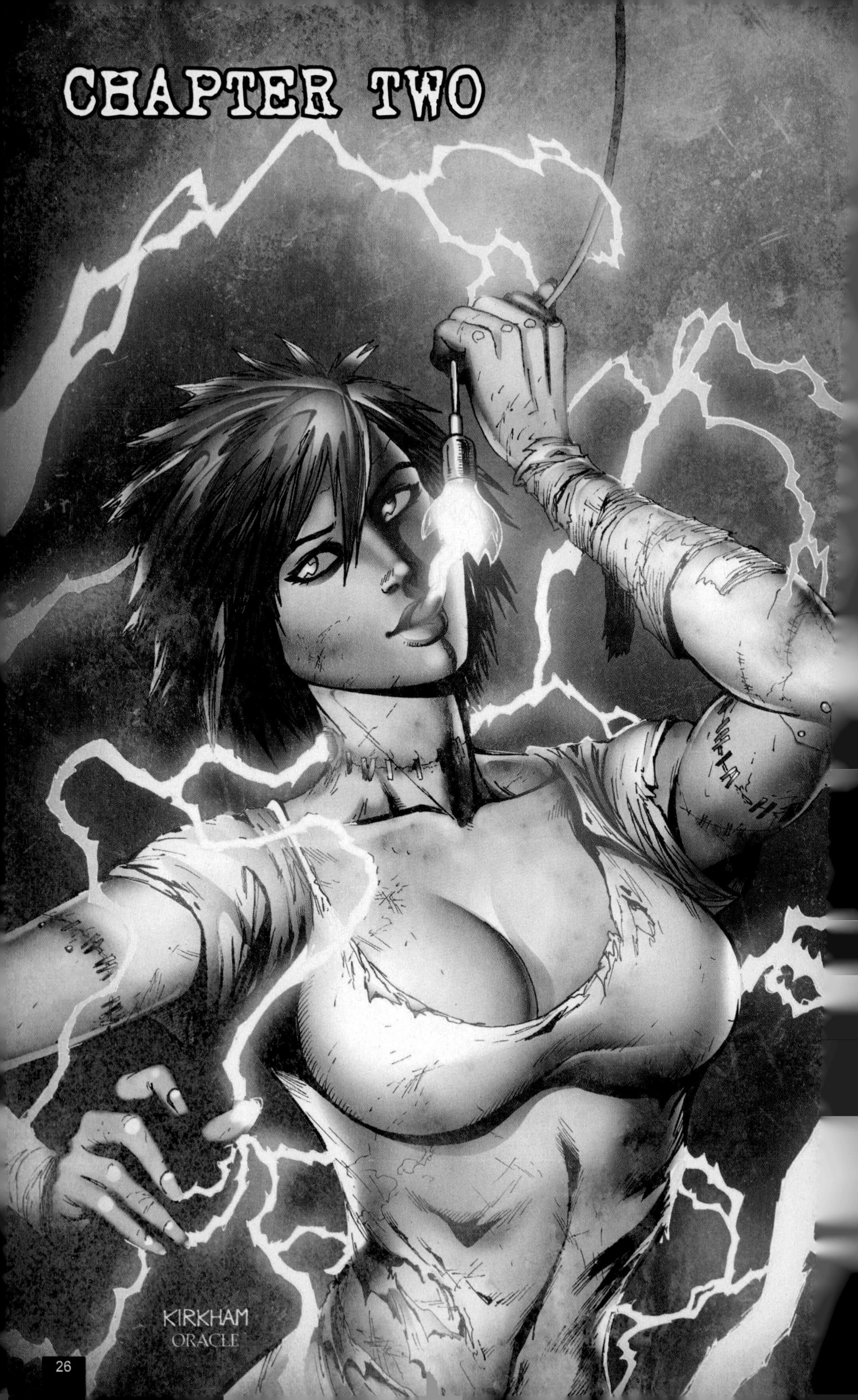
KIRKHAM
ORACLE

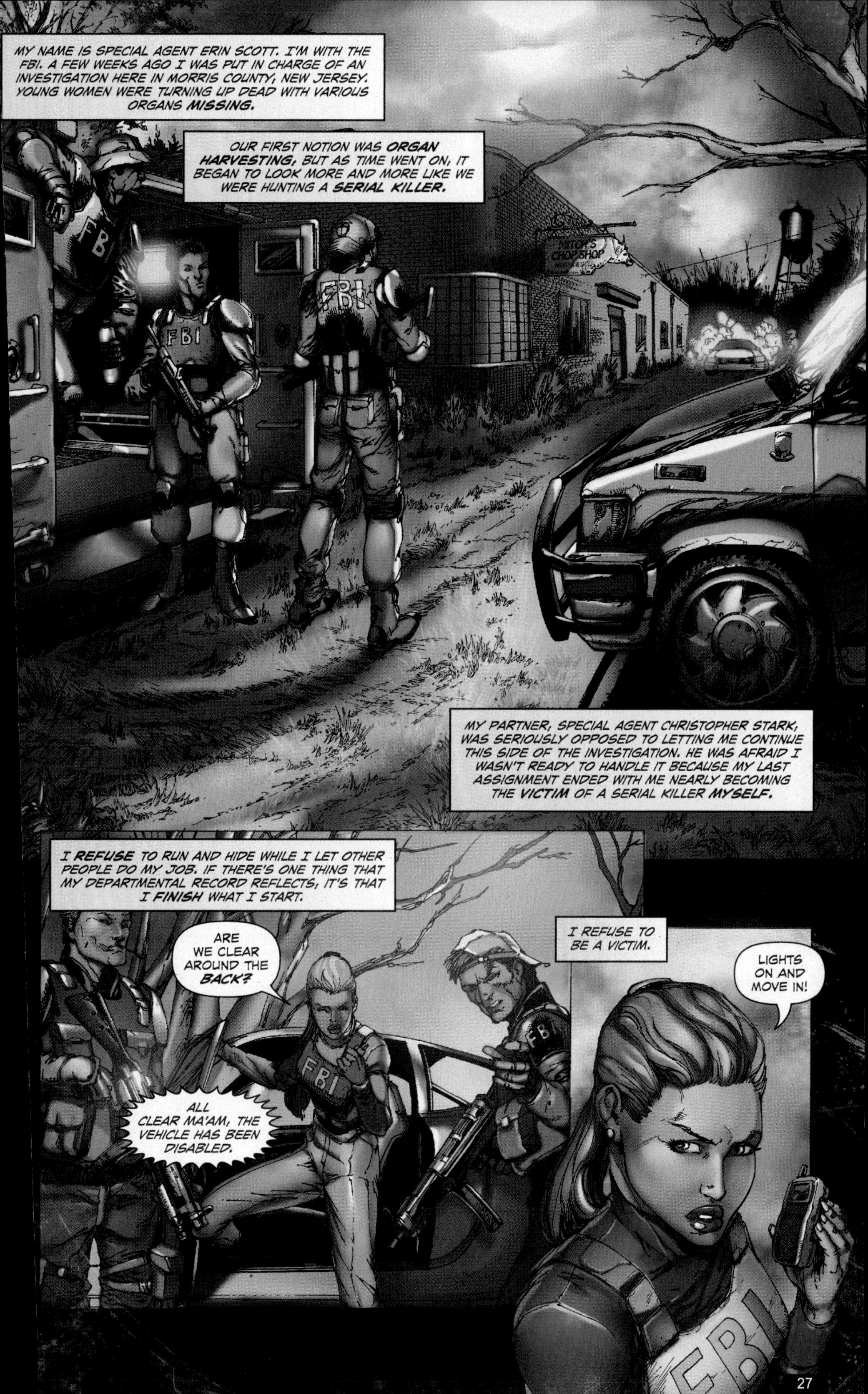
MY NAME IS SPECIAL AGENT ERIN SCOTT. I'M WITH THE FBI. A FEW WEEKS AGO I WAS PUT IN CHARGE OF AN INVESTIGATION HERE IN MORRIS COUNTY, NEW JERSEY. YOUNG WOMEN WERE TURNING UP DEAD WITH VARIOUS ORGANS MISSING.
OUR FIRST NOTION WAS ORGAN HARVESTING, BUT AS TIME WENT ON, IT BEGAN TO LOOK MORE AND MORE LIKE WE WERE HUNTING A SERIAL KILLER.
FBI
FBI
FBI
MITCH'S CHOP SHOP
MY PARTNER, SPECIAL AGENT CHRISTOPHER STARK, WAS SERIOUSLY OPPOSED TO LETTING ME CONTINUE THIS SIDE OF THE INVESTIGATION. HE WAS AFRAID I WASN'T READY TO HANDLE IT BECAUSE MY LAST ASSIGNMENT ENDED WITH ME NEARLY BECOMING THE VICTIM OF A SERIAL KILLER MYSELF.
I REFUSE TO RUN AND HIDE WHILE I LET OTHER PEOPLE DO MY JOB. IF THERE'S ONE THING THAT MY DEPARTMENTAL RECORD REFLECTS, IT'S THAT I FINISH WHAT I START.
ARE WE CLEAR AROUND THE BACK?
ALL CLEAR MA'AM, THE VEHICLE HAS BEEN DISABLED.
FBI
FBI
I REFUSE TO BE A VICTIM.
LIGHTS ON AND MOVE IN!
FBI

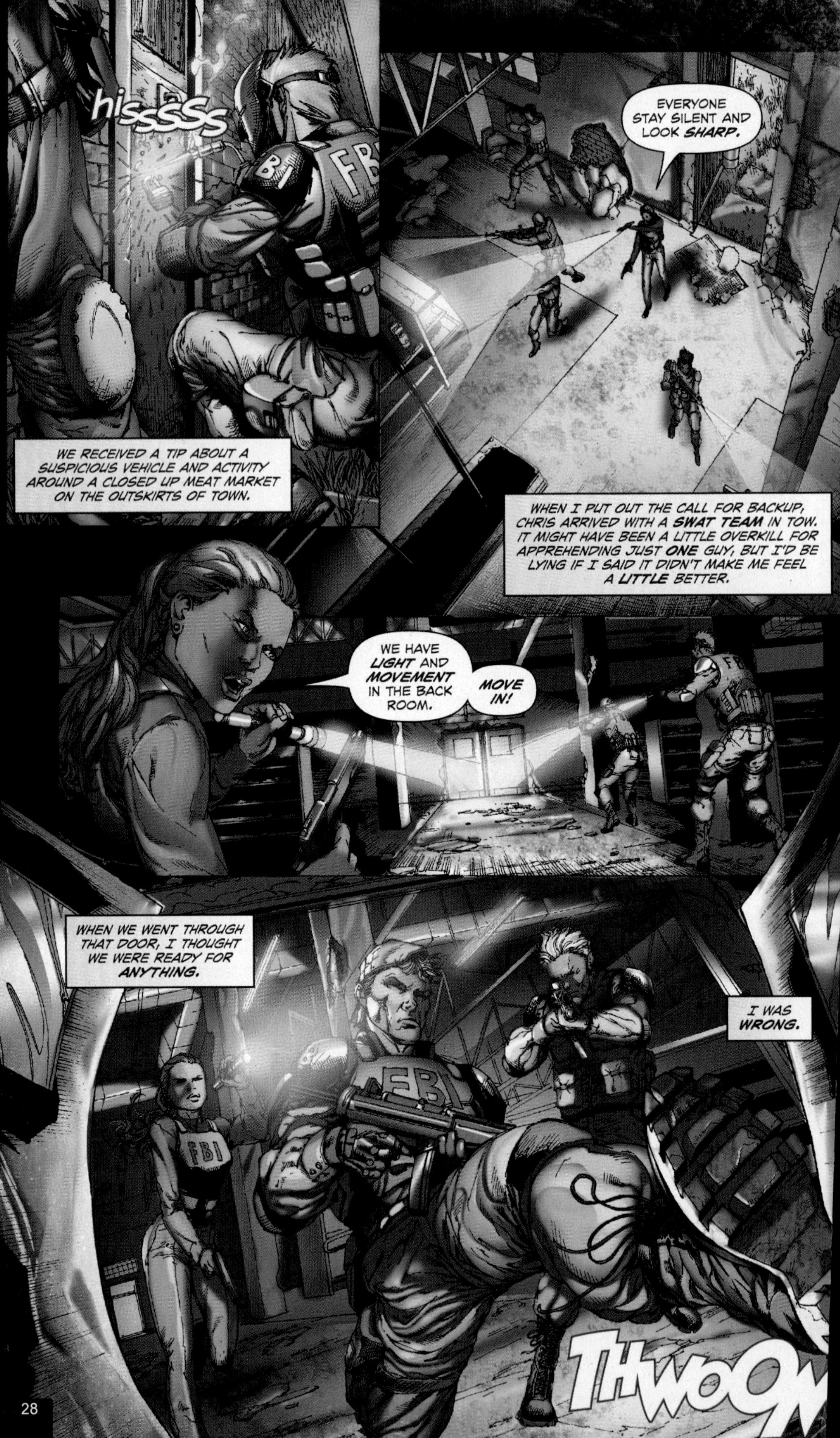
hisssSs
EVERYONE STAY SILENT AND LOOK SHARP.
WE RECEIVED A TIP ABOUT A SUSPICIOUS VEHICLE AND ACTIVITY AROUND A CLOSED UP MEAT MARKET ON THE OUTSKIRTS OF TOWN.
WHEN I PUT OUT THE CALL FOR BACKUP, CHRIS ARRIVED WITH A SWAT TEAM IN TOW. IT MIGHT HAVE BEEN A LITTLE OVERKILL FOR APPREHENDING JUST ONE GUY, BUT I'D BE LYING IF I SAID IT DIDN'T MAKE ME FEEL A LITTLE BETTER.
WE HAVE LIGHT AND MOVEMENT IN THE BACK ROOM.
MOVE IN!
WHEN WE WENT THROUGH THAT DOOR, I THOUGHT WE WERE READY FOR ANYTHING.
I WAS WRONG.
THWOOM

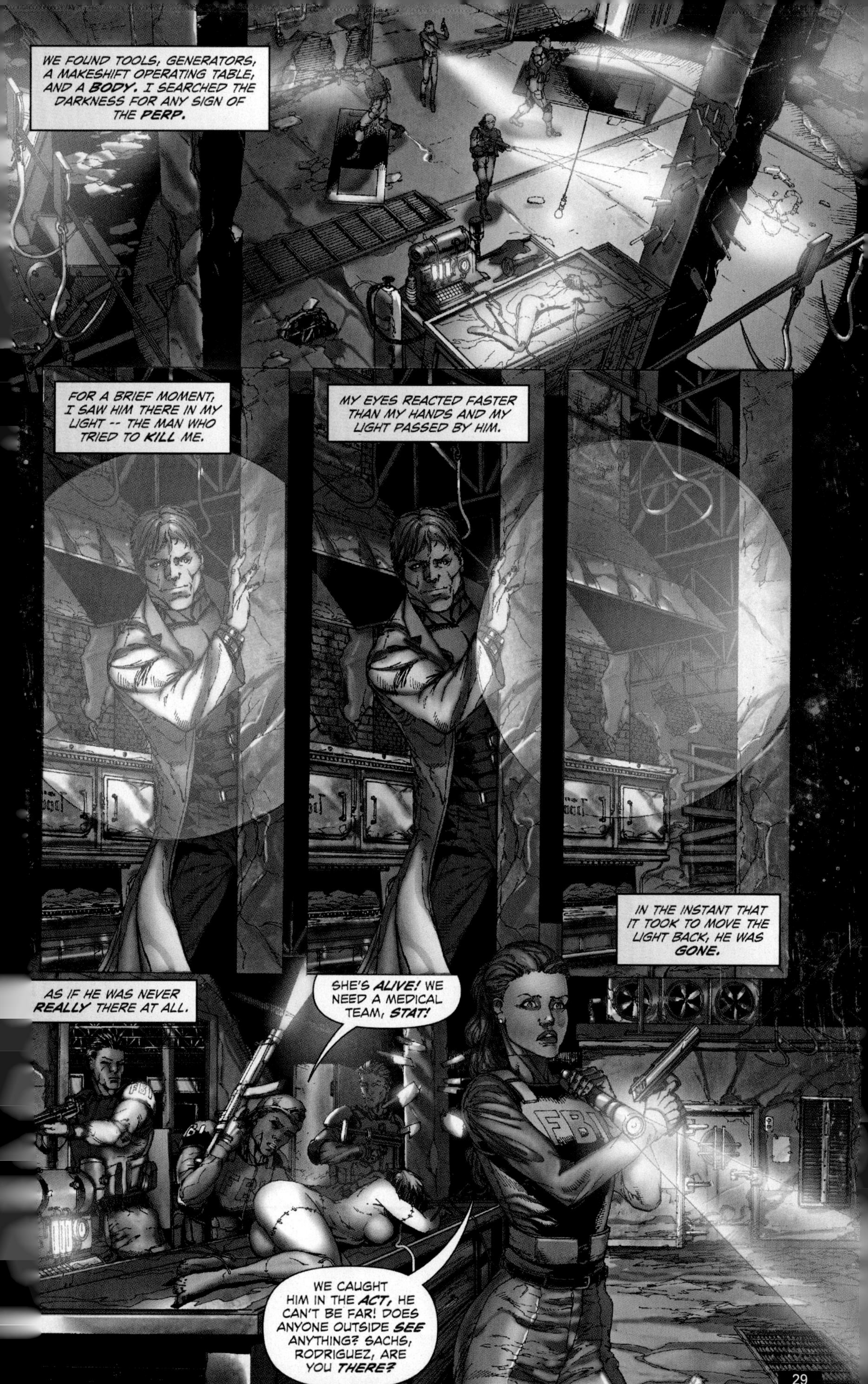
WE FOUND TOOLS, GENERATORS, A MAKESHIFT OPERATING TABLE, AND A **BODY.** I SEARCHED THE DARKNESS FOR ANY SIGN OF THE **PERP.**
FOR A BRIEF MOMENT, I SAW HIM THERE IN MY LIGHT -- THE MAN WHO TRIED TO **KILL** ME.
MY EYES REACTED FASTER THAN MY HANDS AND MY LIGHT PASSED BY HIM.
IN THE INSTANT THAT IT TOOK TO MOVE THE LIGHT BACK, HE WAS **GONE.**
AS IF HE WAS NEVER **REALLY** THERE AT ALL.
SHE'S **ALIVE!** WE NEED A MEDICAL TEAM, **STAT!**
WE CAUGHT HIM IN THE **ACT,** HE CAN'T BE FAR! DOES ANYONE OUTSIDE **SEE** ANYTHING? SACHS, RODRIGUEZ, ARE YOU **THERE?**
FBI

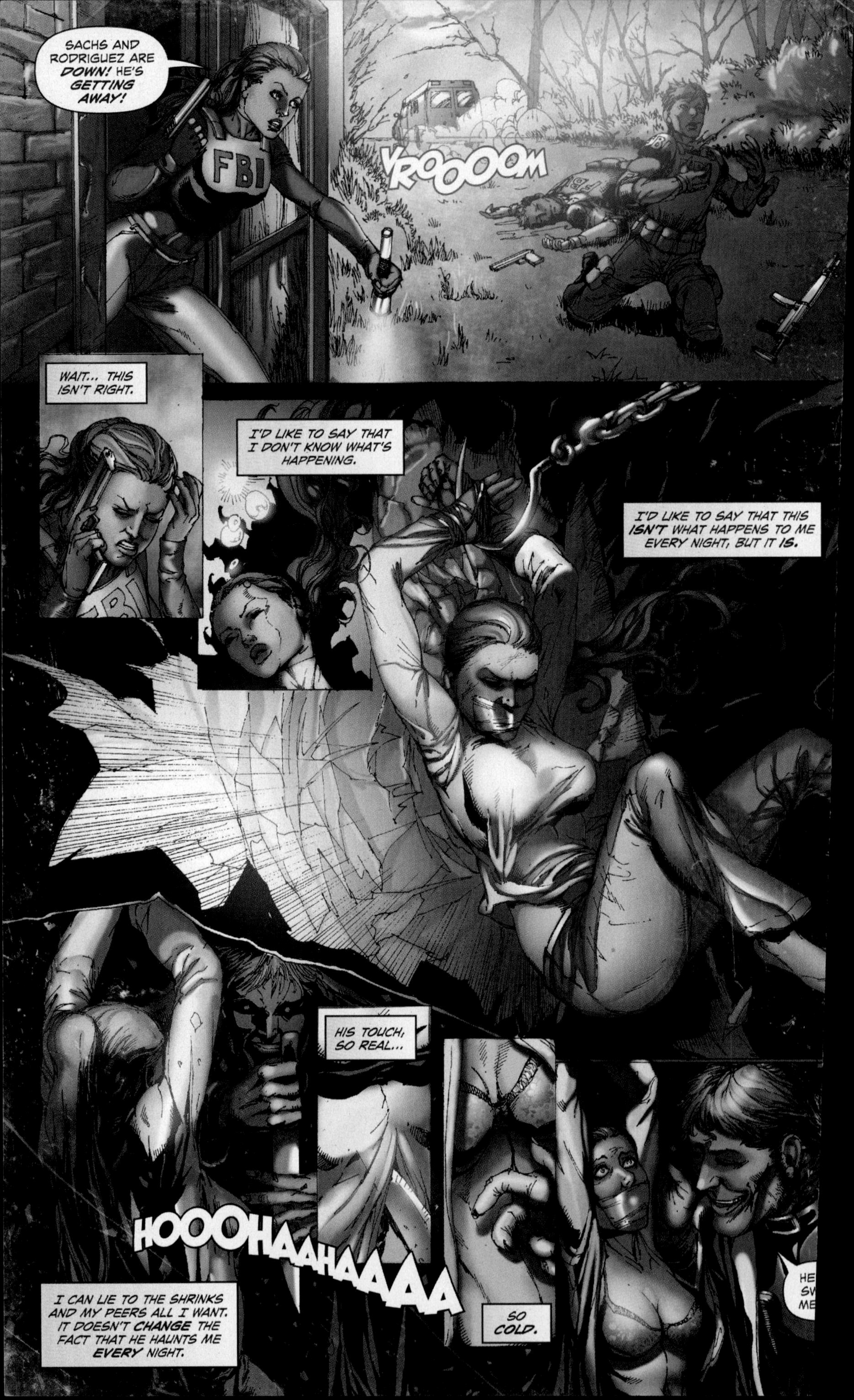
SACHS AND RODRIGUEZ ARE DOWN! HE'S GETTING AWAY!
VROOOOM
FBI
WAIT... THIS ISN'T RIGHT.
I'D LIKE TO SAY THAT I DON'T KNOW WHAT'S HAPPENING.
I'D LIKE TO SAY THAT THIS ISN'T WHAT HAPPENS TO ME EVERY NIGHT, BUT IT IS.
HIS TOUCH, SO REAL...
HOOOHAAHAAAAA
I CAN LIE TO THE SHRINKS AND MY PEERS ALL I WANT. IT DOESN'T CHANGE THE FACT THAT HE HAUNTS ME EVERY NIGHT.
SO COLD.

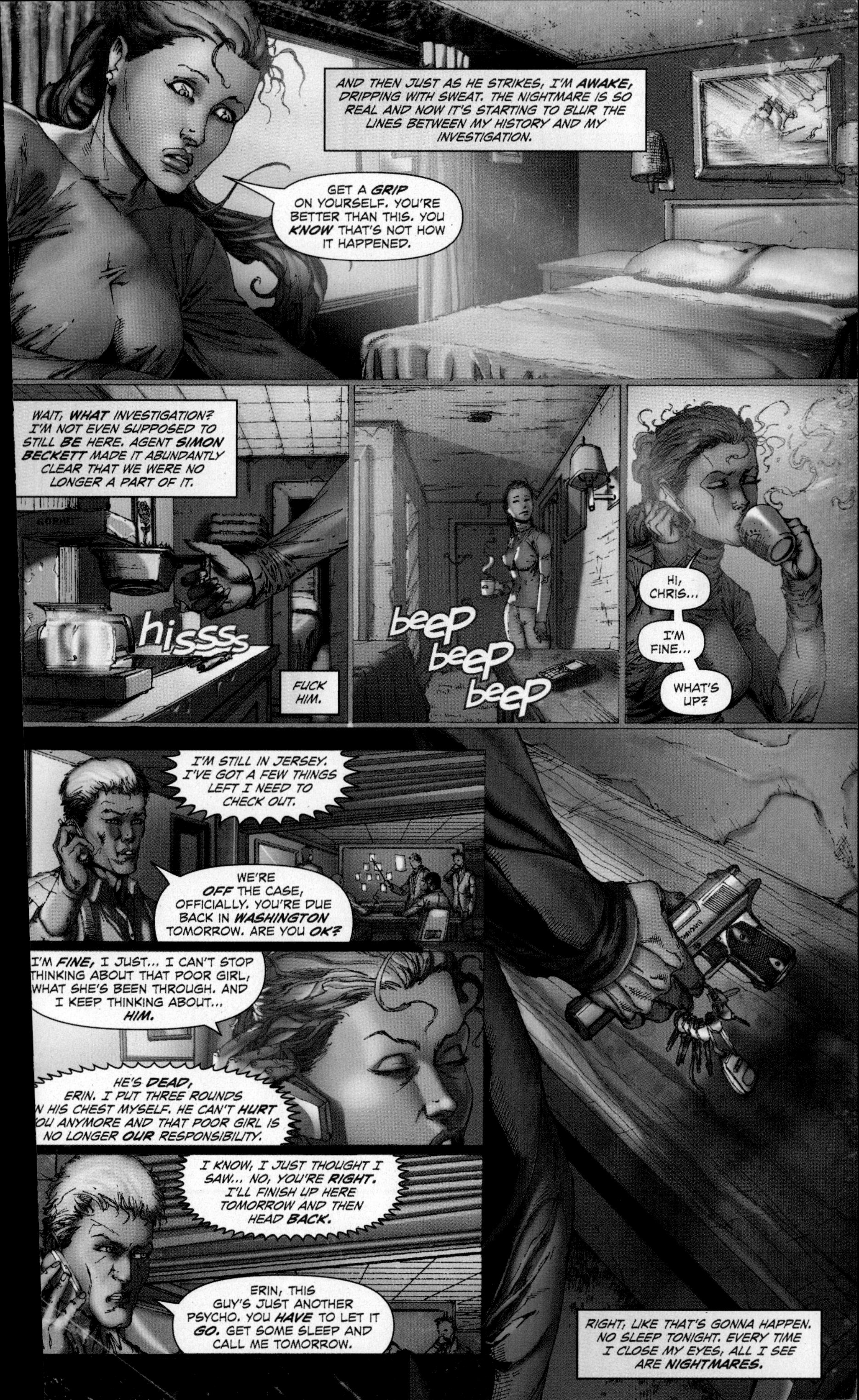
AND THEN JUST AS HE STRIKES, I'M AWAKE, DRIPPING WITH SWEAT. THE NIGHTMARE IS SO REAL AND NOW IT'S STARTING TO BLUR THE LINES BETWEEN MY HISTORY AND MY INVESTIGATION.
GET A GRIP ON YOURSELF. YOU'RE BETTER THAN THIS. YOU KNOW THAT'S NOT HOW IT HAPPENED.
WAIT, WHAT INVESTIGATION? I'M NOT EVEN SUPPOSED TO STILL BE HERE. AGENT SIMON BECKETT MADE IT ABUNDANTLY CLEAR THAT WE WERE NO LONGER A PART OF IT.
hissss
FUCK HIM.
beep beep beep
HI, CHRIS...
I'M FINE...
WHAT'S UP?
I'M STILL IN JERSEY. I'VE GOT A FEW THINGS LEFT I NEED TO CHECK OUT.
WE'RE OFF THE CASE, OFFICIALLY. YOU'RE DUE BACK IN WASHINGTON TOMORROW. ARE YOU OK?
I'M FINE, I JUST... I CAN'T STOP THINKING ABOUT THAT POOR GIRL, WHAT SHE'S BEEN THROUGH. AND I KEEP THINKING ABOUT... HIM.
HE'S DEAD, ERIN. I PUT THREE ROUNDS IN HIS CHEST MYSELF. HE CAN'T HURT YOU ANYMORE AND THAT POOR GIRL IS NO LONGER OUR RESPONSIBILITY.
I KNOW, I JUST THOUGHT I SAW... NO, YOU'RE RIGHT. I'LL FINISH UP HERE TOMORROW AND THEN HEAD BACK.
ERIN, THIS GUY'S JUST ANOTHER PSYCHO. YOU HAVE TO LET IT GO. GET SOME SLEEP AND CALL ME TOMORROW.
RIGHT, LIKE THAT'S GONNA HAPPEN. NO SLEEP TONIGHT. EVERY TIME I CLOSE MY EYES, ALL I SEE ARE NIGHTMARES.

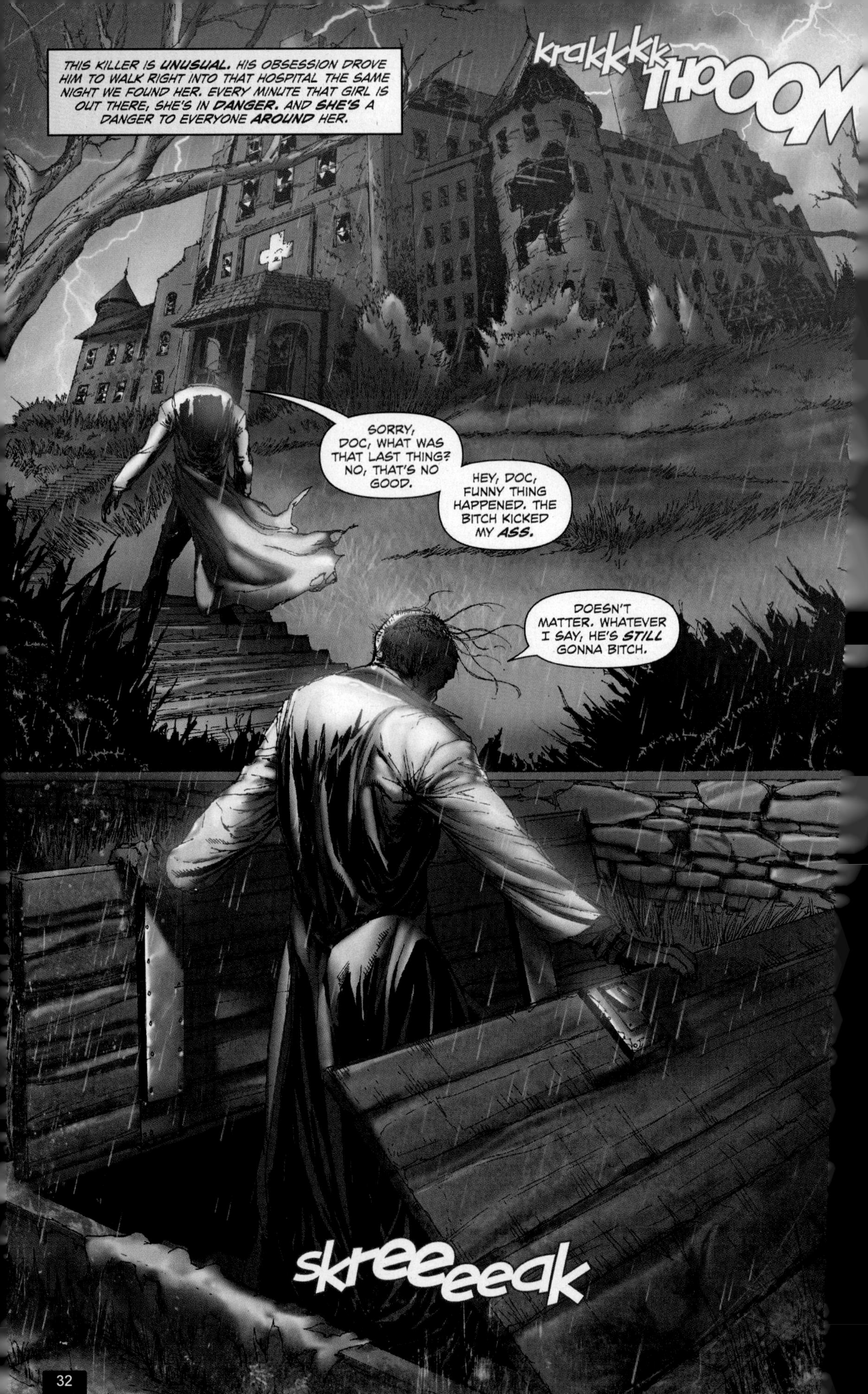

THIS KILLER IS UNUSUAL. HIS OBSESSION DROVE HIM TO WALK RIGHT INTO THAT HOSPITAL THE SAME NIGHT WE FOUND HER. EVERY MINUTE THAT GIRL IS OUT THERE, SHE'S IN DANGER. AND SHE'S A DANGER TO EVERYONE AROUND HER.
krakkkkk THOOOM
SORRY, DOC, WHAT WAS THAT LAST THING? NO, THAT'S NO GOOD.
HEY, DOC, FUNNY THING HAPPENED. THE BITCH KICKED MY ASS.
DOESN'T MATTER. WHATEVER I SAY, HE'S STILL GONNA BITCH.
skreeeeeak

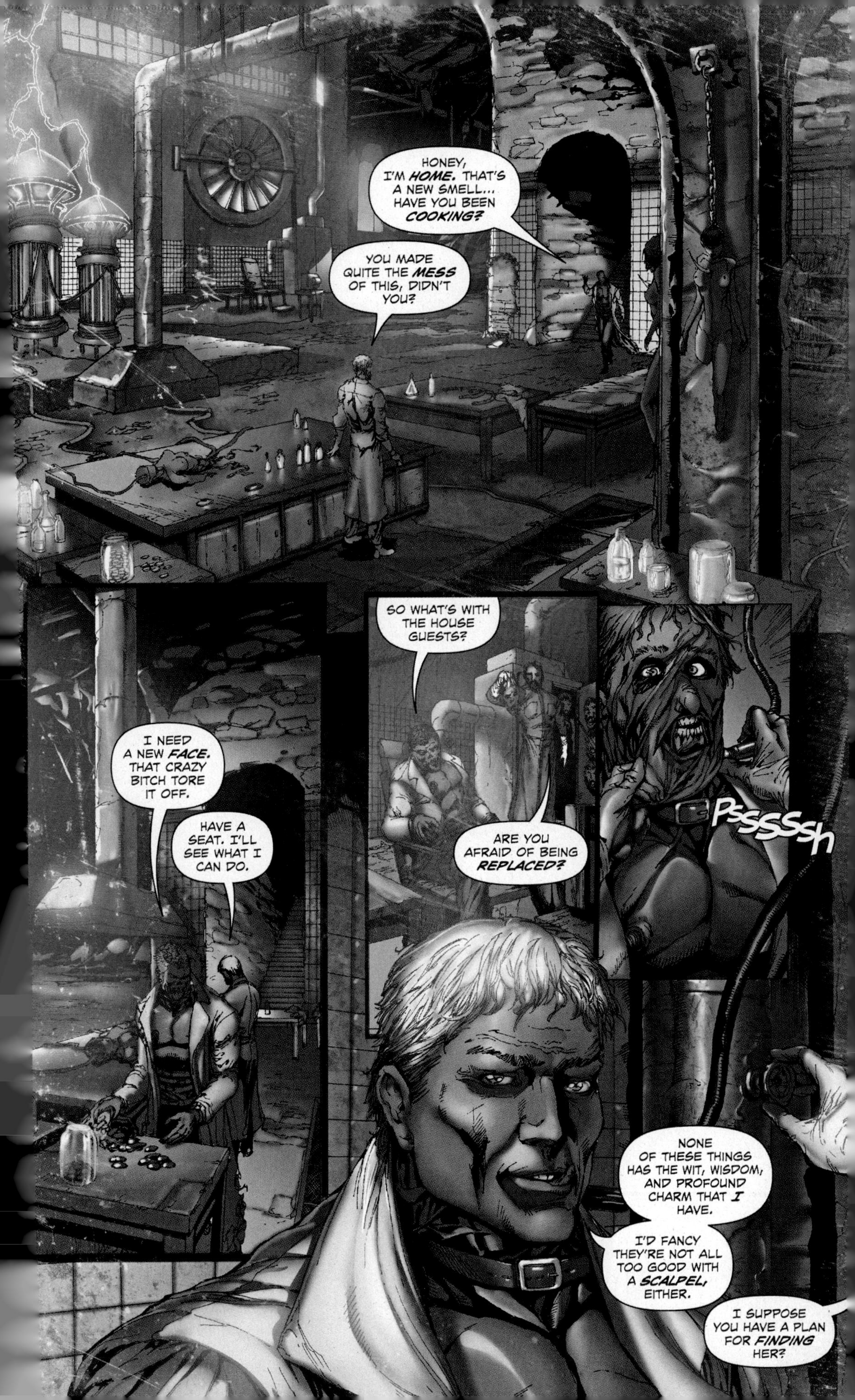
HONEY, I'M HOME. THAT'S A NEW SMELL... HAVE YOU BEEN COOKING?
YOU MADE QUITE THE MESS OF THIS, DIDN'T YOU?
I NEED A NEW FACE. THAT CRAZY BITCH TORE IT OFF.
HAVE A SEAT. I'LL SEE WHAT I CAN DO.
SO WHAT'S WITH THE HOUSE GUESTS?
ARE YOU AFRAID OF BEING REPLACED?
PSSSSSh
NONE OF THESE THINGS HAS THE WIT, WISDOM, AND PROFOUND CHARM THAT I HAVE.
I'D FANCY THEY'RE NOT ALL TOO GOOD WITH A SCALPEL, EITHER.
I SUPPOSE YOU HAVE A PLAN FOR FINDING HER?

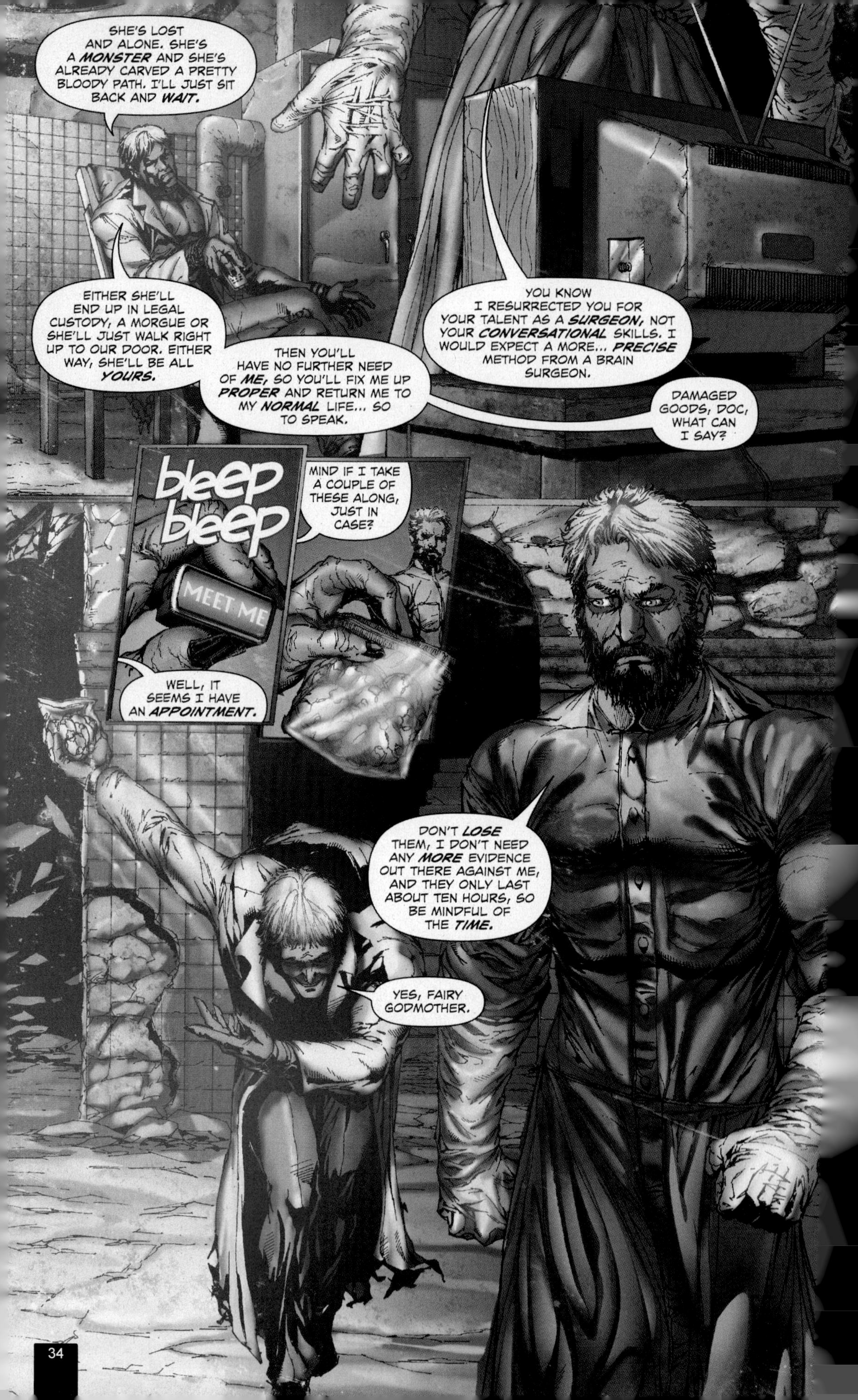
SHE'S LOST AND ALONE. SHE'S A MONSTER AND SHE'S ALREADY CARVED A PRETTY BLOODY PATH. I'LL JUST SIT BACK AND WAIT.
EITHER SHE'LL END UP IN LEGAL CUSTODY, A MORGUE OR SHE'LL JUST WALK RIGHT UP TO OUR DOOR. EITHER WAY, SHE'LL BE ALL YOURS.
THEN YOU'LL HAVE NO FURTHER NEED OF ME, SO YOU'LL FIX ME UP PROPER AND RETURN ME TO MY NORMAL LIFE... SO TO SPEAK.
YOU KNOW I RESURRECTED YOU FOR YOUR TALENT AS A SURGEON, NOT YOUR CONVERSATIONAL SKILLS. I WOULD EXPECT A MORE... PRECISE METHOD FROM A BRAIN SURGEON.
DAMAGED GOODS, DOC, WHAT CAN I SAY?
bleep bleep
MEET ME
MIND IF I TAKE A COUPLE OF THESE ALONG, JUST IN CASE?
WELL, IT SEEMS I HAVE AN APPOINTMENT.
DON'T LOSE THEM, I DON'T NEED ANY MORE EVIDENCE OUT THERE AGAINST ME, AND THEY ONLY LAST ABOUT TEN HOURS, SO BE MINDFUL OF THE TIME.
YES, FAIRY GODMOTHER.

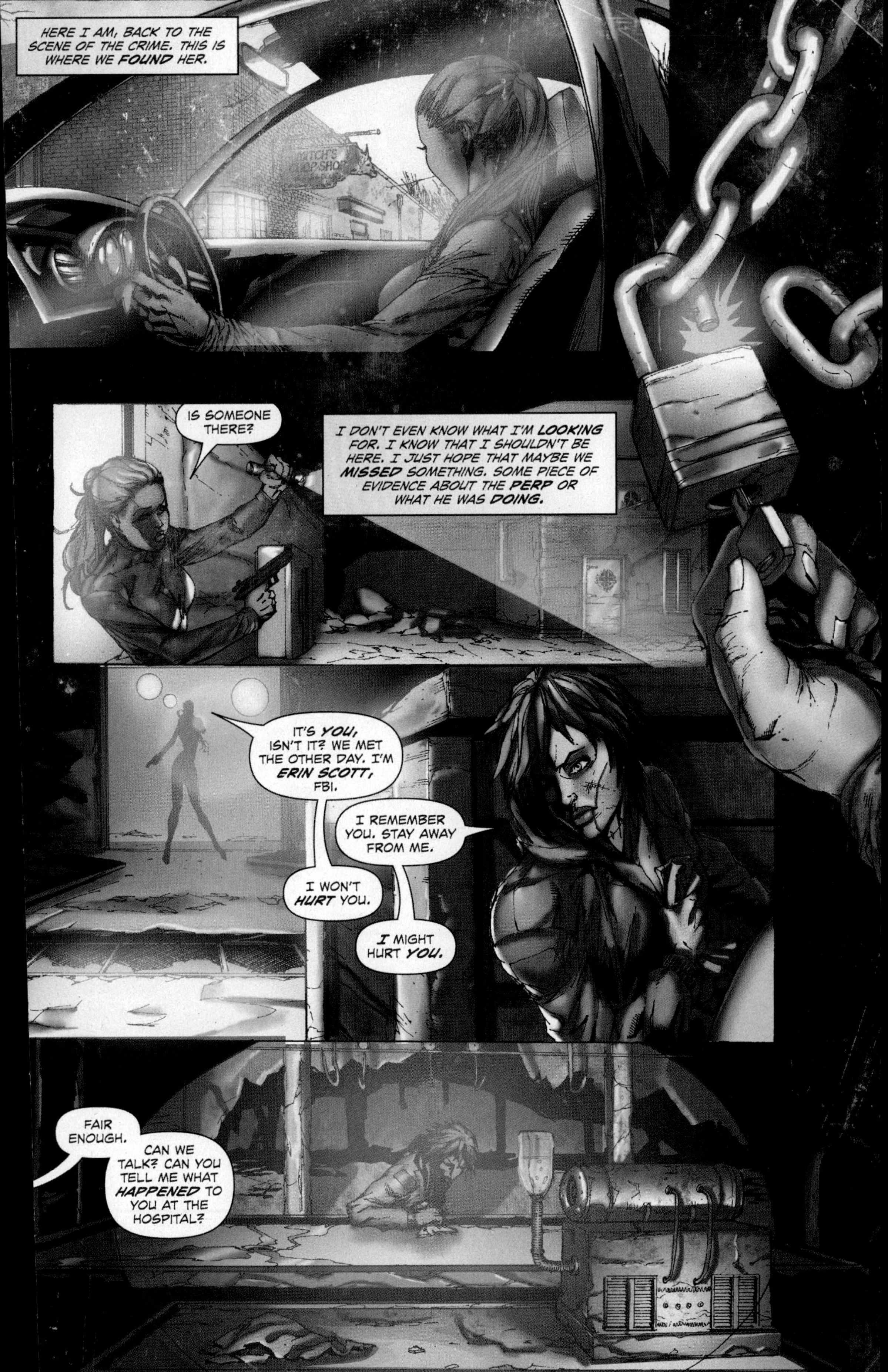
HERE I AM, BACK TO THE SCENE OF THE CRIME. THIS IS WHERE WE FOUND HER.
MITCH'S
IS SOMEONE THERE?
I DON'T EVEN KNOW WHAT I'M LOOKING FOR. I KNOW THAT I SHOULDN'T BE HERE. I JUST HOPE THAT MAYBE WE MISSED SOMETHING. SOME PIECE OF EVIDENCE ABOUT THE PERP OR WHAT HE WAS DOING.
IT'S YOU, ISN'T IT? WE MET THE OTHER DAY. I'M ERIN SCOTT, FBI.
I REMEMBER YOU. STAY AWAY FROM ME.
I WON'T HURT YOU.
I MIGHT HURT YOU.
FAIR ENOUGH.
CAN WE TALK? CAN YOU TELL ME WHAT HAPPENED TO YOU AT THE HOSPITAL?

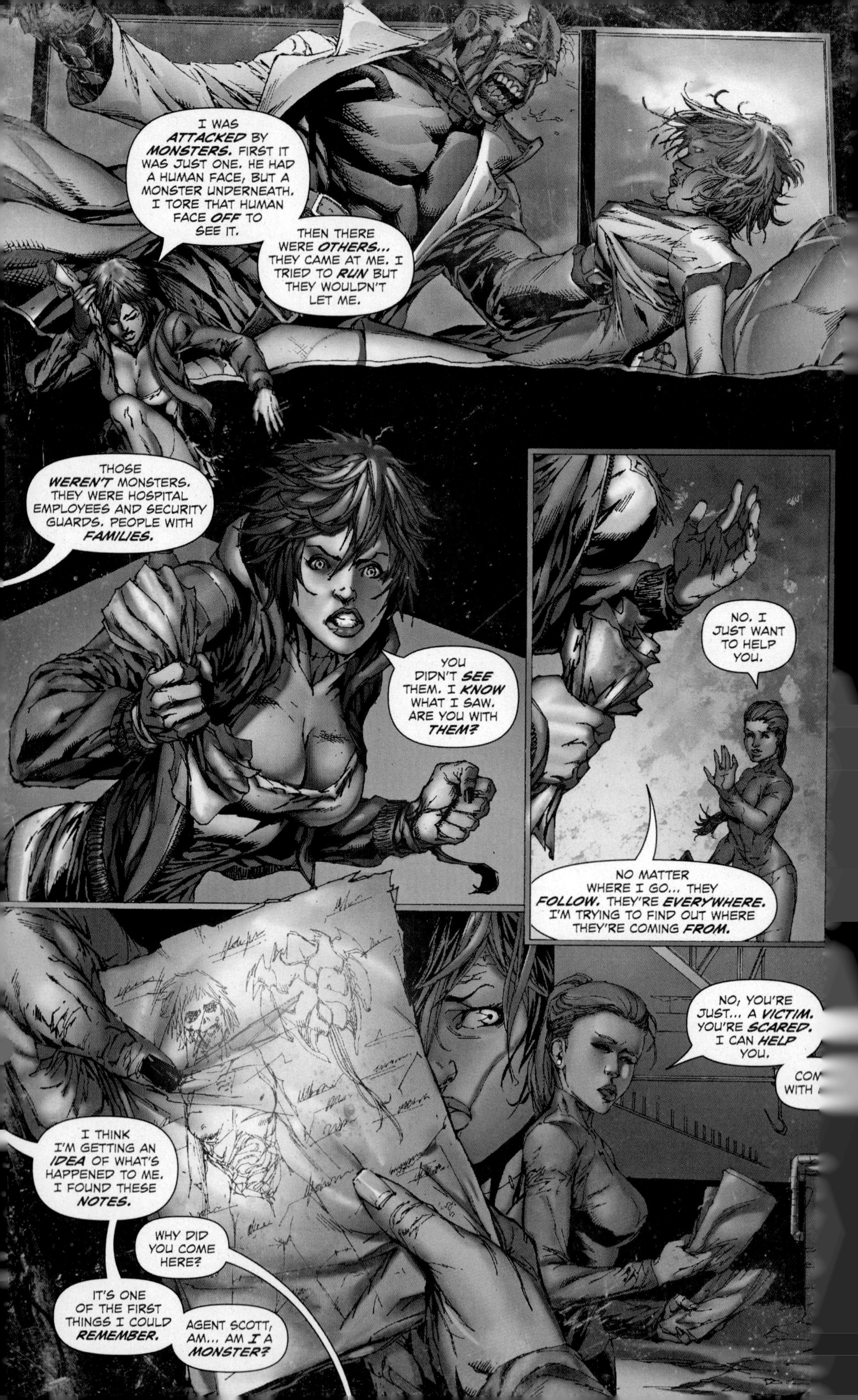
I WAS ATTACKED BY MONSTERS. FIRST IT WAS JUST ONE. HE HAD A HUMAN FACE, BUT A MONSTER UNDERNEATH. I TORE THAT HUMAN FACE OFF TO SEE IT.
THEN THERE WERE OTHERS... THEY CAME AT ME. I TRIED TO RUN BUT THEY WOULDN'T LET ME.
THOSE WEREN'T MONSTERS. THEY WERE HOSPITAL EMPLOYEES AND SECURITY GUARDS. PEOPLE WITH FAMILIES.
YOU DIDN'T SEE THEM. I KNOW WHAT I SAW. ARE YOU WITH THEM?
NO. I JUST WANT TO HELP YOU.
NO MATTER WHERE I GO... THEY FOLLOW. THEY'RE EVERYWHERE. I'M TRYING TO FIND OUT WHERE THEY'RE COMING FROM.
NO, YOU'RE JUST... A VICTIM. YOU'RE SCARED. I CAN HELP YOU.
I THINK I'M GETTING AN IDEA OF WHAT'S HAPPENED TO ME. I FOUND THESE NOTES.
WHY DID YOU COME HERE?
IT'S ONE OF THE FIRST THINGS I COULD REMEMBER.
AGENT SCOTT, AM... AM I A MONSTER?

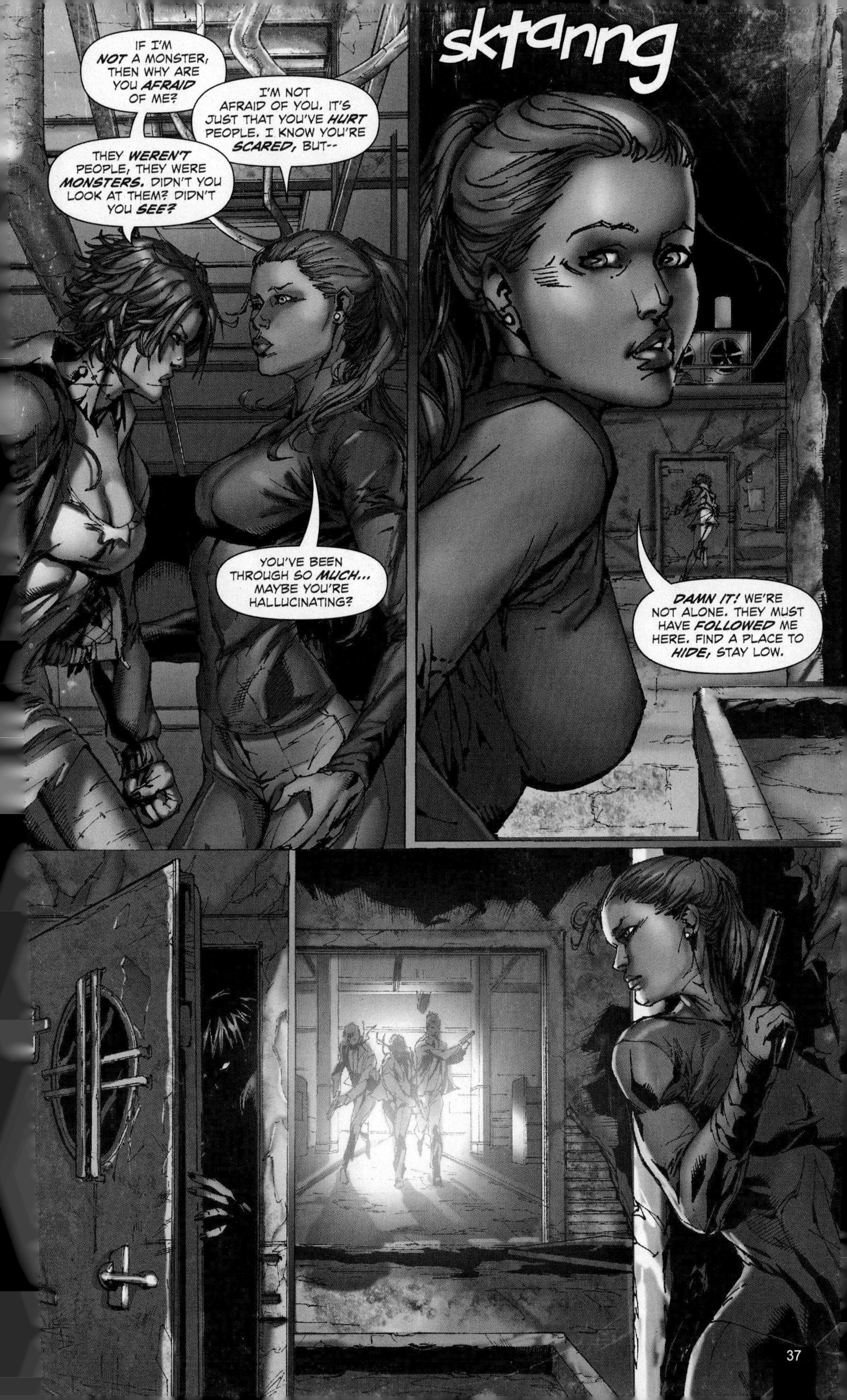

IF I'M NOT A MONSTER, THEN WHY ARE YOU AFRAID OF ME?
I'M NOT AFRAID OF YOU. IT'S JUST THAT YOU'VE HURT PEOPLE. I KNOW YOU'RE SCARED, BUT--
THEY WEREN'T PEOPLE, THEY WERE MONSTERS. DIDN'T YOU LOOK AT THEM? DIDN'T YOU SEE?
YOU'VE BEEN THROUGH SO MUCH... MAYBE YOU'RE HALLUCINATING?
sktanng
DAMN IT! WE'RE NOT ALONE. THEY MUST HAVE FOLLOWED ME HERE. FIND A PLACE TO HIDE, STAY LOW.

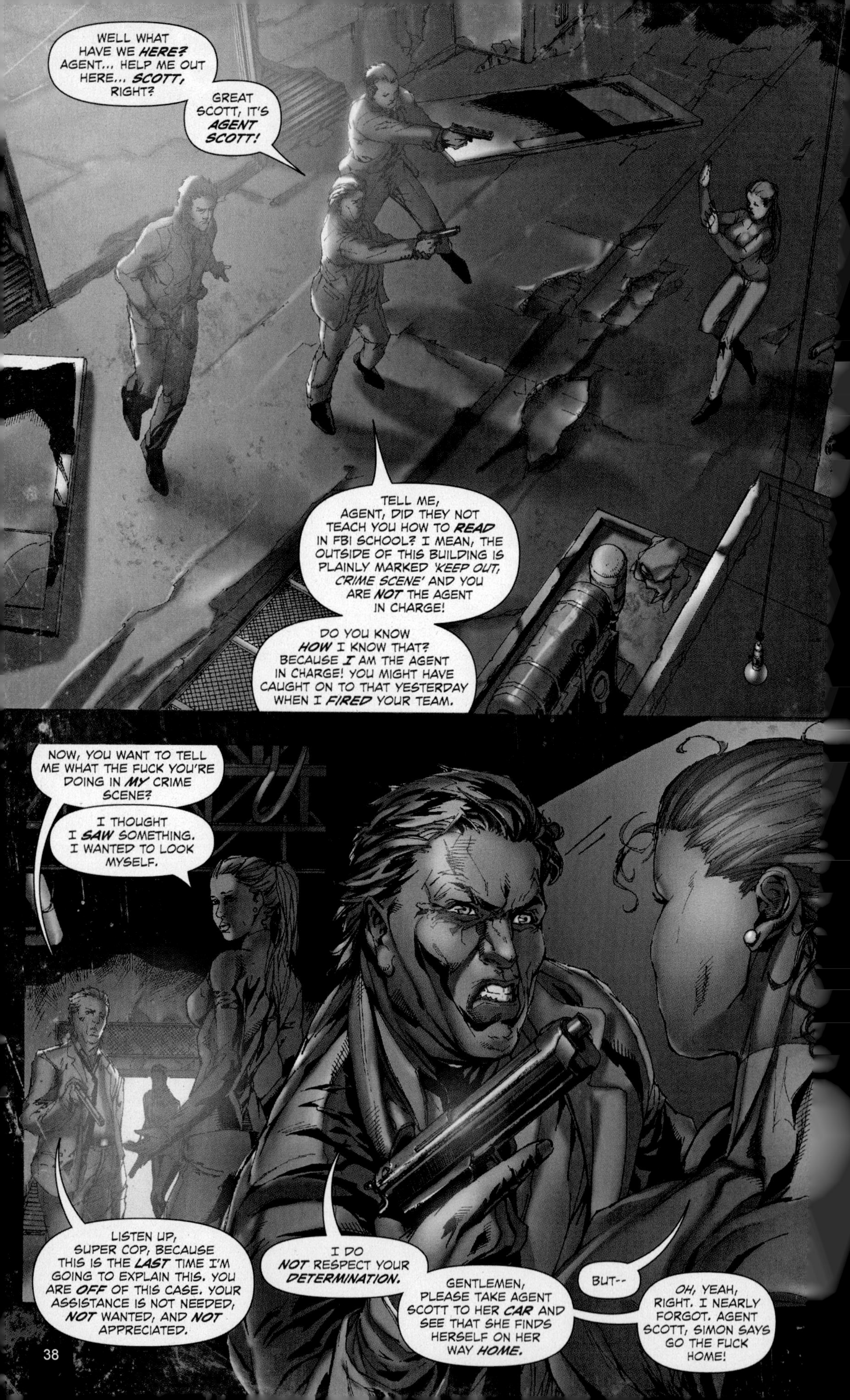
WELL WHAT HAVE WE HERE? AGENT... HELP ME OUT HERE... SCOTT, RIGHT?
GREAT SCOTT, IT'S AGENT SCOTT!
TELL ME, AGENT, DID THEY NOT TEACH YOU HOW TO READ IN FBI SCHOOL? I MEAN, THE OUTSIDE OF THIS BUILDING IS PLAINLY MARKED 'KEEP OUT, CRIME SCENE' AND YOU ARE NOT THE AGENT IN CHARGE!
DO YOU KNOW HOW I KNOW THAT? BECAUSE I AM THE AGENT IN CHARGE! YOU MIGHT HAVE CAUGHT ON TO THAT YESTERDAY WHEN I FIRED YOUR TEAM.
NOW, YOU WANT TO TELL ME WHAT THE FUCK YOU'RE DOING IN MY CRIME SCENE?
I THOUGHT I SAW SOMETHING. I WANTED TO LOOK MYSELF.
LISTEN UP, SUPER COP, BECAUSE THIS IS THE LAST TIME I'M GOING TO EXPLAIN THIS. YOU ARE OFF OF THIS CASE. YOUR ASSISTANCE IS NOT NEEDED, NOT WANTED, AND NOT APPRECIATED.
I DO NOT RESPECT YOUR DETERMINATION.
GENTLEMEN, PLEASE TAKE AGENT SCOTT TO HER CAR AND SEE THAT SHE FINDS HERSELF ON HER WAY HOME.
BUT--
OH, YEAH, RIGHT. I NEARLY FORGOT. AGENT SCOTT, SIMON SAYS GO THE FUCK HOME!

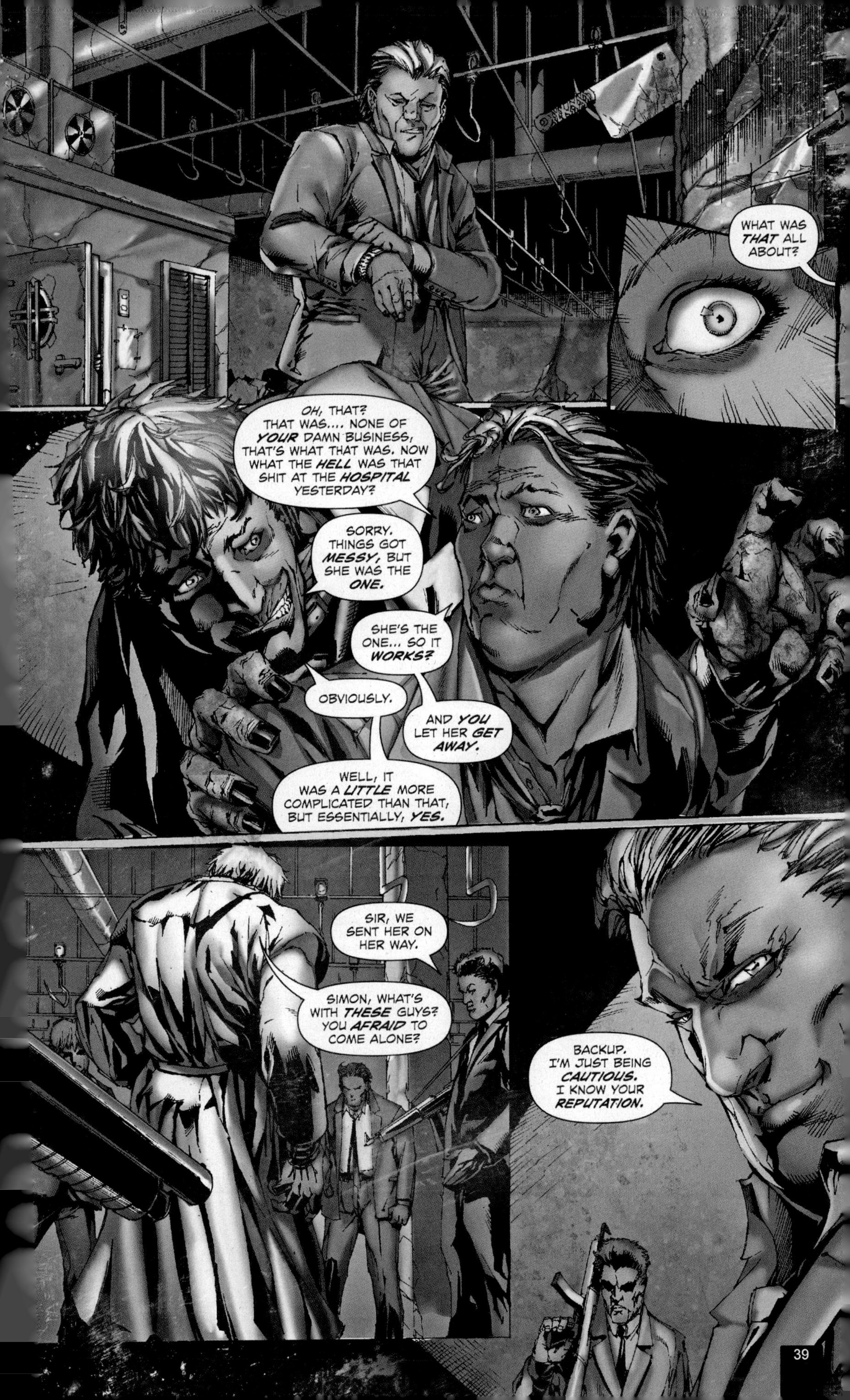
WHAT WAS THAT ALL ABOUT?
OH, THAT? THAT WAS.... NONE OF YOUR DAMN BUSINESS, THAT'S WHAT THAT WAS. NOW WHAT THE HELL WAS THAT SHIT AT THE HOSPITAL YESTERDAY?
SORRY. THINGS GOT MESSY, BUT SHE WAS THE ONE.
SHE'S THE ONE... SO IT WORKS?
OBVIOUSLY.
AND YOU LET HER GET AWAY.
WELL, IT WAS A LITTLE MORE COMPLICATED THAN THAT, BUT ESSENTIALLY, YES.
SIR, WE SENT HER ON HER WAY.
SIMON, WHAT'S WITH THESE GUYS? YOU AFRAID TO COME ALONE?
BACKUP. I'M JUST BEING CAUTIOUS. I KNOW YOUR REPUTATION.

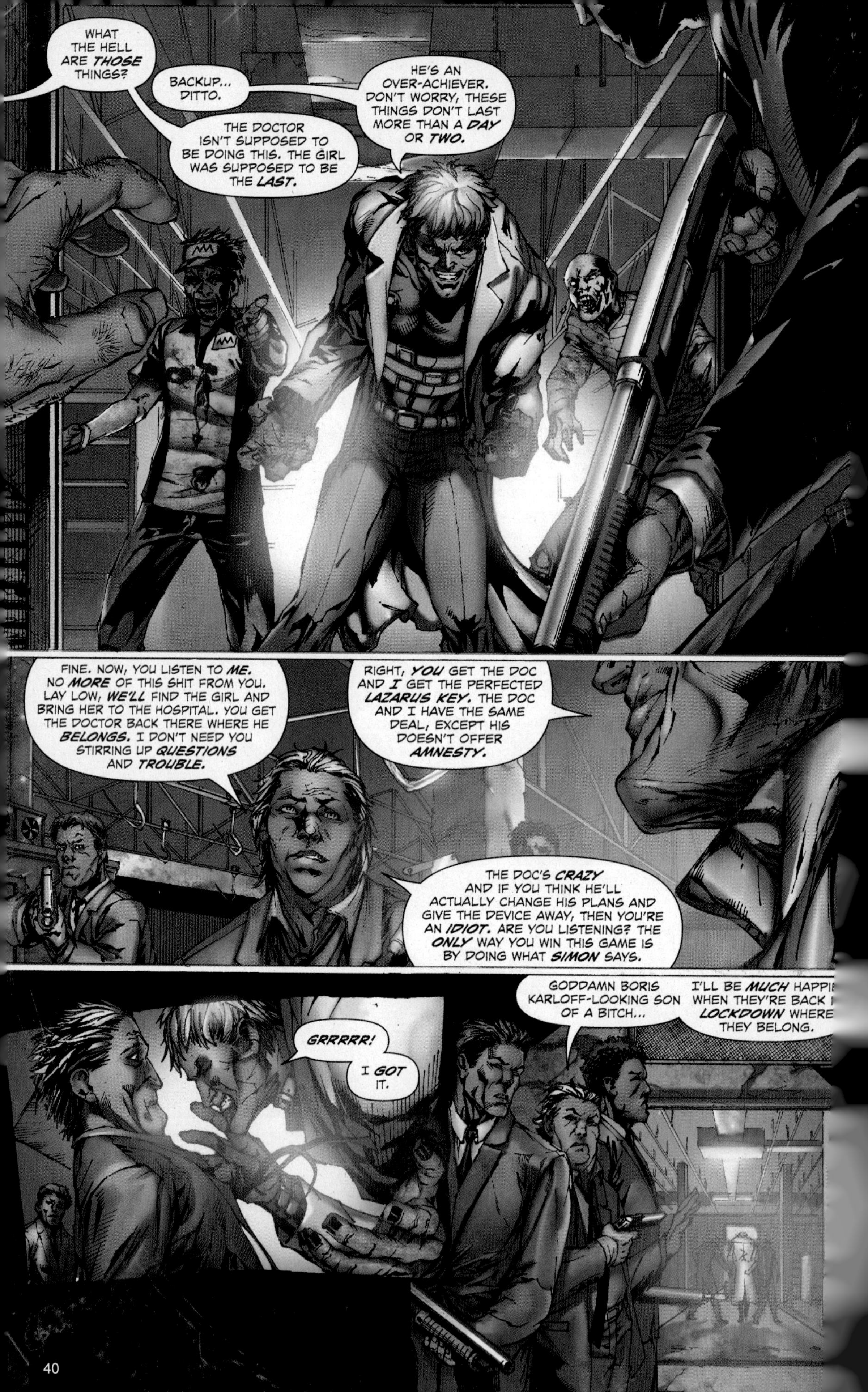
WHAT THE HELL ARE *THOSE* THINGS?
BACKUP... DITTO.
THE DOCTOR ISN'T SUPPOSED TO BE DOING THIS. THE GIRL WAS SUPPOSED TO BE THE *LAST.*
HE'S AN OVER-ACHIEVER. DON'T WORRY, THESE THINGS DON'T LAST MORE THAN A *DAY* OR *TWO.*
FINE. NOW, YOU LISTEN TO *ME.* NO *MORE* OF THIS SHIT FROM YOU. LAY LOW, *WE'LL* FIND THE GIRL AND BRING HER TO THE HOSPITAL. YOU GET THE DOCTOR BACK THERE WHERE HE *BELONGS.* I DON'T NEED YOU STIRRING UP *QUESTIONS* AND *TROUBLE.*
RIGHT, *YOU* GET THE DOC AND *I* GET THE PERFECTED *LAZARUS KEY.* THE DOC AND I HAVE THE SAME DEAL, EXCEPT HIS DOESN'T OFFER *AMNESTY.*
THE DOC'S *CRAZY* AND IF YOU THINK HE'LL ACTUALLY CHANGE HIS PLANS AND GIVE THE DEVICE AWAY, THEN YOU'RE AN *IDIOT.* ARE YOU LISTENING? THE *ONLY* WAY YOU WIN THIS GAME IS BY DOING WHAT *SIMON* SAYS.
GRRRRR!
I *GOT* IT.
GODDAMN BORIS KARLOFF-LOOKING SON OF A BITCH...
I'LL BE *MUCH* HAPPI WHEN THEY'RE BACK *LOCKDOWN* WHERE THEY BELONG.

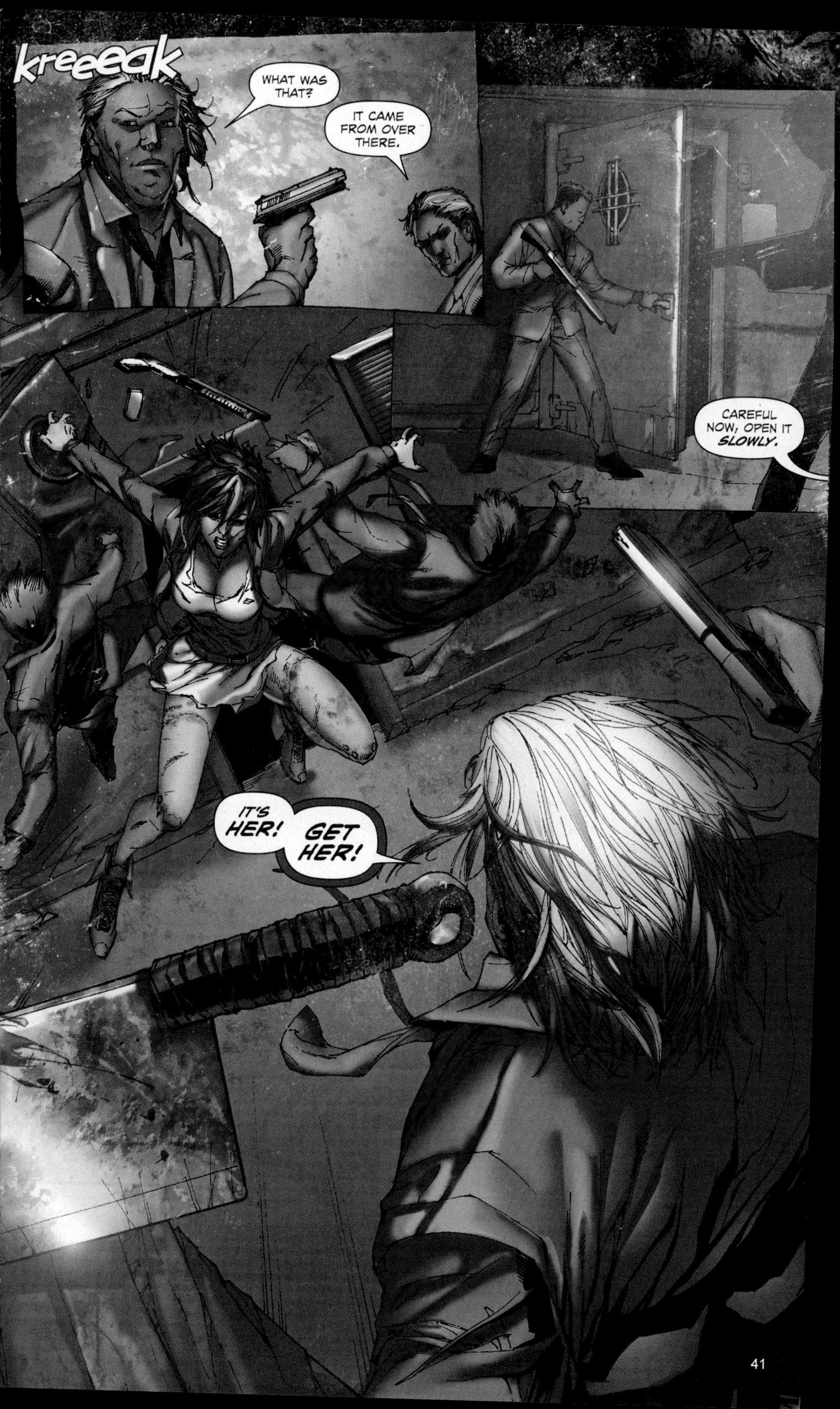
kreeeak
WHAT WAS THAT?
IT CAME FROM OVER THERE.
CAREFUL NOW, OPEN IT SLOWLY.
IT'S HER!
GET HER!

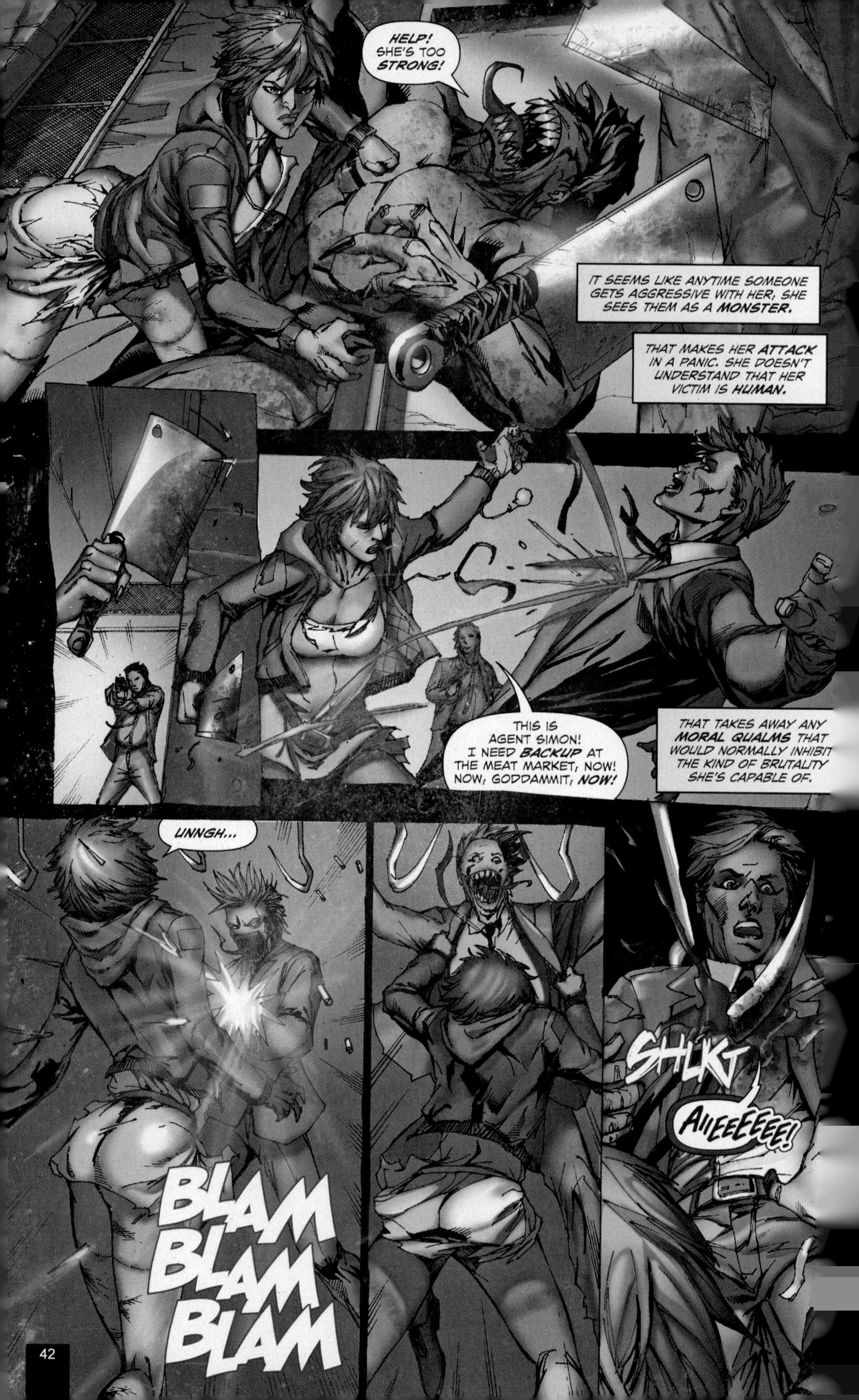
HELP! SHE'S TOO STRONG!
IT SEEMS LIKE ANYTIME SOMEONE GETS AGGRESSIVE WITH HER, SHE SEES THEM AS A MONSTER.
THAT MAKES HER ATTACK IN A PANIC. SHE DOESN'T UNDERSTAND THAT HER VICTIM IS HUMAN.
THIS IS AGENT SIMON! I NEED BACKUP AT THE MEAT MARKET, NOW! NOW, GODDAMMIT, NOW!
THAT TAKES AWAY ANY MORAL QUALMS THAT WOULD NORMALLY INHIBIT THE KIND OF BRUTALITY SHE'S CAPABLE OF.
UNNGH...
BLAM BLAM BLAM
SHLKT
AIIEEEEEE!

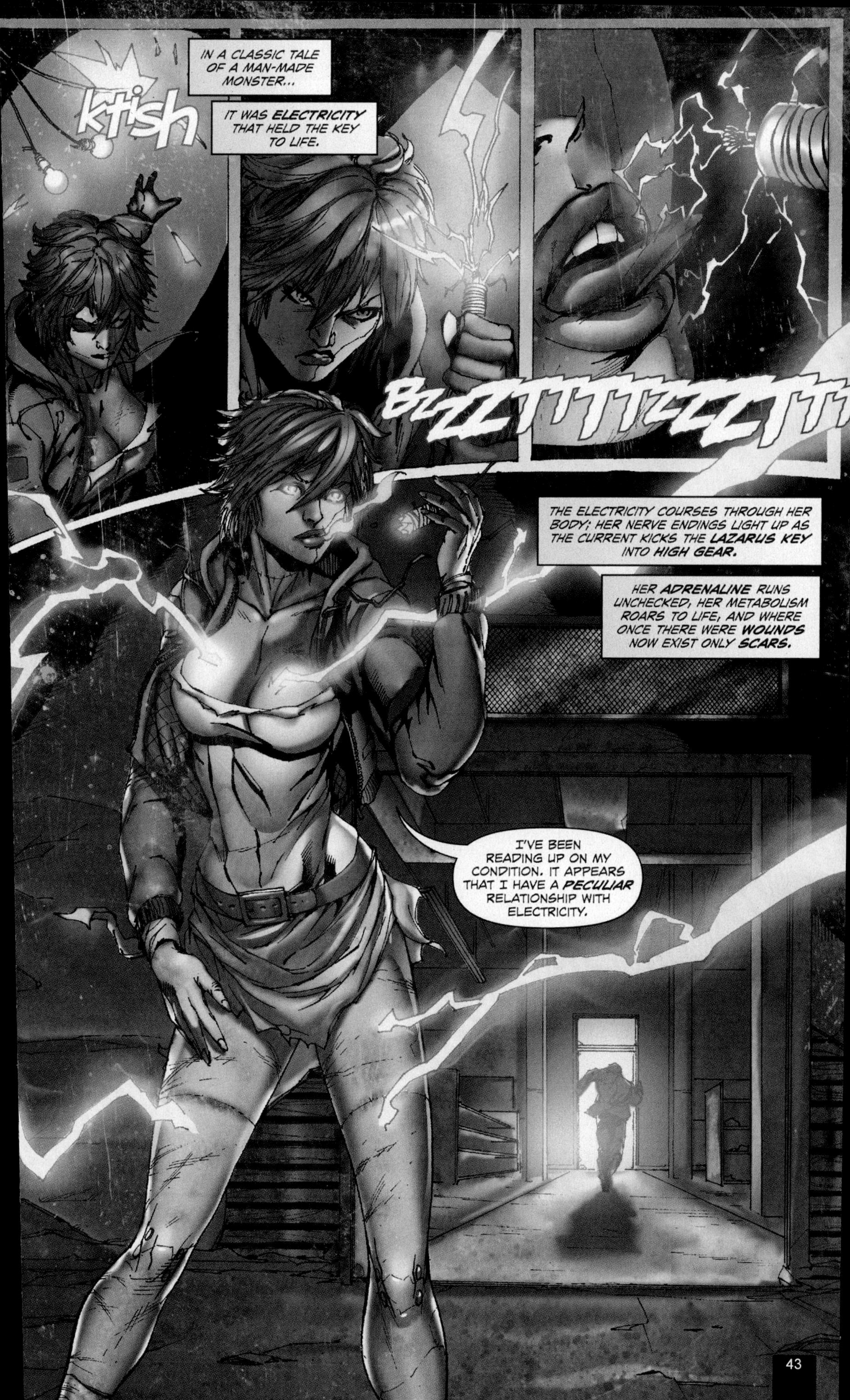
IN A CLASSIC TALE OF A MAN-MADE MONSTER...
KTISH
IT WAS ELECTRICITY THAT HELD THE KEY TO LIFE.
BZZZTTTTZZZZTTT
THE ELECTRICITY COURSES THROUGH HER BODY; HER NERVE ENDINGS LIGHT UP AS THE CURRENT KICKS THE LAZARUS KEY INTO HIGH GEAR.
HER ADRENALINE RUNS UNCHECKED, HER METABOLISM ROARS TO LIFE, AND WHERE ONCE THERE WERE WOUNDS NOW EXIST ONLY SCARS.
I'VE BEEN READING UP ON MY CONDITION. IT APPEARS THAT I HAVE A PECULIAR RELATIONSHIP WITH ELECTRICITY.

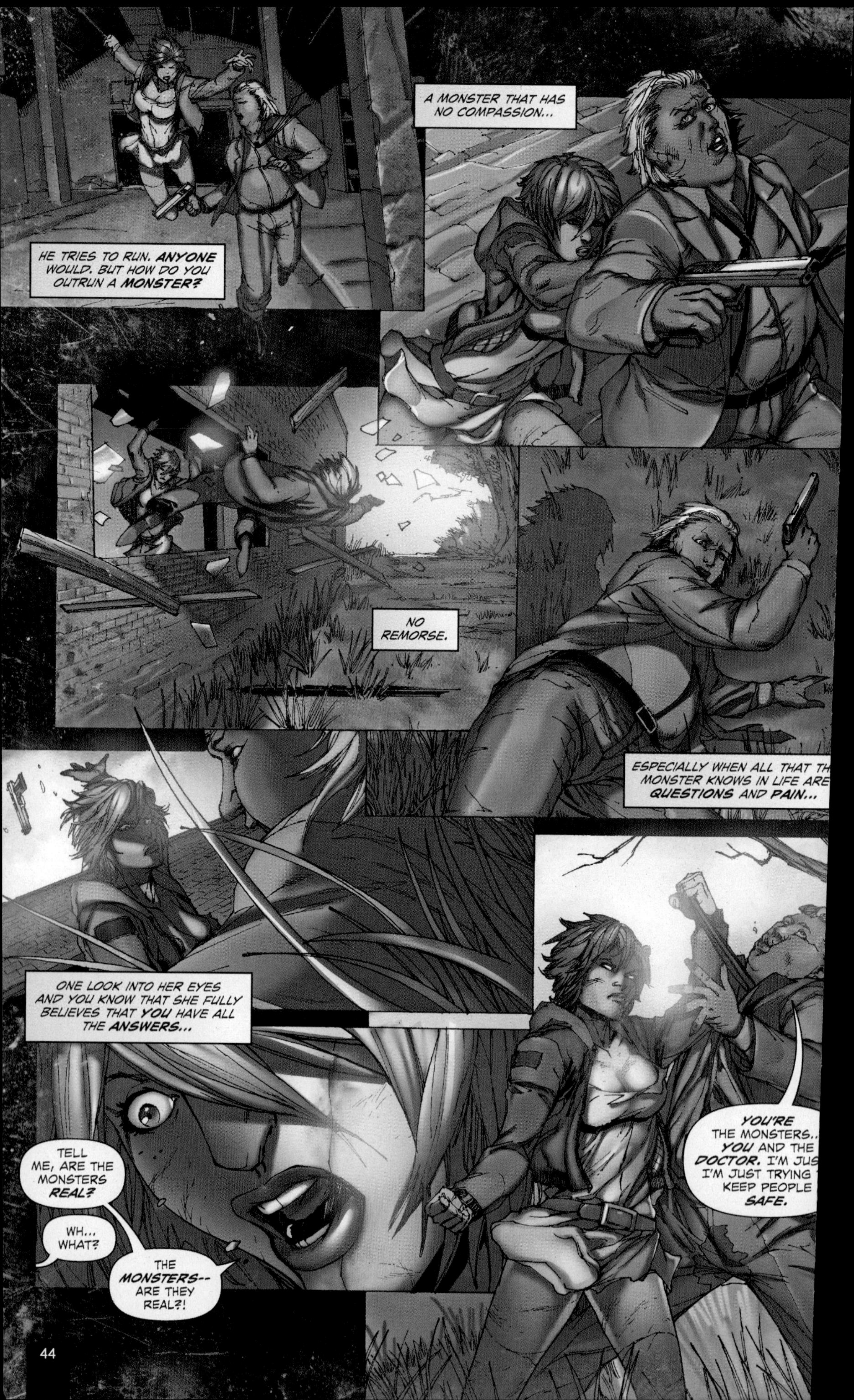

HE TRIES TO RUN. ANYONE WOULD. BUT HOW DO YOU OUTRUN A MONSTER?
A MONSTER THAT HAS NO COMPASSION...
NO REMORSE.
ESPECIALLY WHEN ALL THAT TH MONSTER KNOWS IN LIFE ARE QUESTIONS AND PAIN...
ONE LOOK INTO HER EYES AND YOU KNOW THAT SHE FULLY BELIEVES THAT YOU HAVE ALL THE ANSWERS...
TELL ME, ARE THE MONSTERS REAL?
WH... WHAT?
THE MONSTERS-- ARE THEY REAL?!
YOU'RE THE MONSTERS.. YOU AND THE DOCTOR. I'M JUS I'M JUST TRYING KEEP PEOPLE SAFE.

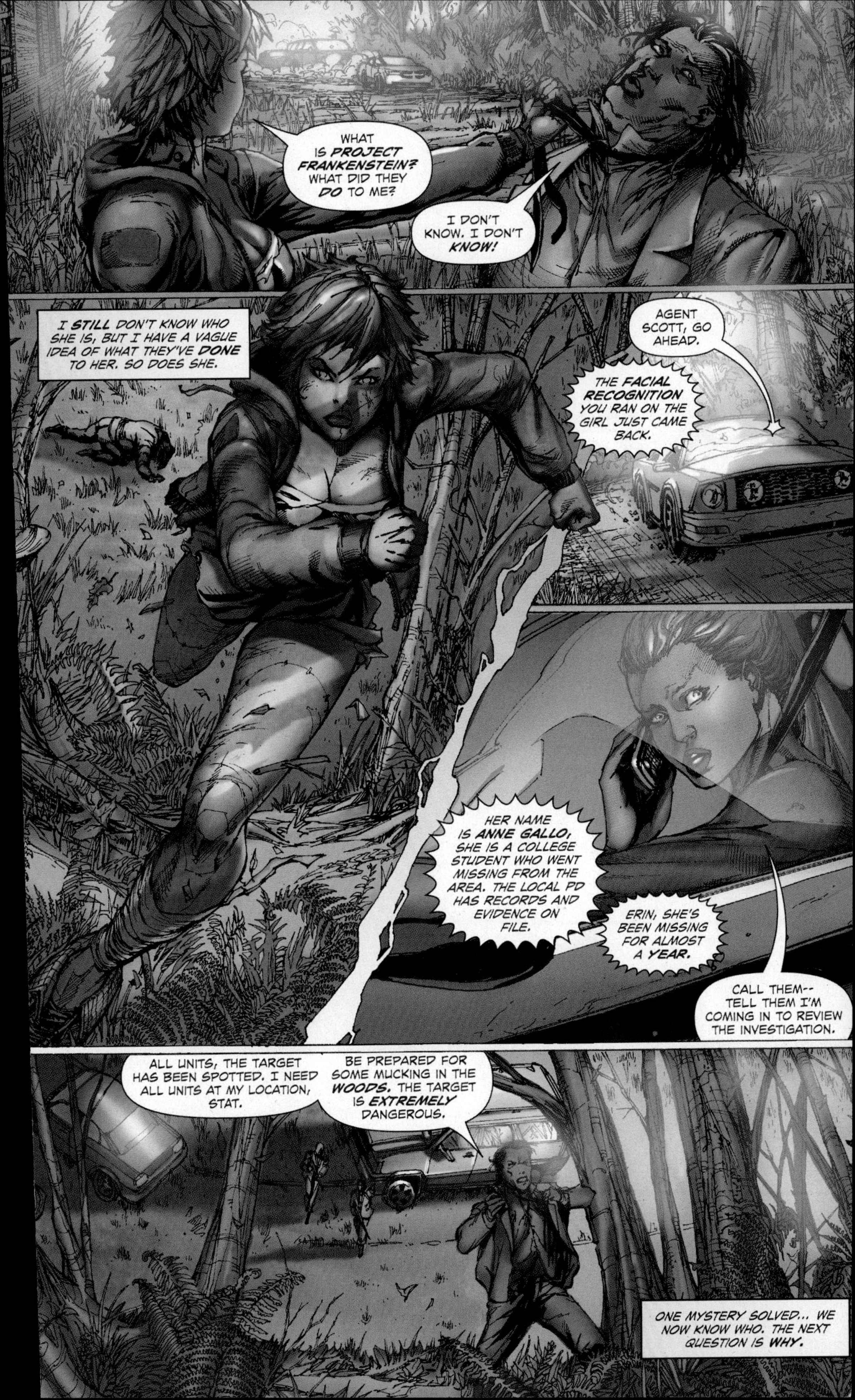
WHAT IS PROJECT FRANKENSTEIN? WHAT DID THEY DO TO ME?
I DON'T KNOW. I DON'T KNOW!
I STILL DON'T KNOW WHO SHE IS, BUT I HAVE A VAGUE IDEA OF WHAT THEY'VE DONE TO HER. SO DOES SHE.
AGENT SCOTT, GO AHEAD.
THE FACIAL RECOGNITION YOU RAN ON THE GIRL JUST CAME BACK.
HER NAME IS ANNE GALLO, SHE IS A COLLEGE STUDENT WHO WENT MISSING FROM THE AREA. THE LOCAL PD HAS RECORDS AND EVIDENCE ON FILE.
ERIN, SHE'S BEEN MISSING FOR ALMOST A YEAR.
CALL THEM--TELL THEM I'M COMING IN TO REVIEW THE INVESTIGATION.
ALL UNITS, THE TARGET HAS BEEN SPOTTED. I NEED ALL UNITS AT MY LOCATION, STAT.
BE PREPARED FOR SOME MUCKING IN THE WOODS. THE TARGET IS EXTREMELY DANGEROUS.
ONE MYSTERY SOLVED... WE NOW KNOW WHO. THE NEXT QUESTION IS WHY.

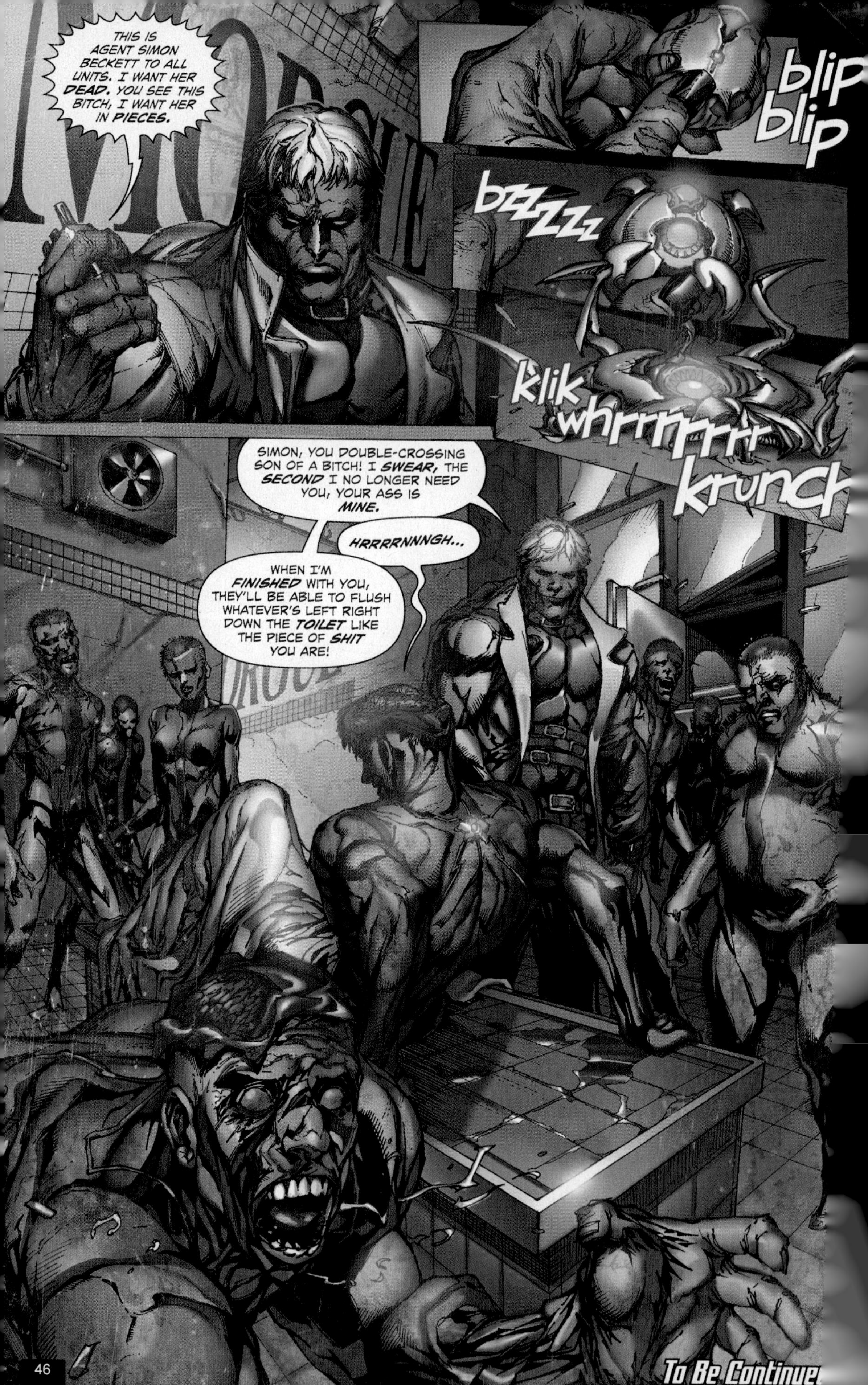
THIS IS AGENT SIMON BECKETT TO ALL UNITS. I WANT HER DEAD. YOU SEE THIS BITCH, I WANT HER IN PIECES.
blip blip
bzzzzz
klik
whrrrrrrrr
krunch
SIMON, YOU DOUBLE-CROSSING SON OF A BITCH! I SWEAR, THE SECOND I NO LONGER NEED YOU, YOUR ASS IS MINE.
HRRRRNNNGH...
WHEN I'M FINISHED WITH YOU, THEY'LL BE ABLE TO FLUSH WHATEVER'S LEFT RIGHT DOWN THE TOILET LIKE THE PIECE OF SHIT YOU ARE!
To Be Continue

SCREWED

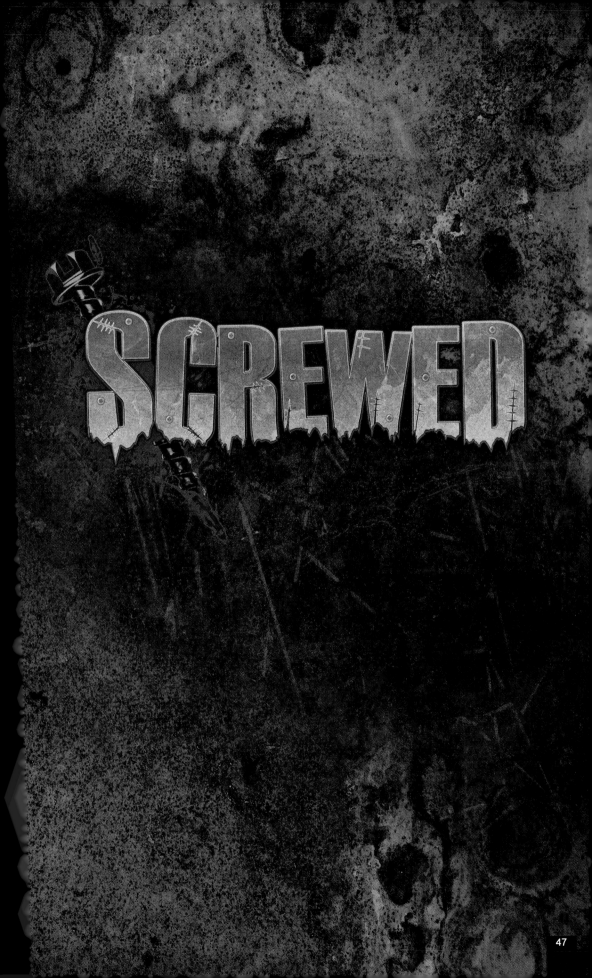

CHAPTER THREE

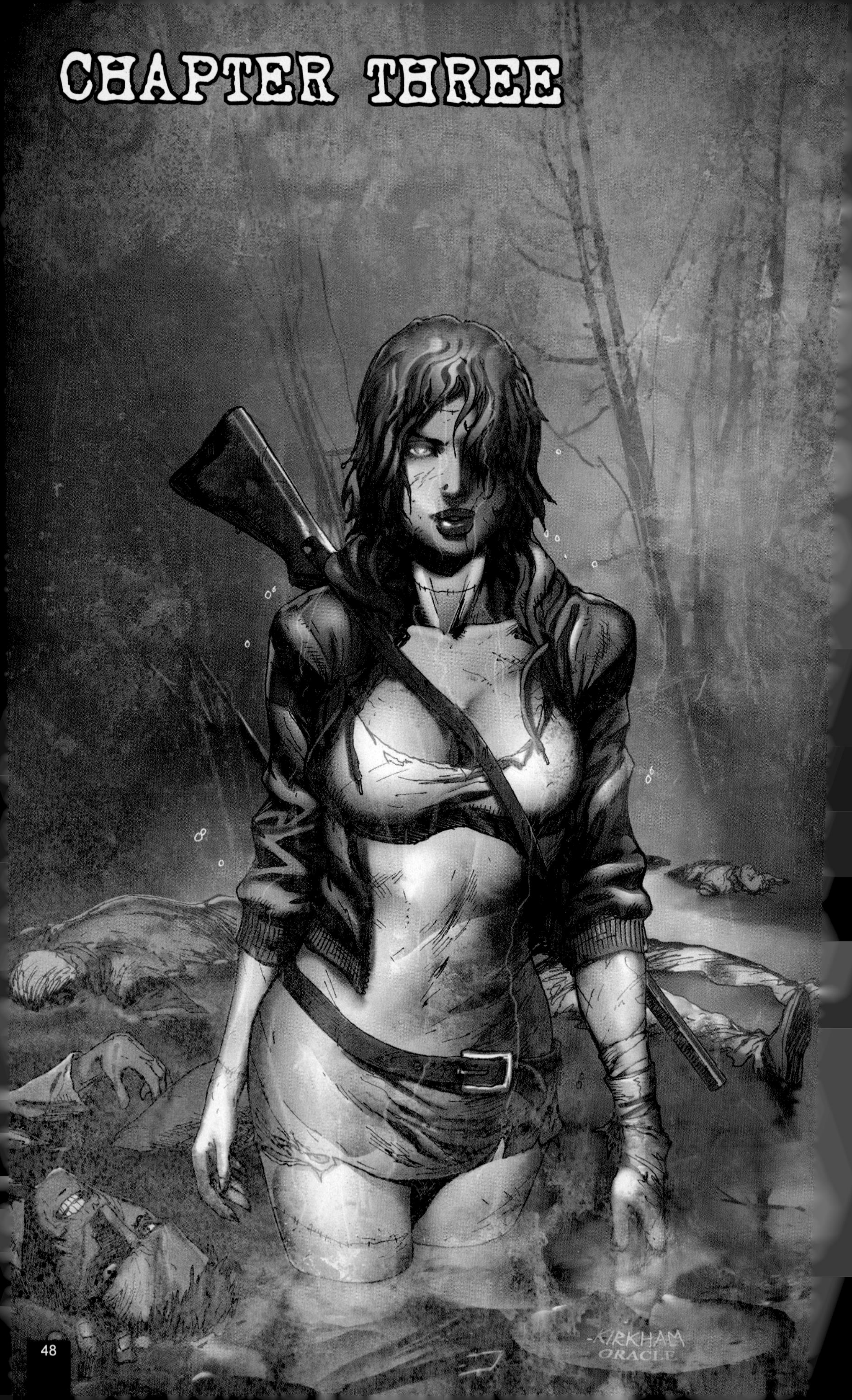
KIRKHAM
ORACLE

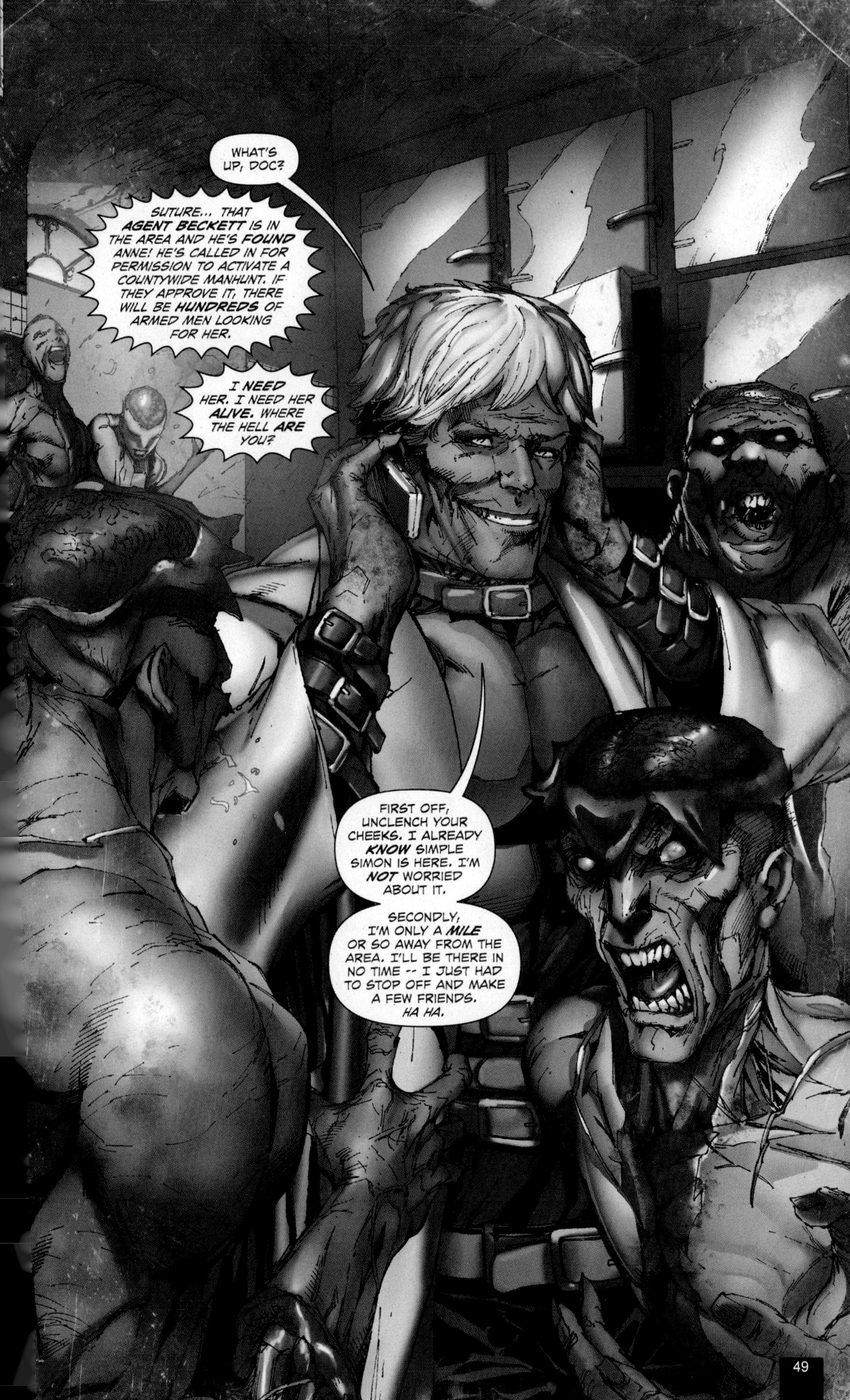
WHAT'S UP, DOC?
SUTURE... THAT AGENT BECKETT IS IN THE AREA AND HE'S FOUND ANNE! HE'S CALLED IN FOR PERMISSION TO ACTIVATE A COUNTYWIDE MANHUNT. IF THEY APPROVE IT, THERE WILL BE HUNDREDS OF ARMED MEN LOOKING FOR HER.
I NEED HER. I NEED HER ALIVE. WHERE THE HELL ARE YOU?
FIRST OFF, UNCLENCH YOUR CHEEKS. I ALREADY KNOW SIMPLE SIMON IS HERE. I'M NOT WORRIED ABOUT IT.
SECONDLY, I'M ONLY A MILE OR SO AWAY FROM THE AREA. I'LL BE THERE IN NO TIME -- I JUST HAD TO STOP OFF AND MAKE A FEW FRIENDS. HA HA.

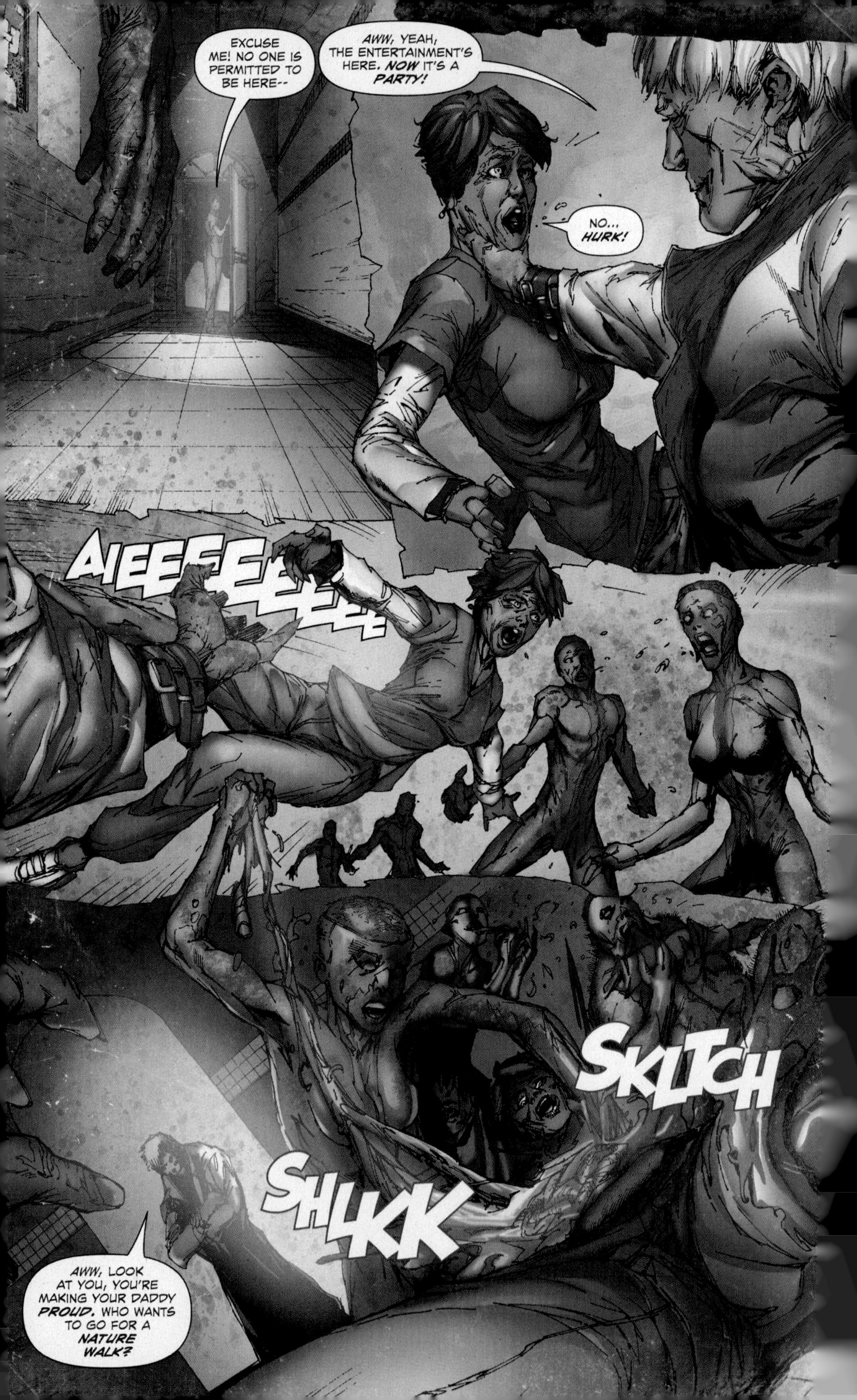
EXCUSE ME! NO ONE IS PERMITTED TO BE HERE--
AWW, YEAH, THE ENTERTAINMENT'S HERE. NOW IT'S A PARTY!
NO... HURK!
AIEEEEEEEEE
SKLTCH
SHLKK
AWW, LOOK AT YOU, YOU'RE MAKING YOUR DADDY PROUD. WHO WANTS TO GO FOR A NATURE WALK?

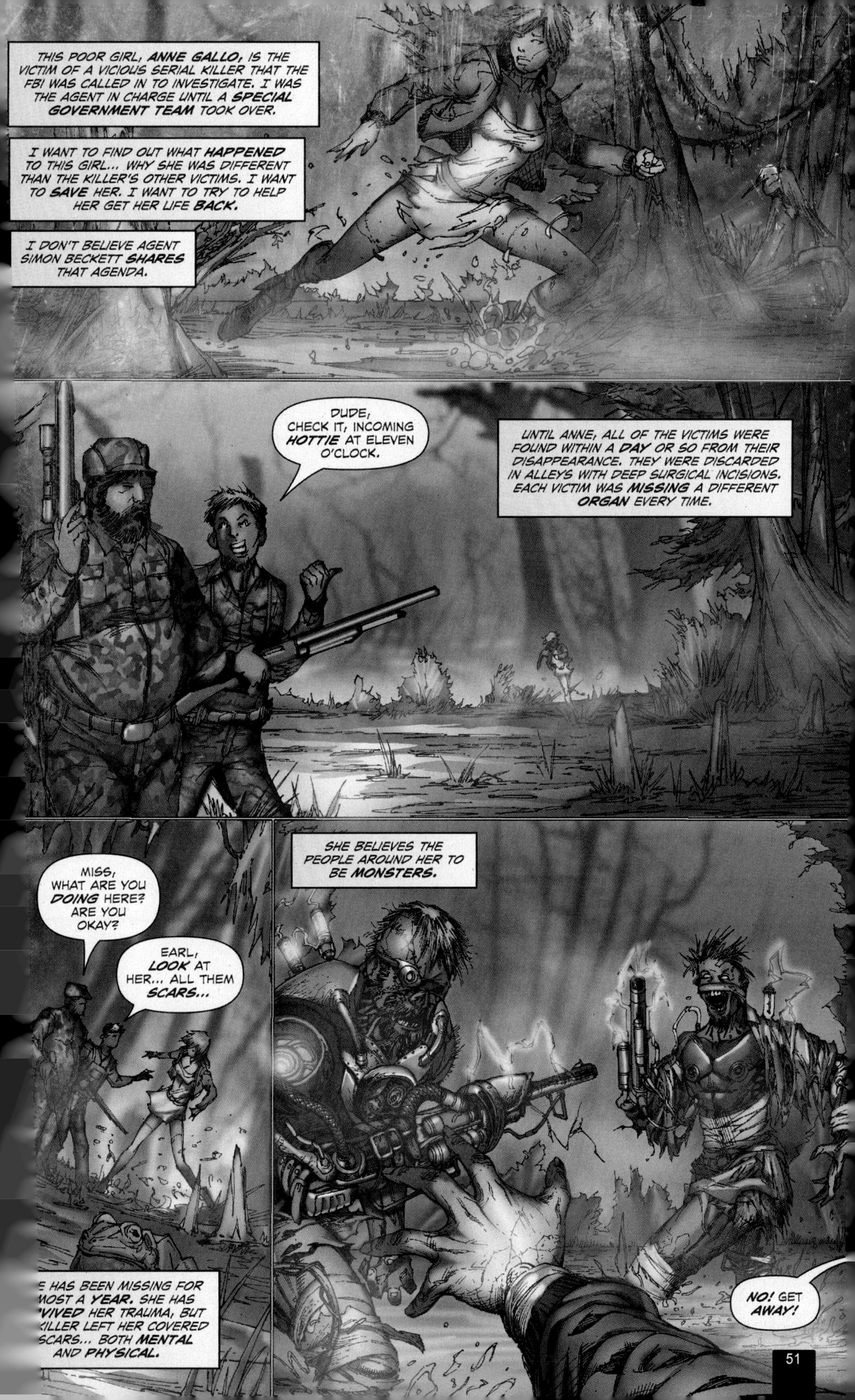

THIS POOR GIRL, ANNE GALLO, IS THE VICTIM OF A VICIOUS SERIAL KILLER THAT THE FBI WAS CALLED IN TO INVESTIGATE. I WAS THE AGENT IN CHARGE UNTIL A SPECIAL GOVERNMENT TEAM TOOK OVER.
I WANT TO FIND OUT WHAT HAPPENED TO THIS GIRL... WHY SHE WAS DIFFERENT THAN THE KILLER'S OTHER VICTIMS. I WANT TO SAVE HER. I WANT TO TRY TO HELP HER GET HER LIFE BACK.
I DON'T BELIEVE AGENT SIMON BECKETT SHARES THAT AGENDA.
DUDE, CHECK IT, INCOMING HOTTIE AT ELEVEN O'CLOCK.
UNTIL ANNE, ALL OF THE VICTIMS WERE FOUND WITHIN A DAY OR SO FROM THEIR DISAPPEARANCE. THEY WERE DISCARDED IN ALLEYS WITH DEEP SURGICAL INCISIONS. EACH VICTIM WAS MISSING A DIFFERENT ORGAN EVERY TIME.
MISS, WHAT ARE YOU DOING HERE? ARE YOU OKAY?
EARL, LOOK AT HER... ALL THEM SCARS...
E HAS BEEN MISSING FOR MOST A YEAR. SHE HAS VIVED HER TRAUMA, BUT KILLER LEFT HER COVERED SCARS... BOTH MENTAL AND PHYSICAL.
SHE BELIEVES THE PEOPLE AROUND HER TO BE MONSTERS.
NO! GET AWAY!

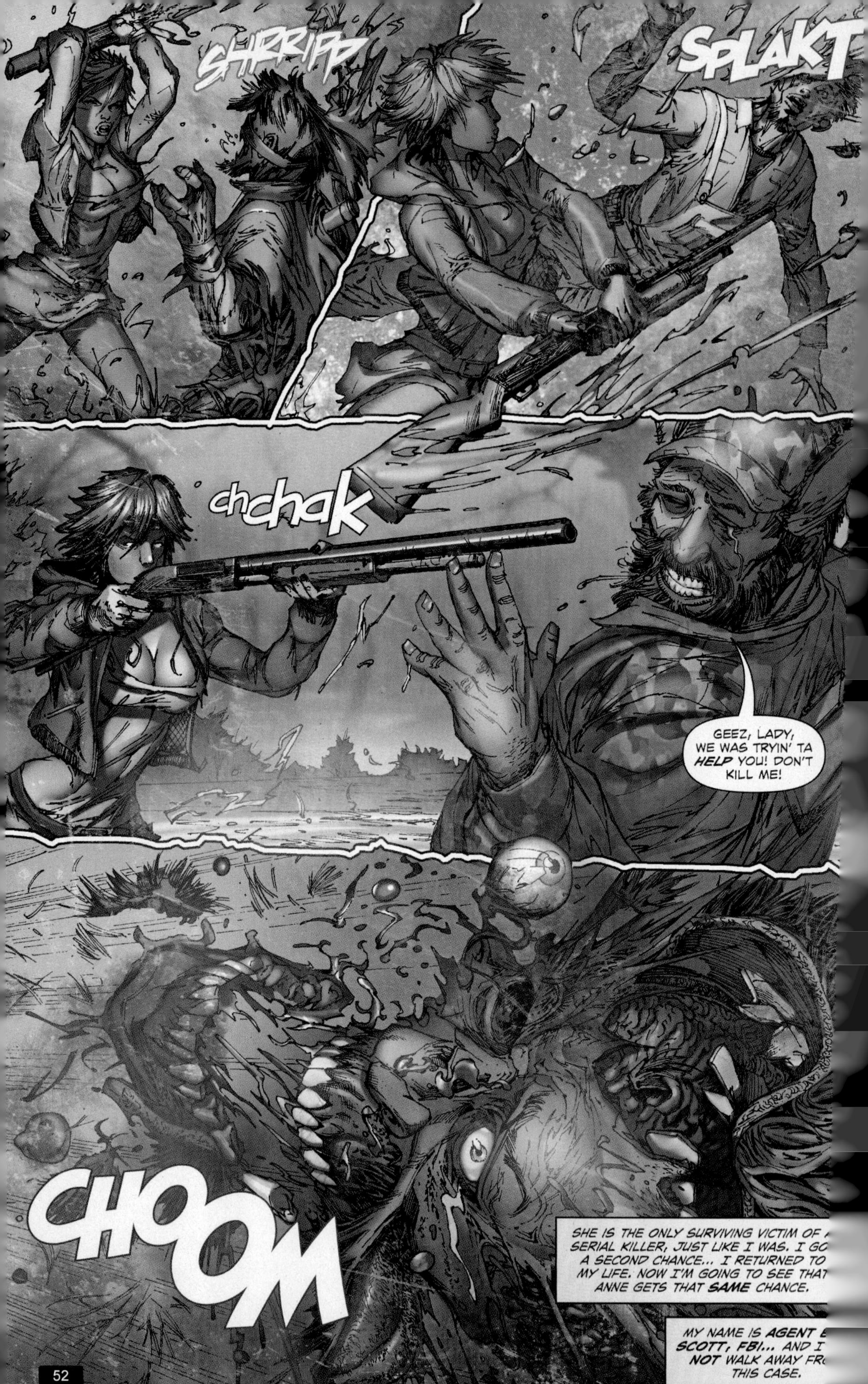
SHRRIPP
SPLAKT
chchak
GEEZ, LADY, WE WAS TRYIN' TA **HELP** YOU! DON'T KILL ME!
CHOOM
SHE IS THE ONLY SURVIVING VICTIM OF A SERIAL KILLER, JUST LIKE I WAS. I GO A SECOND CHANCE... I RETURNED TO MY LIFE. NOW I'M GOING TO SEE THAT ANNE GETS THAT **SAME** CHANCE.
MY NAME IS **AGENT** **SCOTT, FBI**... AND I **NOT** WALK AWAY FR THIS CASE.

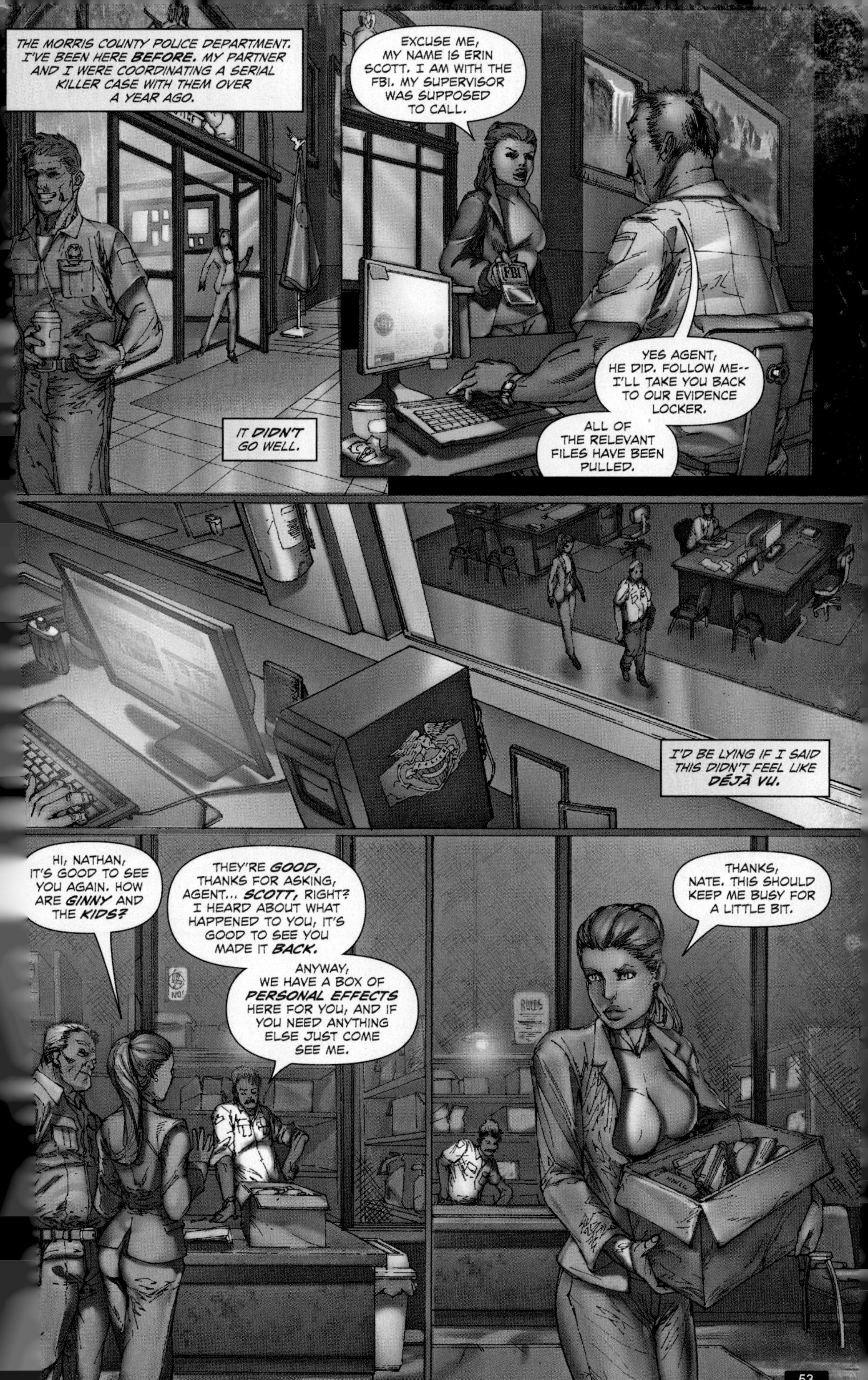
THE MORRIS COUNTY POLICE DEPARTMENT. I'VE BEEN HERE **BEFORE.** MY PARTNER AND I WERE COORDINATING A SERIAL KILLER CASE WITH THEM OVER A YEAR AGO.
IT **DIDN'T** GO WELL.
EXCUSE ME, MY NAME IS ERIN SCOTT. I AM WITH THE FBI. MY SUPERVISOR WAS SUPPOSED TO CALL.
YES AGENT, HE DID. FOLLOW ME-- I'LL TAKE YOU BACK TO OUR EVIDENCE LOCKER.
ALL OF THE RELEVANT FILES HAVE BEEN PULLED.
I'D BE LYING IF I SAID THIS DIDN'T FEEL LIKE **DÉJÀ VU.**
HI, NATHAN, IT'S GOOD TO SEE YOU AGAIN. HOW ARE **GINNY** AND THE **KIDS?**
THEY'RE **GOOD,** THANKS FOR ASKING, AGENT... **SCOTT,** RIGHT? I HEARD ABOUT WHAT HAPPENED TO YOU, IT'S GOOD TO SEE YOU MADE IT **BACK.**
ANYWAY, WE HAVE A BOX OF **PERSONAL EFFECTS** HERE FOR YOU, AND IF YOU NEED ANYTHING ELSE JUST COME SEE ME.
THANKS, NATE. THIS SHOULD KEEP ME BUSY FOR A LITTLE BIT.

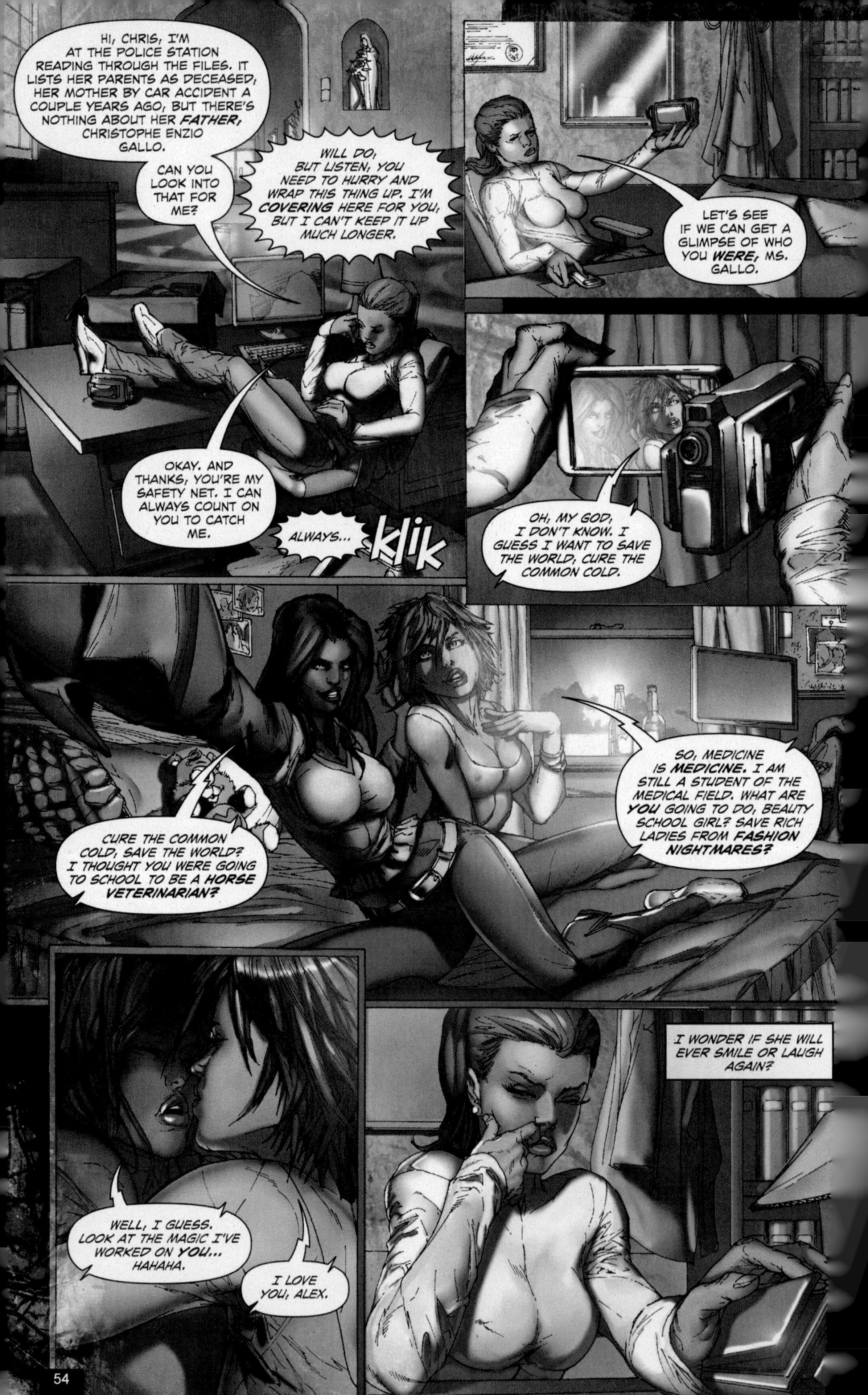
HI, CHRIS, I'M AT THE POLICE STATION READING THROUGH THE FILES. IT LISTS HER PARENTS AS DECEASED, HER MOTHER BY CAR ACCIDENT A COUPLE YEARS AGO, BUT THERE'S NOTHING ABOUT HER FATHER, CHRISTOPHE ENZIO GALLO.
CAN YOU LOOK INTO THAT FOR ME?
WILL DO, BUT LISTEN, YOU NEED TO HURRY AND WRAP THIS THING UP. I'M COVERING HERE FOR YOU, BUT I CAN'T KEEP IT UP MUCH LONGER.
OKAY. AND THANKS, YOU'RE MY SAFETY NET. I CAN ALWAYS COUNT ON YOU TO CATCH ME.
ALWAYS...
KLIK
LET'S SEE IF WE CAN GET A GLIMPSE OF WHO YOU WERE, MS. GALLO.
OH, MY GOD, I DON'T KNOW. I GUESS I WANT TO SAVE THE WORLD, CURE THE COMMON COLD.
CURE THE COMMON COLD, SAVE THE WORLD? I THOUGHT YOU WERE GOING TO SCHOOL TO BE A HORSE VETERINARIAN?
SO, MEDICINE IS MEDICINE. I AM STILL A STUDENT OF THE MEDICAL FIELD. WHAT ARE YOU GOING TO DO, BEAUTY SCHOOL GIRL? SAVE RICH LADIES FROM FASHION NIGHTMARES?
WELL, I GUESS. LOOK AT THE MAGIC I'VE WORKED ON YOU... HAHAHA.
I LOVE YOU, ALEX.
I WONDER IF SHE WILL EVER SMILE OR LAUGH AGAIN?

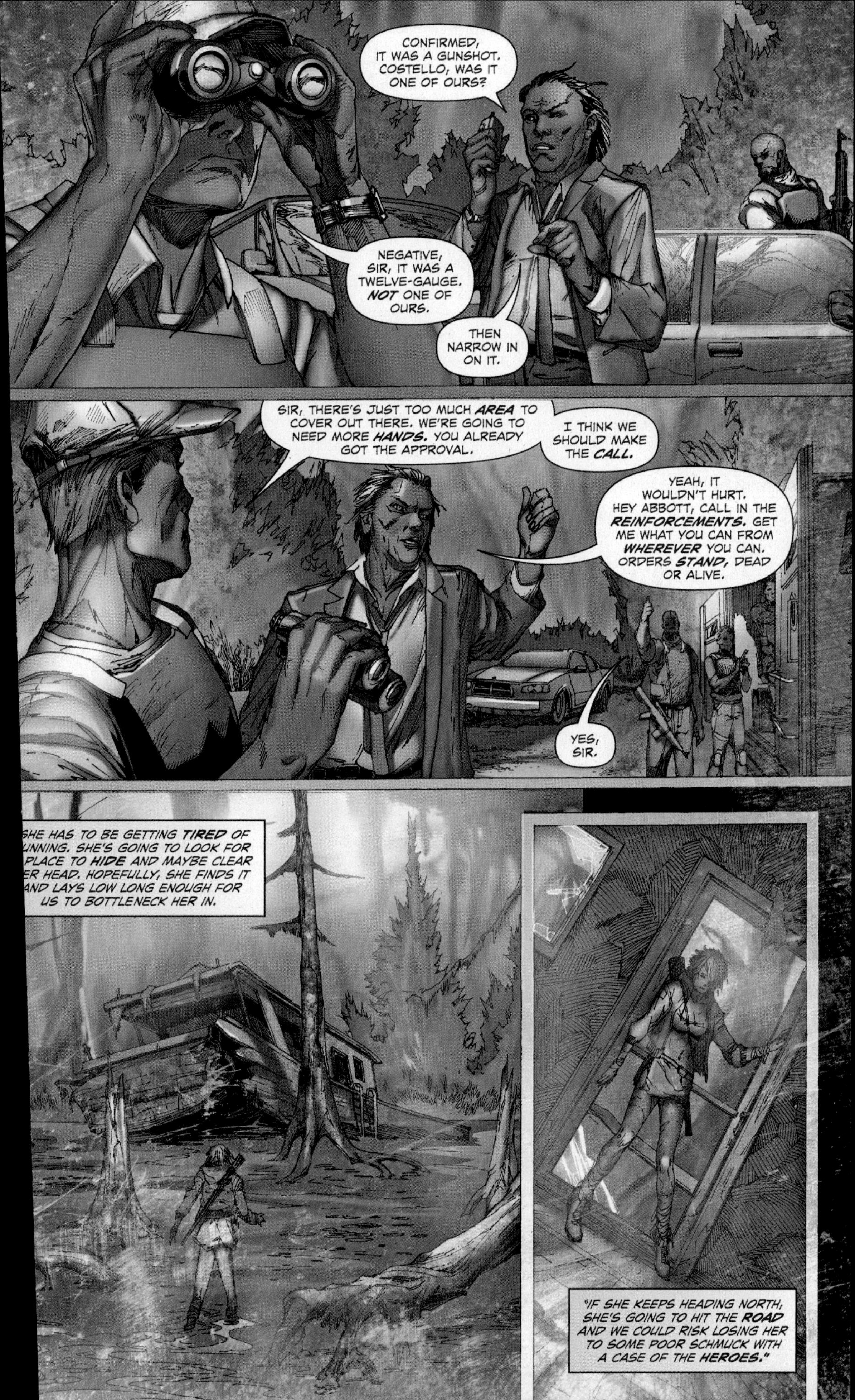
CONFIRMED, IT WAS A GUNSHOT. COSTELLO, WAS IT ONE OF OURS?
NEGATIVE, SIR, IT WAS A TWELVE-GAUGE. NOT ONE OF OURS.
THEN NARROW IN ON IT.
SIR, THERE'S JUST TOO MUCH AREA TO COVER OUT THERE. WE'RE GOING TO NEED MORE HANDS. YOU ALREADY GOT THE APPROVAL.
I THINK WE SHOULD MAKE THE CALL.
YEAH, IT WOULDN'T HURT. HEY ABBOTT, CALL IN THE REINFORCEMENTS. GET ME WHAT YOU CAN FROM WHEREVER YOU CAN. ORDERS STAND, DEAD OR ALIVE.
YES, SIR.
SHE HAS TO BE GETTING TIRED OF UNNING. SHE'S GOING TO LOOK FOR PLACE TO HIDE AND MAYBE CLEAR ER HEAD. HOPEFULLY, SHE FINDS IT AND LAYS LOW LONG ENOUGH FOR US TO BOTTLENECK HER IN.
"IF SHE KEEPS HEADING NORTH, SHE'S GOING TO HIT THE ROAD AND WE COULD RISK LOSING HER TO SOME POOR SCHMUCK WITH A CASE OF THE HEROES."

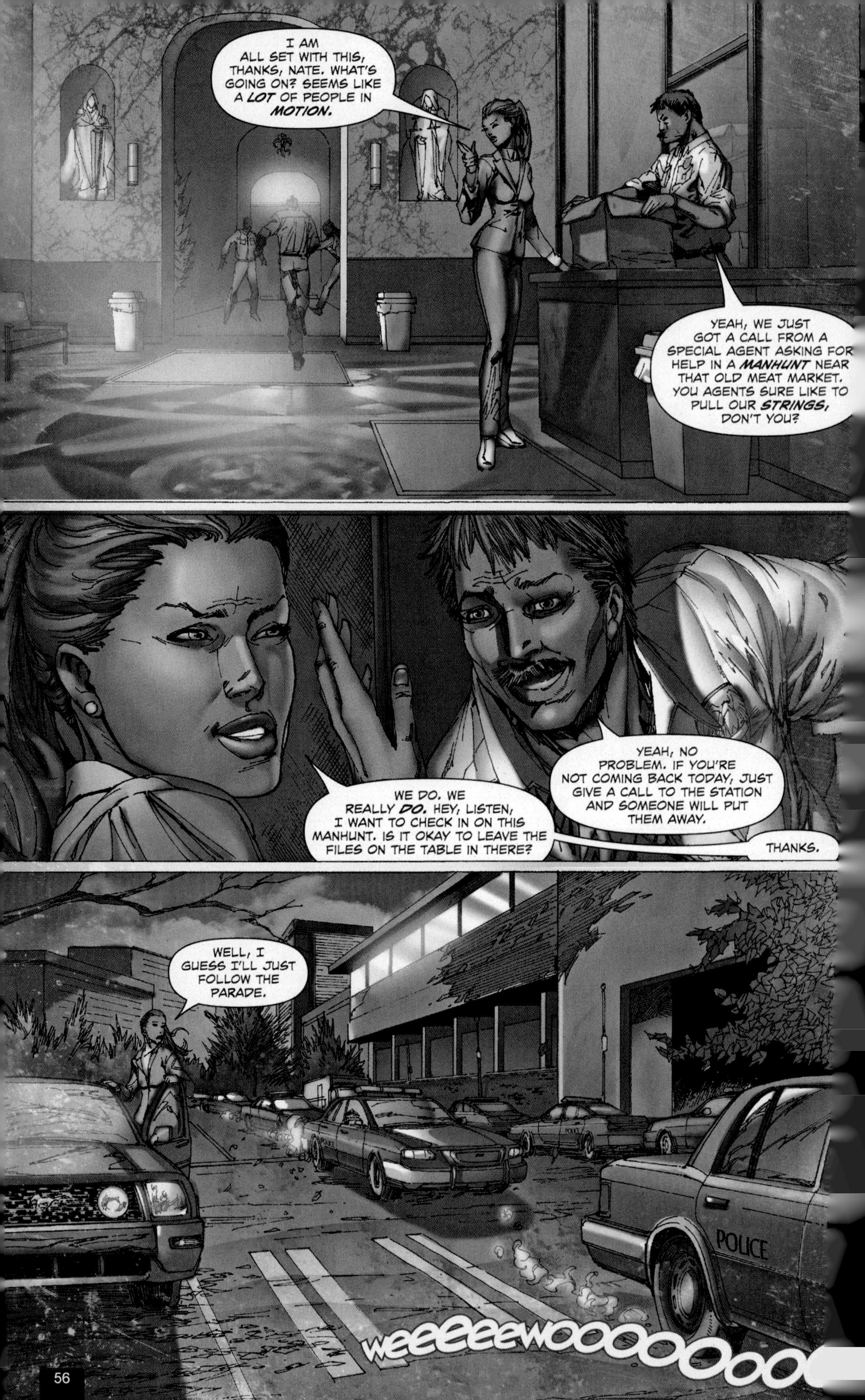
I AM ALL SET WITH THIS, THANKS, NATE. WHAT'S GOING ON? SEEMS LIKE A LOT OF PEOPLE IN MOTION.
YEAH, WE JUST GOT A CALL FROM A SPECIAL AGENT ASKING FOR HELP IN A MANHUNT NEAR THAT OLD MEAT MARKET. YOU AGENTS SURE LIKE TO PULL OUR STRINGS, DON'T YOU?
WE DO. WE REALLY DO. HEY, LISTEN, I WANT TO CHECK IN ON THIS MANHUNT. IS IT OKAY TO LEAVE THE FILES ON THE TABLE IN THERE?
YEAH, NO PROBLEM. IF YOU'RE NOT COMING BACK TODAY, JUST GIVE A CALL TO THE STATION AND SOMEONE WILL PUT THEM AWAY.
THANKS.
WELL, I GUESS I'LL JUST FOLLOW THE PARADE.
POLICE
WEEEEEEWOOOOOOOOOO

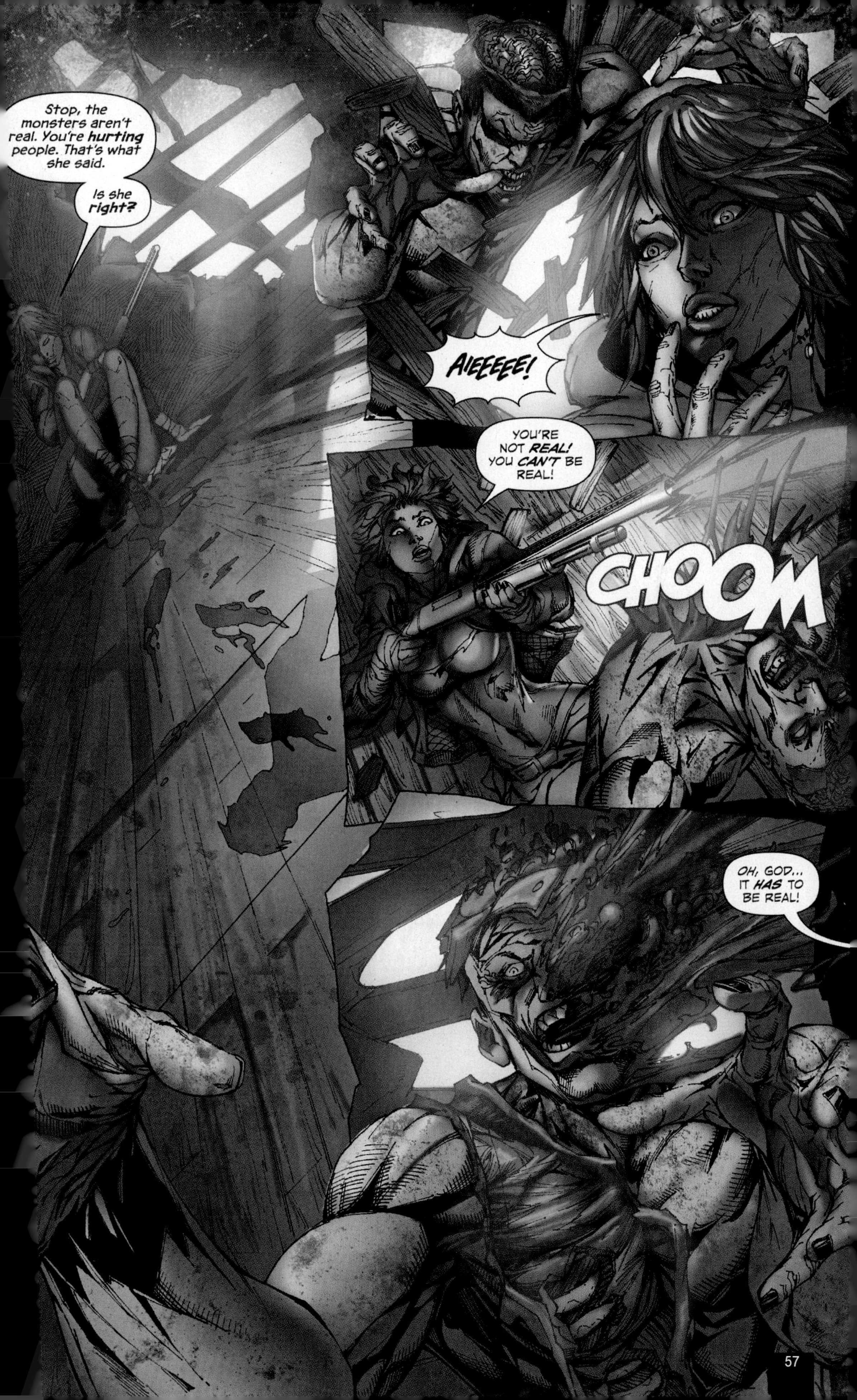
Stop, the monsters aren't real. You're **hurting** people. That's what she said.
Is she **right?**
AIEEEEE!
YOU'RE NOT ***REAL!*** YOU ***CAN'T*** BE REAL!
CHOOM
OH, GOD... IT ***HAS*** TO BE REAL!

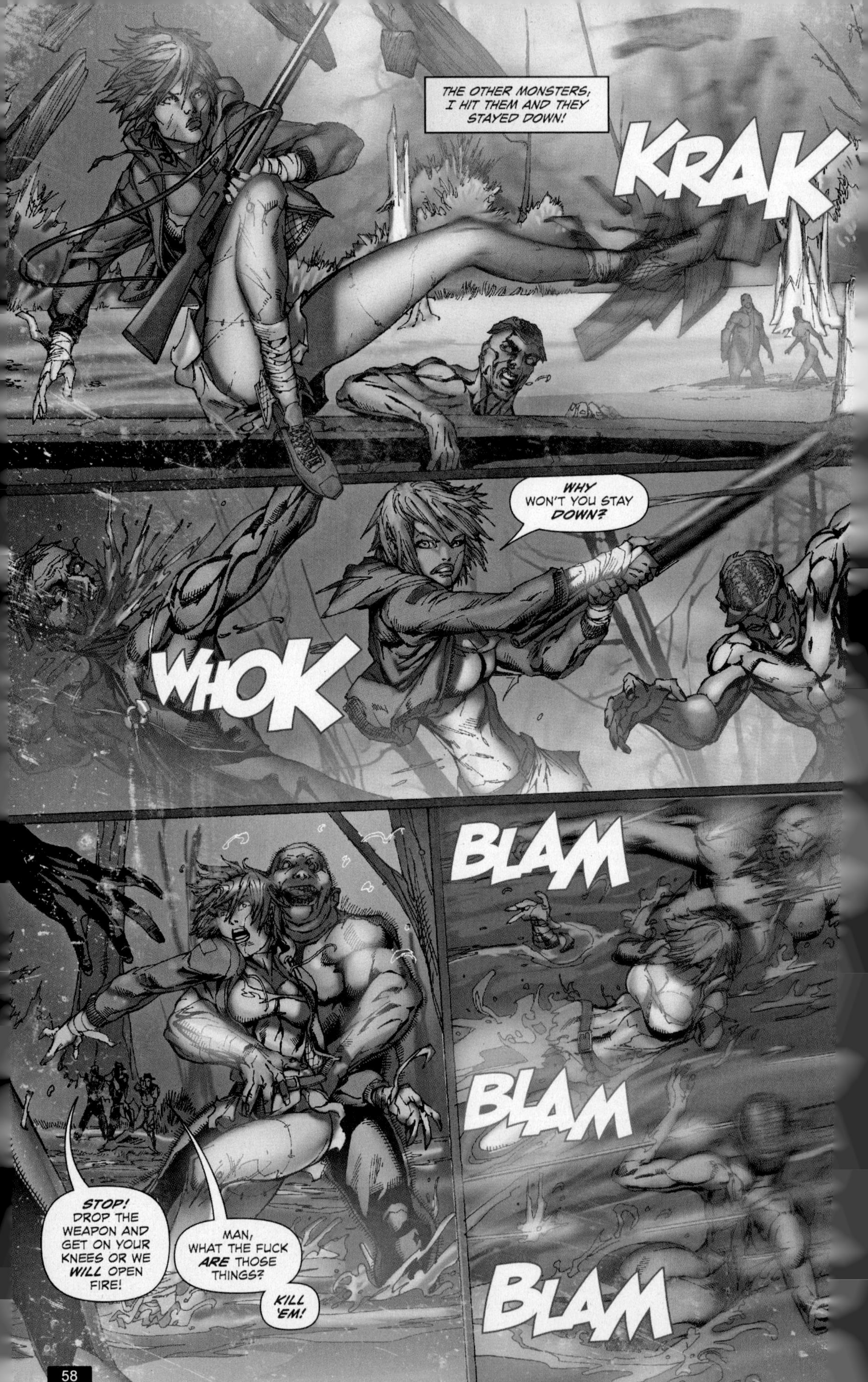
THE OTHER MONSTERS; I HIT THEM AND THEY STAYED DOWN!
KRAK
WHY WON'T YOU STAY DOWN?
WHOK
STOP! DROP THE WEAPON AND GET ON YOUR KNEES OR WE WILL OPEN FIRE!
MAN, WHAT THE FUCK ARE THOSE THINGS?
KILL 'EM!
BLAM
BLAM
BLAM

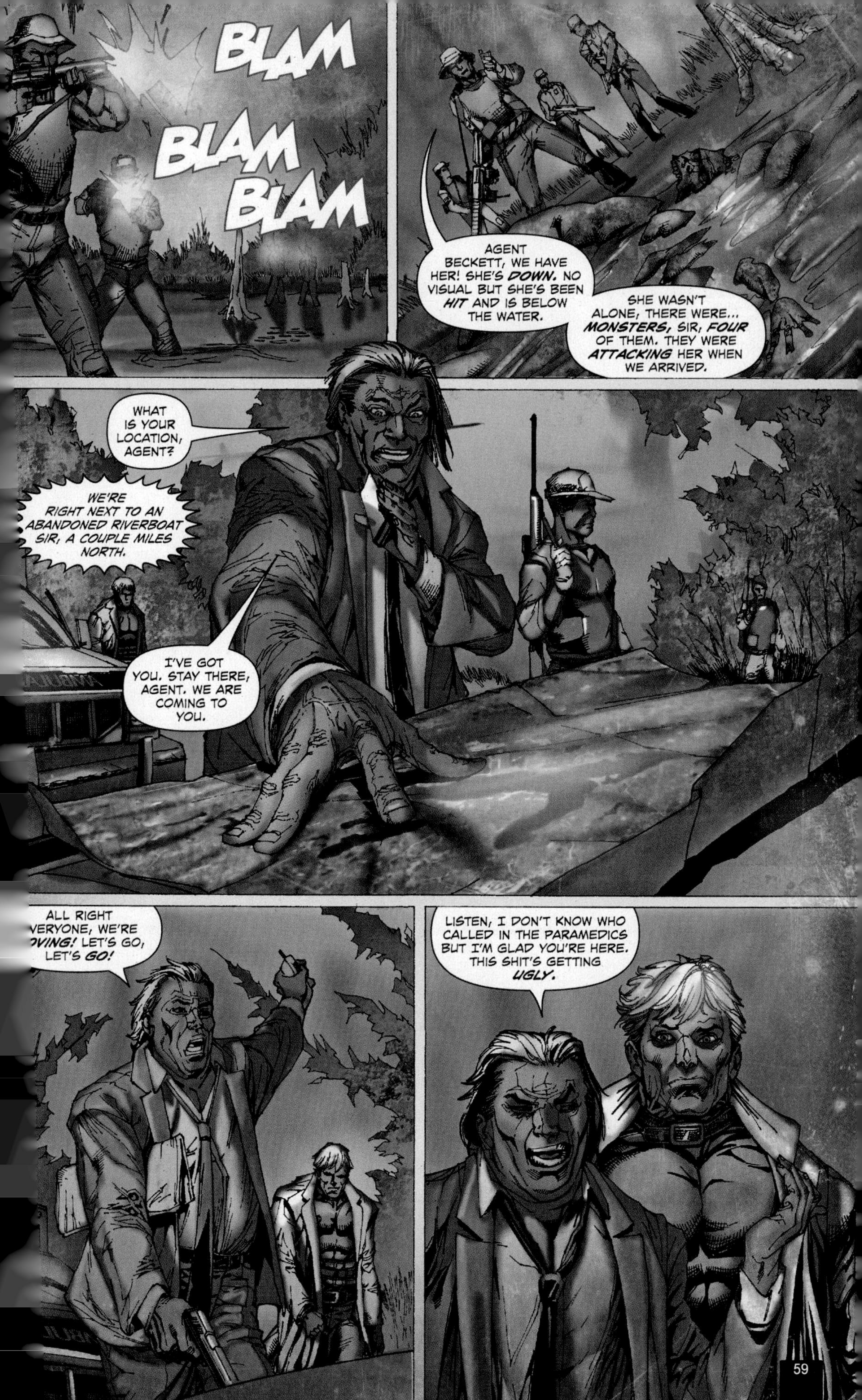
BLAM
BLAM
BLAM
AGENT BECKETT, WE HAVE HER! SHE'S DOWN. NO VISUAL BUT SHE'S BEEN HIT AND IS BELOW THE WATER.
SHE WASN'T ALONE, THERE WERE... MONSTERS, SIR, FOUR OF THEM. THEY WERE ATTACKING HER WHEN WE ARRIVED.
WHAT IS YOUR LOCATION, AGENT?
WE'RE RIGHT NEXT TO AN ABANDONED RIVERBOAT SIR, A COUPLE MILES NORTH.
I'VE GOT YOU. STAY THERE, AGENT. WE ARE COMING TO YOU.
ALL RIGHT VERYONE, WE'RE OVING! LET'S GO, LET'S GO!
LISTEN, I DON'T KNOW WHO CALLED IN THE PARAMEDICS BUT I'M GLAD YOU'RE HERE. THIS SHIT'S GETTING UGLY.

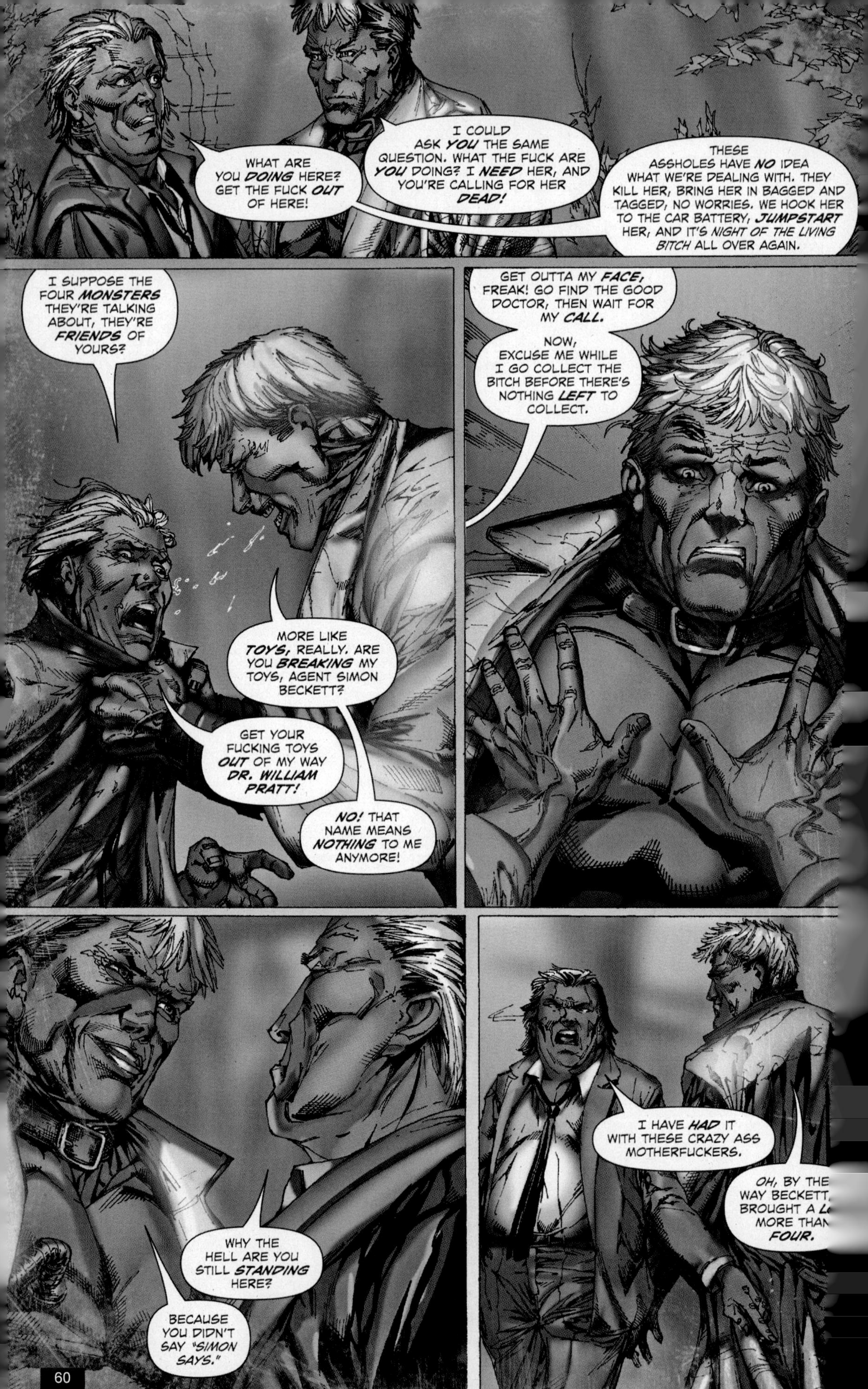

WHAT ARE YOU DOING HERE? GET THE FUCK OUT OF HERE!
I COULD ASK YOU THE SAME QUESTION. WHAT THE FUCK ARE YOU DOING? I NEED HER, AND YOU'RE CALLING FOR HER DEAD!
THESE ASSHOLES HAVE NO IDEA WHAT WE'RE DEALING WITH. THEY KILL HER, BRING HER IN BAGGED AND TAGGED, NO WORRIES. WE HOOK HER TO THE CAR BATTERY, JUMPSTART HER, AND IT'S NIGHT OF THE LIVING BITCH ALL OVER AGAIN.
I SUPPOSE THE FOUR MONSTERS THEY'RE TALKING ABOUT, THEY'RE FRIENDS OF YOURS?
MORE LIKE TOYS, REALLY. ARE YOU BREAKING MY TOYS, AGENT SIMON BECKETT?
GET YOUR FUCKING TOYS OUT OF MY WAY DR. WILLIAM PRATT!
NO! THAT NAME MEANS NOTHING TO ME ANYMORE!
GET OUTTA MY FACE, FREAK! GO FIND THE GOOD DOCTOR, THEN WAIT FOR MY CALL.
NOW, EXCUSE ME WHILE I GO COLLECT THE BITCH BEFORE THERE'S NOTHING LEFT TO COLLECT.
WHY THE HELL ARE YOU STILL STANDING HERE?
BECAUSE YOU DIDN'T SAY "SIMON SAYS."
I HAVE HAD IT WITH THESE CRAZY ASS MOTHERFUCKERS.
OH, BY THE WAY BECKETT, BROUGHT A
MORE THAN FOUR.

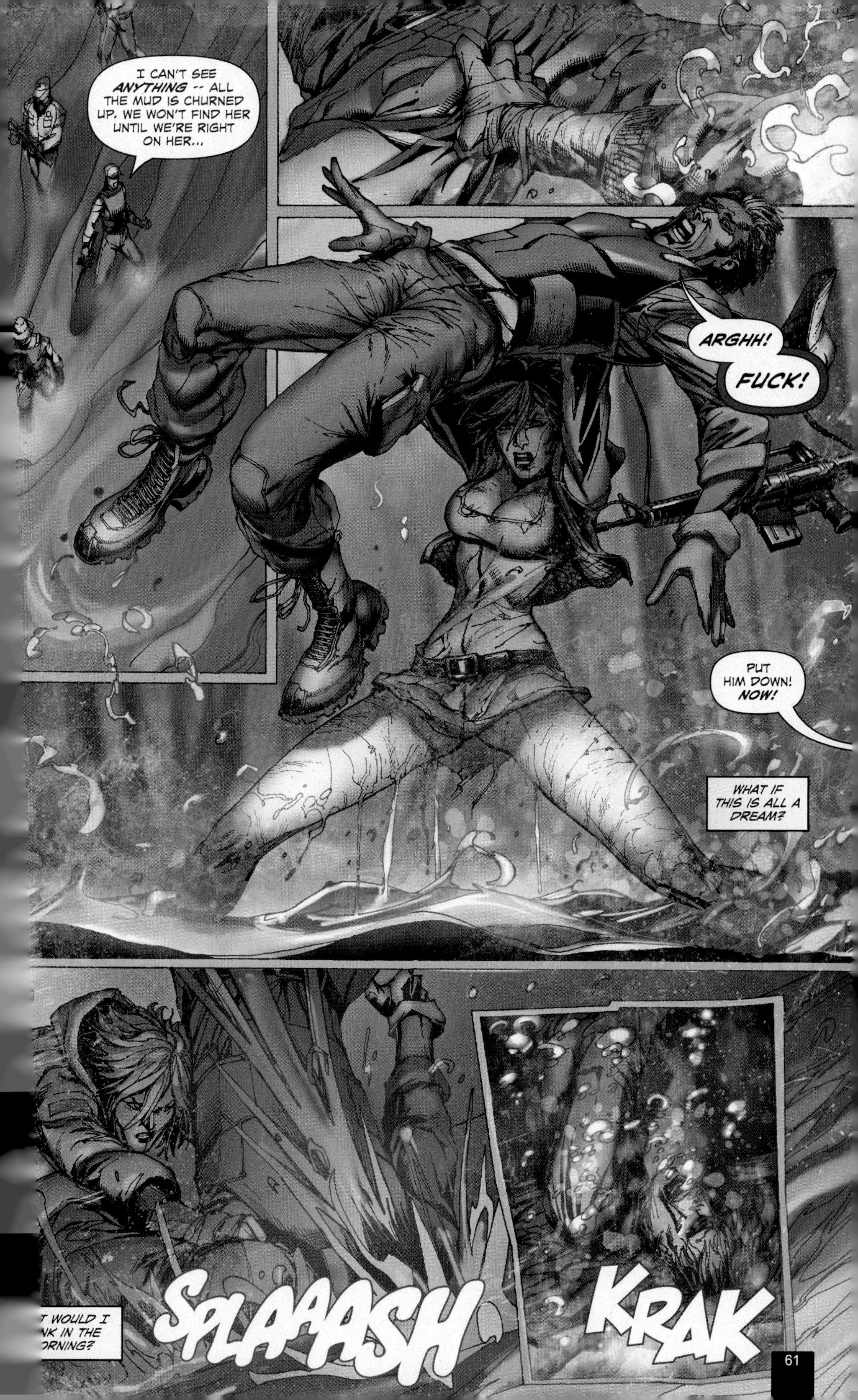

I CAN'T SEE *ANYTHING* -- ALL THE MUD IS CHURNED UP. WE WON'T FIND HER UNTIL WE'RE RIGHT ON HER...
ARGHH!
FUCK!
PUT HIM DOWN! *NOW!*
WHAT IF THIS IS ALL A DREAM?
T WOULD I NK IN THE ORNING?
SPLAAASH
KRAK

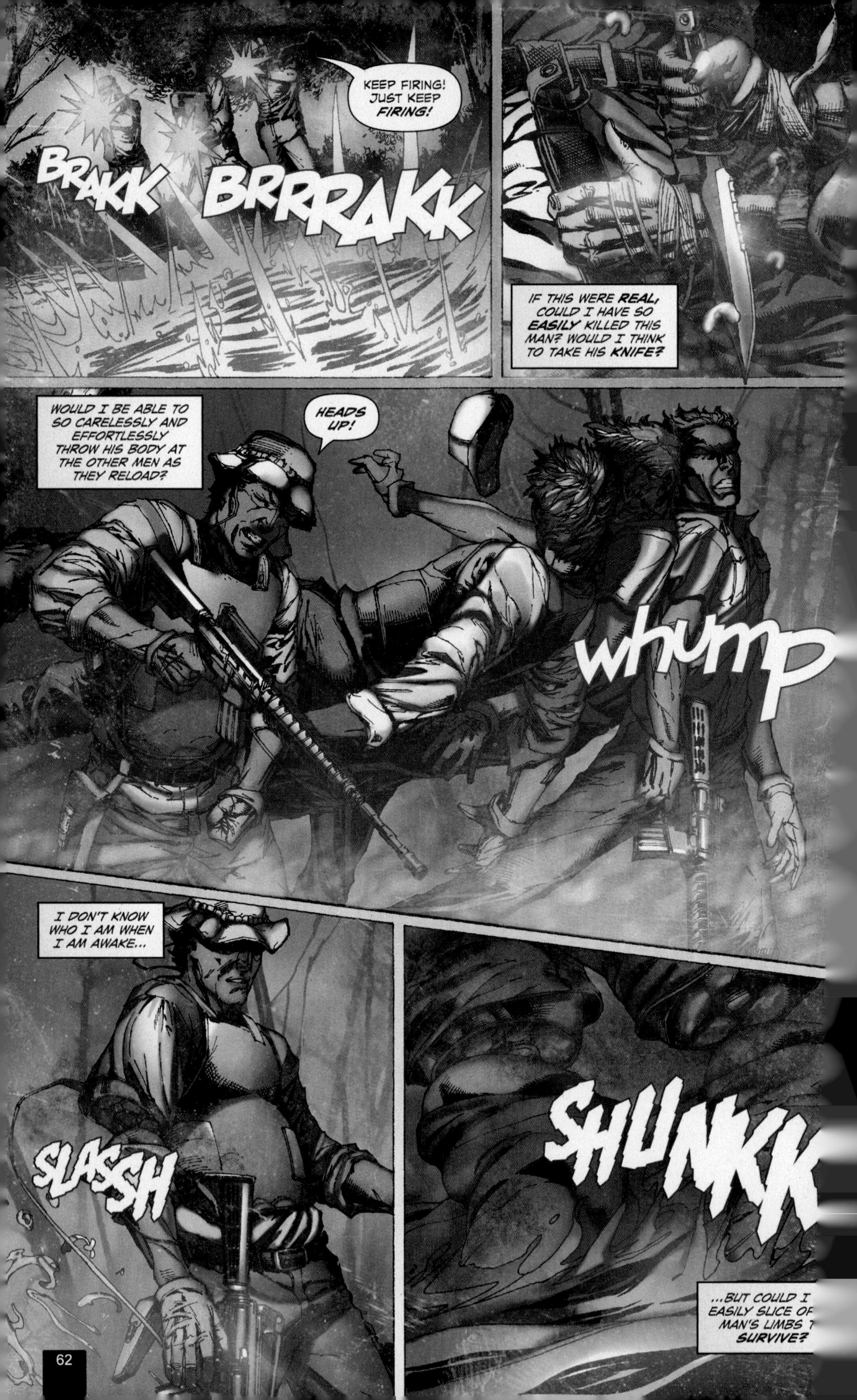
KEEP FIRING! JUST KEEP FIRING!
BRAKK
BRRRAKK
IF THIS WERE REAL, COULD I HAVE SO EASILY KILLED THIS MAN? WOULD I THINK TO TAKE HIS KNIFE?
WOULD I BE ABLE TO SO CARELESSLY AND EFFORTLESSLY THROW HIS BODY AT THE OTHER MEN AS THEY RELOAD?
HEADS UP!
whump
I DON'T KNOW WHO I AM WHEN I AM AWAKE...
SLASSH
SHUNKK
...BUT COULD I EASILY SLICE OF MAN'S LIMBS T SURVIVE?

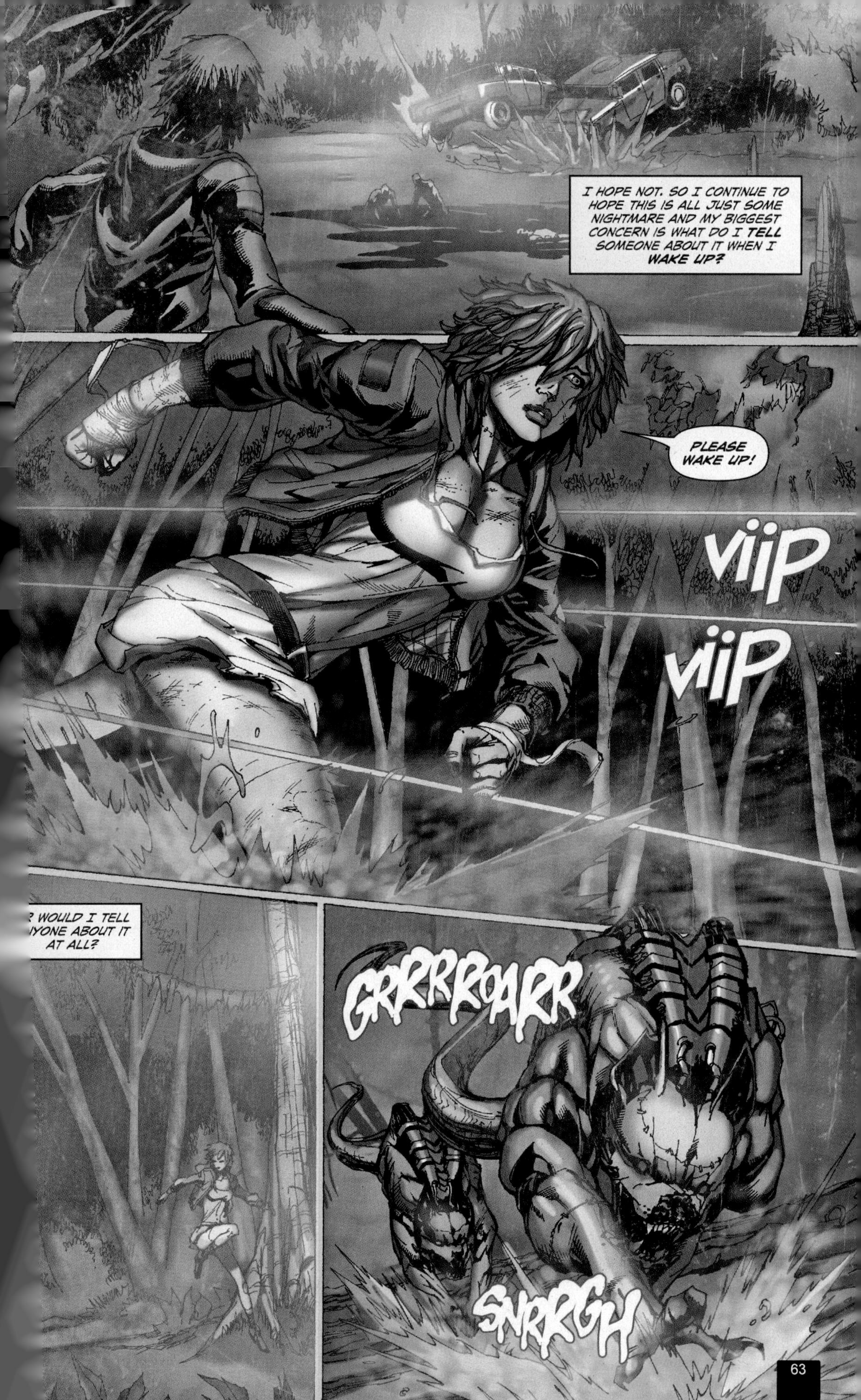
I HOPE NOT. SO I CONTINUE TO HOPE THIS IS ALL JUST SOME NIGHTMARE AND MY BIGGEST CONCERN IS WHAT DO I TELL SOMEONE ABOUT IT WHEN I WAKE UP?
PLEASE WAKE UP!
VIIP
VIIP
R WOULD I TELL NYONE ABOUT IT AT ALL?
GRRRROARR
SNRRGH

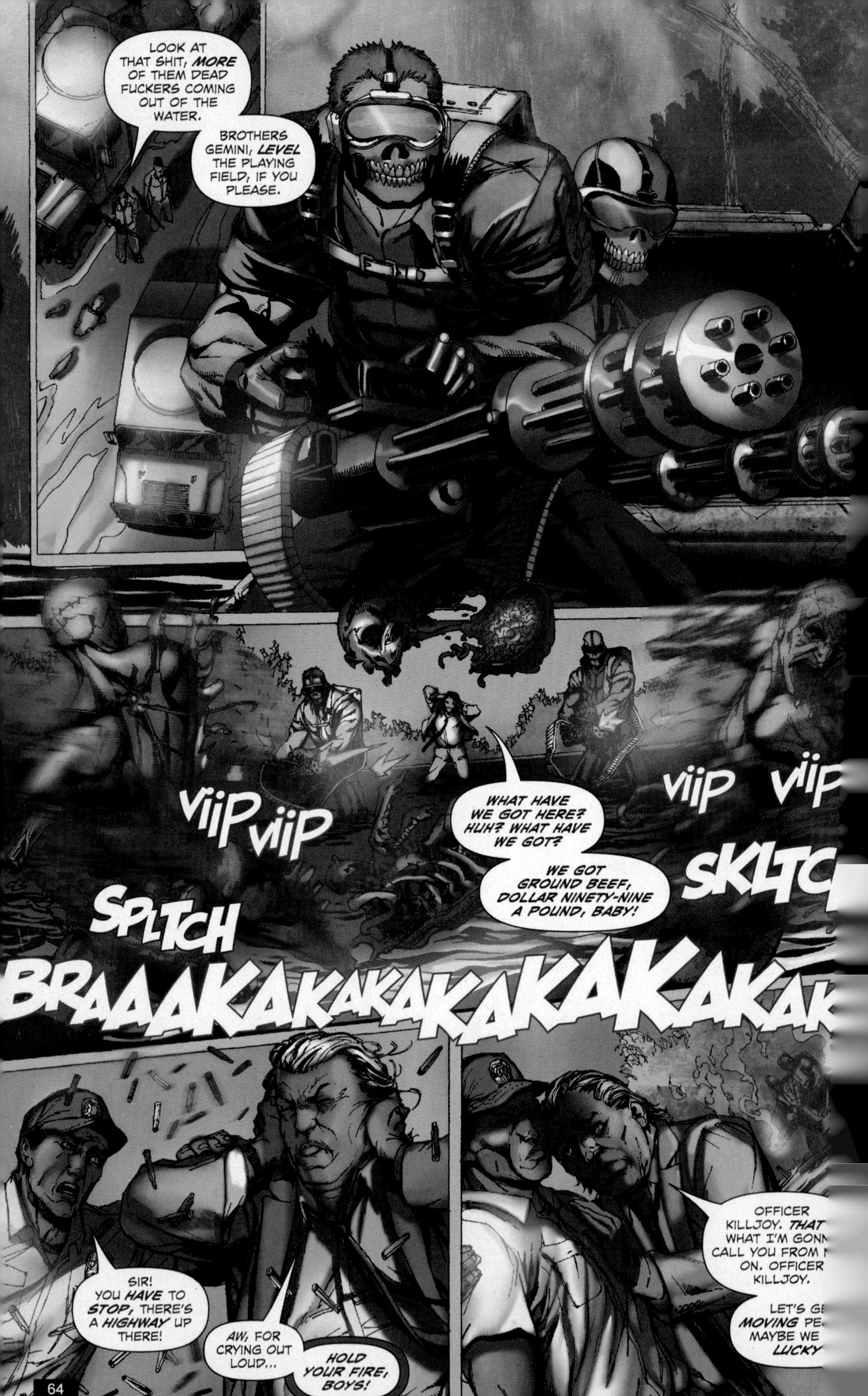

LOOK AT THAT SHIT, MORE OF THEM DEAD FUCKERS COMING OUT OF THE WATER.
BROTHERS GEMINI, LEVEL THE PLAYING FIELD, IF YOU PLEASE.
VIIP VIIP
WHAT HAVE WE GOT HERE? HUH? WHAT HAVE WE GOT?
WE GOT GROUND BEEF, DOLLAR NINETY-NINE A POUND, BABY!
VIIP VIIP
SPLTCH
SKLTC
BRAAAKAKAKAKAKAKAKAK
SIR! YOU HAVE TO STOP, THERE'S A HIGHWAY UP THERE!
AW, FOR CRYING OUT LOUD...
HOLD YOUR FIRE, BOYS!
OFFICER KILLJOY. THAT WHAT I'M GONN CALL YOU FROM ON. OFFICER KILLJOY.
LET'S GE MOVING PE MAYBE WE LUCKY

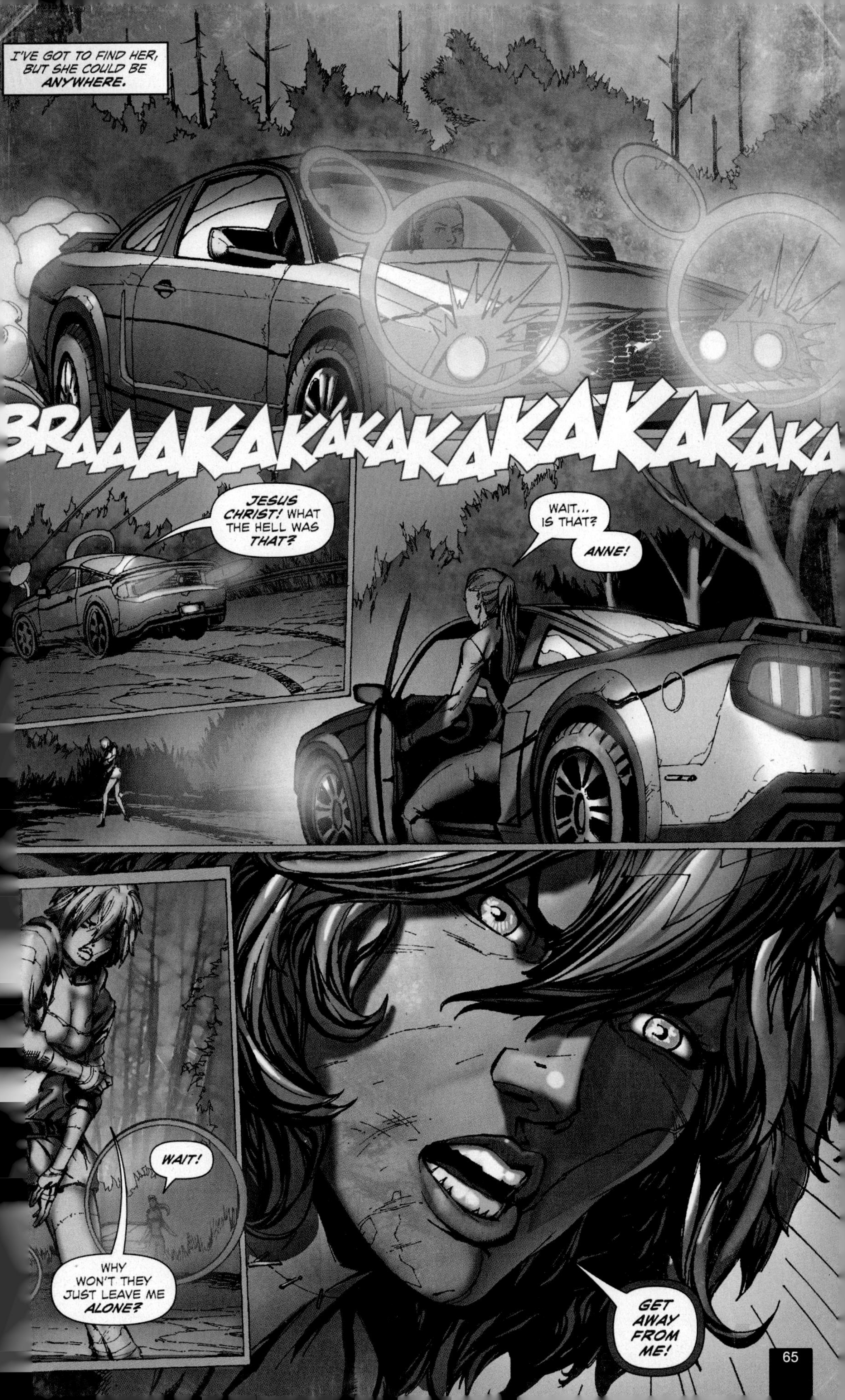
I'VE GOT TO FIND HER, BUT SHE COULD BE ANYWHERE.
BRAAAKAKAKAKAKAKAKAKA
JESUS CHRIST! WHAT THE HELL WAS THAT?
WAIT... IS THAT?
ANNE!
WAIT!
WHY WON'T THEY JUST LEAVE ME ALONE?
GET AWAY FROM ME!

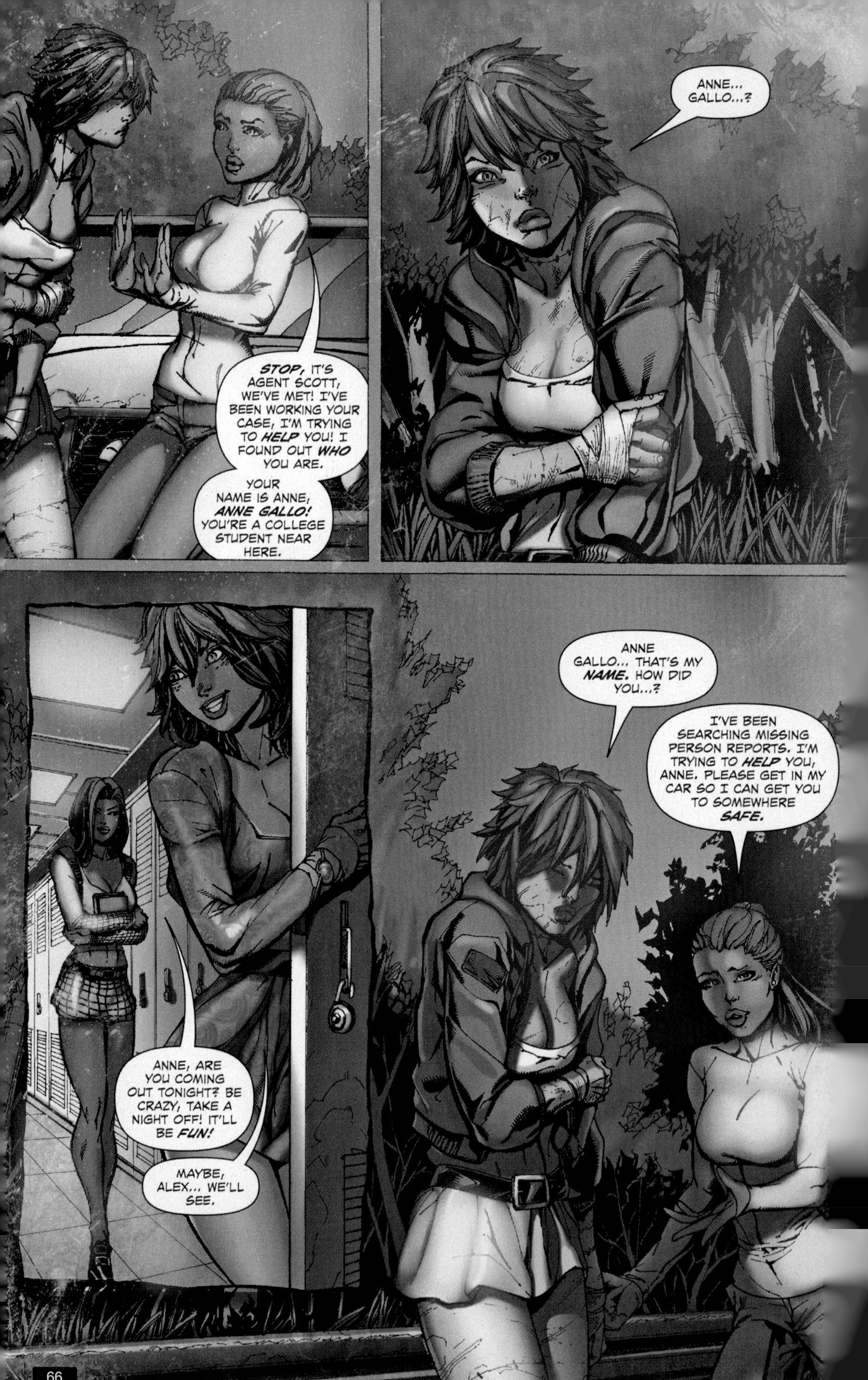

STOP, IT'S AGENT SCOTT, WE'VE MET! I'VE BEEN WORKING YOUR CASE, I'M TRYING TO HELP YOU! I FOUND OUT WHO YOU ARE.
YOUR NAME IS ANNE, ANNE GALLO! YOU'RE A COLLEGE STUDENT NEAR HERE.
ANNE... GALLO...?
ANNE, ARE YOU COMING OUT TONIGHT? BE CRAZY, TAKE A NIGHT OFF! IT'LL BE FUN!
MAYBE, ALEX... WE'LL SEE.
ANNE GALLO... THAT'S MY NAME. HOW DID YOU...?
I'VE BEEN SEARCHING MISSING PERSON REPORTS. I'M TRYING TO HELP YOU, ANNE. PLEASE GET IN MY CAR SO I CAN GET YOU TO SOMEWHERE SAFE.

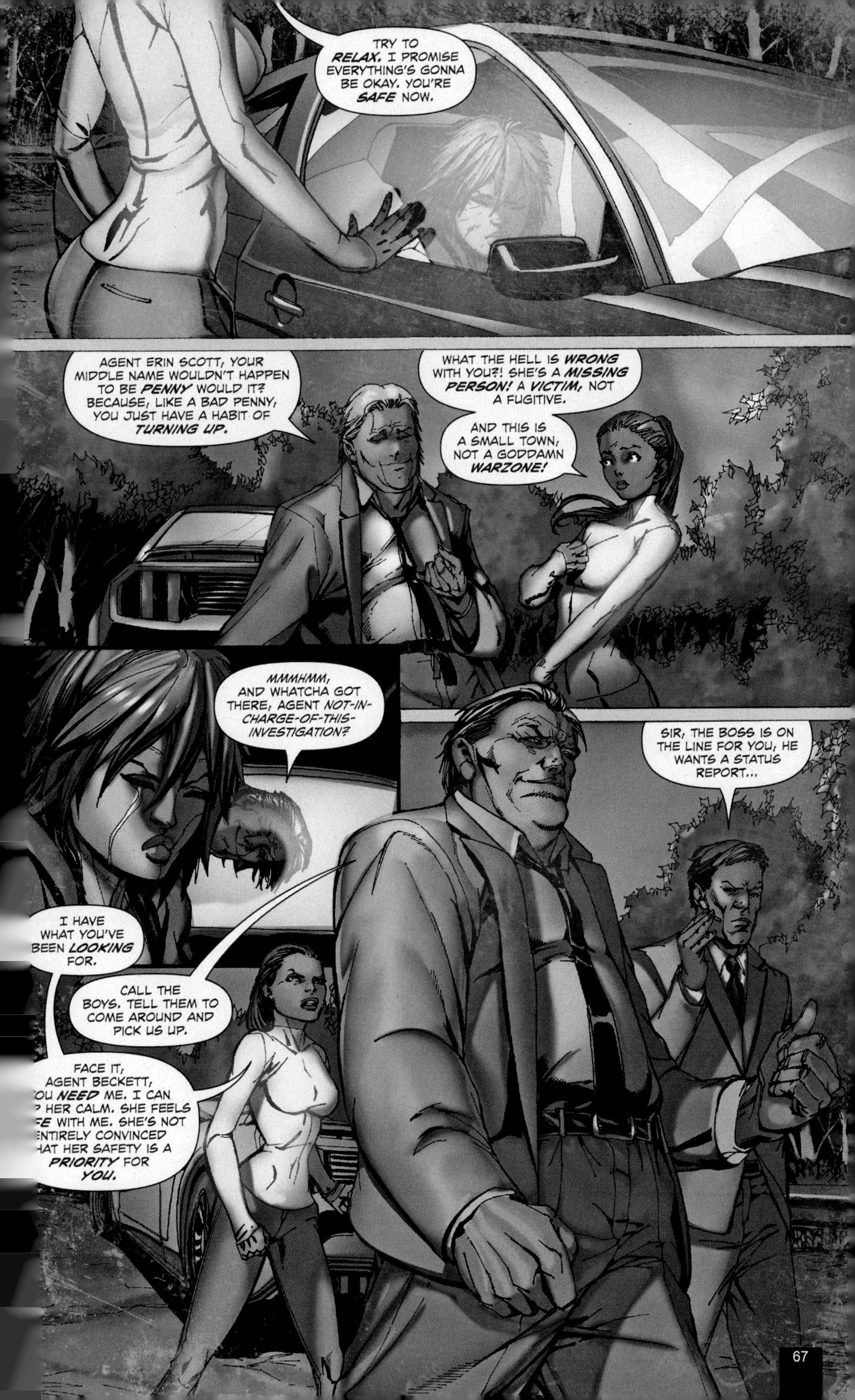
TRY TO RELAX. I PROMISE EVERYTHING'S GONNA BE OKAY. YOU'RE SAFE NOW.
AGENT ERIN SCOTT, YOUR MIDDLE NAME WOULDN'T HAPPEN TO BE PENNY WOULD IT? BECAUSE, LIKE A BAD PENNY, YOU JUST HAVE A HABIT OF TURNING UP.
WHAT THE HELL IS WRONG WITH YOU?! SHE'S A MISSING PERSON! A VICTIM, NOT A FUGITIVE.
AND THIS IS A SMALL TOWN, NOT A GODDAMN WARZONE!
MMMHMM, AND WHATCHA GOT THERE, AGENT NOT-IN-CHARGE-OF-THIS-INVESTIGATION?
I HAVE WHAT YOU'VE BEEN LOOKING FOR.
SIR, THE BOSS IS ON THE LINE FOR YOU, HE WANTS A STATUS REPORT...
CALL THE BOYS. TELL THEM TO COME AROUND AND PICK US UP.
FACE IT, AGENT BECKETT, OU NEED ME. I CAN HER CALM. SHE FEELS FE WITH ME. SHE'S NOT NTIRELY CONVINCED HAT HER SAFETY IS A PRIORITY FOR YOU.

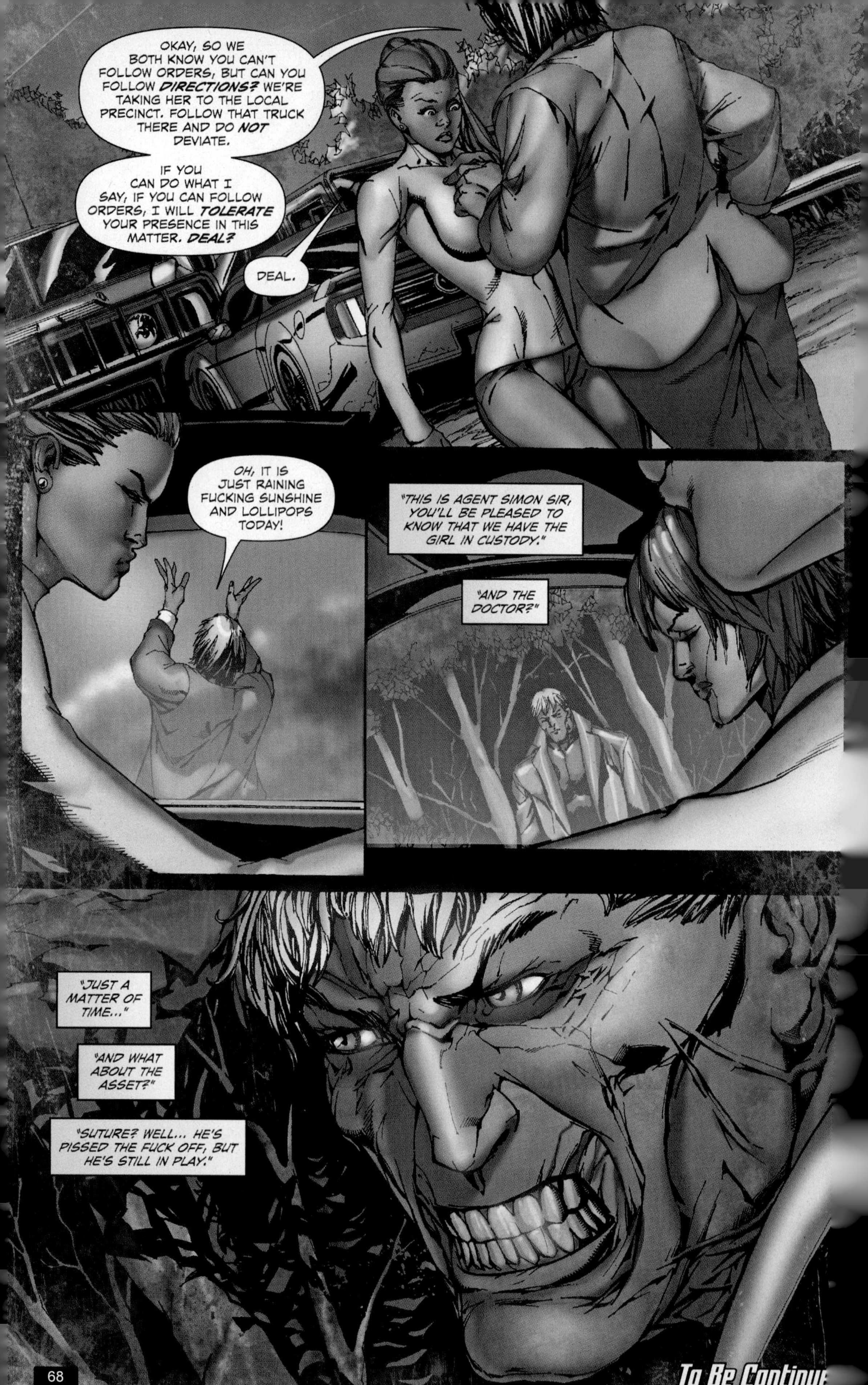
OKAY, SO WE BOTH KNOW YOU CAN'T FOLLOW ORDERS, BUT CAN YOU FOLLOW DIRECTIONS? WE'RE TAKING HER TO THE LOCAL PRECINCT. FOLLOW THAT TRUCK THERE AND DO NOT DEVIATE.
IF YOU CAN DO WHAT I SAY, IF YOU CAN FOLLOW ORDERS, I WILL TOLERATE YOUR PRESENCE IN THIS MATTER. DEAL?
DEAL.
OH, IT IS JUST RAINING FUCKING SUNSHINE AND LOLLIPOPS TODAY!
"THIS IS AGENT SIMON SIR, YOU'LL BE PLEASED TO KNOW THAT WE HAVE THE GIRL IN CUSTODY."
"AND THE DOCTOR?"
"JUST A MATTER OF TIME..."
"AND WHAT ABOUT THE ASSET?"
"SUTURE? WELL... HE'S PISSED THE FUCK OFF, BUT HE'S STILL IN PLAY."
To Be Continue

SCREWED

CHAPTER FOUR

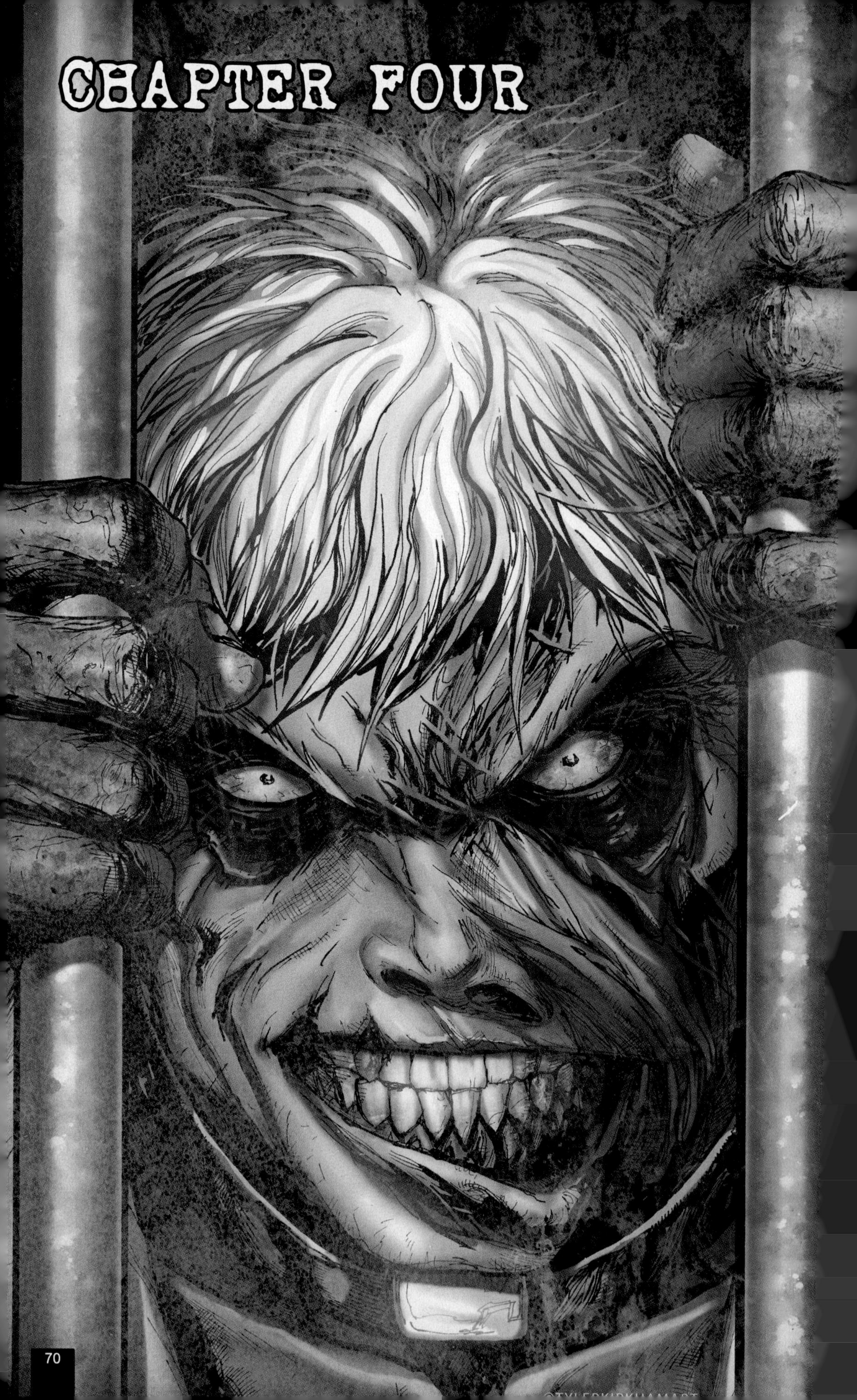

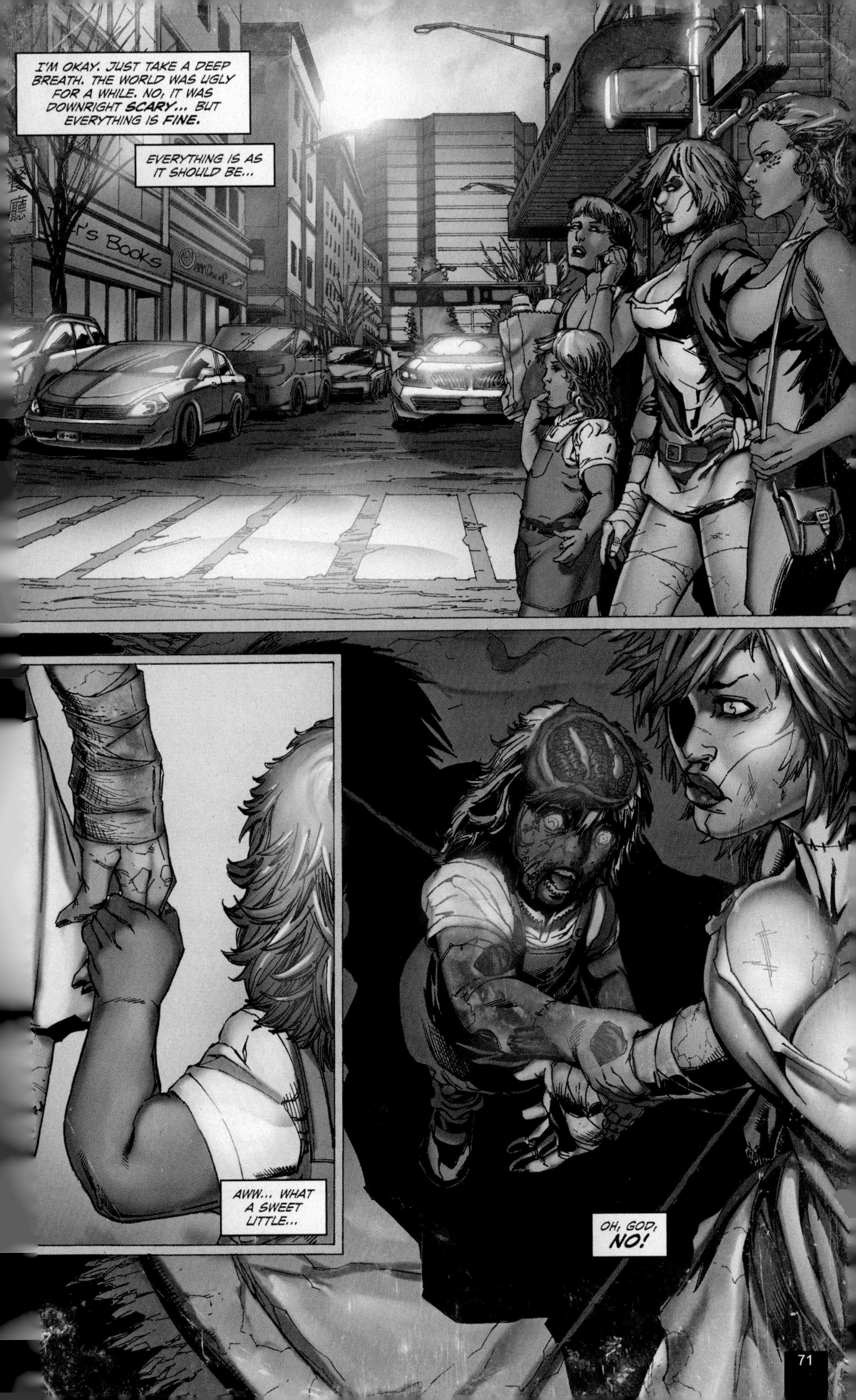
I'M OKAY. JUST TAKE A DEEP BREATH. THE WORLD WAS UGLY FOR A WHILE. NO, IT WAS DOWNRIGHT SCARY... BUT EVERYTHING IS FINE.
EVERYTHING IS AS IT SHOULD BE...
AWW... WHAT A SWEET LITTLE...
OH, GOD, NO!

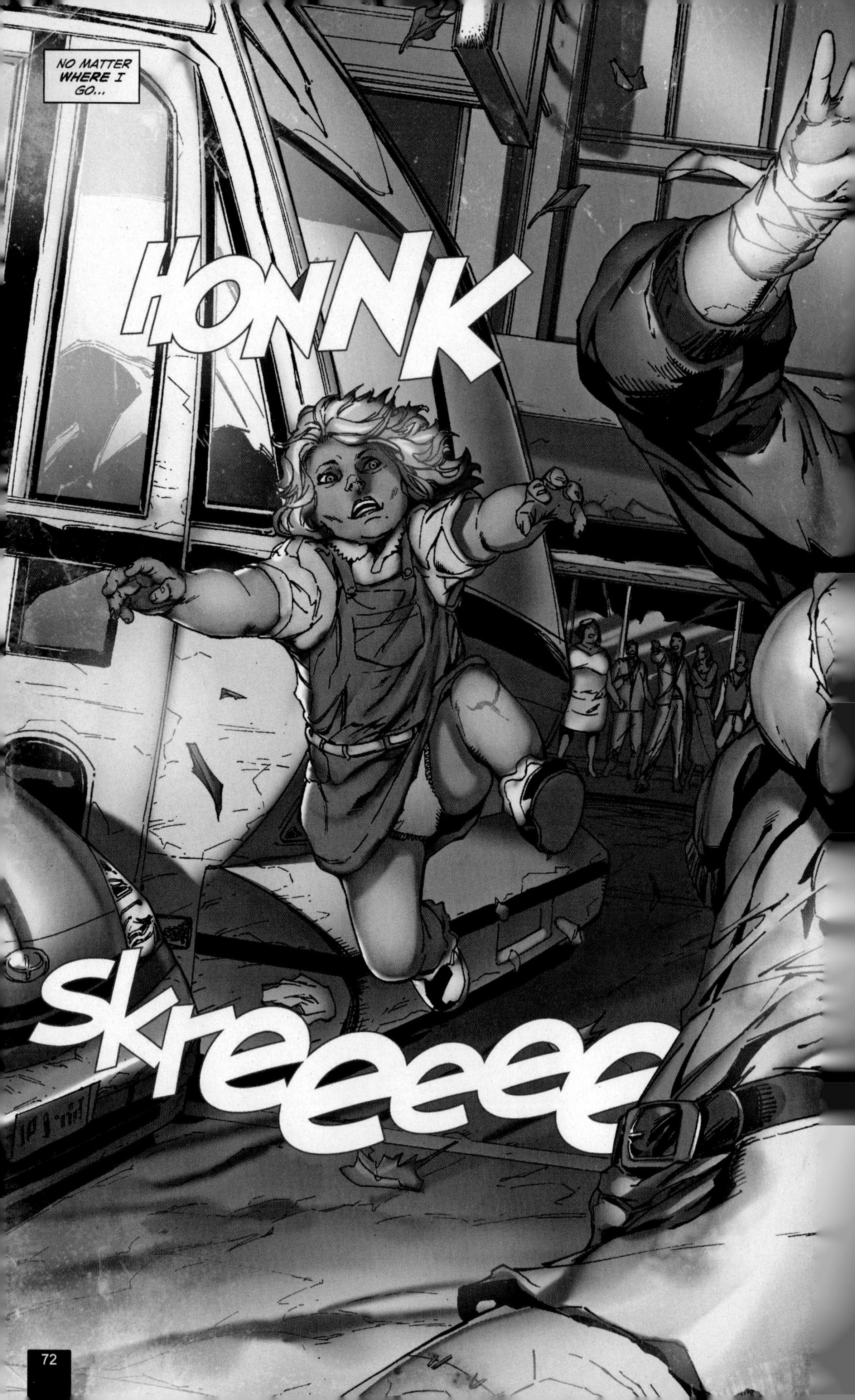
NO MATTER WHERE I GO...
HONNK
Skreeeee

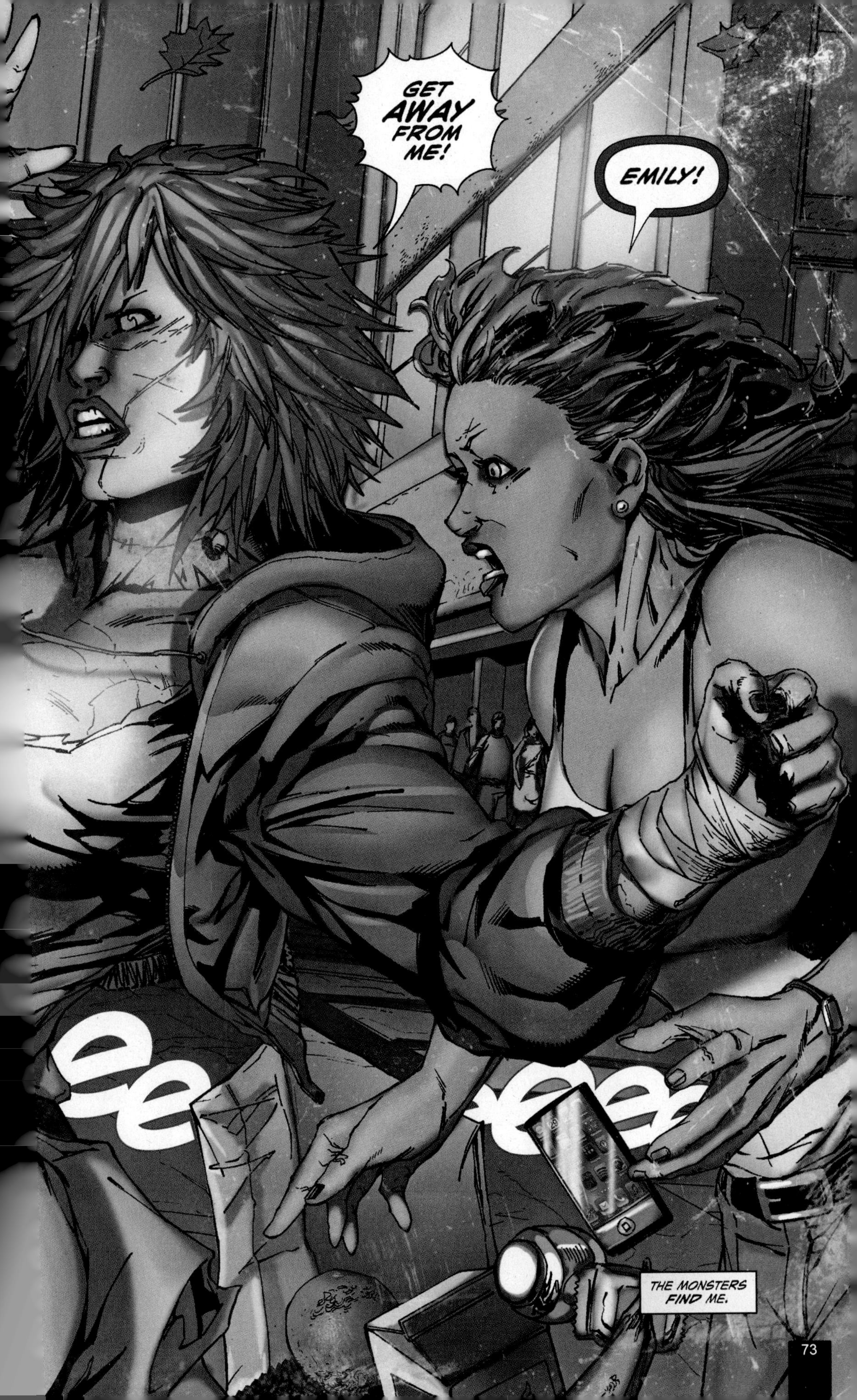
GET AWAY FROM ME!
EMILY!
eeeeee
THE MONSTERS FIND ME.

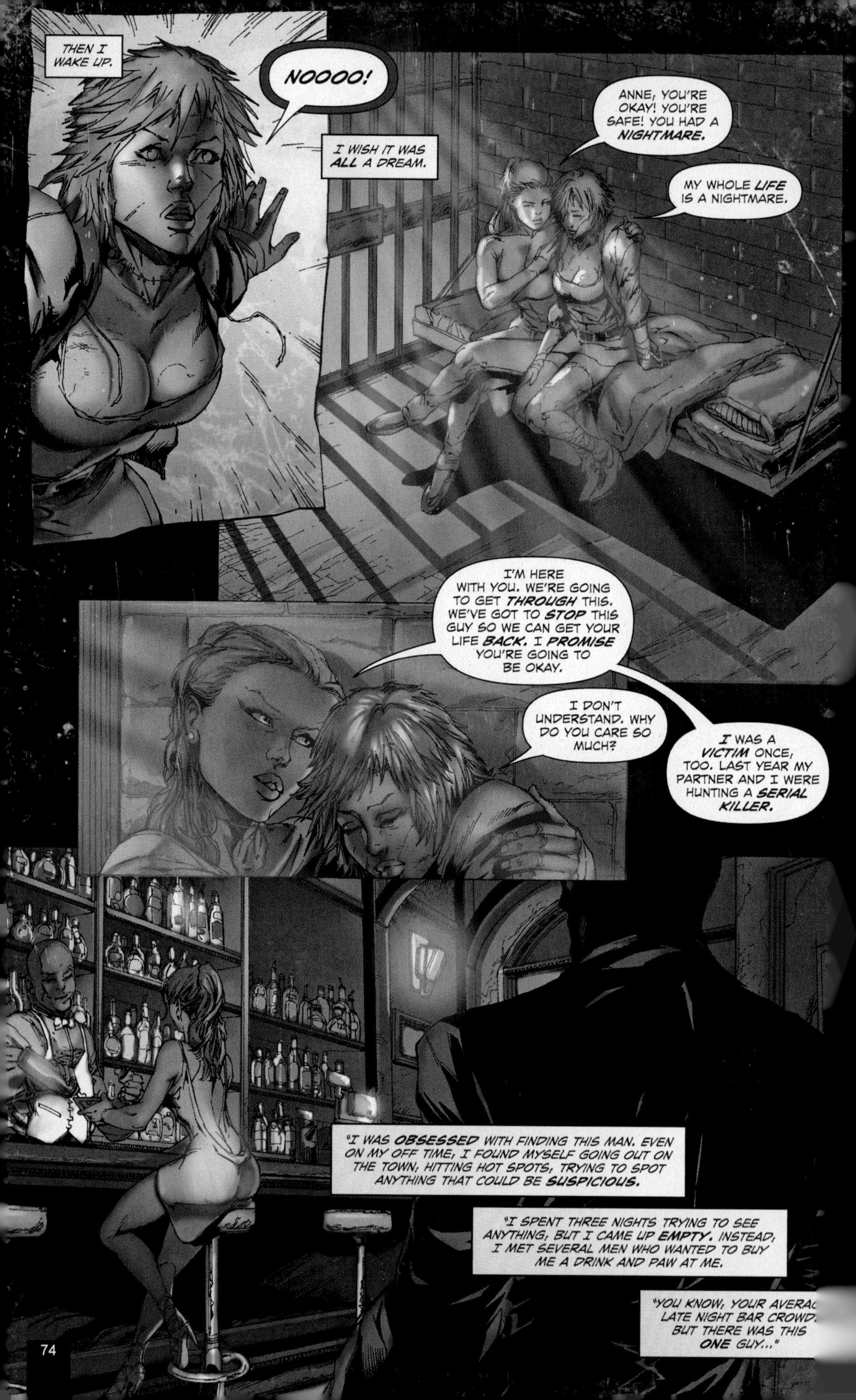
THEN I WAKE UP.
NOOOO!
I WISH IT WAS ALL A DREAM.
ANNE, YOU'RE OKAY! YOU'RE SAFE! YOU HAD A NIGHTMARE.
MY WHOLE LIFE IS A NIGHTMARE.
I'M HERE WITH YOU. WE'RE GOING TO GET THROUGH THIS. WE'VE GOT TO STOP THIS GUY SO WE CAN GET YOUR LIFE BACK. I PROMISE YOU'RE GOING TO BE OKAY.
I DON'T UNDERSTAND. WHY DO YOU CARE SO MUCH?
I WAS A VICTIM ONCE, TOO. LAST YEAR MY PARTNER AND I WERE HUNTING A SERIAL KILLER.
"I WAS OBSESSED WITH FINDING THIS MAN. EVEN ON MY OFF TIME, I FOUND MYSELF GOING OUT ON THE TOWN, HITTING HOT SPOTS, TRYING TO SPOT ANYTHING THAT COULD BE SUSPICIOUS.
"I SPENT THREE NIGHTS TRYING TO SEE ANYTHING, BUT I CAME UP EMPTY. INSTEAD, I MET SEVERAL MEN WHO WANTED TO BUY ME A DRINK AND PAW AT ME.
"YOU KNOW, YOUR AVERAG LATE NIGHT BAR CROWD. BUT THERE WAS THIS ONE GUY..."

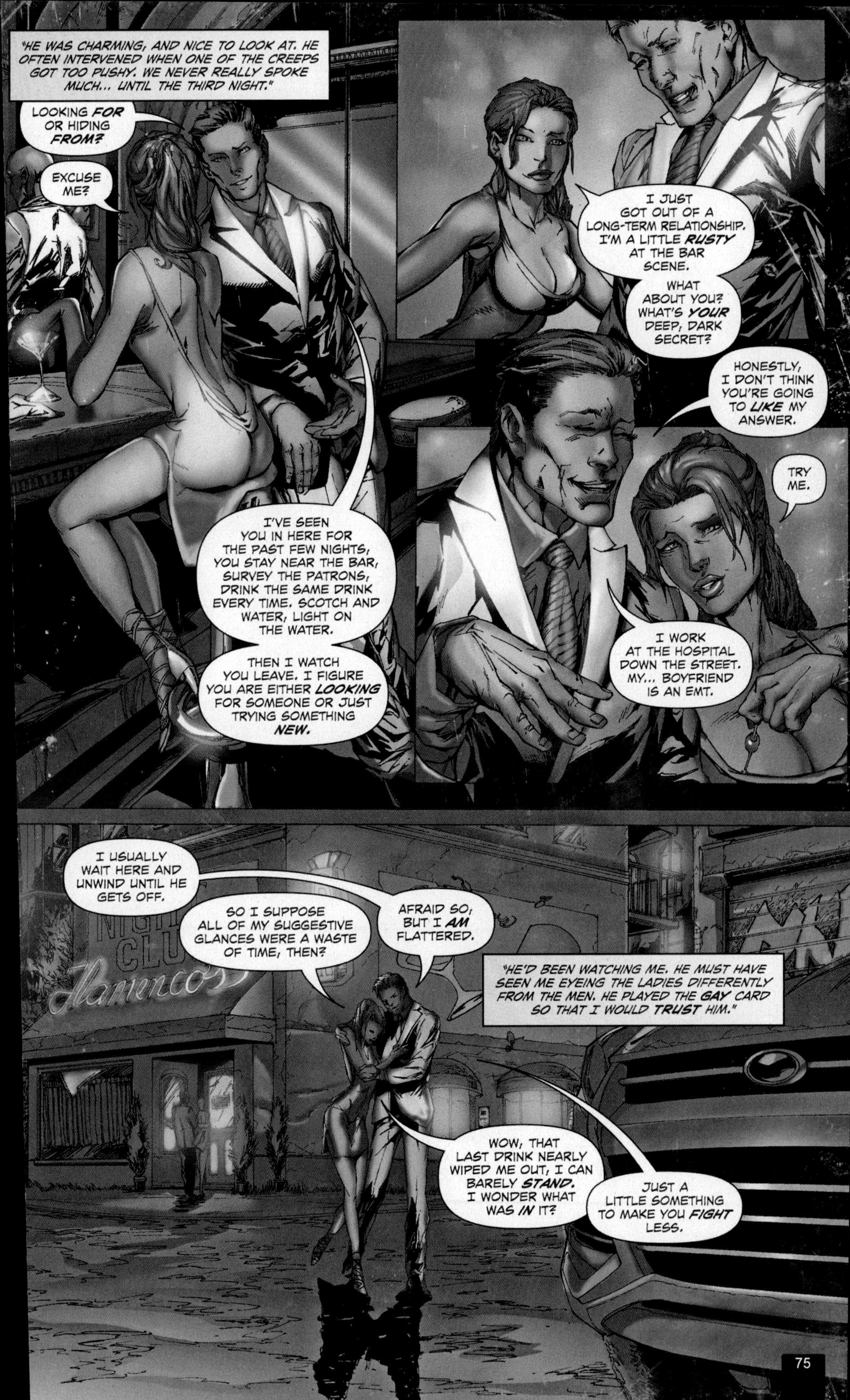
"HE WAS CHARMING, AND NICE TO LOOK AT. HE OFTEN INTERVENED WHEN ONE OF THE CREEPS GOT TOO PUSHY. WE NEVER REALLY SPOKE MUCH... UNTIL THE THIRD NIGHT."
LOOKING FOR OR HIDING FROM?
EXCUSE ME?
I'VE SEEN YOU IN HERE FOR THE PAST FEW NIGHTS, YOU STAY NEAR THE BAR, SURVEY THE PATRONS, DRINK THE SAME DRINK EVERY TIME. SCOTCH AND WATER, LIGHT ON THE WATER.
THEN I WATCH YOU LEAVE. I FIGURE YOU ARE EITHER LOOKING FOR SOMEONE OR JUST TRYING SOMETHING NEW.
I JUST GOT OUT OF A LONG-TERM RELATIONSHIP. I'M A LITTLE RUSTY AT THE BAR SCENE.
WHAT ABOUT YOU? WHAT'S YOUR DEEP, DARK SECRET?
HONESTLY, I DON'T THINK YOU'RE GOING TO LIKE MY ANSWER.
TRY ME.
I WORK AT THE HOSPITAL DOWN THE STREET. MY... BOYFRIEND IS AN EMT.
I USUALLY WAIT HERE AND UNWIND UNTIL HE GETS OFF.
SO I SUPPOSE ALL OF MY SUGGESTIVE GLANCES WERE A WASTE OF TIME, THEN?
AFRAID SO, BUT I AM FLATTERED.
"HE'D BEEN WATCHING ME. HE MUST HAVE SEEN ME EYEING THE LADIES DIFFERENTLY FROM THE MEN. HE PLAYED THE GAY CARD SO THAT I WOULD TRUST HIM."
WOW, THAT LAST DRINK NEARLY WIPED ME OUT, I CAN BARELY STAND. I WONDER WHAT WAS IN IT?
JUST A LITTLE SOMETHING TO MAKE YOU FIGHT LESS.

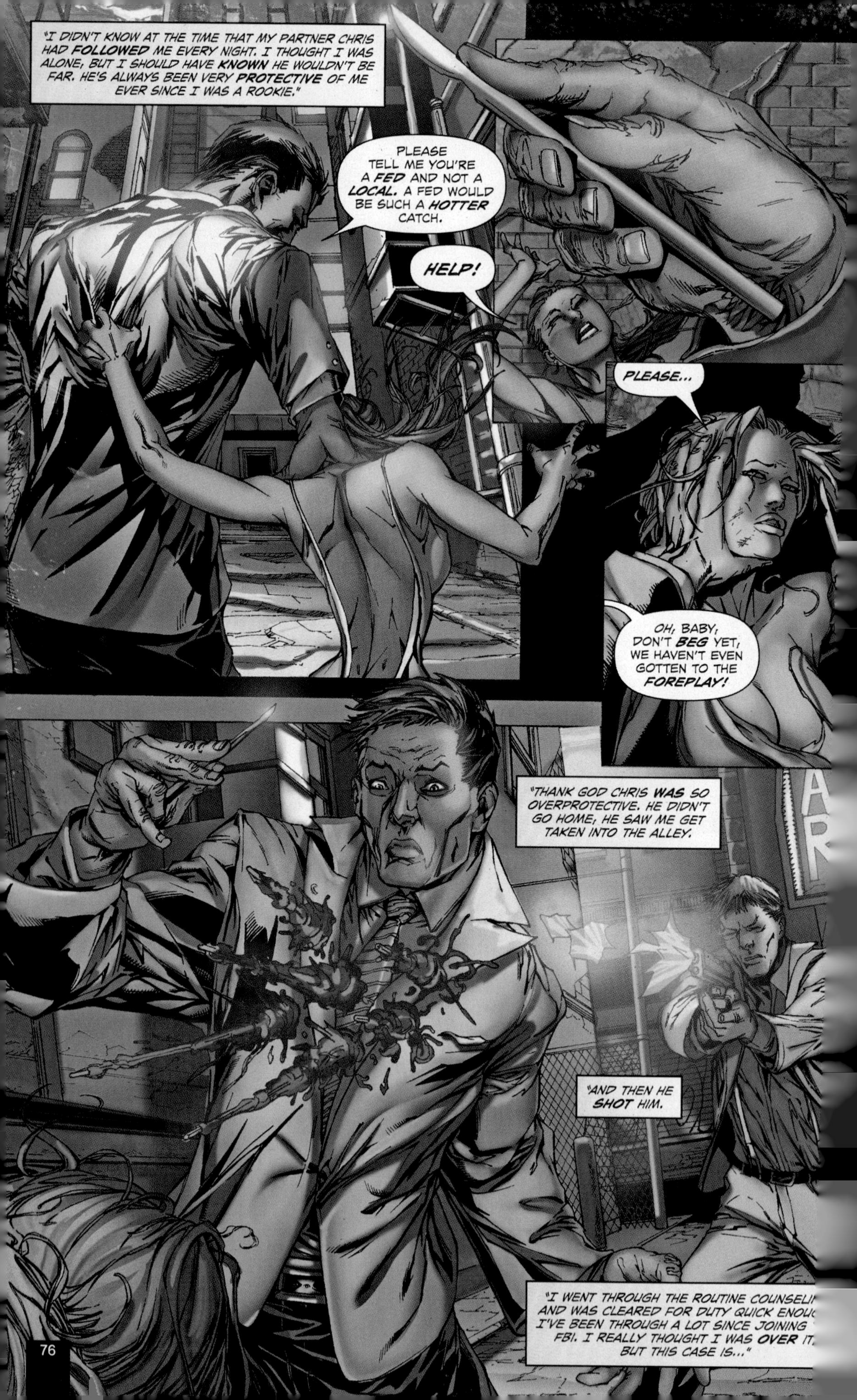
"I DIDN'T KNOW AT THE TIME THAT MY PARTNER CHRIS HAD FOLLOWED ME EVERY NIGHT. I THOUGHT I WAS ALONE, BUT I SHOULD HAVE KNOWN HE WOULDN'T BE FAR. HE'S ALWAYS BEEN VERY PROTECTIVE OF ME EVER SINCE I WAS A ROOKIE."
PLEASE TELL ME YOU'RE A FED AND NOT A LOCAL. A FED WOULD BE SUCH A HOTTER CATCH.
HELP!
PLEASE...
OH, BABY, DON'T BEG YET, WE HAVEN'T EVEN GOTTEN TO THE FOREPLAY!
"THANK GOD CHRIS WAS SO OVERPROTECTIVE. HE DIDN'T GO HOME; HE SAW ME GET TAKEN INTO THE ALLEY.
"AND THEN HE SHOT HIM.
"I WENT THROUGH THE ROUTINE COUNSELI AND WAS CLEARED FOR DUTY QUICK ENOUG I'VE BEEN THROUGH A LOT SINCE JOINING FBI. I REALLY THOUGHT I WAS OVER IT BUT THIS CASE IS..."

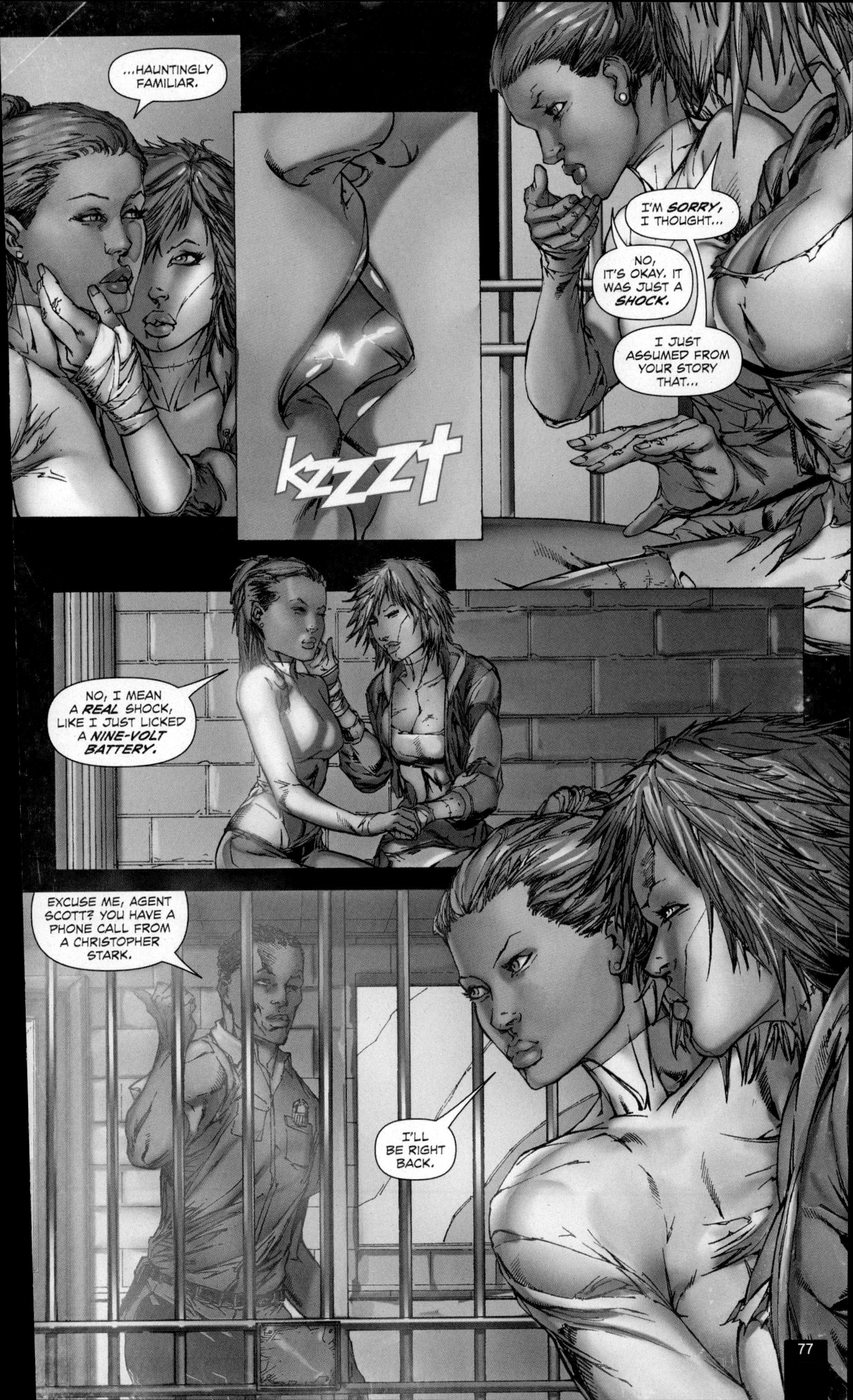
...HAUNTINGLY FAMILIAR.
KZZZT
I'M SORRY, I THOUGHT...
NO, IT'S OKAY. IT WAS JUST A SHOCK.
I JUST ASSUMED FROM YOUR STORY THAT...
NO, I MEAN A REAL SHOCK, LIKE I JUST LICKED A NINE-VOLT BATTERY.
EXCUSE ME, AGENT SCOTT? YOU HAVE A PHONE CALL FROM A CHRISTOPHER STARK.
I'LL BE RIGHT BACK.

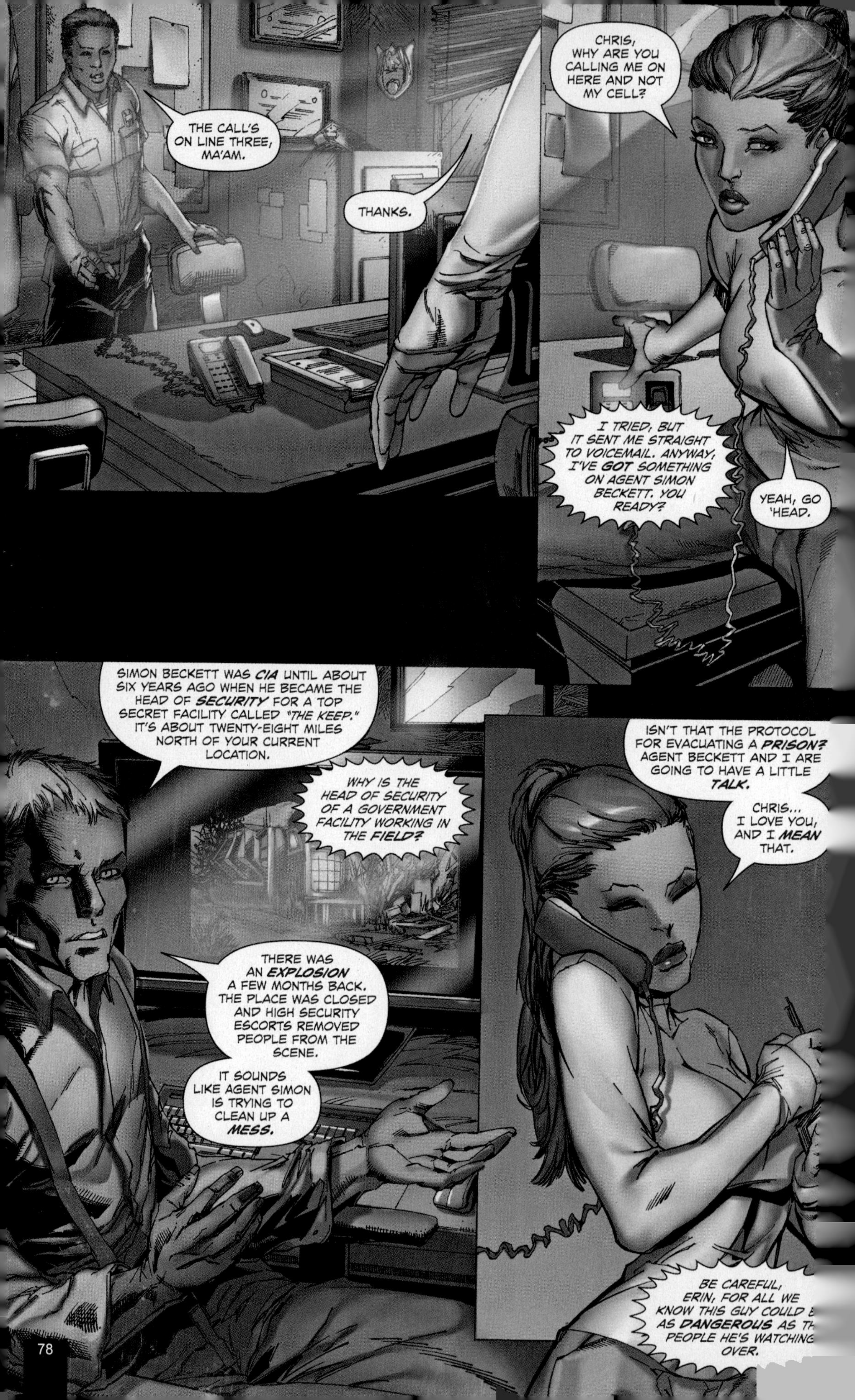

THE CALL'S ON LINE THREE, MA'AM.
THANKS.
CHRIS, WHY ARE YOU CALLING ME ON HERE AND NOT MY CELL?
I TRIED, BUT IT SENT ME STRAIGHT TO VOICEMAIL. ANYWAY, I'VE GOT SOMETHING ON AGENT SIMON BECKETT. YOU READY?
YEAH, GO 'HEAD.
SIMON BECKETT WAS CIA UNTIL ABOUT SIX YEARS AGO WHEN HE BECAME THE HEAD OF SECURITY FOR A TOP SECRET FACILITY CALLED "THE KEEP." IT'S ABOUT TWENTY-EIGHT MILES NORTH OF YOUR CURRENT LOCATION.
WHY IS THE HEAD OF SECURITY OF A GOVERNMENT FACILITY WORKING IN THE FIELD?
THERE WAS AN EXPLOSION A FEW MONTHS BACK. THE PLACE WAS CLOSED AND HIGH SECURITY ESCORTS REMOVED PEOPLE FROM THE SCENE.
IT SOUNDS LIKE AGENT SIMON IS TRYING TO CLEAN UP A MESS.
ISN'T THAT THE PROTOCOL FOR EVACUATING A PRISON? AGENT BECKETT AND I ARE GOING TO HAVE A LITTLE TALK.
CHRIS... I LOVE YOU, AND I MEAN THAT.
BE CAREFUL, ERIN, FOR ALL WE KNOW THIS GUY COULD B AS DANGEROUS AS TH PEOPLE HE'S WATCHING OVER.

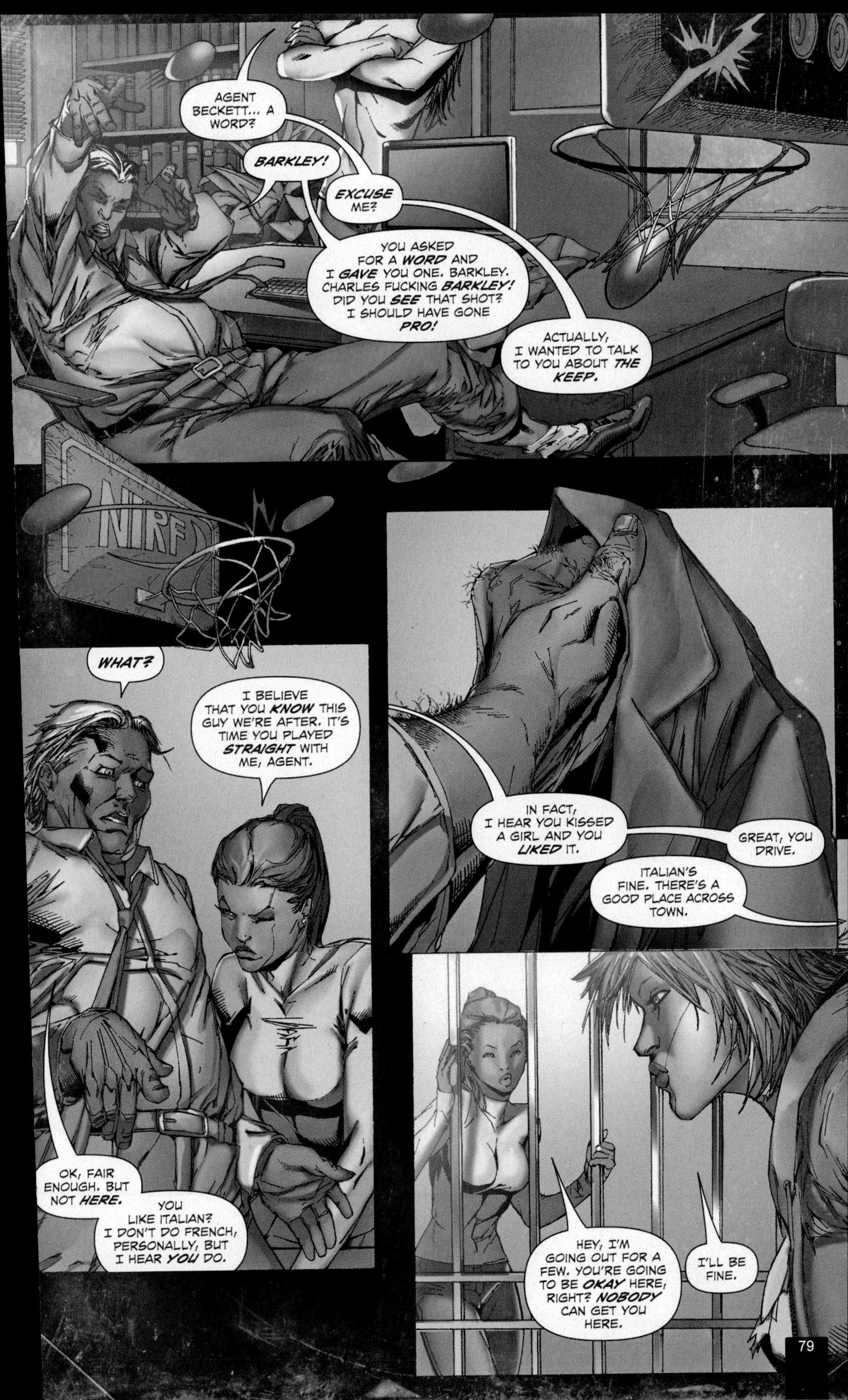
AGENT BECKETT... A WORD?
BARKLEY!
EXCUSE ME?
YOU ASKED FOR A WORD AND I GAVE YOU ONE. BARKLEY. CHARLES FUCKING BARKLEY! DID YOU SEE THAT SHOT? I SHOULD HAVE GONE PRO!
ACTUALLY, I WANTED TO TALK TO YOU ABOUT THE KEEP.
NIRF
WHAT?
I BELIEVE THAT YOU KNOW THIS GUY WE'RE AFTER. IT'S TIME YOU PLAYED STRAIGHT WITH ME, AGENT.
OK, FAIR ENOUGH. BUT NOT HERE.
YOU LIKE ITALIAN? I DON'T DO FRENCH, PERSONALLY, BUT I HEAR YOU DO.
IN FACT, I HEAR YOU KISSED A GIRL AND YOU LIKED IT.
ITALIAN'S FINE. THERE'S A GOOD PLACE ACROSS TOWN.
GREAT, YOU DRIVE.
HEY, I'M GOING OUT FOR A FEW. YOU'RE GOING TO BE OKAY HERE, RIGHT? NOBODY CAN GET YOU HERE.
I'LL BE FINE.

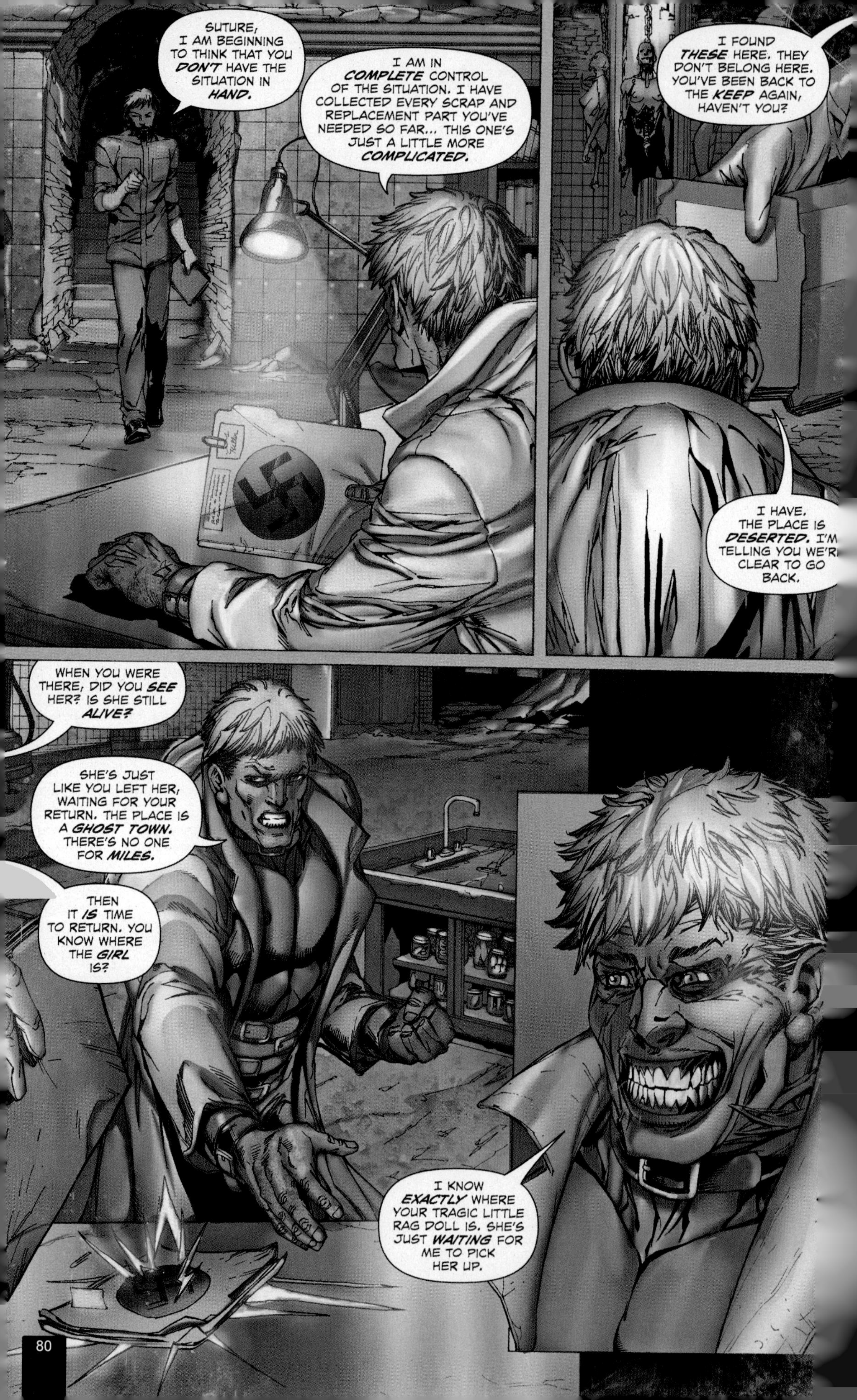

SUTURE, I AM BEGINNING TO THINK THAT YOU DON'T HAVE THE SITUATION IN HAND.
I AM IN COMPLETE CONTROL OF THE SITUATION. I HAVE COLLECTED EVERY SCRAP AND REPLACEMENT PART YOU'VE NEEDED SO FAR... THIS ONE'S JUST A LITTLE MORE COMPLICATED.
I FOUND THESE HERE. THEY DON'T BELONG HERE. YOU'VE BEEN BACK TO THE KEEP AGAIN, HAVEN'T YOU?
I HAVE. THE PLACE IS DESERTED. I'M TELLING YOU WE'R CLEAR TO GO BACK.
WHEN YOU WERE THERE, DID YOU SEE HER? IS SHE STILL ALIVE?
SHE'S JUST LIKE YOU LEFT HER, WAITING FOR YOUR RETURN. THE PLACE IS A GHOST TOWN. THERE'S NO ONE FOR MILES.
THEN IT IS TIME TO RETURN. YOU KNOW WHERE THE GIRL IS?
I KNOW EXACTLY WHERE YOUR TRAGIC LITTLE RAG DOLL IS. SHE'S JUST WAITING FOR ME TO PICK HER UP.

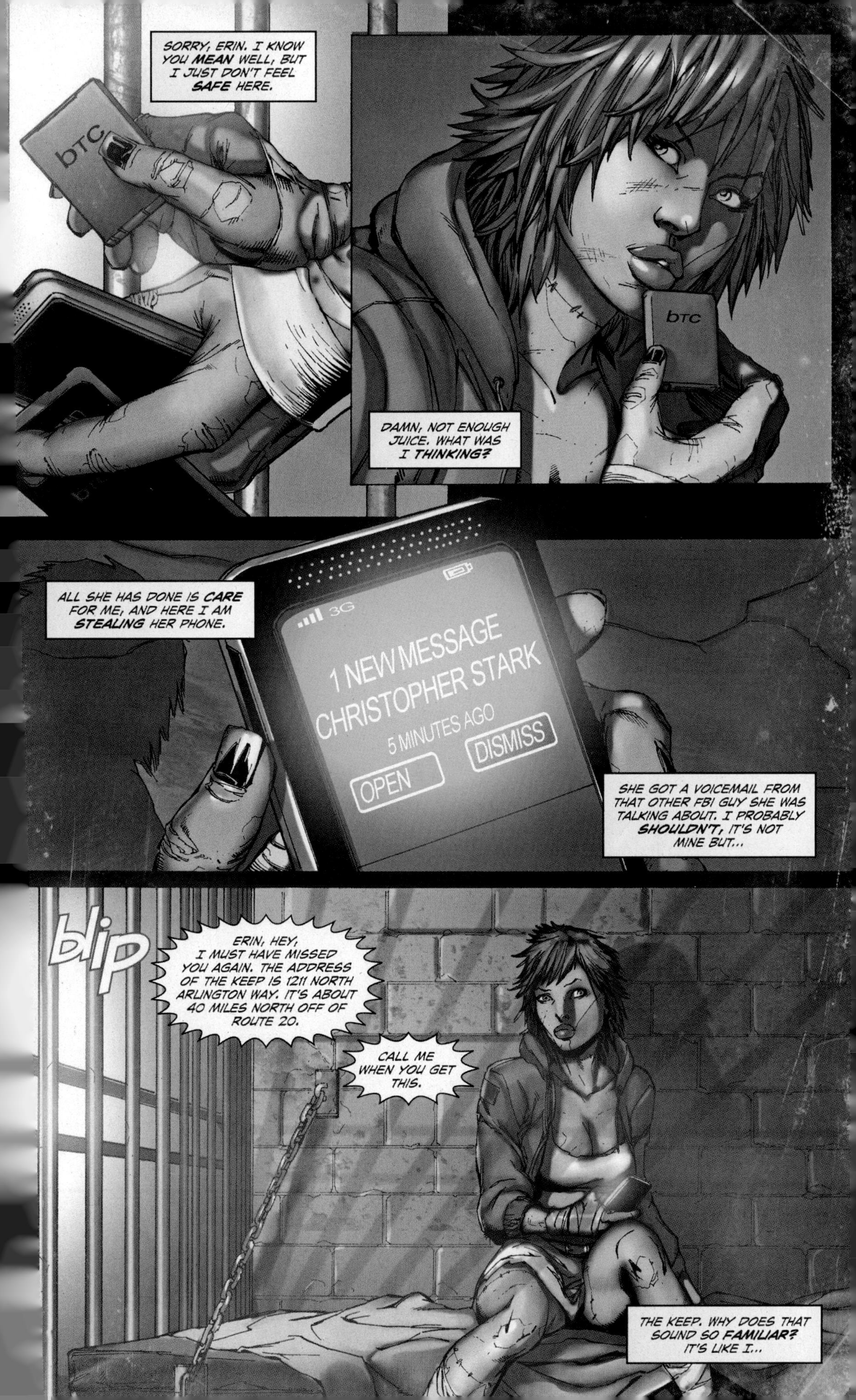

SORRY, ERIN. I KNOW YOU MEAN WELL, BUT I JUST DON'T FEEL SAFE HERE.
bTC
bTC
DAMN, NOT ENOUGH JUICE. WHAT WAS I THINKING?
ALL SHE HAS DONE IS CARE FOR ME, AND HERE I AM STEALING HER PHONE.
3G
1 NEW MESSAGE
CHRISTOPHER STARK
5 MINUTES AGO
OPEN
DISMISS
SHE GOT A VOICEMAIL FROM THAT OTHER FBI GUY SHE WAS TALKING ABOUT. I PROBABLY SHOULDN'T, IT'S NOT MINE BUT...
blip
ERIN, HEY, I MUST HAVE MISSED YOU AGAIN. THE ADDRESS OF THE KEEP IS 1211 NORTH ARLINGTON WAY. IT'S ABOUT 40 MILES NORTH OFF OF ROUTE 20.
CALL ME WHEN YOU GET THIS.
THE KEEP. WHY DOES THAT SOUND SO FAMILIAR? IT'S LIKE I...

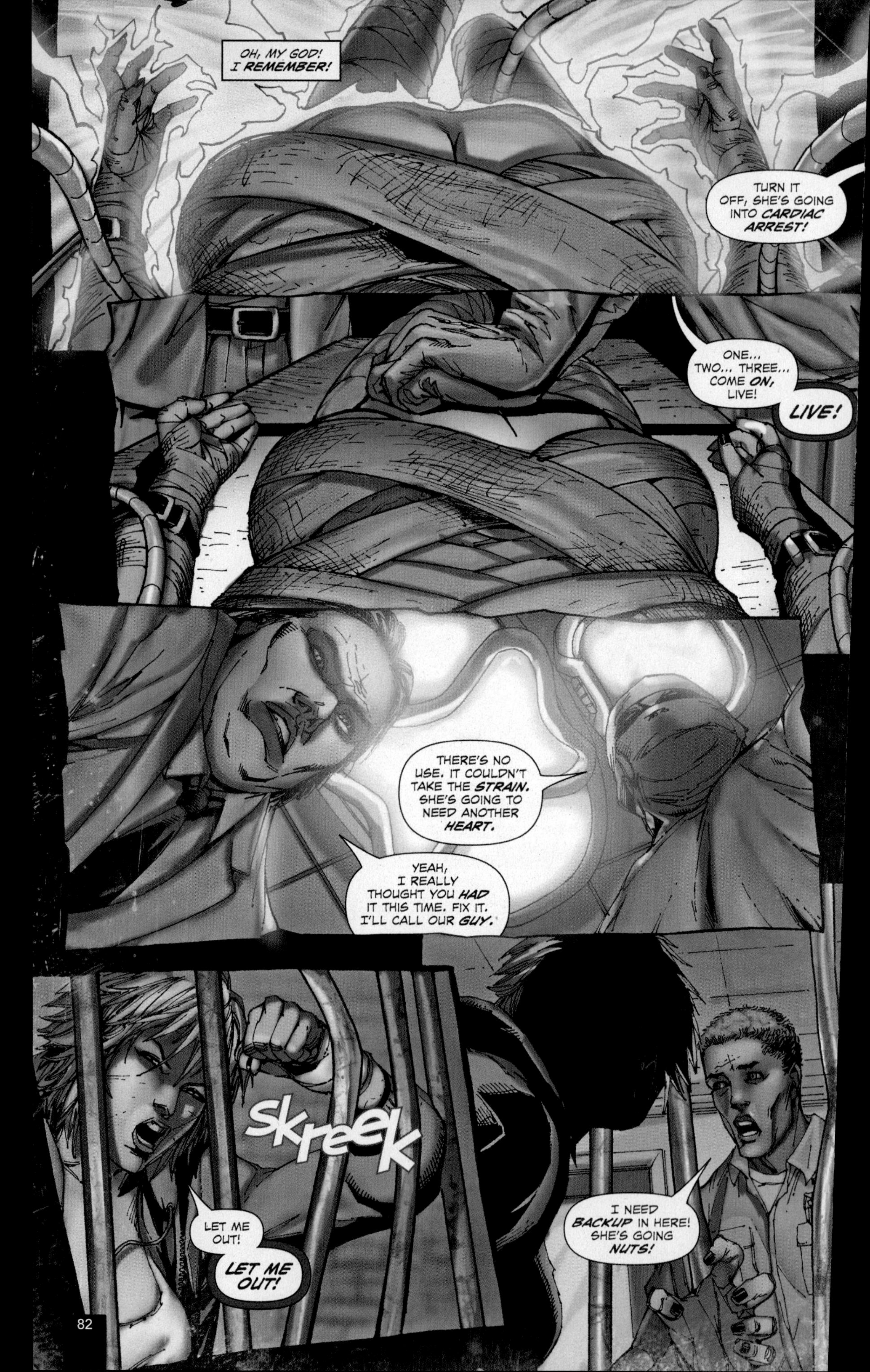
OH, MY GOD! I REMEMBER!
TURN IT OFF, SHE'S GOING INTO CARDIAC ARREST!
ONE... TWO... THREE... COME ON, LIVE!
LIVE!
THERE'S NO USE. IT COULDN'T TAKE THE STRAIN. SHE'S GOING TO NEED ANOTHER HEART.
YEAH, I REALLY THOUGHT YOU HAD IT THIS TIME. FIX IT. I'LL CALL OUR GUY.
SKREEK
LET ME OUT!
LET ME OUT!
I NEED BACKUP IN HERE! SHE'S GOING NUTS!

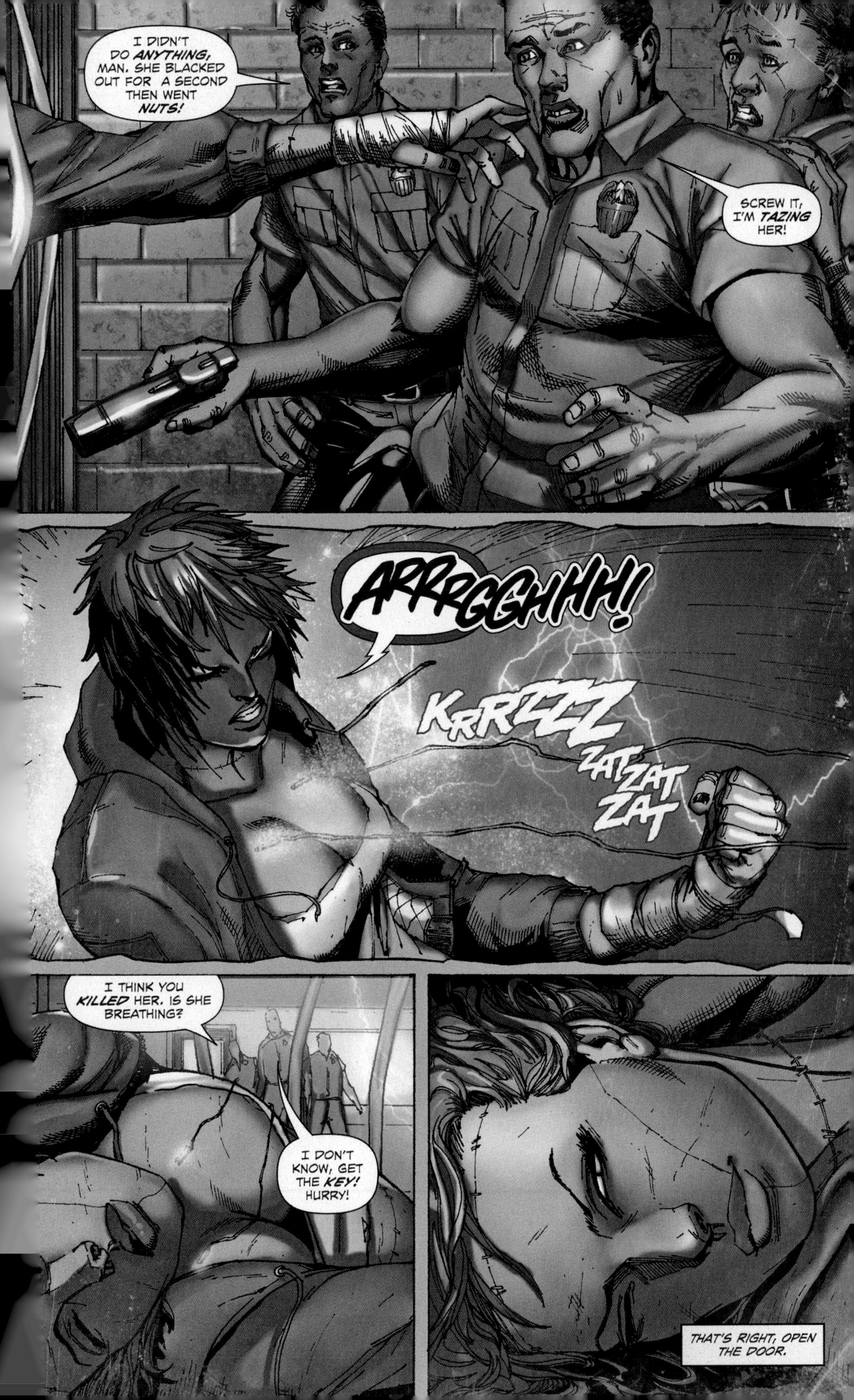

I DIDN'T DO ANYTHING, MAN. SHE BLACKED OUT FOR A SECOND THEN WENT NUTS!
SCREW IT, I'M TAZING HER!
ARRRGGHHH!
KRRZZZ
ZAT ZAT ZAT
I THINK YOU KILLED HER. IS SHE BREATHING?
I DON'T KNOW, GET THE KEY! HURRY!
THAT'S RIGHT, OPEN THE DOOR.

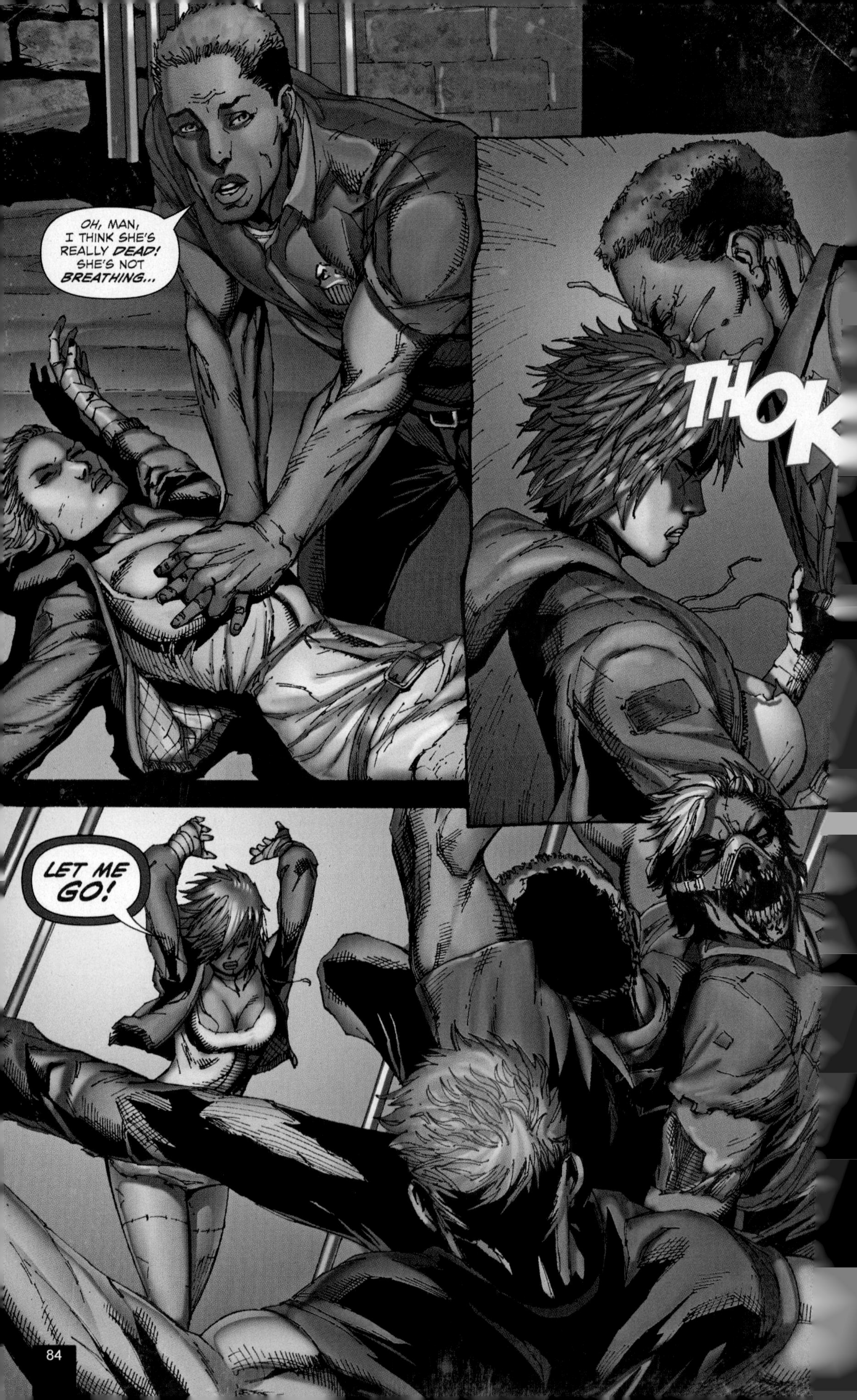

OH, MAN, I THINK SHE'S REALLY *DEAD!* SHE'S NOT *BREATHING...*
THOK
LET ME GO!

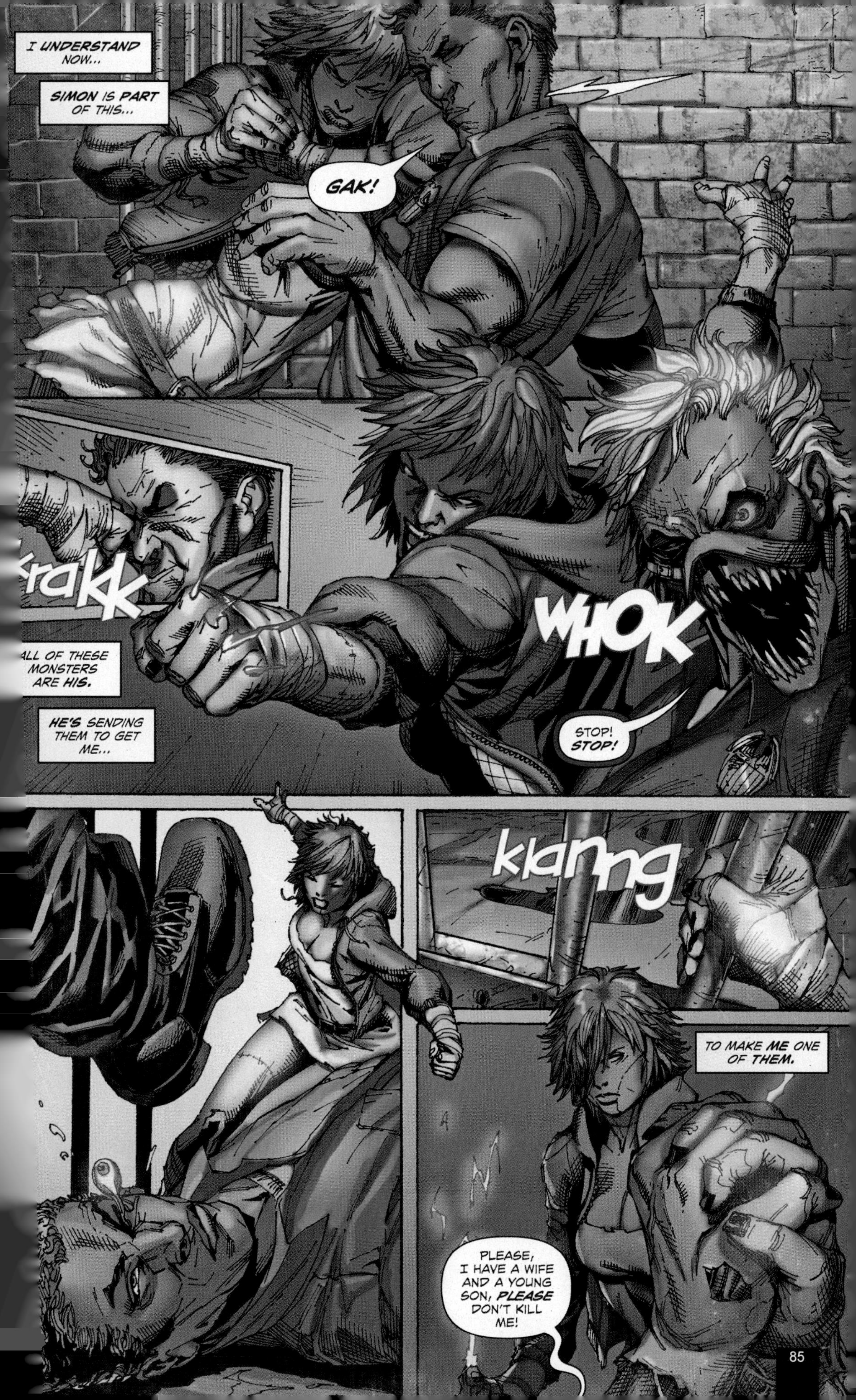

I UNDERSTAND NOW...
SIMON IS PART OF THIS...
GAK!
KRAKK
WHOK
ALL OF THESE MONSTERS ARE HIS.
HE'S SENDING THEM TO GET ME...
STOP! STOP!
KLANNG
TO MAKE ME ONE OF THEM.
PLEASE, I HAVE A WIFE AND A YOUNG SON, PLEASE DON'T KILL ME!

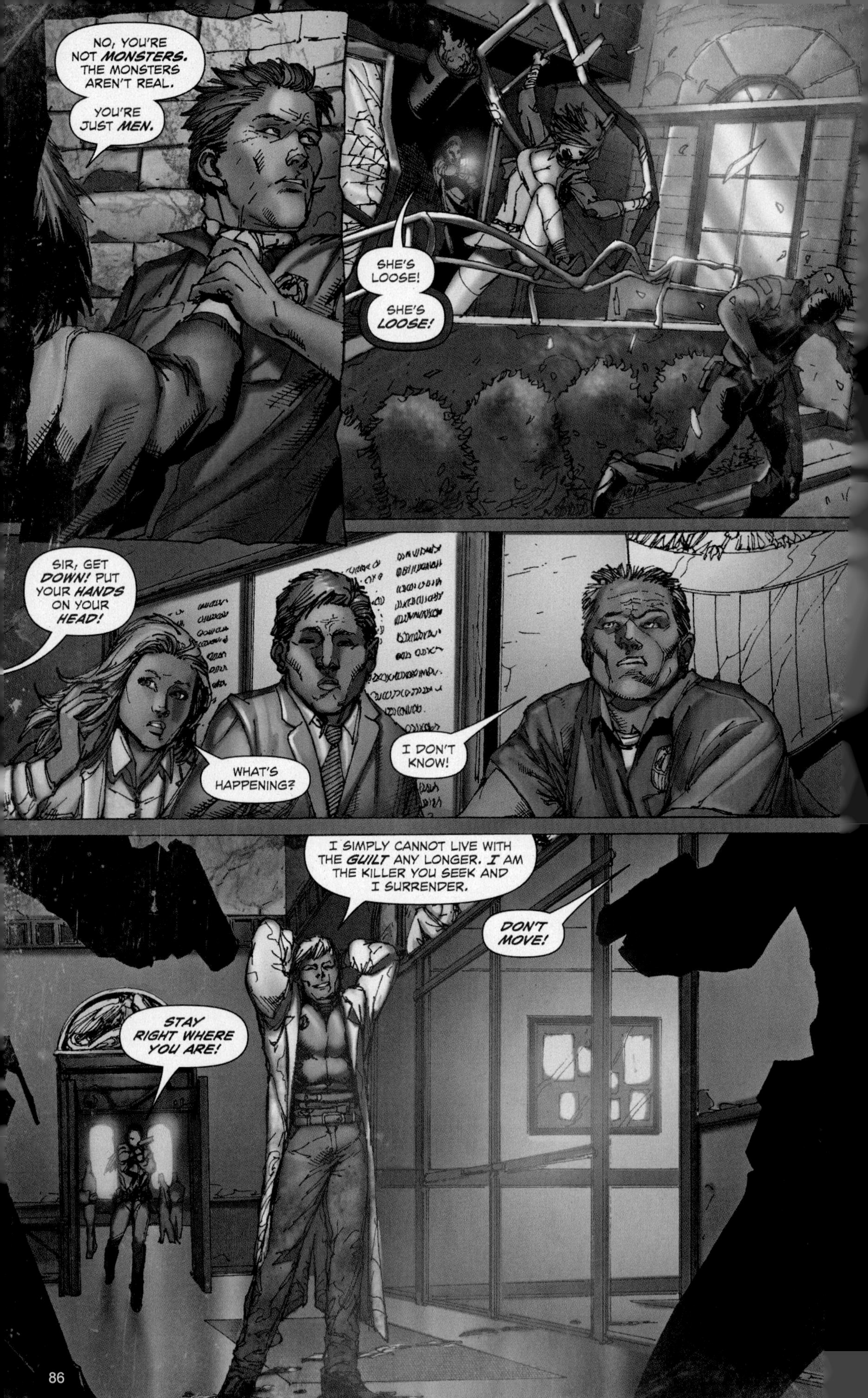
NO, YOU'RE NOT MONSTERS. THE MONSTERS AREN'T REAL.
YOU'RE JUST MEN.
SHE'S LOOSE!
SHE'S LOOSE!
SIR, GET DOWN! PUT YOUR HANDS ON YOUR HEAD!
WHAT'S HAPPENING?
I DON'T KNOW!
I SIMPLY CANNOT LIVE WITH THE GUILT ANY LONGER. I AM THE KILLER YOU SEEK AND I SURRENDER.
DON'T MOVE!
STAY RIGHT WHERE YOU ARE!

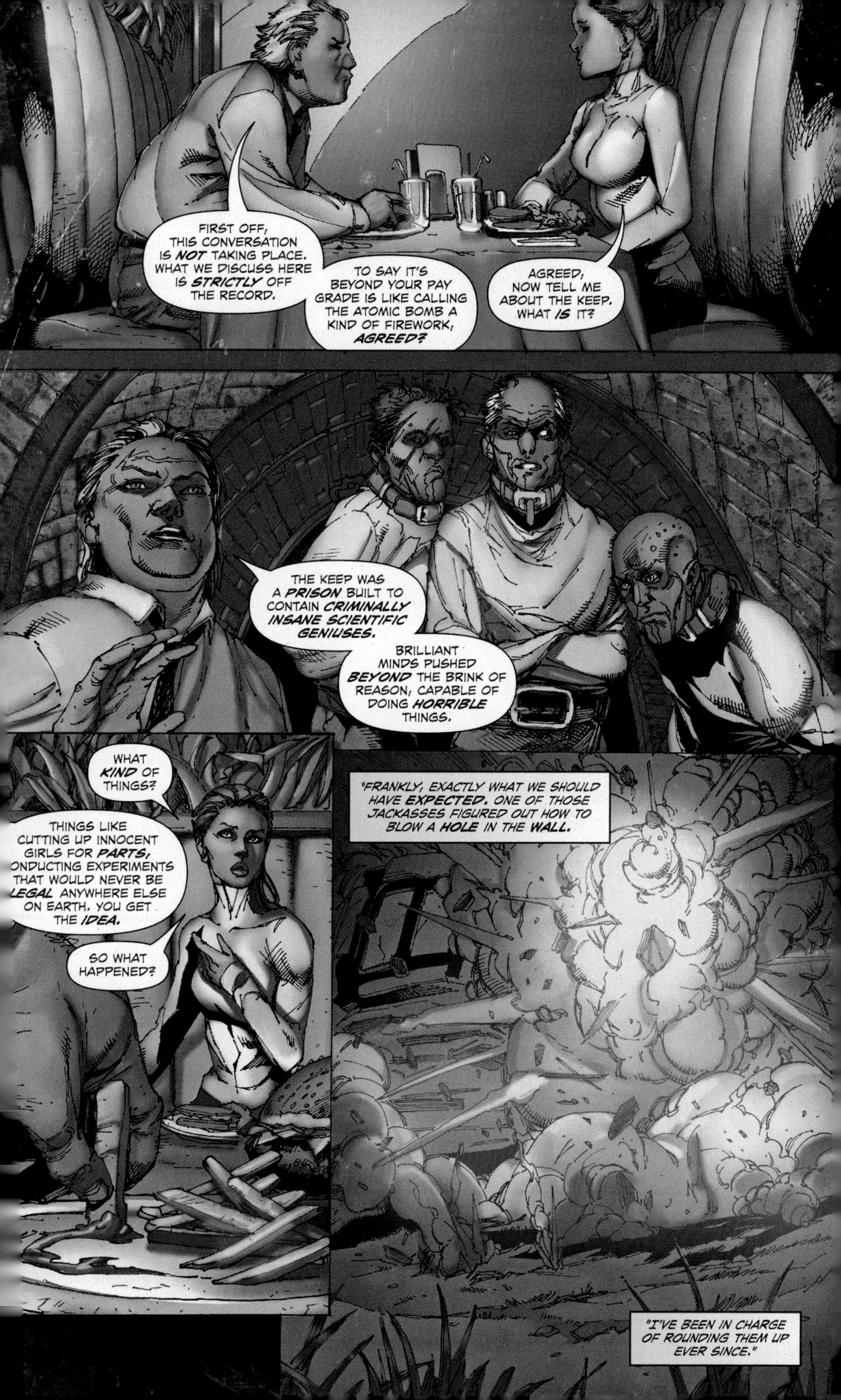
FIRST OFF, THIS CONVERSATION IS NOT TAKING PLACE. WHAT WE DISCUSS HERE IS STRICTLY OFF THE RECORD.
TO SAY IT'S BEYOND YOUR PAY GRADE IS LIKE CALLING THE ATOMIC BOMB A KIND OF FIREWORK, AGREED?
AGREED, NOW TELL ME ABOUT THE KEEP. WHAT IS IT?
THE KEEP WAS A PRISON BUILT TO CONTAIN CRIMINALLY INSANE SCIENTIFIC GENIUSES.
BRILLIANT MINDS PUSHED BEYOND THE BRINK OF REASON, CAPABLE OF DOING HORRIBLE THINGS.
WHAT KIND OF THINGS?
THINGS LIKE CUTTING UP INNOCENT GIRLS FOR PARTS, CONDUCTING EXPERIMENTS THAT WOULD NEVER BE LEGAL ANYWHERE ELSE ON EARTH. YOU GET THE IDEA.
SO WHAT HAPPENED?
"FRANKLY, EXACTLY WHAT WE SHOULD HAVE EXPECTED. ONE OF THOSE JACKASSES FIGURED OUT HOW TO BLOW A HOLE IN THE WALL.
"I'VE BEEN IN CHARGE OF ROUNDING THEM UP EVER SINCE."

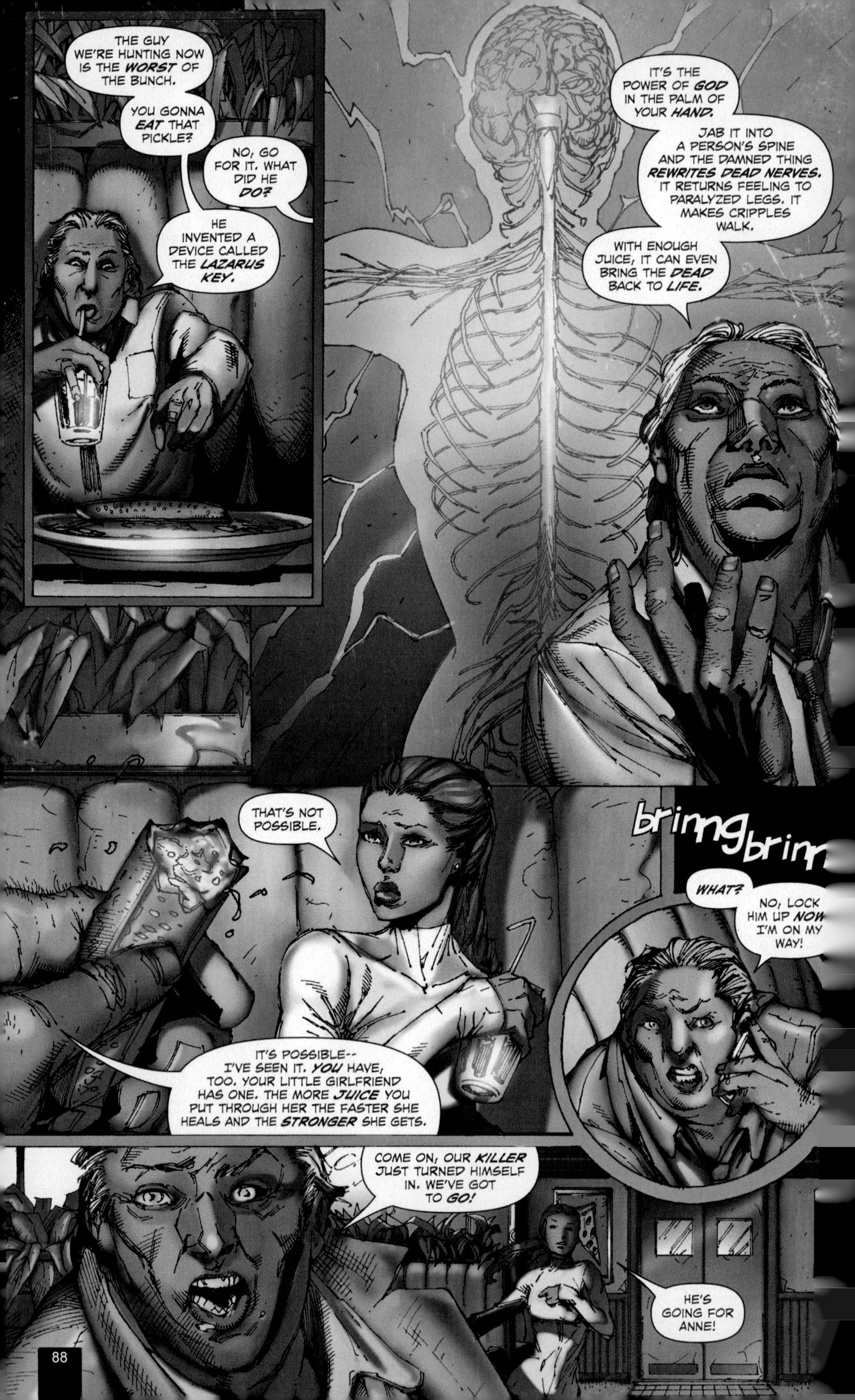
THE GUY WE'RE HUNTING NOW IS THE WORST OF THE BUNCH.
YOU GONNA EAT THAT PICKLE?
NO, GO FOR IT. WHAT DID HE DO?
HE INVENTED A DEVICE CALLED THE LAZARUS KEY.
IT'S THE POWER OF GOD IN THE PALM OF YOUR HAND.
JAB IT INTO A PERSON'S SPINE AND THE DAMNED THING REWRITES DEAD NERVES. IT RETURNS FEELING TO PARALYZED LEGS. IT MAKES CRIPPLES WALK.
WITH ENOUGH JUICE, IT CAN EVEN BRING THE DEAD BACK TO LIFE.
THAT'S NOT POSSIBLE.
IT'S POSSIBLE-- I'VE SEEN IT. YOU HAVE, TOO. YOUR LITTLE GIRLFRIEND HAS ONE. THE MORE JUICE YOU PUT THROUGH HER THE FASTER SHE HEALS AND THE STRONGER SHE GETS.
brinngbrinn
WHAT?
NO, LOCK HIM UP NOW I'M ON MY WAY!
COME ON, OUR KILLER JUST TURNED HIMSELF IN. WE'VE GOT TO GO!
HE'S GOING FOR ANNE!

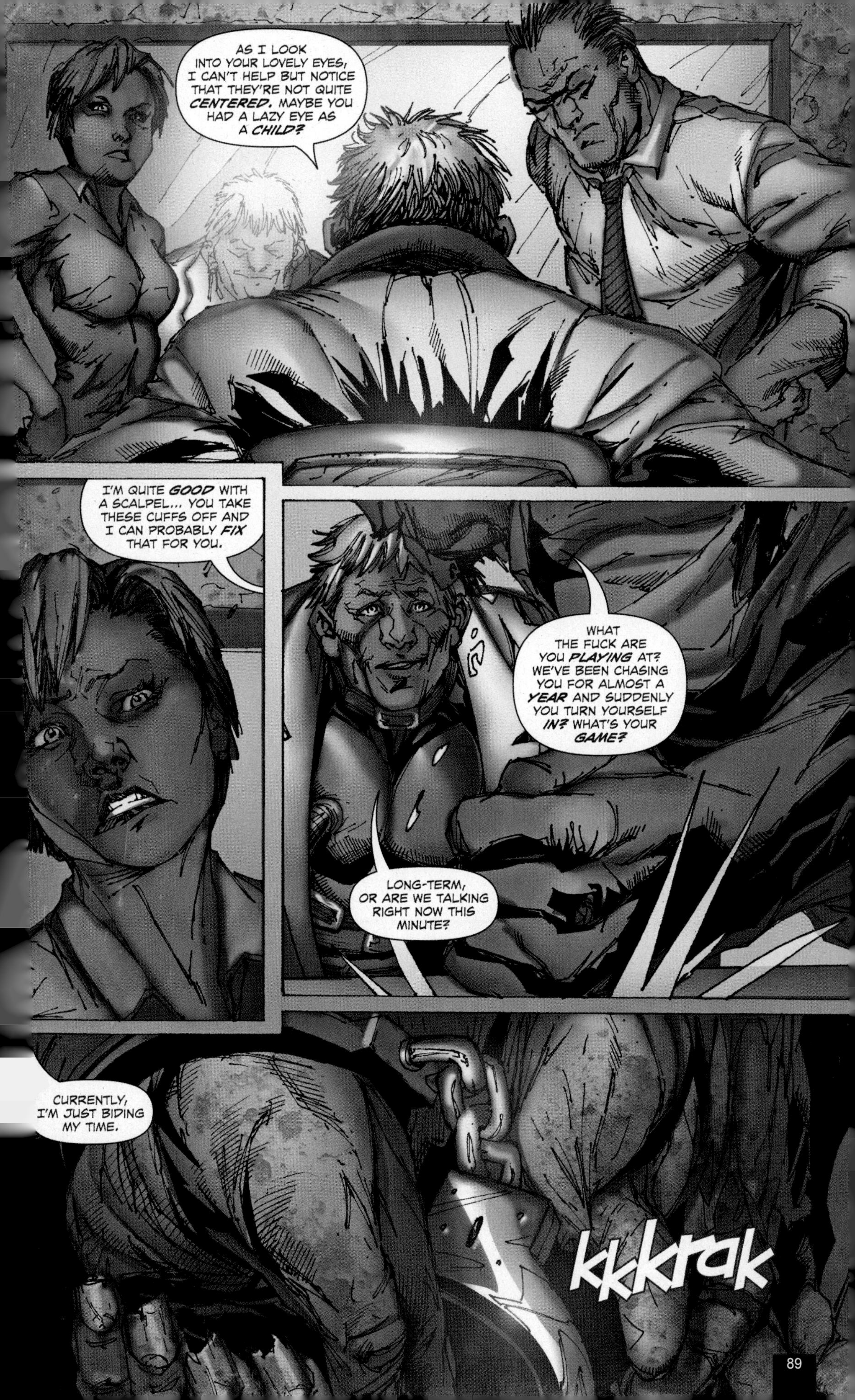

AS I LOOK INTO YOUR LOVELY EYES, I CAN'T HELP BUT NOTICE THAT THEY'RE NOT QUITE CENTERED. MAYBE YOU HAD A LAZY EYE AS A CHILD?
I'M QUITE GOOD WITH A SCALPEL... YOU TAKE THESE CUFFS OFF AND I CAN PROBABLY FIX THAT FOR YOU.
WHAT THE FUCK ARE YOU PLAYING AT? WE'VE BEEN CHASING YOU FOR ALMOST A YEAR AND SUDDENLY YOU TURN YOURSELF IN? WHAT'S YOUR GAME?
LONG-TERM, OR ARE WE TALKING RIGHT NOW THIS MINUTE?
CURRENTLY, I'M JUST BIDING MY TIME.
KKKRAK

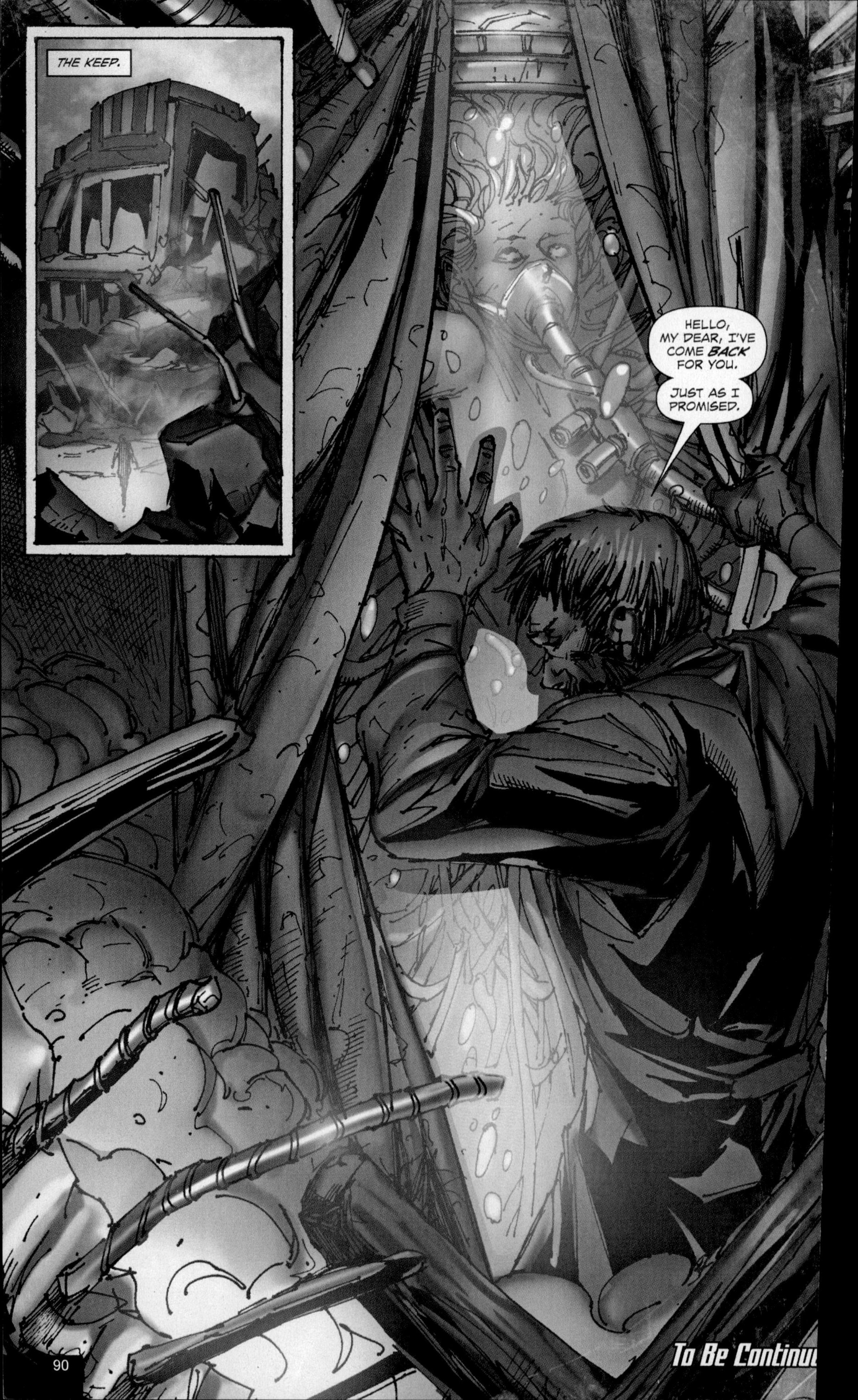
THE KEEP.
HELLO, MY DEAR, I'VE COME BACK FOR YOU.
JUST AS I PROMISED.
To Be Continu

SCREWED

CHAPTER FIVE

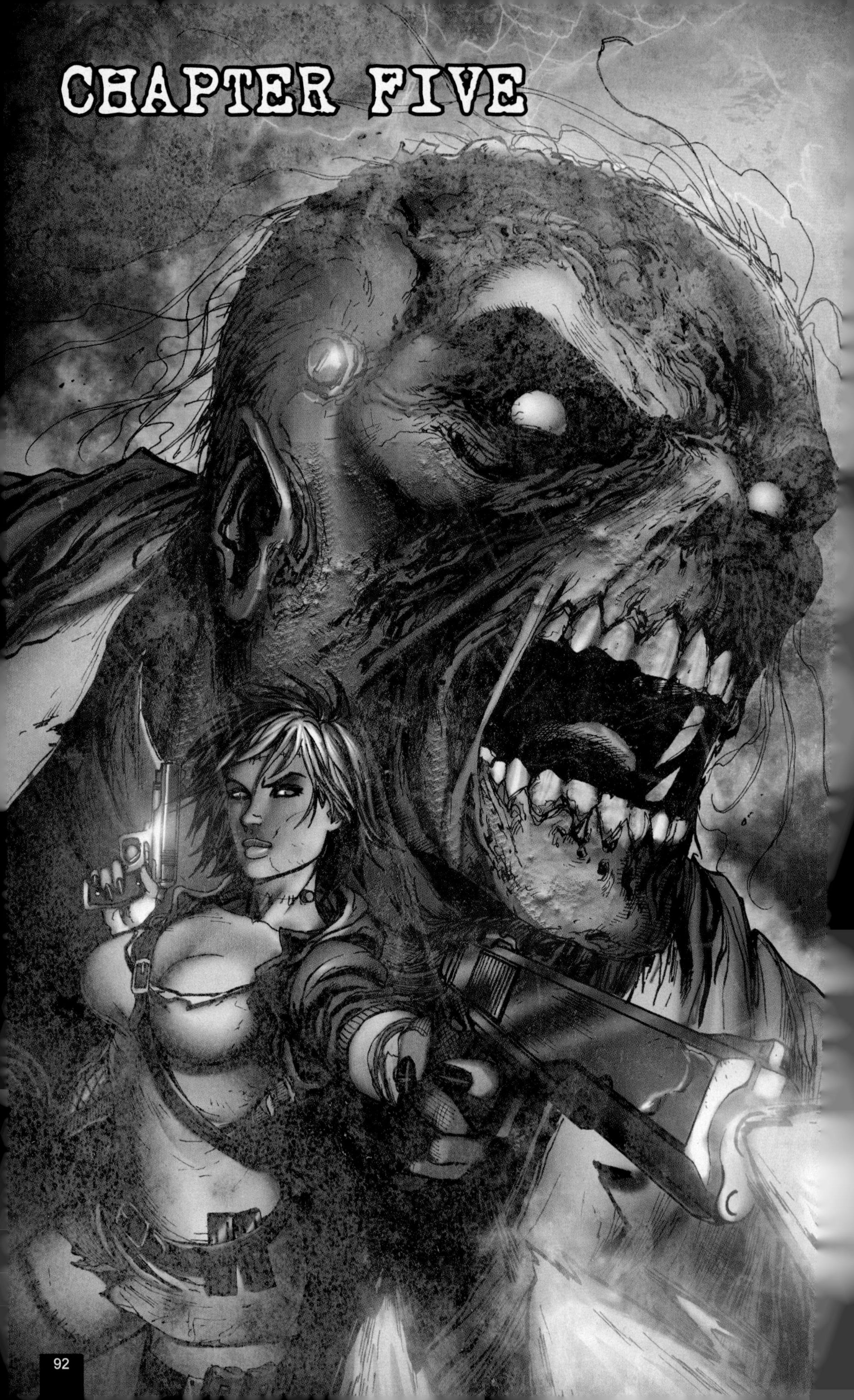

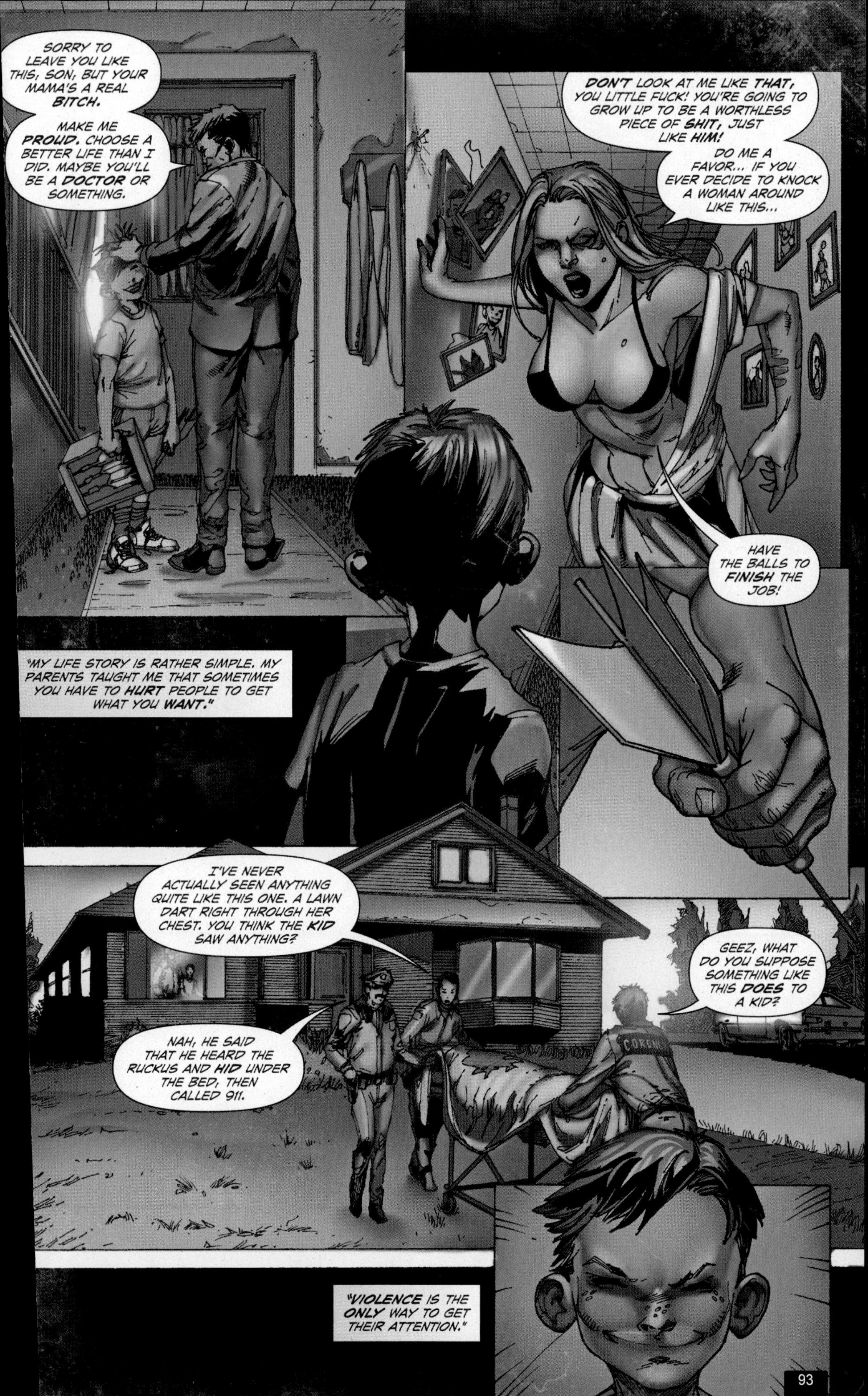
SORRY TO LEAVE YOU LIKE THIS, SON, BUT YOUR MAMA'S A REAL **BITCH.**
MAKE ME **PROUD.** CHOOSE A BETTER LIFE THAN I DID. MAYBE YOU'LL BE A **DOCTOR** OR SOMETHING.
DON'T LOOK AT ME LIKE **THAT,** YOU LITTLE FUCK! YOU'RE GOING TO GROW UP TO BE A WORTHLESS PIECE OF **SHIT,** JUST LIKE **HIM!**
DO ME A FAVOR... IF YOU EVER DECIDE TO KNOCK A WOMAN AROUND LIKE THIS...
HAVE THE BALLS TO **FINISH** THE JOB!
"MY LIFE STORY IS RATHER SIMPLE. MY PARENTS TAUGHT ME THAT SOMETIMES YOU HAVE TO **HURT** PEOPLE TO GET WHAT YOU **WANT.**"
I'VE NEVER ACTUALLY SEEN ANYTHING QUITE LIKE THIS ONE. A LAWN DART RIGHT THROUGH HER CHEST. YOU THINK THE **KID** SAW ANYTHING?
NAH, HE SAID THAT HE HEARD THE **RUCKUS** AND **HID** UNDER THE BED, THEN CALLED 911.
GEEZ, WHAT DO YOU SUPPOSE SOMETHING LIKE THIS **DOES** TO A KID?
"**VIOLENCE** IS THE **ONLY** WAY TO GET THEIR ATTENTION."

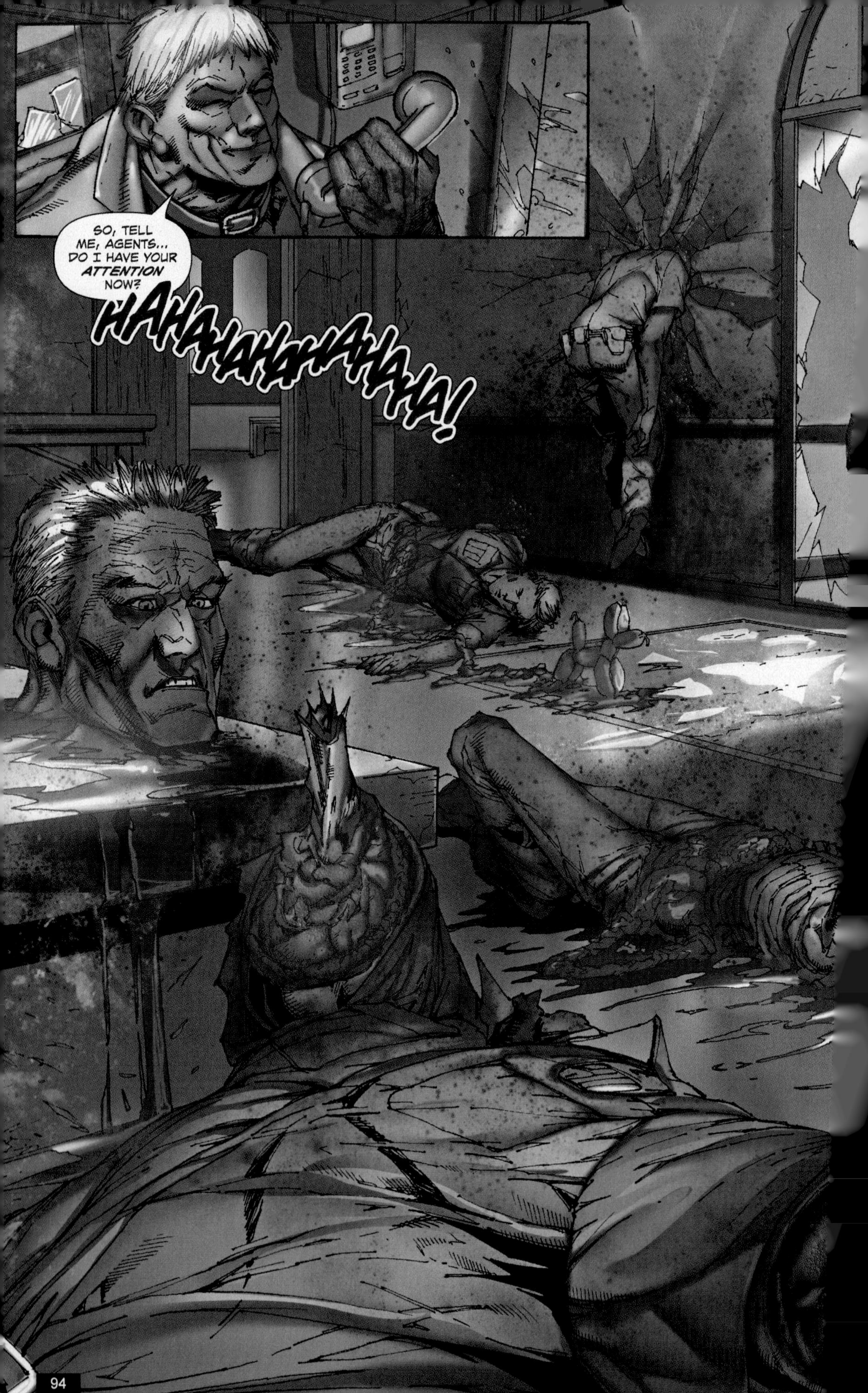
SO, TELL ME, AGENTS... DO I HAVE YOUR ATTENTION NOW?
HAHAHAHAHAHAHAHAHA!

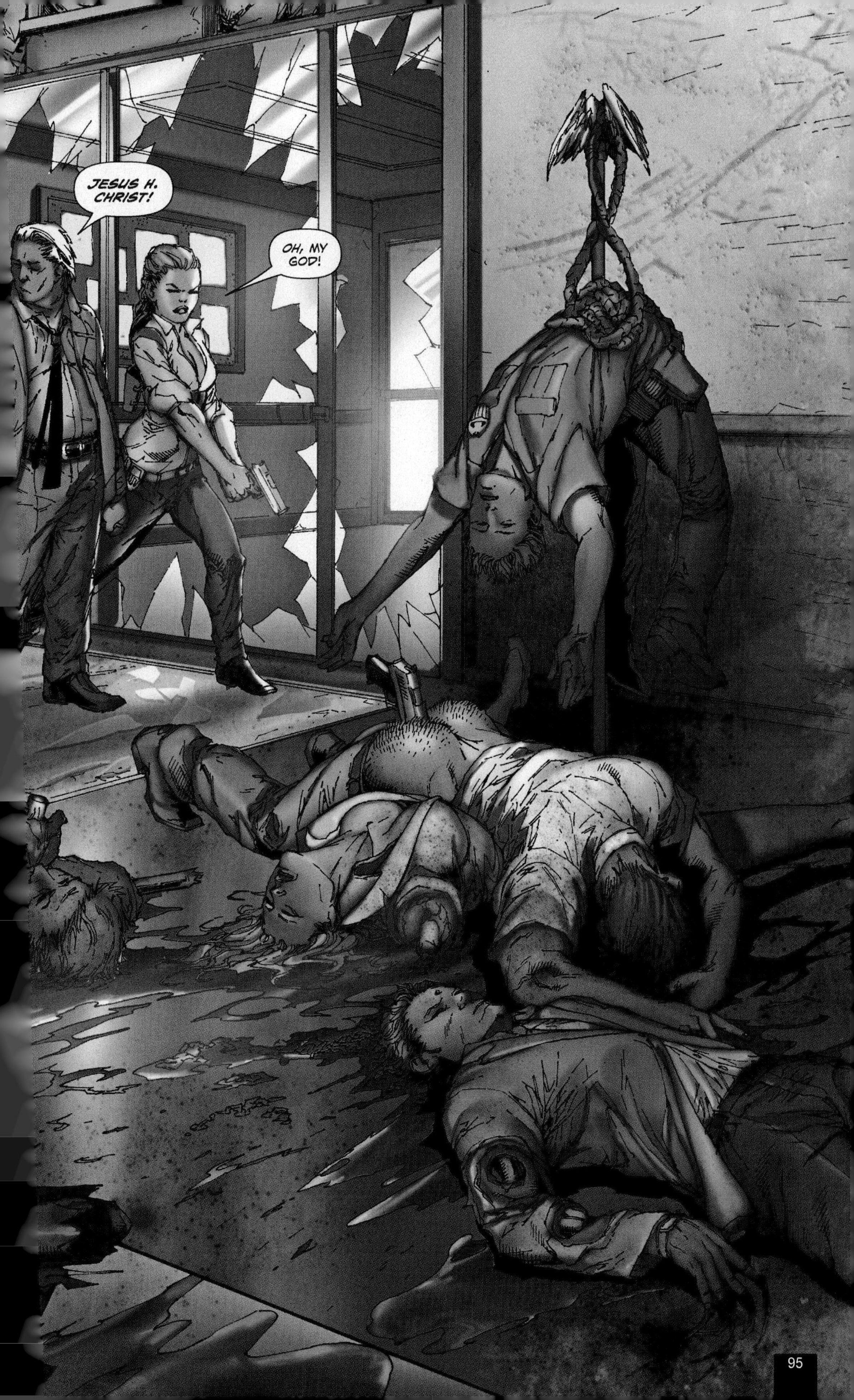
JESUS H. CHRIST!
OH, MY GOD!

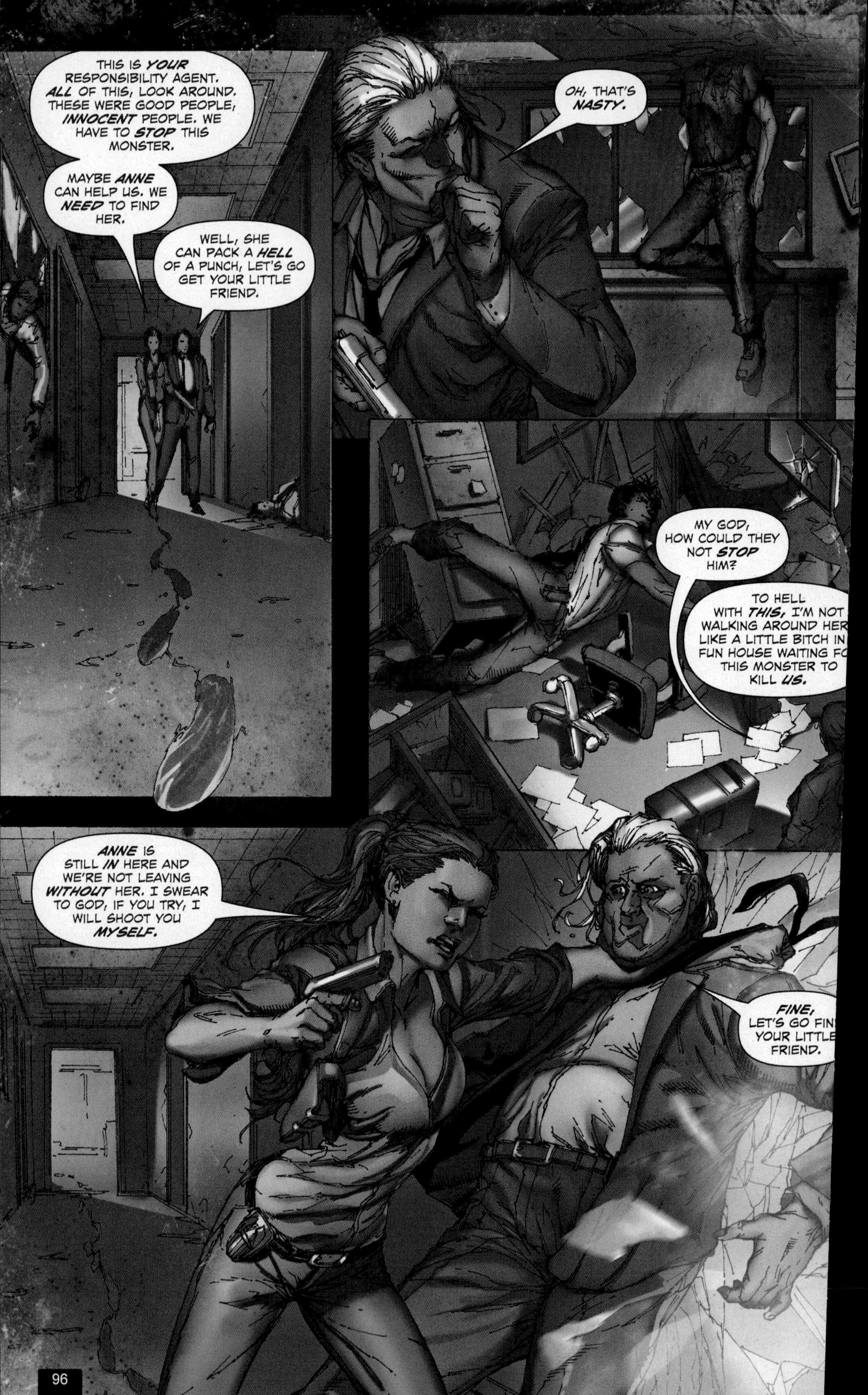
THIS IS YOUR RESPONSIBILITY AGENT. ALL OF THIS, LOOK AROUND. THESE WERE GOOD PEOPLE, INNOCENT PEOPLE. WE HAVE TO STOP THIS MONSTER.
MAYBE ANNE CAN HELP US. WE NEED TO FIND HER.
WELL, SHE CAN PACK A HELL OF A PUNCH, LET'S GO GET YOUR LITTLE FRIEND.
OH, THAT'S NASTY.
MY GOD, HOW COULD THEY NOT STOP HIM?
ANNE IS STILL IN HERE AND WE'RE NOT LEAVING WITHOUT HER. I SWEAR TO GOD, IF YOU TRY, I WILL SHOOT YOU MYSELF.

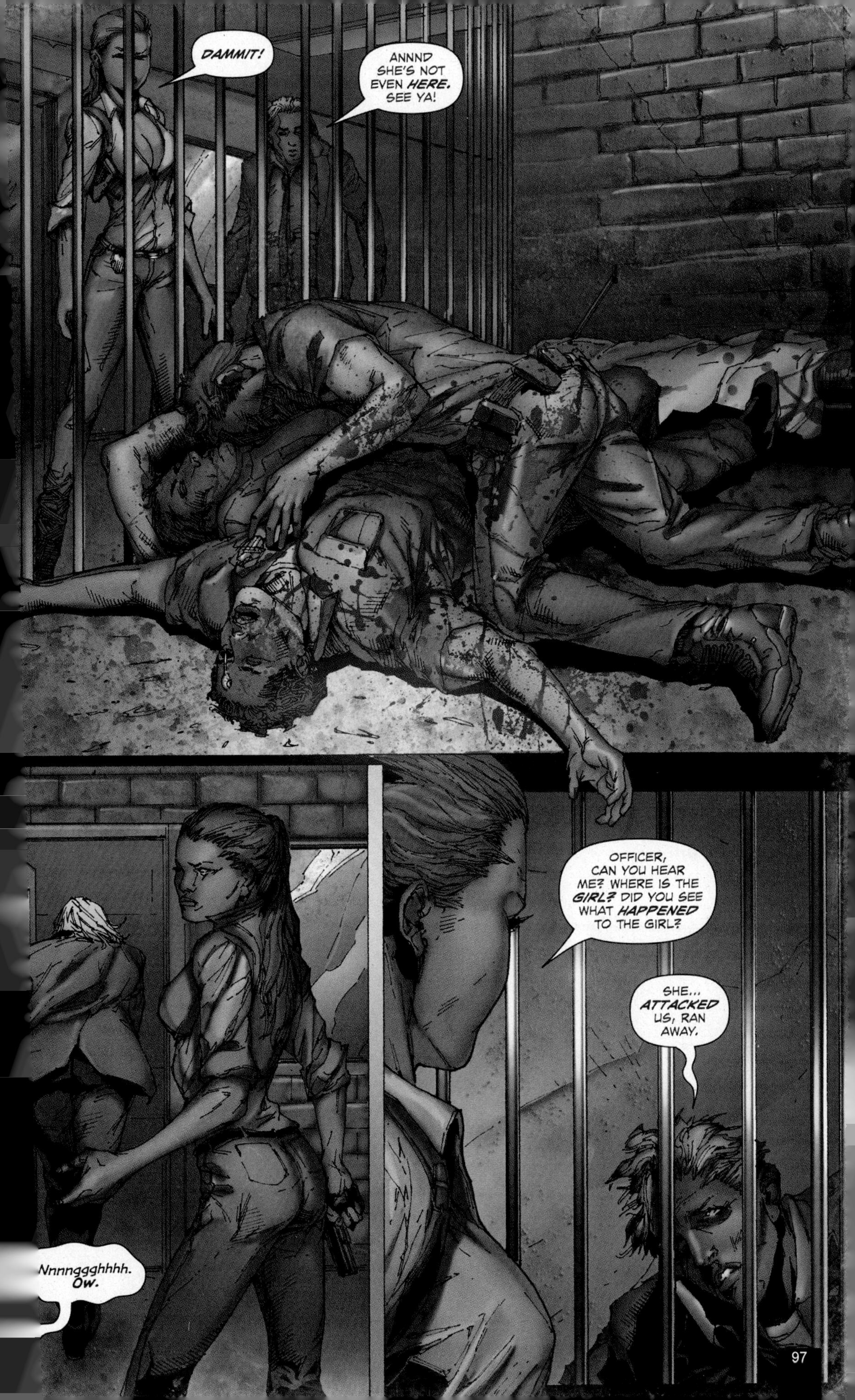

DAMMIT!
ANNND SHE'S NOT EVEN HERE. SEE YA!
OFFICER, CAN YOU HEAR ME? WHERE IS THE GIRL? DID YOU SEE WHAT HAPPENED TO THE GIRL?
SHE... ATTACKED US, RAN AWAY.
Nnnngggghhhh. Ow.

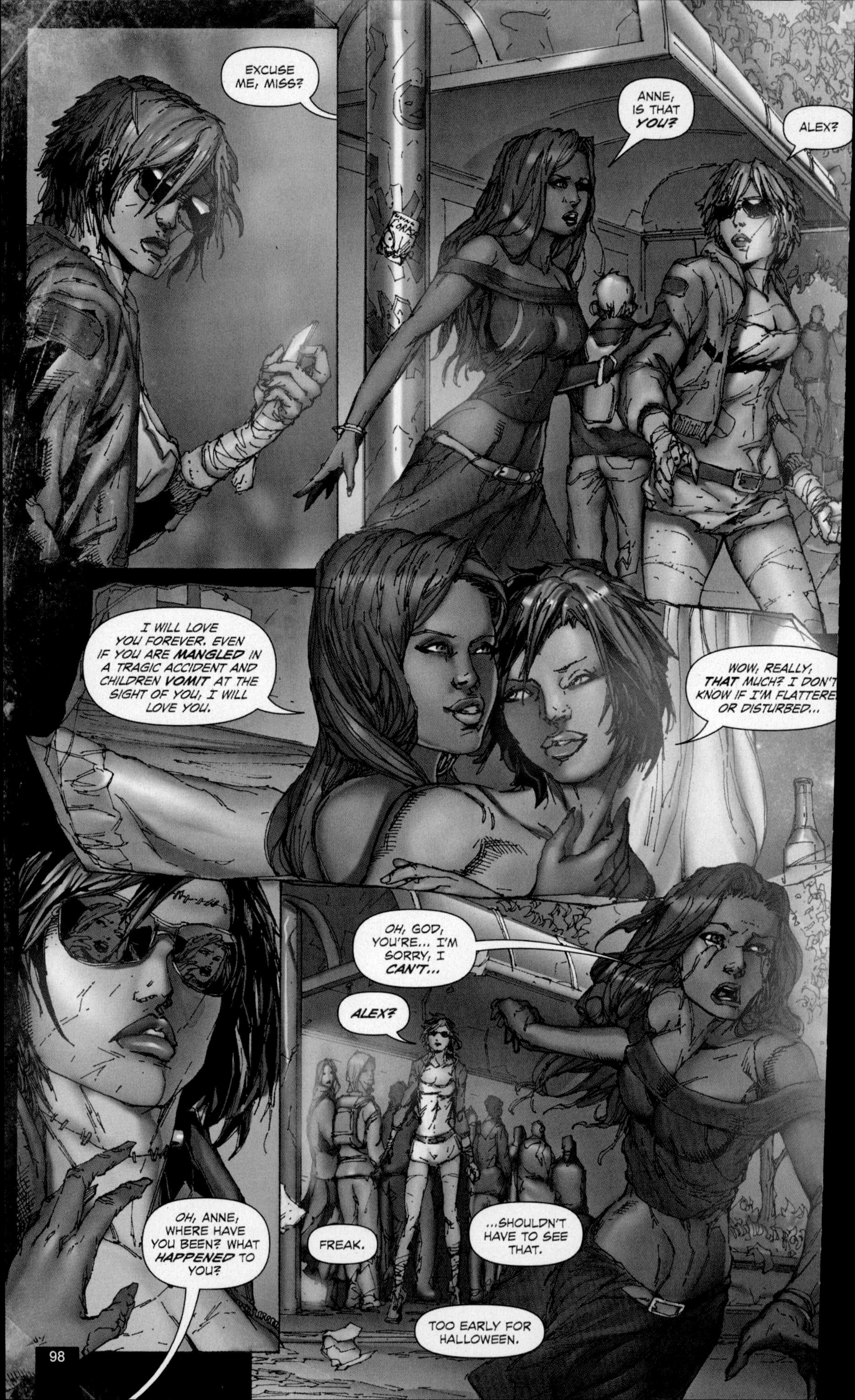
EXCUSE ME, MISS?
ANNE, IS THAT YOU?
ALEX?
I WILL LOVE YOU FOREVER. EVEN IF YOU ARE MANGLED IN A TRAGIC ACCIDENT AND CHILDREN VOMIT AT THE SIGHT OF YOU, I WILL LOVE YOU.
WOW, REALLY, THAT MUCH? I DON'T KNOW IF I'M FLATTERED OR DISTURBED...
OH, GOD, YOU'RE... I'M SORRY, I CAN'T...
ALEX?
OH, ANNE, WHERE HAVE YOU BEEN? WHAT HAPPENED TO YOU?
FREAK.
...SHOULDN'T HAVE TO SEE THAT.
TOO EARLY FOR HALLOWEEN.

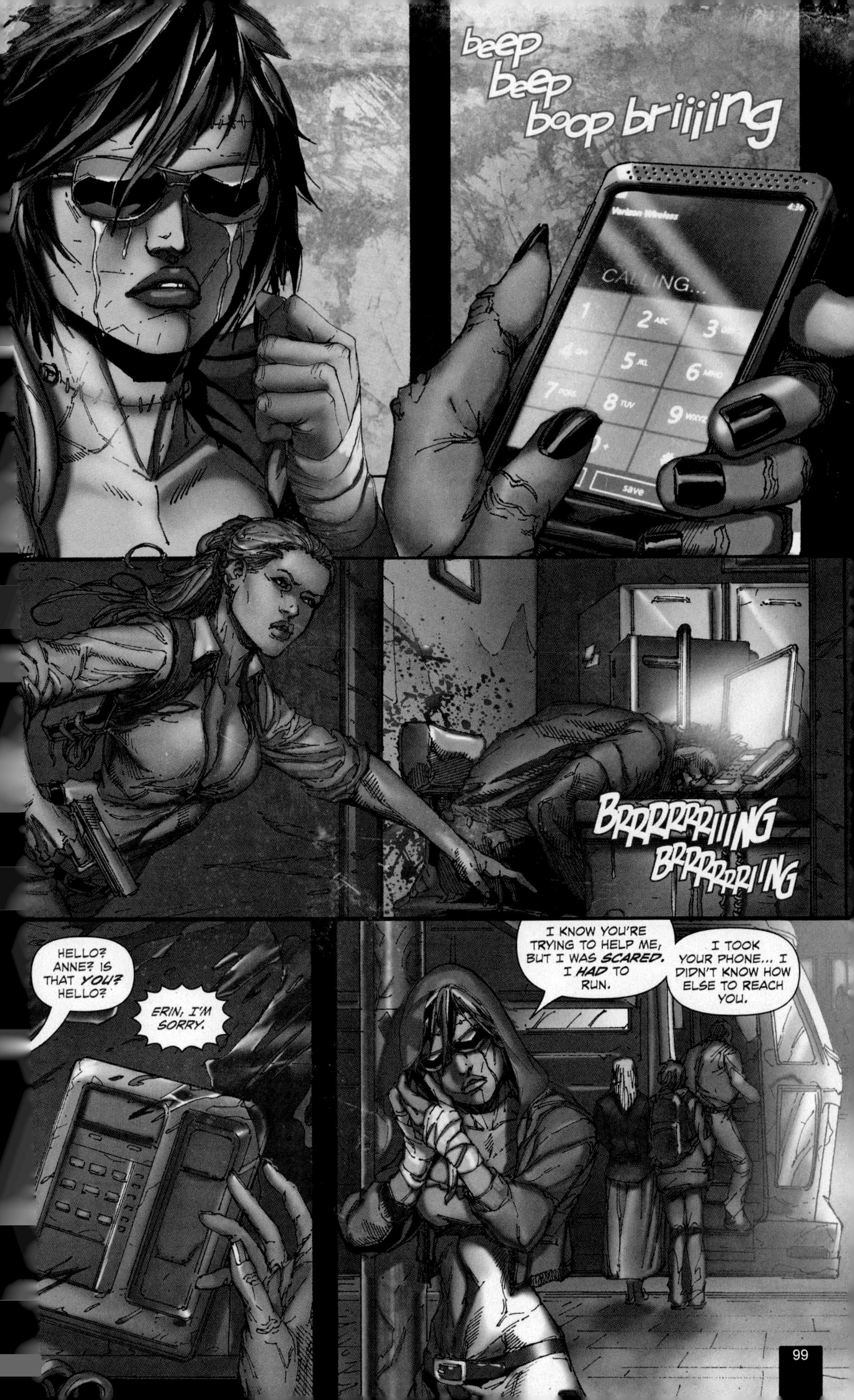
beep
beep
boop briiiing
CALLING...
save
BRRRRRRRIIING
BRRRRRRRIING
HELLO? ANNE? IS THAT YOU? HELLO?
ERIN, I'M SORRY.
I KNOW YOU'RE TRYING TO HELP ME, BUT I WAS SCARED. I HAD TO RUN.
I TOOK YOUR PHONE... I DIDN'T KNOW HOW ELSE TO REACH YOU.

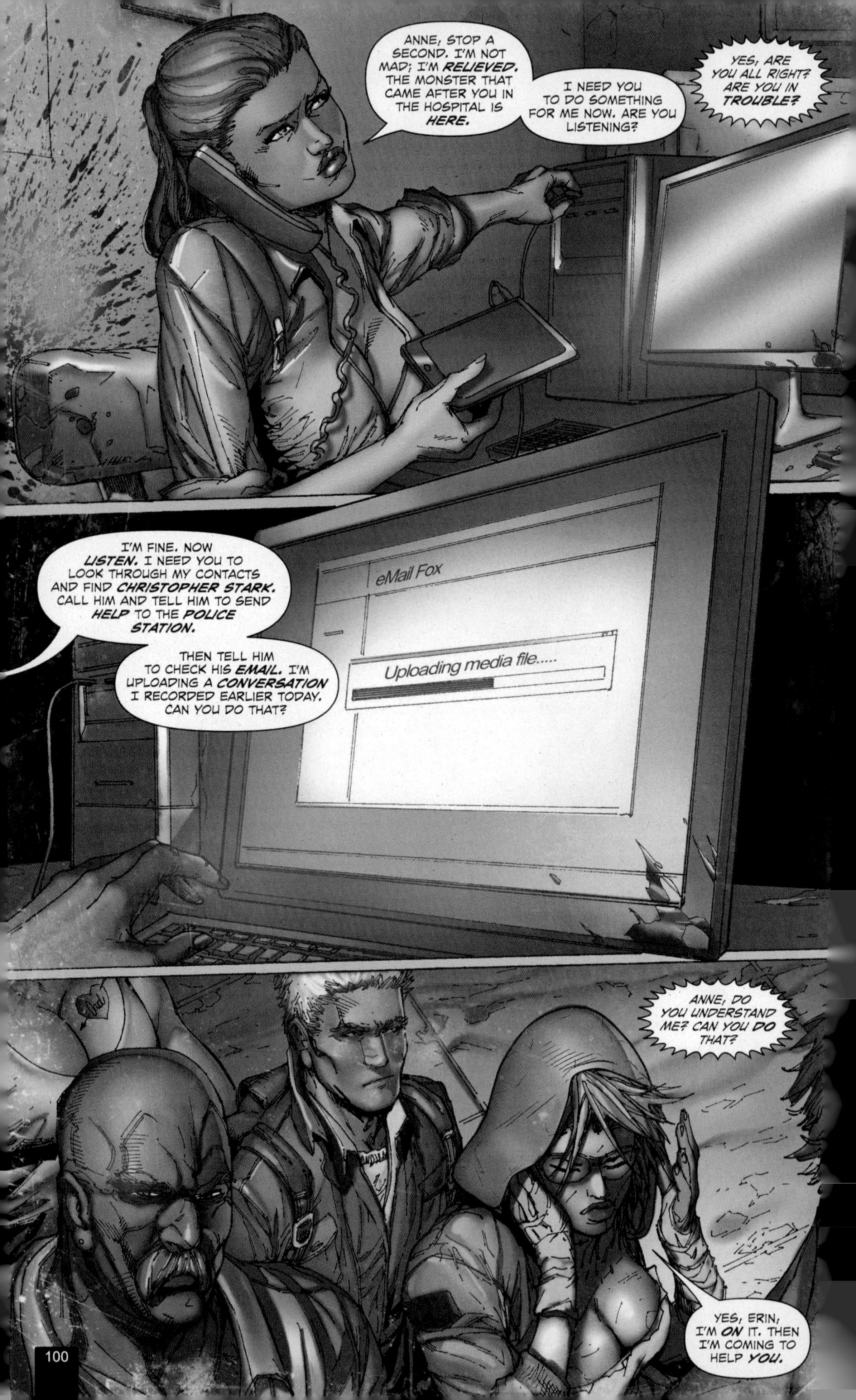
ANNE, STOP A SECOND. I'M NOT MAD; I'M **RELIEVED.** THE MONSTER THAT CAME AFTER YOU IN THE HOSPITAL IS **HERE.**
I NEED YOU TO DO SOMETHING FOR ME NOW. ARE YOU LISTENING?
YES, ARE YOU ALL RIGHT? ARE YOU IN **TROUBLE?**
I'M FINE. NOW **LISTEN.** I NEED YOU TO LOOK THROUGH MY CONTACTS AND FIND **CHRISTOPHER STARK.** CALL HIM AND TELL HIM TO SEND **HELP** TO THE **POLICE STATION.**
THEN TELL HIM TO CHECK HIS **EMAIL.** I'M UPLOADING A **CONVERSATION** I RECORDED EARLIER TODAY. CAN YOU DO THAT?
eMail Fox
Uploading media file.....
ANNE, DO YOU UNDERSTAND ME? CAN YOU **DO** THAT?
YES, ERIN, I'M **ON** IT. THEN I'M COMING TO HELP **YOU.**

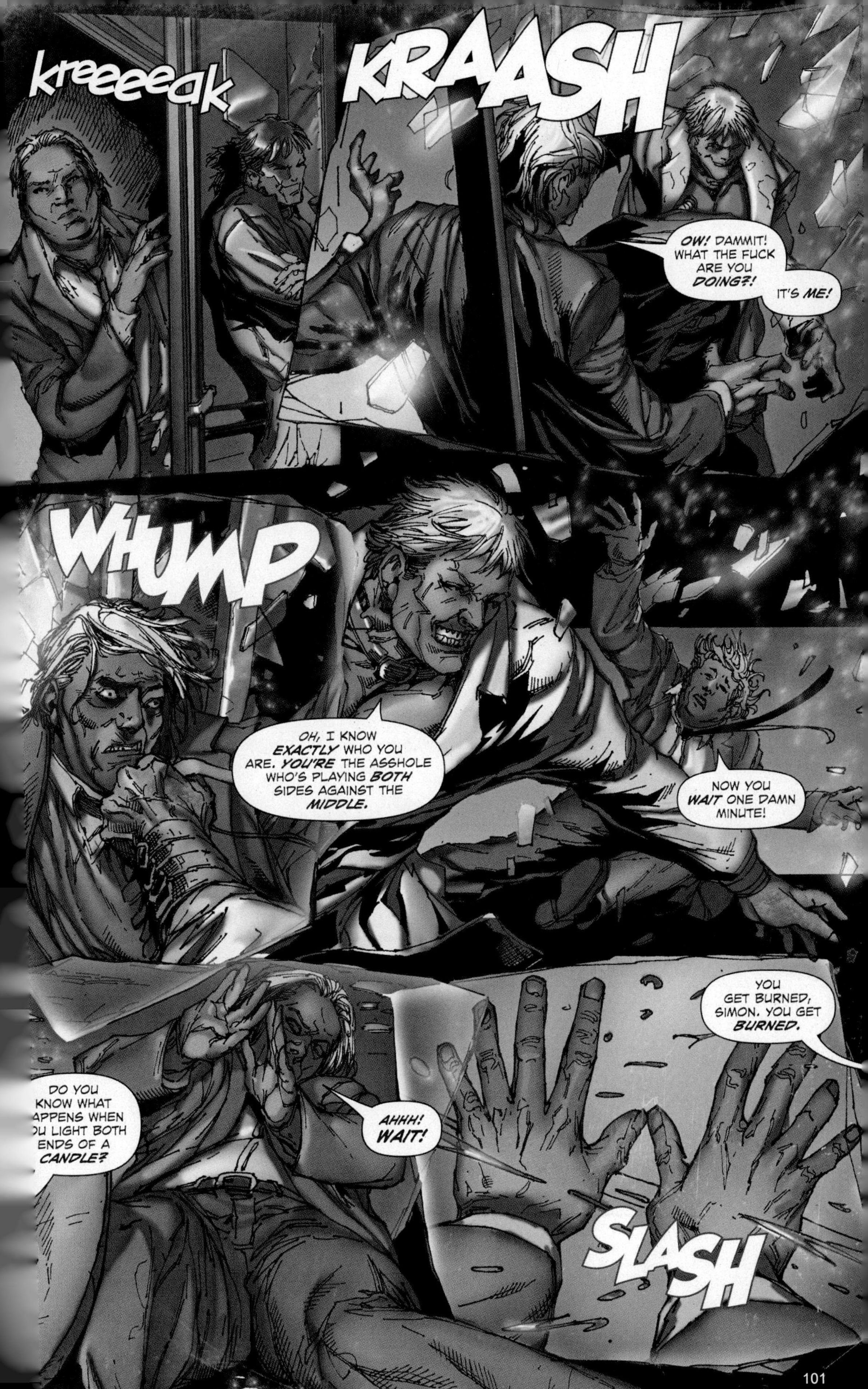
kreeeeeak
KRAASH
OW! DAMMIT! WHAT THE FUCK ARE YOU DOING?!
IT'S ME!
WHUMP
OH, I KNOW EXACTLY WHO YOU ARE. YOU'RE THE ASSHOLE WHO'S PLAYING BOTH SIDES AGAINST THE MIDDLE.
NOW YOU WAIT ONE DAMN MINUTE!
DO YOU KNOW WHAT APPENS WHEN OU LIGHT BOTH ENDS OF A CANDLE?
AHHH! WAIT!
YOU GET BURNED, SIMON. YOU GET BURNED.
SLASH

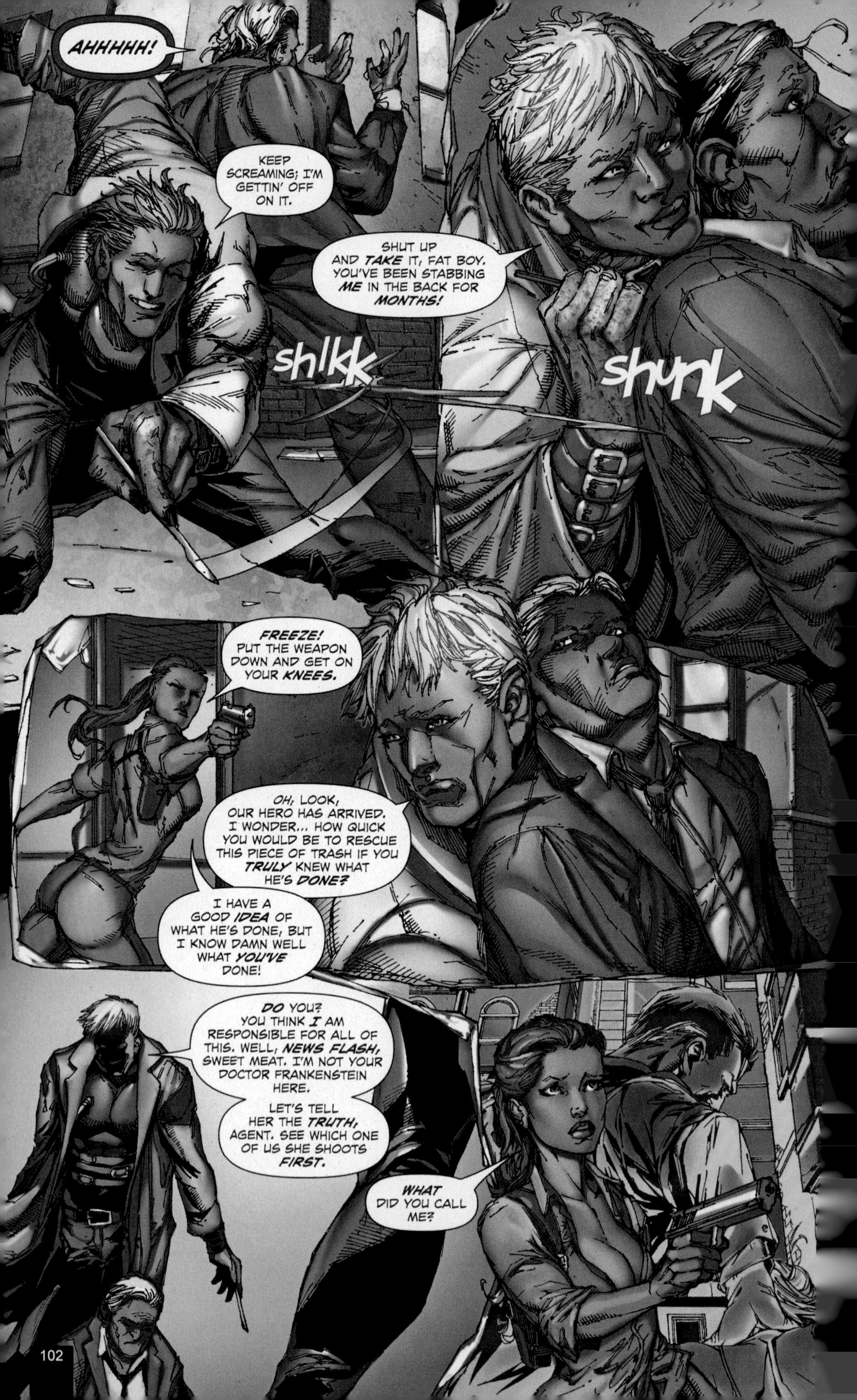
AHHHHH!
KEEP SCREAMING; I'M GETTIN' OFF ON IT.
SHUT UP AND TAKE IT, FAT BOY. YOU'VE BEEN STABBING ME IN THE BACK FOR MONTHS!
shlkk
shunk
FREEZE! PUT THE WEAPON DOWN AND GET ON YOUR KNEES.
OH, LOOK, OUR HERO HAS ARRIVED. I WONDER... HOW QUICK YOU WOULD BE TO RESCUE THIS PIECE OF TRASH IF YOU TRULY KNEW WHAT HE'S DONE?
I HAVE A GOOD IDEA OF WHAT HE'S DONE, BUT I KNOW DAMN WELL WHAT YOU'VE DONE!
DO YOU? YOU THINK I AM RESPONSIBLE FOR ALL OF THIS. WELL, NEWS FLASH, SWEET MEAT. I'M NOT YOUR DOCTOR FRANKENSTEIN HERE.
LET'S TELL HER THE TRUTH, AGENT. SEE WHICH ONE OF US SHE SHOOTS FIRST.
WHAT DID YOU CALL ME?

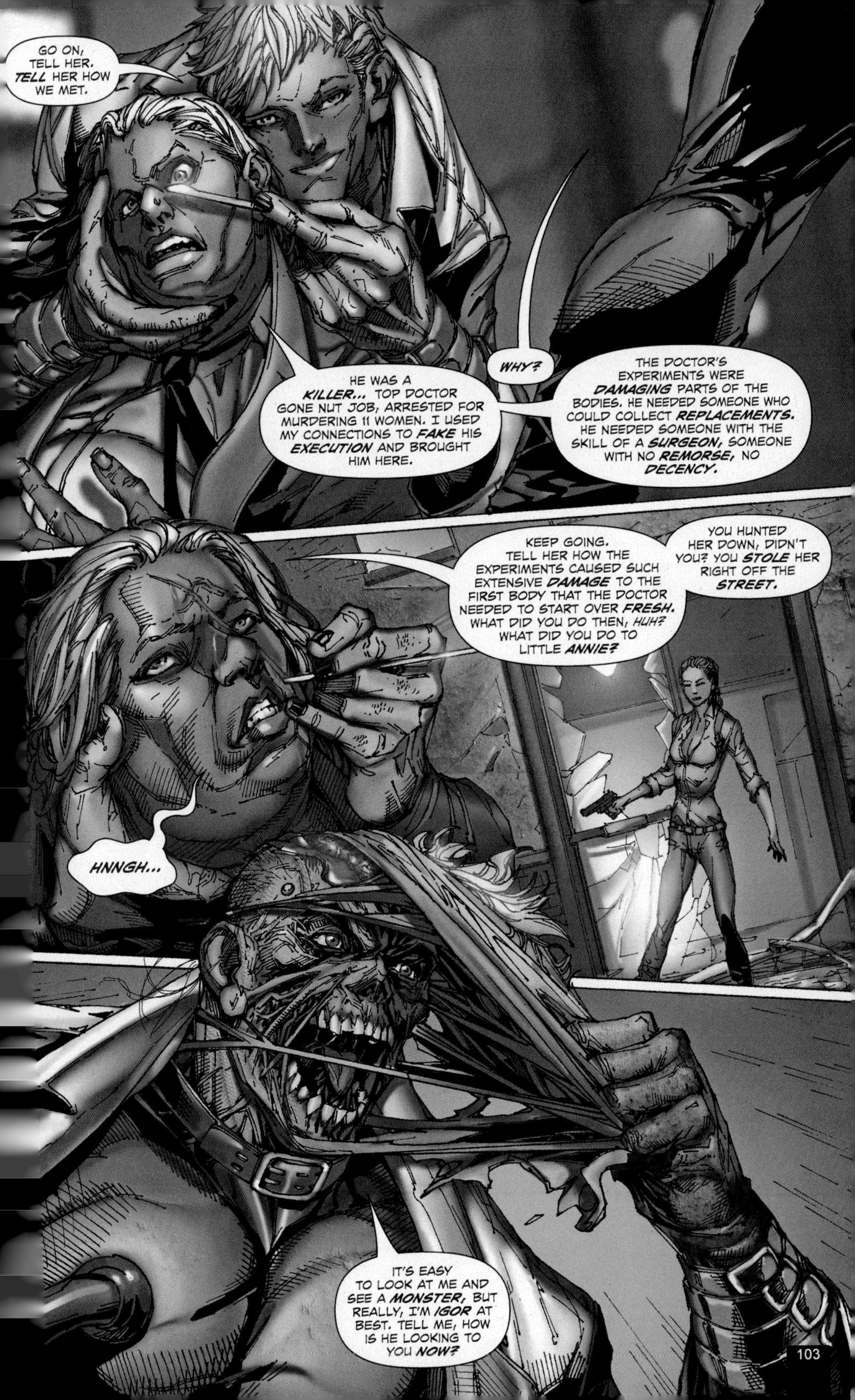
GO ON, TELL HER. TELL HER HOW WE MET.
HE WAS A KILLER... TOP DOCTOR GONE NUT JOB, ARRESTED FOR MURDERING 11 WOMEN. I USED MY CONNECTIONS TO FAKE HIS EXECUTION AND BROUGHT HIM HERE.
WHY?
THE DOCTOR'S EXPERIMENTS WERE DAMAGING PARTS OF THE BODIES. HE NEEDED SOMEONE WHO COULD COLLECT REPLACEMENTS. HE NEEDED SOMEONE WITH THE SKILL OF A SURGEON, SOMEONE WITH NO REMORSE, NO DECENCY.
KEEP GOING. TELL HER HOW THE EXPERIMENTS CAUSED SUCH EXTENSIVE DAMAGE TO THE FIRST BODY THAT THE DOCTOR NEEDED TO START OVER FRESH. WHAT DID YOU DO THEN, HUH? WHAT DID YOU DO TO LITTLE ANNIE?
YOU HUNTED HER DOWN, DIDN'T YOU? YOU STOLE HER RIGHT OFF THE STREET.
HNNGH...
IT'S EASY TO LOOK AT ME AND SEE A MONSTER, BUT REALLY, I'M IGOR AT BEST. TELL ME, HOW IS HE LOOKING TO YOU NOW?

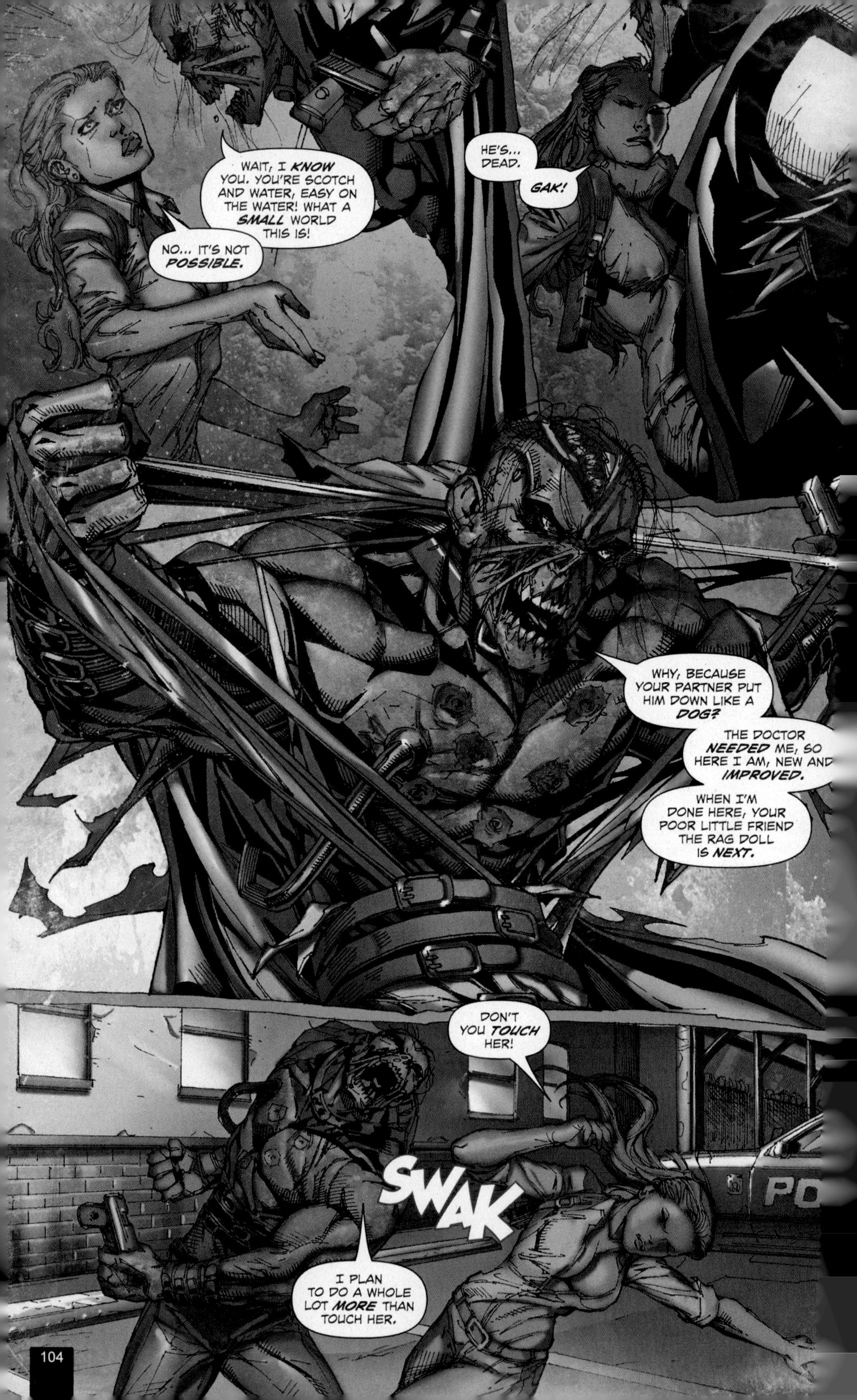
WAIT, I KNOW YOU. YOU'RE SCOTCH AND WATER, EASY ON THE WATER! WHAT A SMALL WORLD THIS IS!
NO... IT'S NOT POSSIBLE.
HE'S... DEAD.
GAK!
WHY, BECAUSE YOUR PARTNER PUT HIM DOWN LIKE A DOG?
THE DOCTOR NEEDED ME, SO HERE I AM, NEW AND IMPROVED.
WHEN I'M DONE HERE, YOUR POOR LITTLE FRIEND THE RAG DOLL IS NEXT.
DON'T YOU TOUCH HER!
SWAK
I PLAN TO DO A WHOLE LOT MORE THAN TOUCH HER.
PD

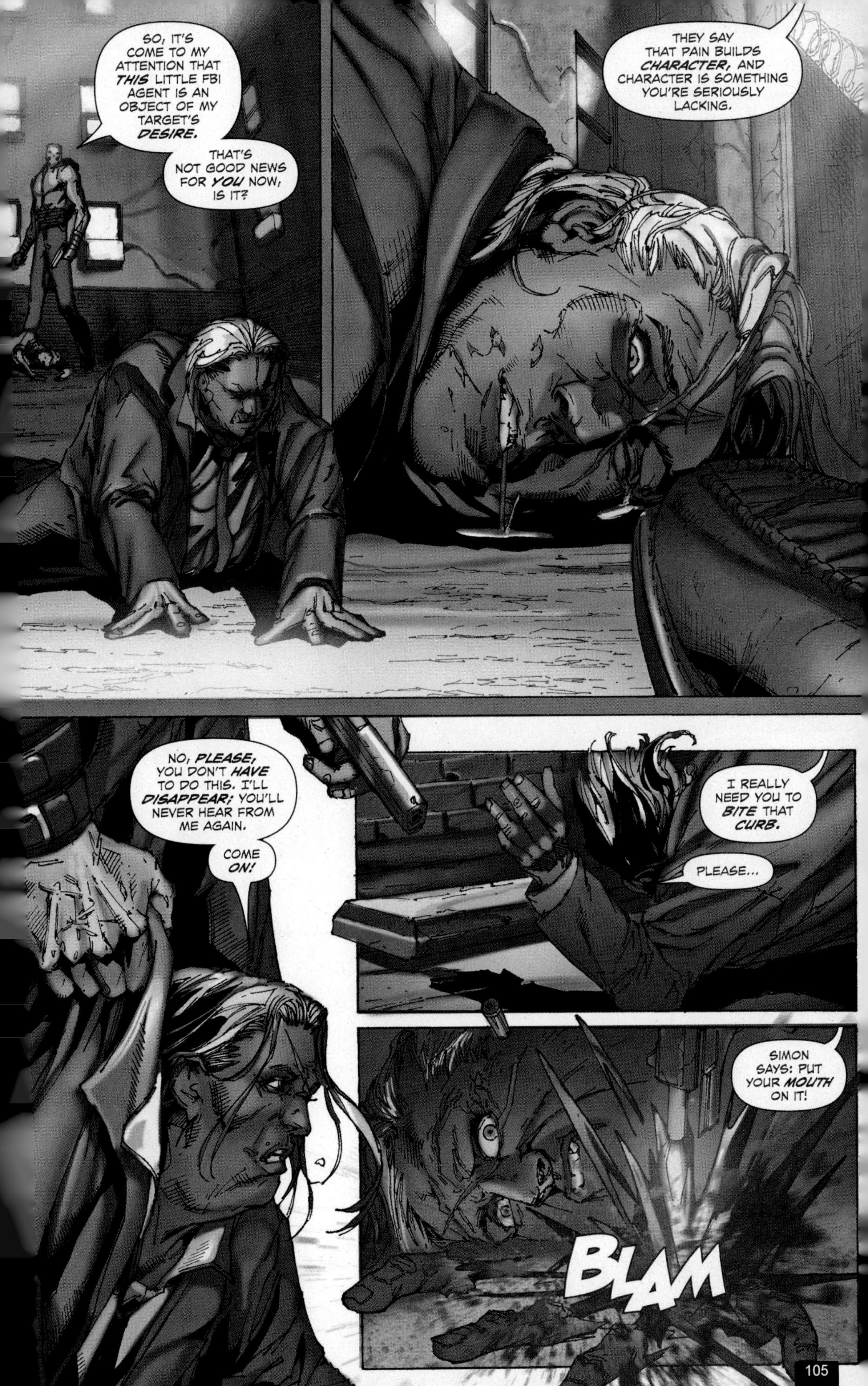
SO, IT'S COME TO MY ATTENTION THAT *THIS* LITTLE FBI AGENT IS AN OBJECT OF MY TARGET'S *DESIRE.*
THAT'S NOT GOOD NEWS FOR *YOU* NOW, IS IT?
THEY SAY THAT PAIN BUILDS *CHARACTER,* AND CHARACTER IS SOMETHING YOU'RE SERIOUSLY LACKING.
NO, *PLEASE,* YOU DON'T *HAVE* TO DO THIS. I'LL *DISAPPEAR;* YOU'LL NEVER HEAR FROM ME AGAIN.
COME *ON!*
I REALLY NEED YOU TO *BITE* THAT *CURB.*
PLEASE...
SIMON SAYS: PUT YOUR *MOUTH* ON IT!
BLAM

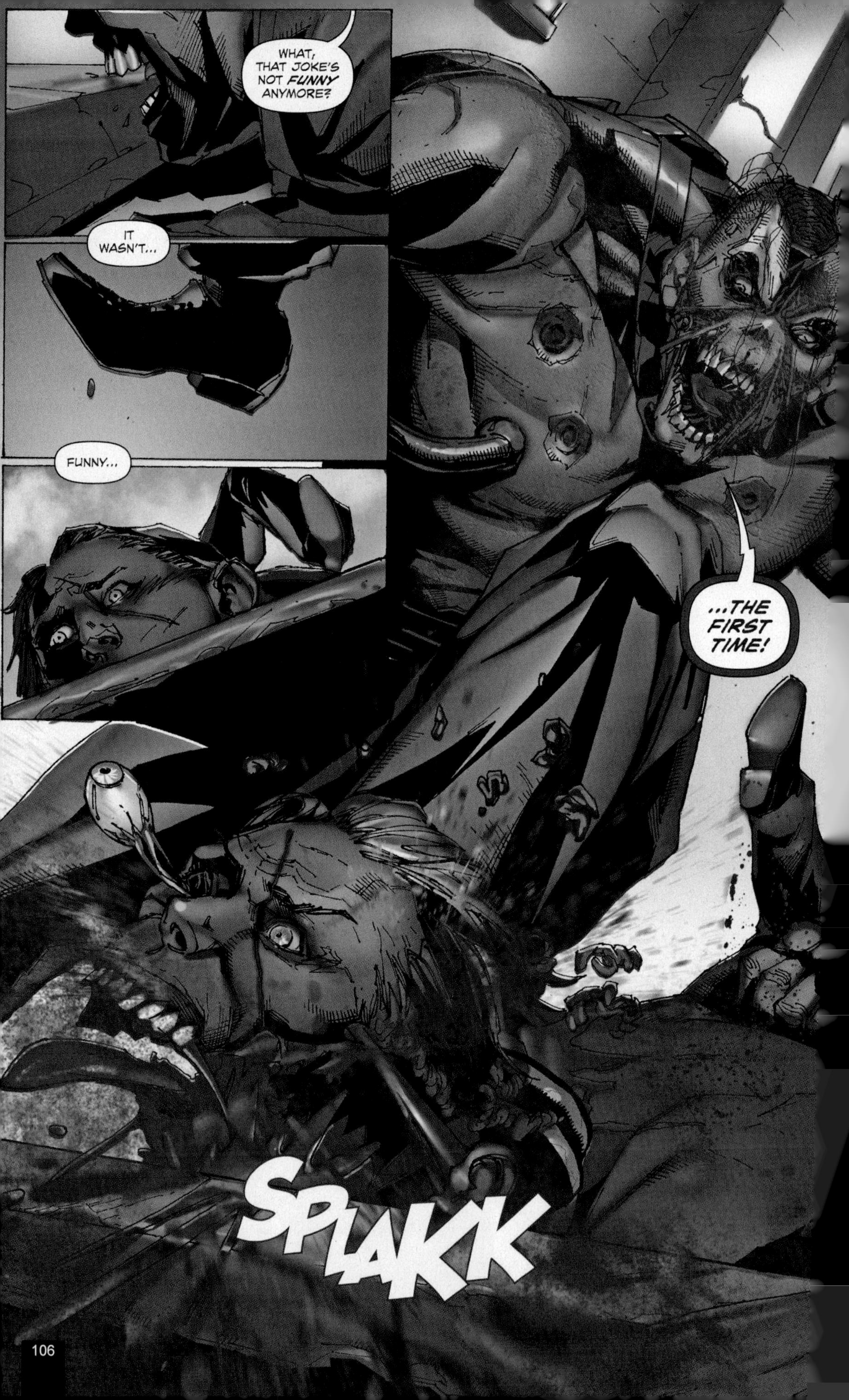
WHAT, THAT JOKE'S NOT FUNNY ANYMORE?
IT WASN'T...
FUNNY...
...THE FIRST TIME!
SPLAKK

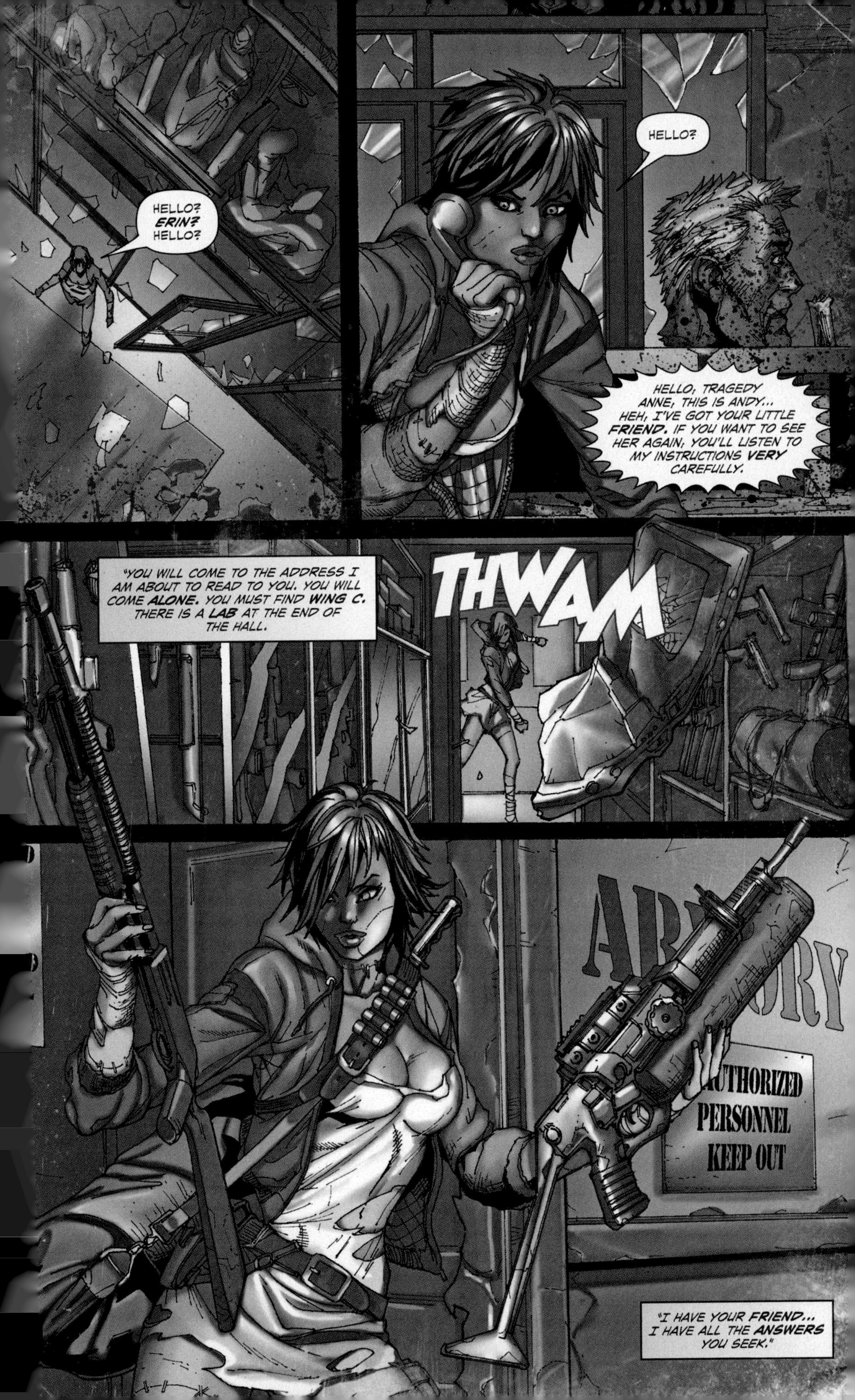

HELLO? ERIN? HELLO?
HELLO?
HELLO, TRAGEDY ANNE, THIS IS ANDY... HEH, I'VE GOT YOUR LITTLE FRIEND. IF YOU WANT TO SEE HER AGAIN, YOU'LL LISTEN TO MY INSTRUCTIONS VERY CAREFULLY.
"YOU WILL COME TO THE ADDRESS I AM ABOUT TO READ TO YOU. YOU WILL COME ALONE. YOU MUST FIND WING C. THERE IS A LAB AT THE END OF THE HALL.
THWAM
PERSONNEL
KEEP OUT
"I HAVE YOUR FRIEND... I HAVE ALL THE ANSWERS YOU SEEK."

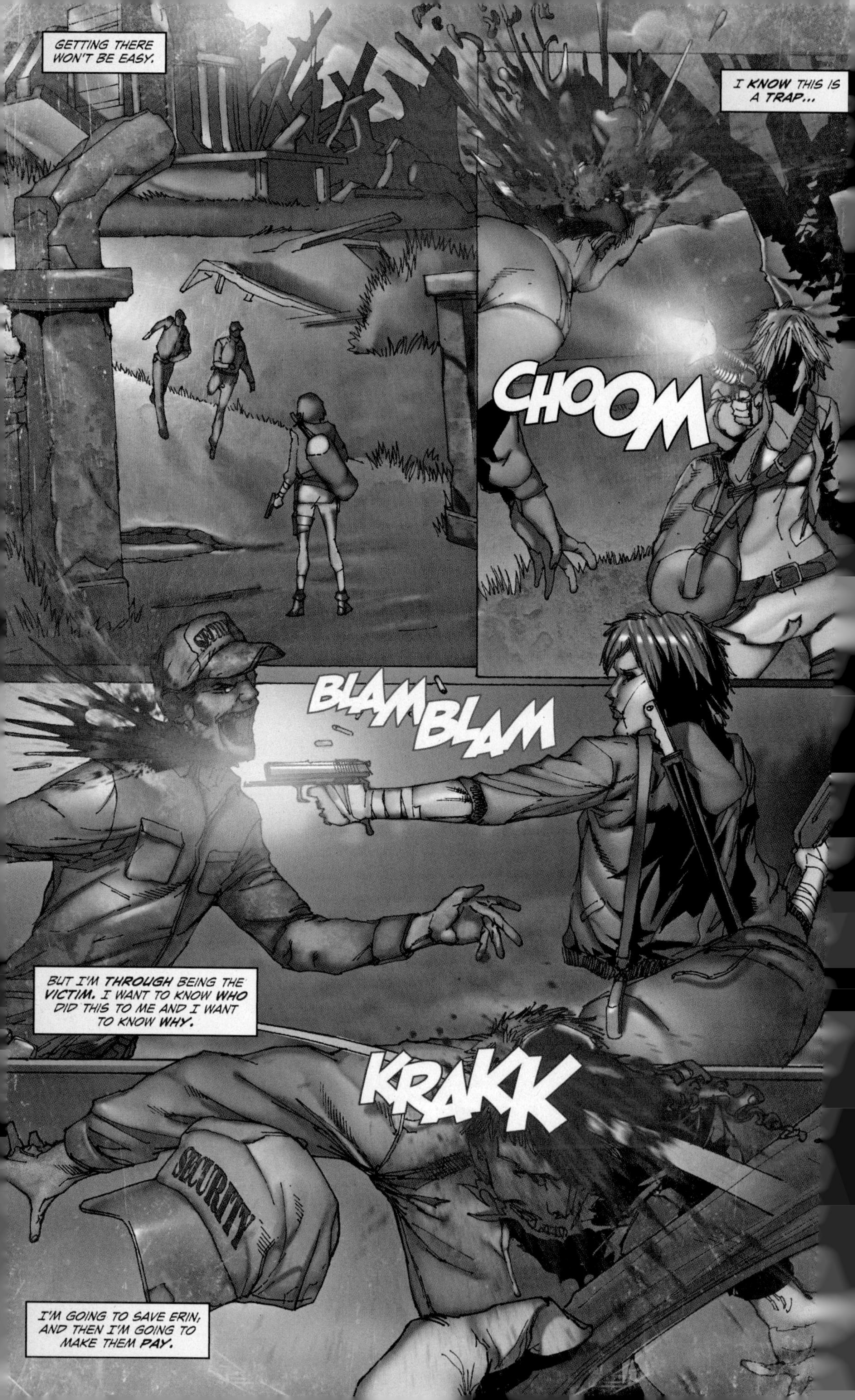
GETTING THERE WON'T BE EASY.
I KNOW THIS IS A TRAP...
CHOOM
BLAM BLAM
BUT I'M THROUGH BEING THE VICTIM. I WANT TO KNOW WHO DID THIS TO ME AND I WANT TO KNOW WHY.
KRAKK
SECURITY
I'M GOING TO SAVE ERIN, AND THEN I'M GOING TO MAKE THEM PAY.

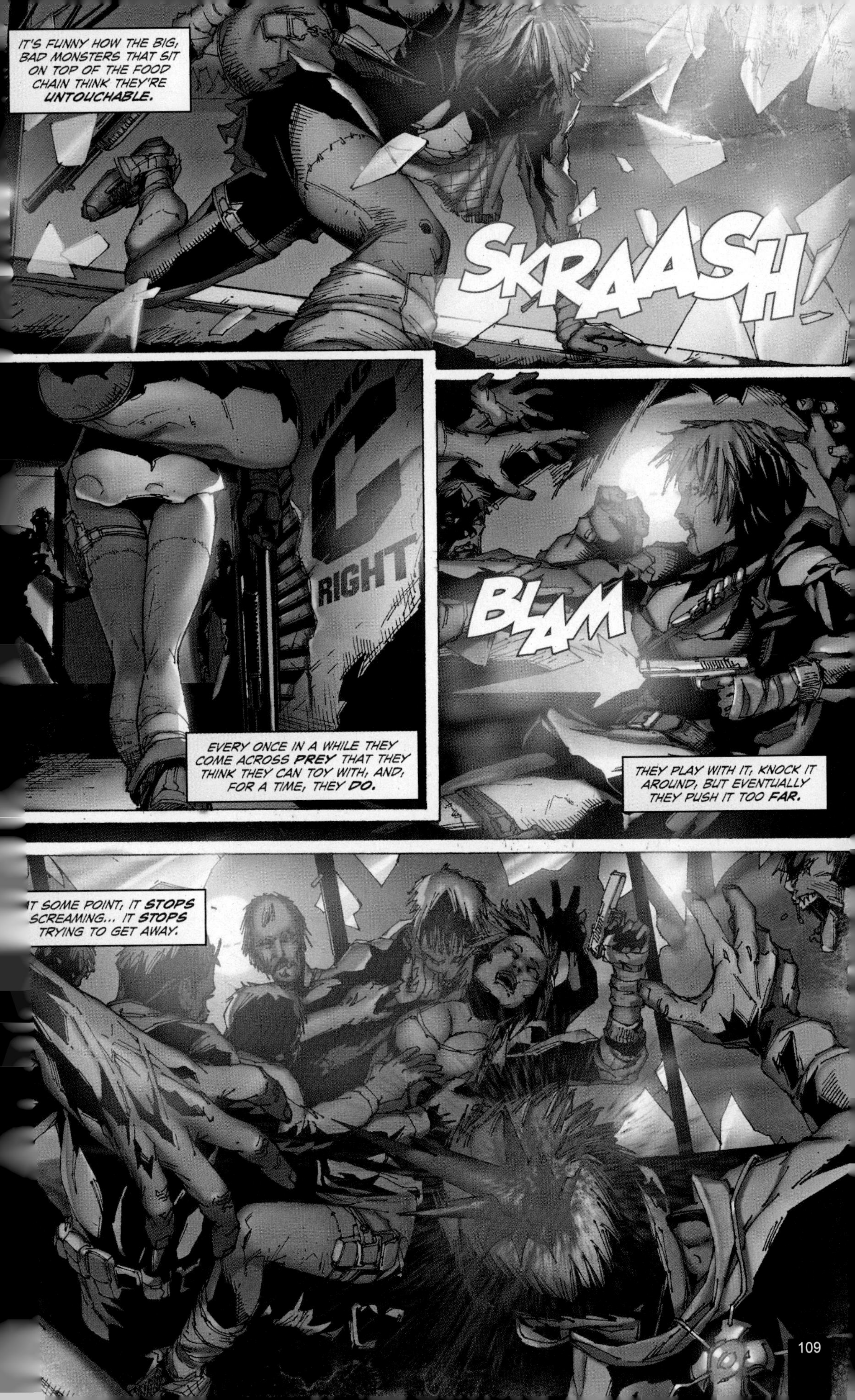
IT'S FUNNY HOW THE BIG, BAD MONSTERS THAT SIT ON TOP OF THE FOOD CHAIN THINK THEY'RE UNTOUCHABLE.
SKRAASH
RIGHT
EVERY ONCE IN A WHILE THEY COME ACROSS PREY THAT THEY THINK THEY CAN TOY WITH, AND, FOR A TIME, THEY DO.
BLAM
THEY PLAY WITH IT, KNOCK IT AROUND, BUT EVENTUALLY THEY PUSH IT TOO FAR.
T SOME POINT, IT STOPS SCREAMING... IT STOPS TRYING TO GET AWAY.

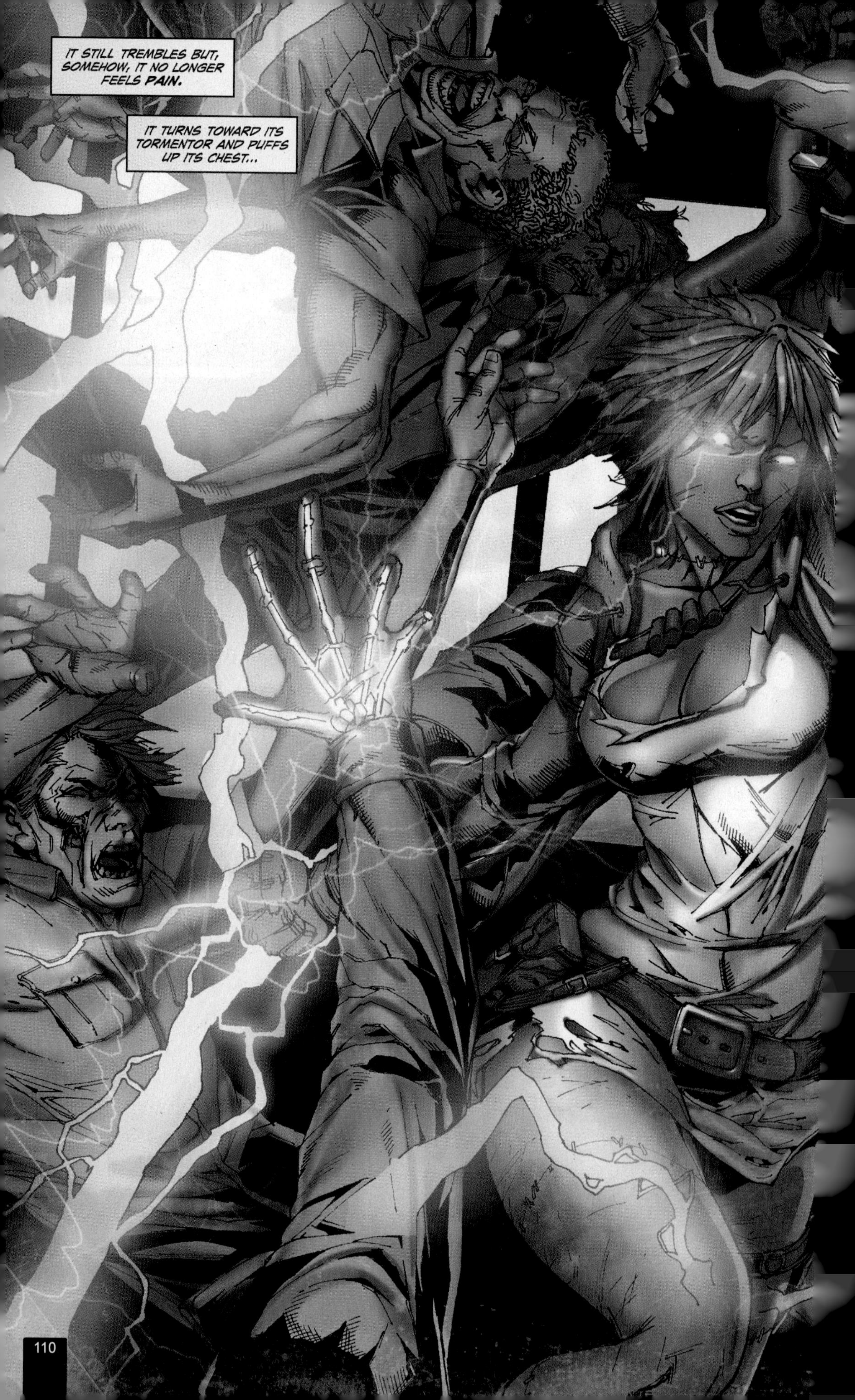
IT STILL TREMBLES BUT, SOMEHOW, IT NO LONGER FEELS PAIN.
IT TURNS TOWARD ITS TORMENTOR AND PUFFS UP ITS CHEST...

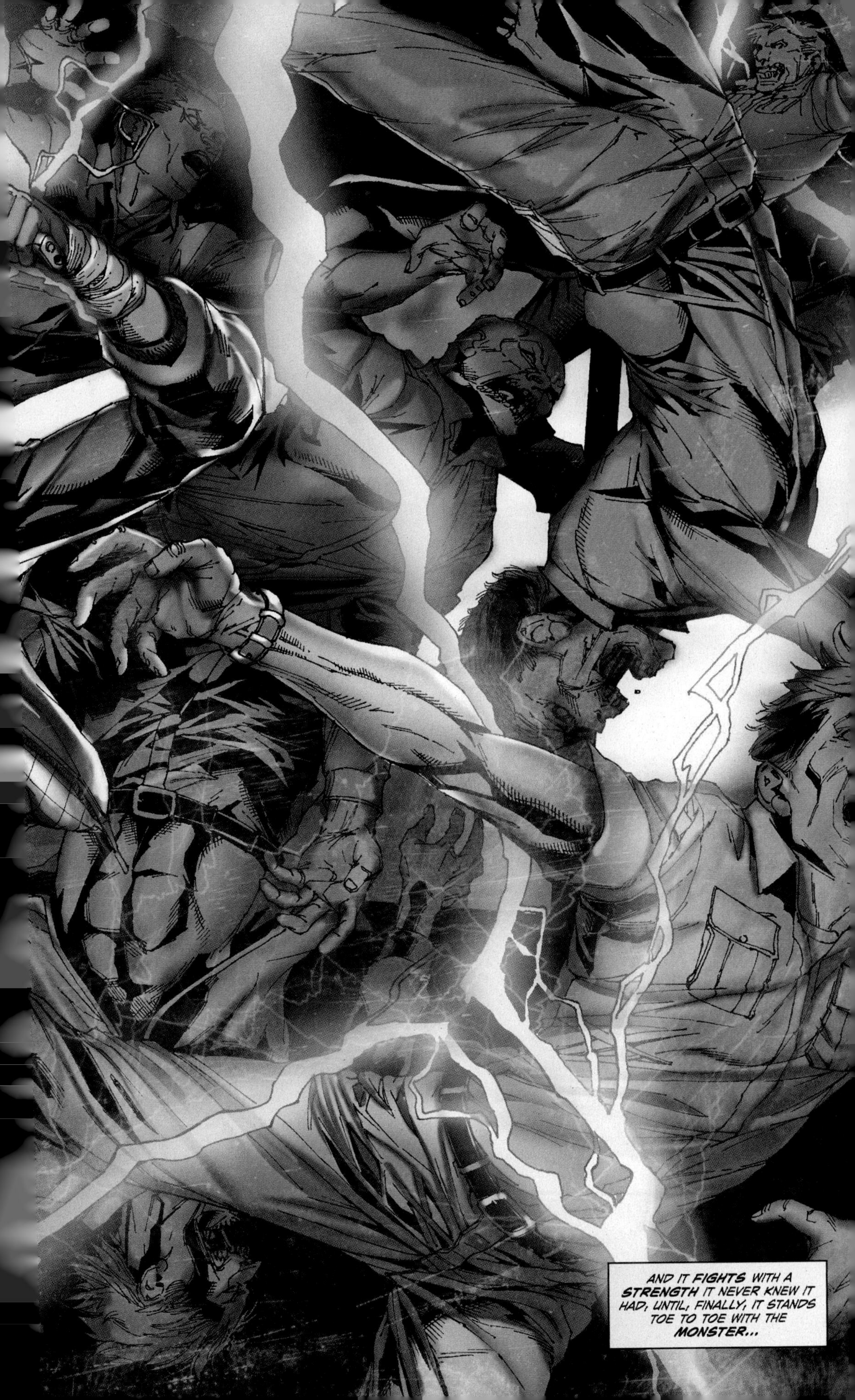
AND IT FIGHTS WITH A STRENGTH IT NEVER KNEW IT HAD, UNTIL, FINALLY, IT STANDS TOE TO TOE WITH THE MONSTER...

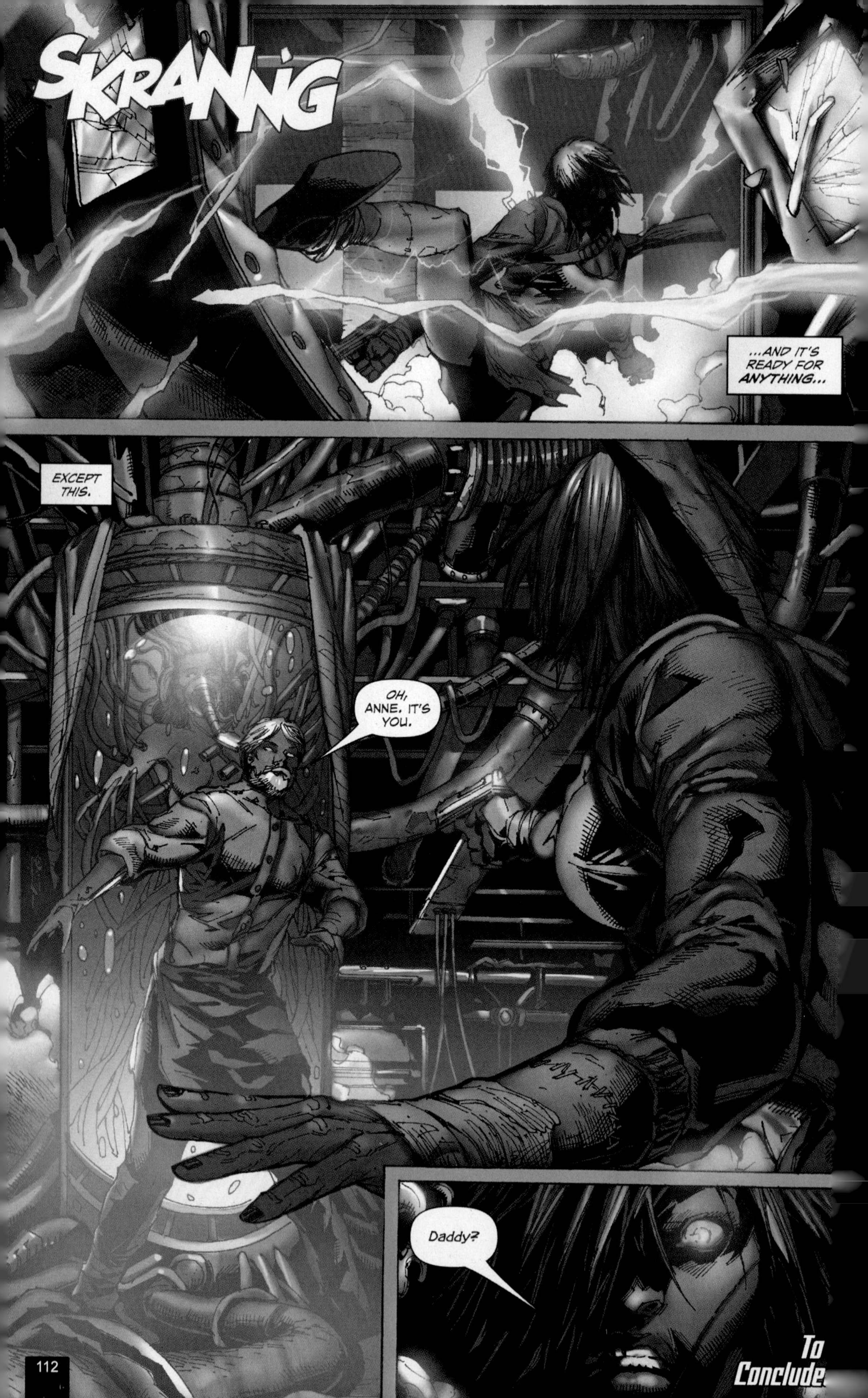
SKRANNG
...AND IT'S READY FOR ANYTHING...
EXCEPT THIS.
OH, ANNE. IT'S YOU.
Daddy?
To Conclude

SCREWED

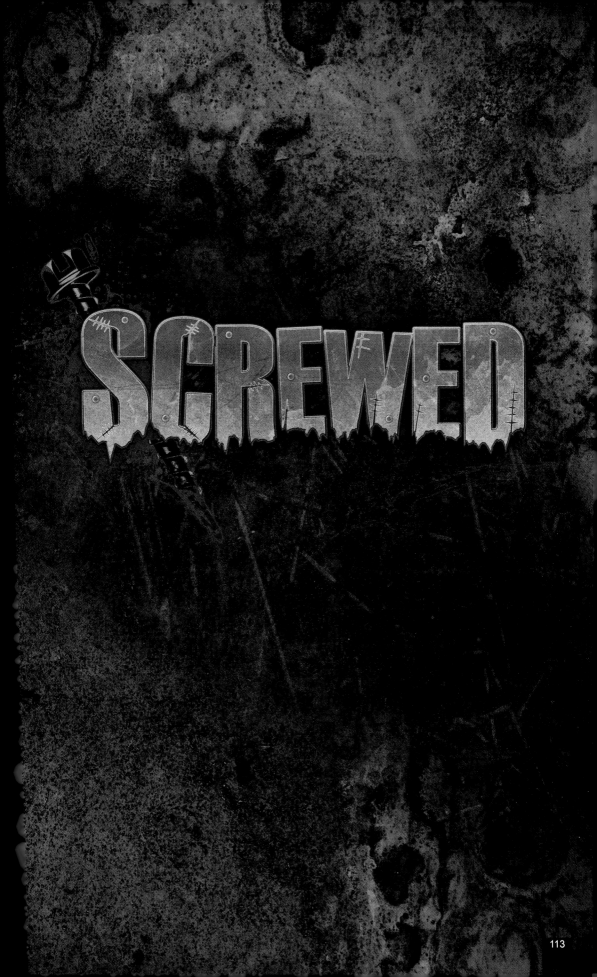

CHAPTER SIX

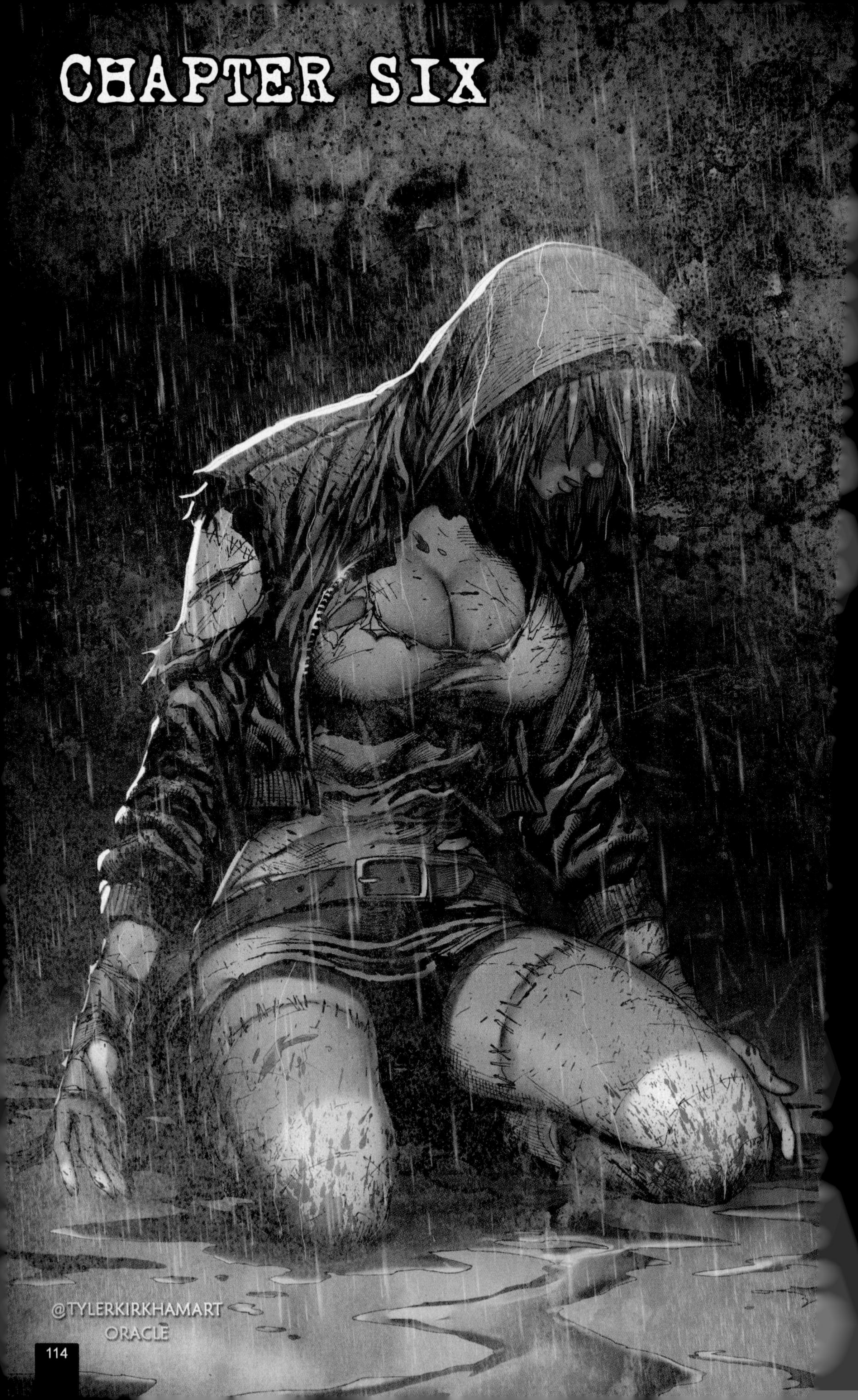
@TYLERKIRKHAMART
ORACLE

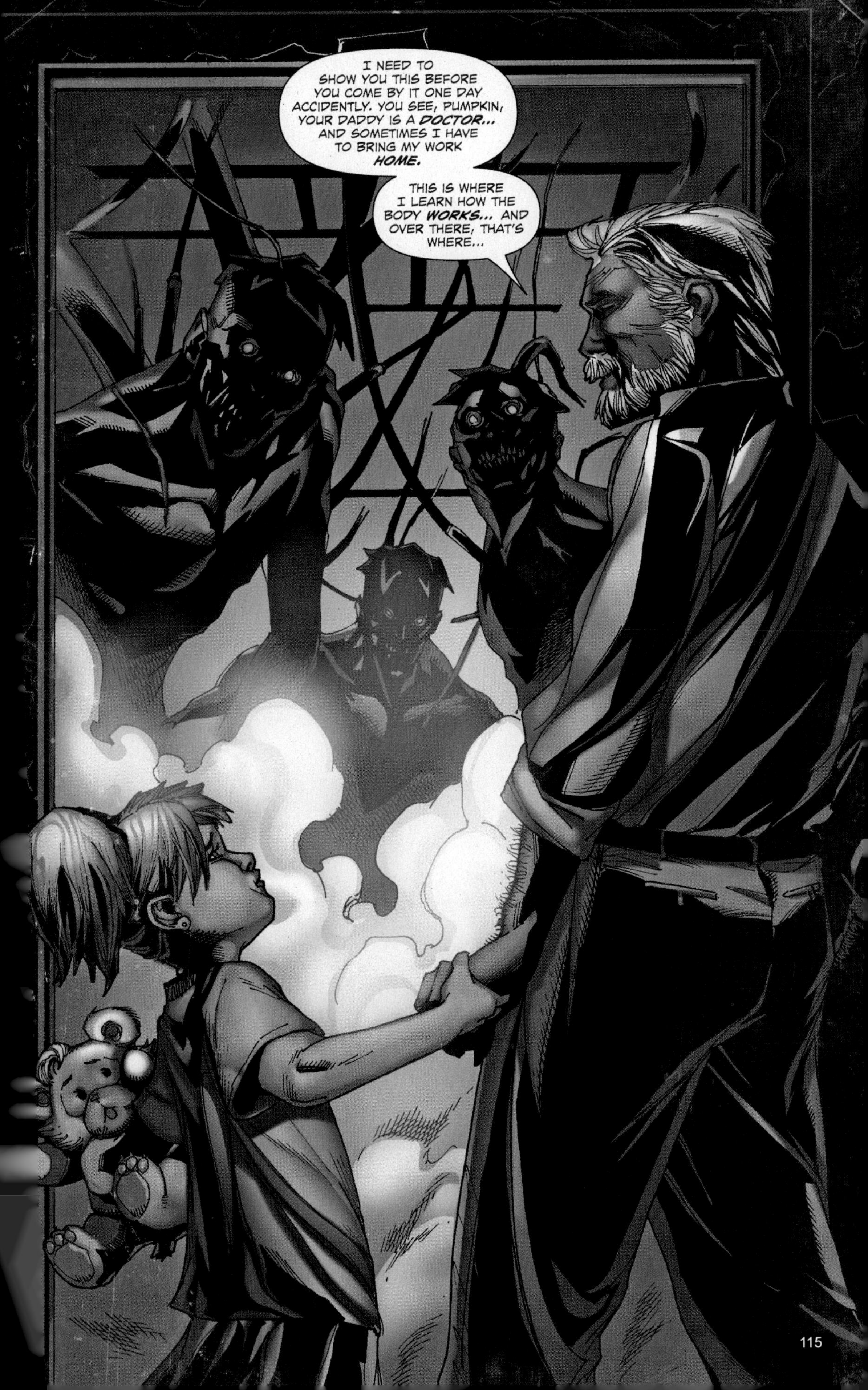
I NEED TO SHOW YOU THIS BEFORE YOU COME BY IT ONE DAY ACCIDENTLY. YOU SEE, PUMPKIN, YOUR DADDY IS A DOCTOR... AND SOMETIMES I HAVE TO BRING MY WORK HOME.
THIS IS WHERE I LEARN HOW THE BODY WORKS... AND OVER THERE, THAT'S WHERE...

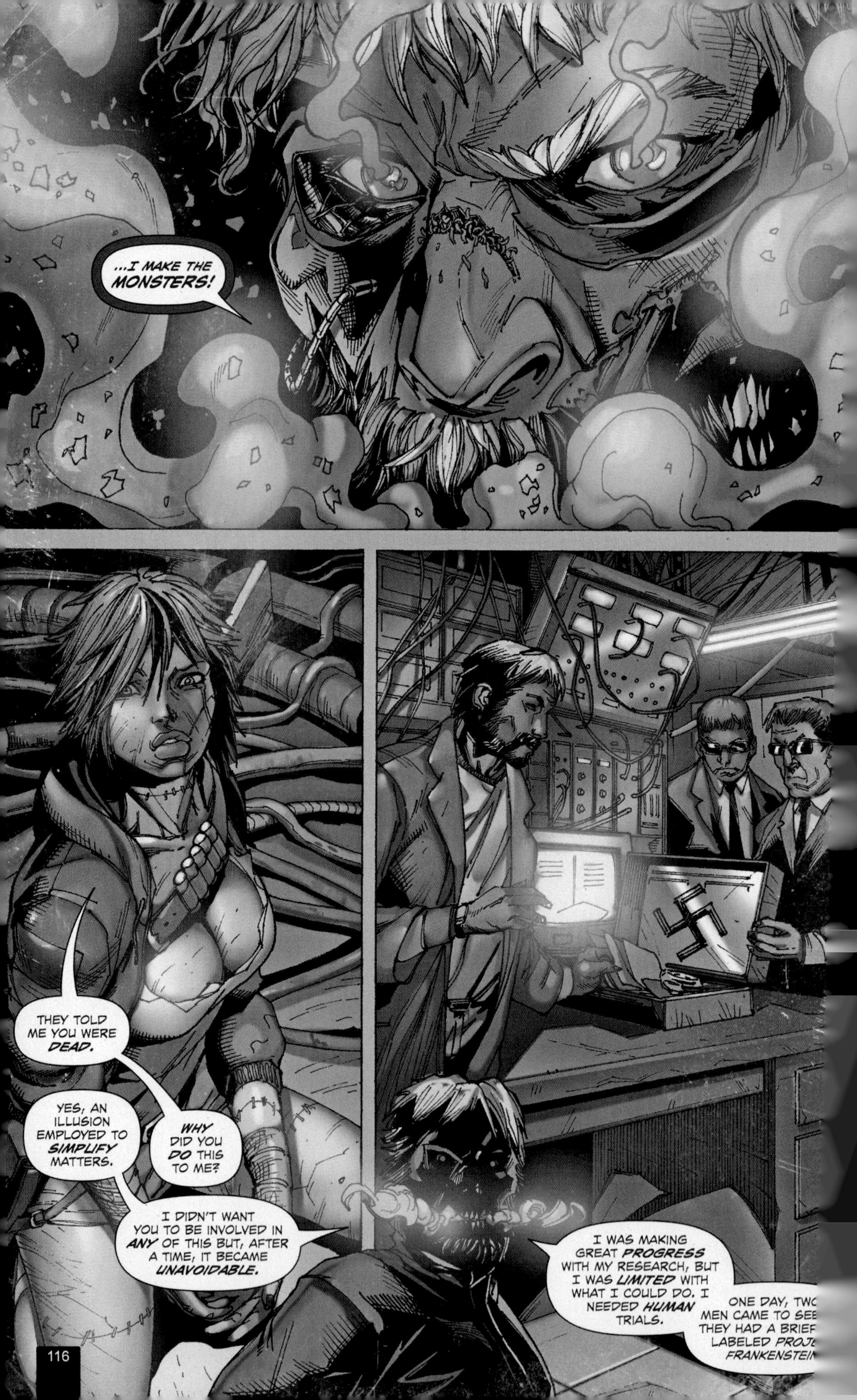
...I MAKE THE MONSTERS!
THEY TOLD ME YOU WERE DEAD.
YES, AN ILLUSION EMPLOYED TO SIMPLIFY MATTERS.
WHY DID YOU DO THIS TO ME?
I DIDN'T WANT YOU TO BE INVOLVED IN ANY OF THIS BUT, AFTER A TIME, IT BECAME UNAVOIDABLE.
I WAS MAKING GREAT PROGRESS WITH MY RESEARCH, BUT I WAS LIMITED WITH WHAT I COULD DO. I NEEDED HUMAN TRIALS.
ONE DAY, TWO MEN CAME TO SEE THEY HAD A BRIEF LABELED PROJE FRANKENSTEIN

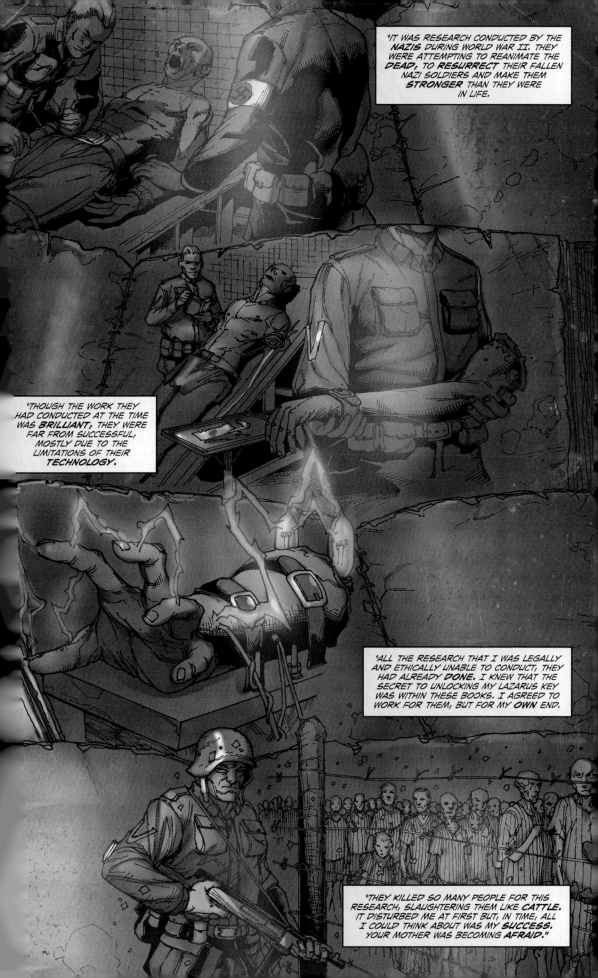

"IT WAS RESEARCH CONDUCTED BY THE **NAZIS** DURING WORLD WAR II. THEY WERE ATTEMPTING TO REANIMATE THE **DEAD**, TO **RESURRECT** THEIR FALLEN NAZI SOLDIERS AND MAKE THEM **STRONGER** THAN THEY WERE IN LIFE.

"THOUGH THE WORK THEY HAD CONDUCTED AT THE TIME WAS **BRILLIANT**, THEY WERE FAR FROM SUCCESSFUL, MOSTLY DUE TO THE LIMITATIONS OF THEIR **TECHNOLOGY**.

"ALL THE RESEARCH THAT I WAS LEGALLY AND ETHICALLY UNABLE TO CONDUCT, THEY HAD ALREADY **DONE**. I KNEW THAT THE SECRET TO UNLOCKING MY LAZARUS KEY WAS WITHIN THESE BOOKS. I AGREED TO WORK FOR THEM, BUT FOR MY **OWN** END.

"THEY KILLED SO MANY PEOPLE FOR THIS RESEARCH, SLAUGHTERING THEM LIKE **CATTLE**. IT DISTURBED ME AT FIRST BUT, IN TIME, ALL I COULD THINK ABOUT WAS MY **SUCCESS**. YOUR MOTHER WAS BECOMING **AFRAID**."

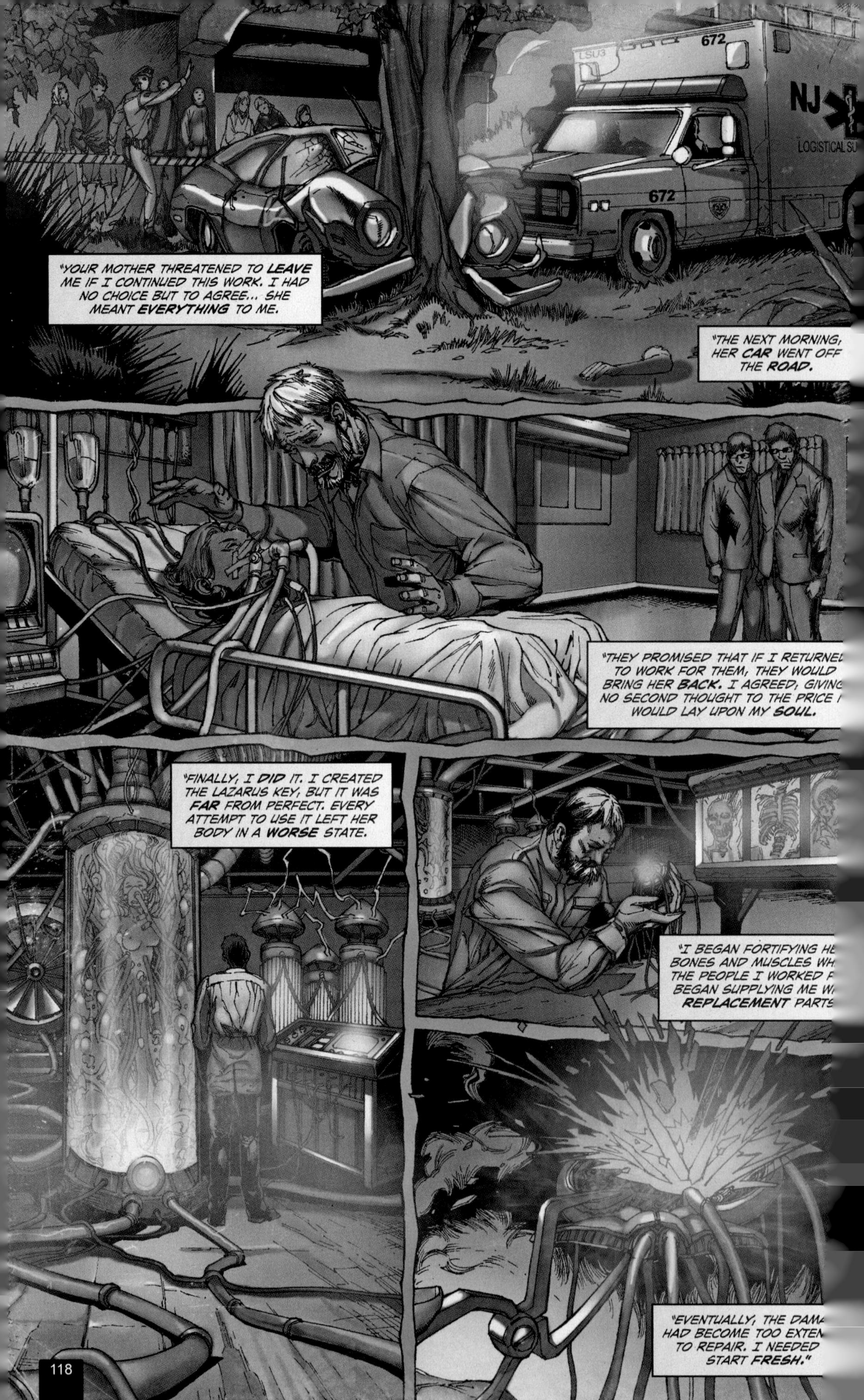
672
LSU3
NJ
LOGISTICAL SU
672
"YOUR MOTHER THREATENED TO LEAVE ME IF I CONTINUED THIS WORK. I HAD NO CHOICE BUT TO AGREE... SHE MEANT EVERYTHING TO ME.
"THE NEXT MORNING, HER CAR WENT OFF THE ROAD.
"THEY PROMISED THAT IF I RETURNED TO WORK FOR THEM, THEY WOULD BRING HER BACK. I AGREED, GIVING NO SECOND THOUGHT TO THE PRICE I WOULD LAY UPON MY SOUL.
"FINALLY, I DID IT. I CREATED THE LAZARUS KEY, BUT IT WAS FAR FROM PERFECT. EVERY ATTEMPT TO USE IT LEFT HER BODY IN A WORSE STATE.
"I BEGAN FORTIFYING HE BONES AND MUSCLES WH THE PEOPLE I WORKED F BEGAN SUPPLYING ME W REPLACEMENT PARTS
"EVENTUALLY, THE DAMA HAD BECOME TOO EXTEN TO REPAIR. I NEEDED START FRESH."

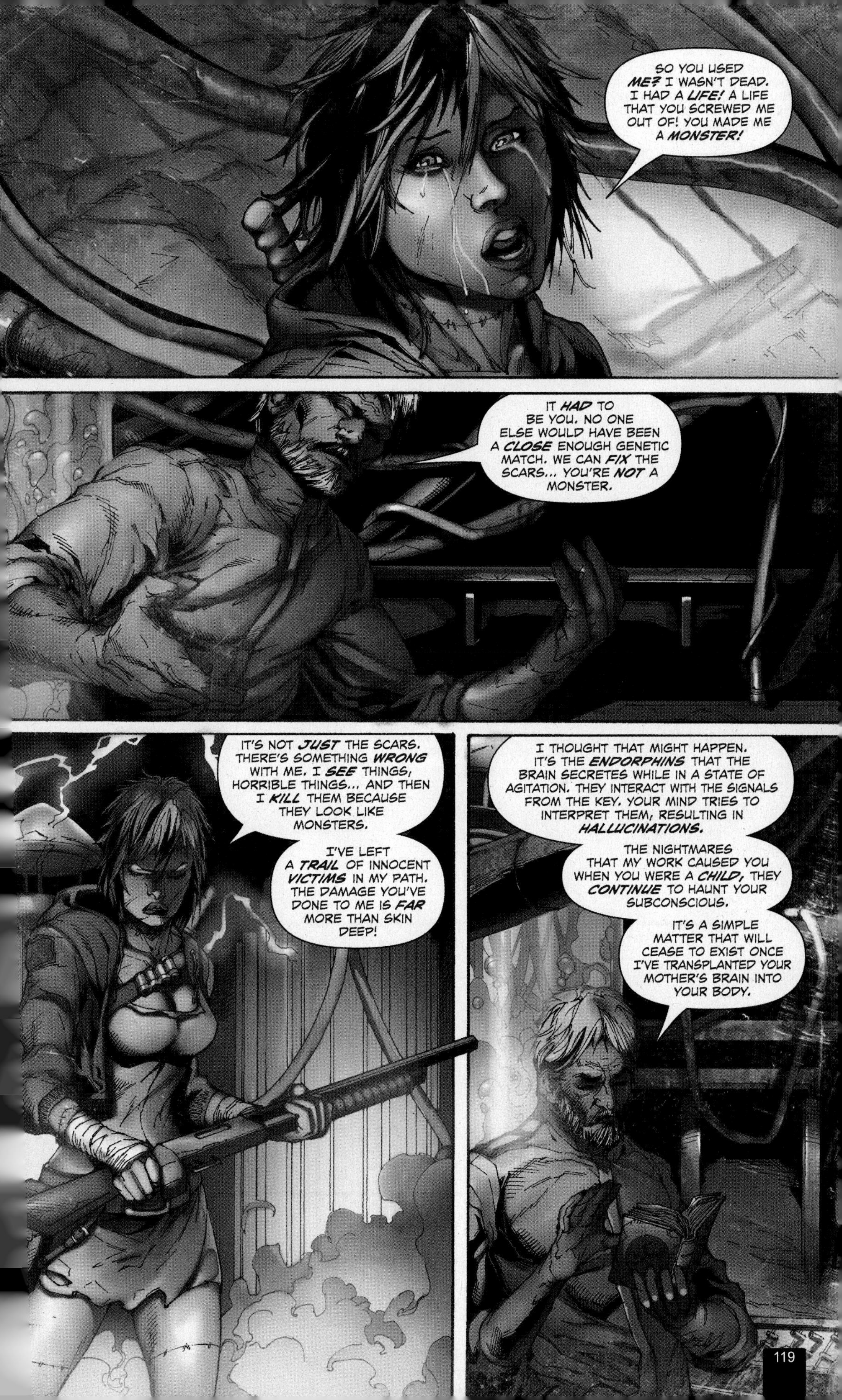
SO YOU USED ME? I WASN'T DEAD. I HAD A LIFE! A LIFE THAT YOU SCREWED ME OUT OF! YOU MADE ME A MONSTER!
IT HAD TO BE YOU. NO ONE ELSE WOULD HAVE BEEN A CLOSE ENOUGH GENETIC MATCH. WE CAN FIX THE SCARS... YOU'RE NOT A MONSTER.
IT'S NOT JUST THE SCARS. THERE'S SOMETHING WRONG WITH ME. I SEE THINGS, HORRIBLE THINGS... AND THEN I KILL THEM BECAUSE THEY LOOK LIKE MONSTERS.
I'VE LEFT A TRAIL OF INNOCENT VICTIMS IN MY PATH. THE DAMAGE YOU'VE DONE TO ME IS FAR MORE THAN SKIN DEEP!
I THOUGHT THAT MIGHT HAPPEN. IT'S THE ENDORPHINS THAT THE BRAIN SECRETES WHILE IN A STATE OF AGITATION. THEY INTERACT WITH THE SIGNALS FROM THE KEY. YOUR MIND TRIES TO INTERPRET THEM, RESULTING IN HALLUCINATIONS.
THE NIGHTMARES THAT MY WORK CAUSED YOU WHEN YOU WERE A CHILD, THEY CONTINUE TO HAUNT YOUR SUBCONSCIOUS.
IT'S A SIMPLE MATTER THAT WILL CEASE TO EXIST ONCE I'VE TRANSPLANTED YOUR MOTHER'S BRAIN INTO YOUR BODY.

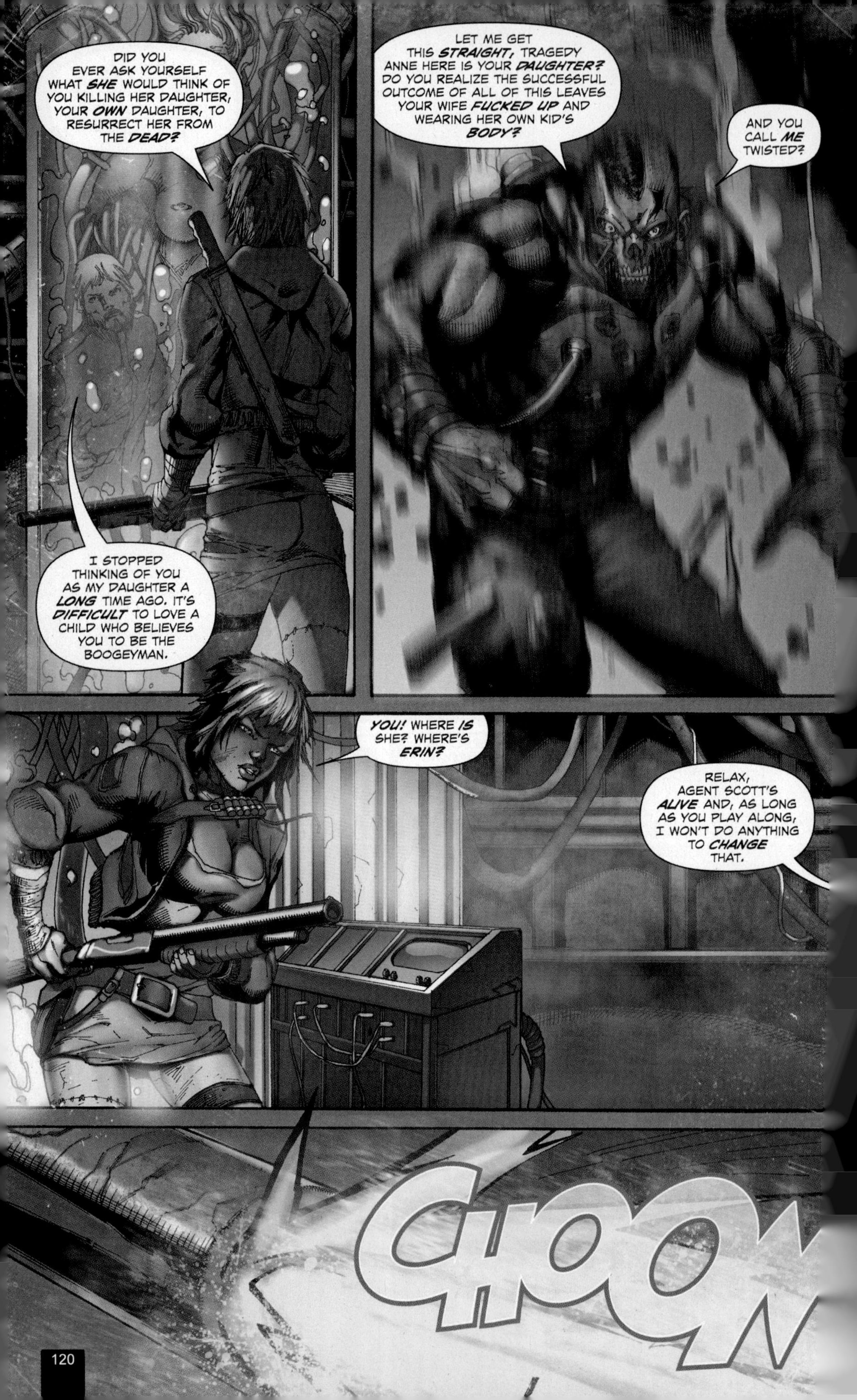
DID YOU EVER ASK YOURSELF WHAT SHE WOULD THINK OF YOU KILLING HER DAUGHTER, YOUR OWN DAUGHTER, TO RESURRECT HER FROM THE DEAD?
I STOPPED THINKING OF YOU AS MY DAUGHTER A LONG TIME AGO. IT'S DIFFICULT TO LOVE A CHILD WHO BELIEVES YOU TO BE THE BOOGEYMAN.
LET ME GET THIS STRAIGHT, TRAGEDY ANNE HERE IS YOUR DAUGHTER? DO YOU REALIZE THE SUCCESSFUL OUTCOME OF ALL OF THIS LEAVES YOUR WIFE FUCKED UP AND WEARING HER OWN KID'S BODY?
AND YOU CALL ME TWISTED?
YOU! WHERE IS SHE? WHERE'S ERIN?
RELAX, AGENT SCOTT'S ALIVE AND, AS LONG AS YOU PLAY ALONG, I WON'T DO ANYTHING TO CHANGE THAT.
CHOOM

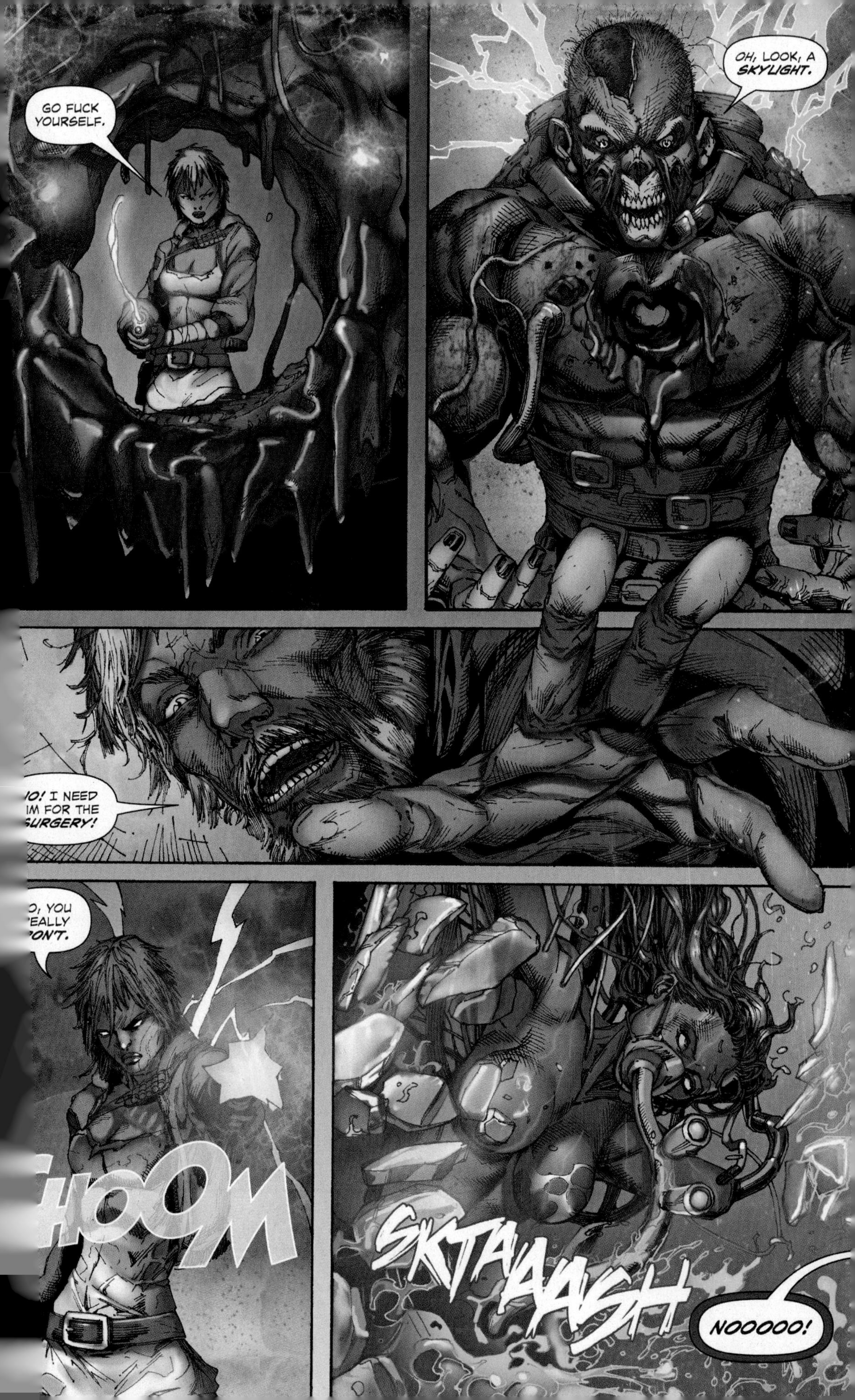

GO FUCK YOURSELF.
OH, LOOK, A SKYLIGHT.
O! I NEED IM FOR THE SURGERY!
O, YOU EALLY ON'T.
HOOM
SKTAAAASH
NOOOOO!

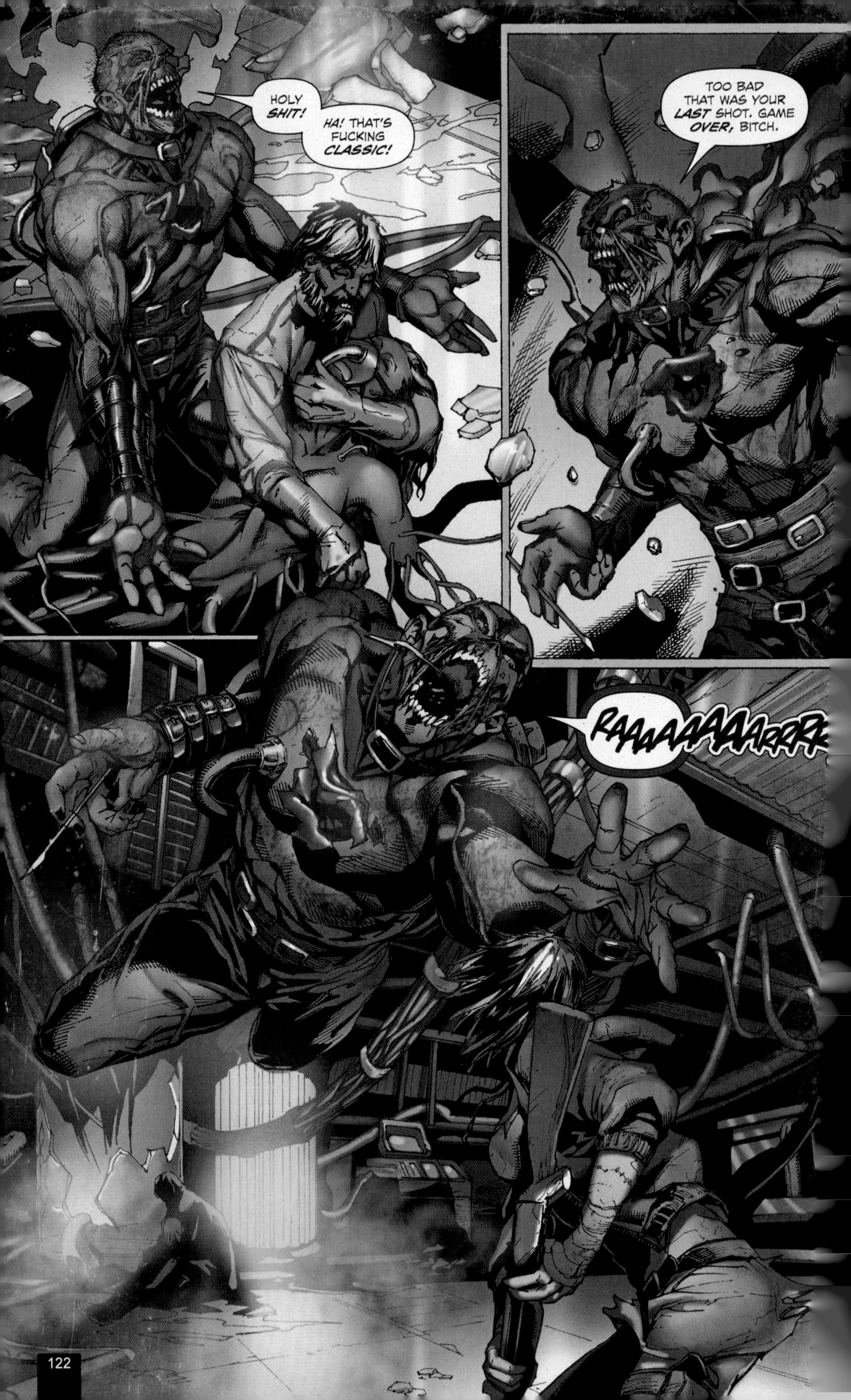
HOLY SHIT!
HA! THAT'S FUCKING CLASSIC!
TOO BAD THAT WAS YOUR LAST SHOT. GAME OVER, BITCH.
RAAAAAAAARRRR

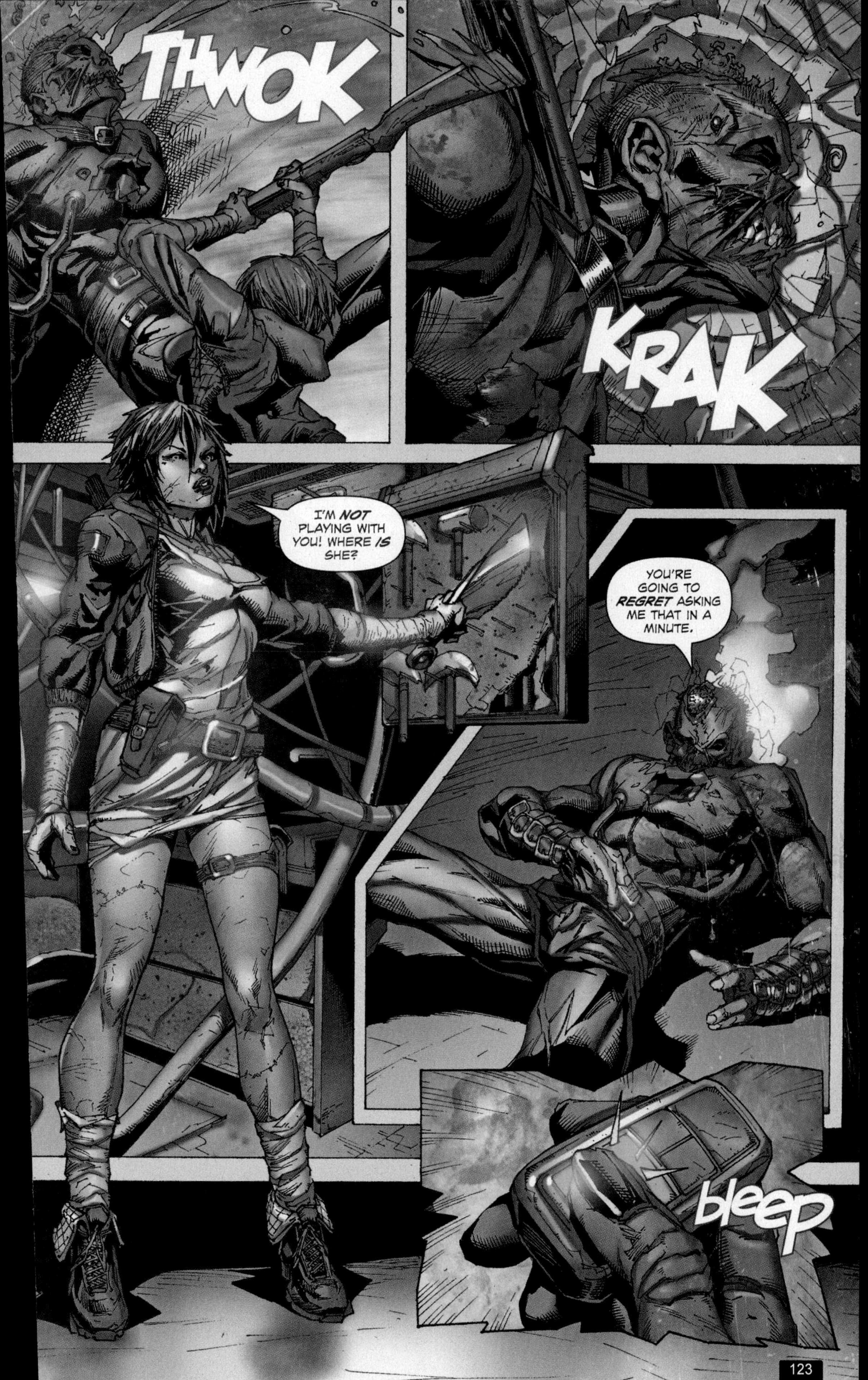
THWOK
KRAK
I'M NOT PLAYING WITH YOU! WHERE IS SHE?
YOU'RE GOING TO REGRET ASKING ME THAT IN A MINUTE.
bleep

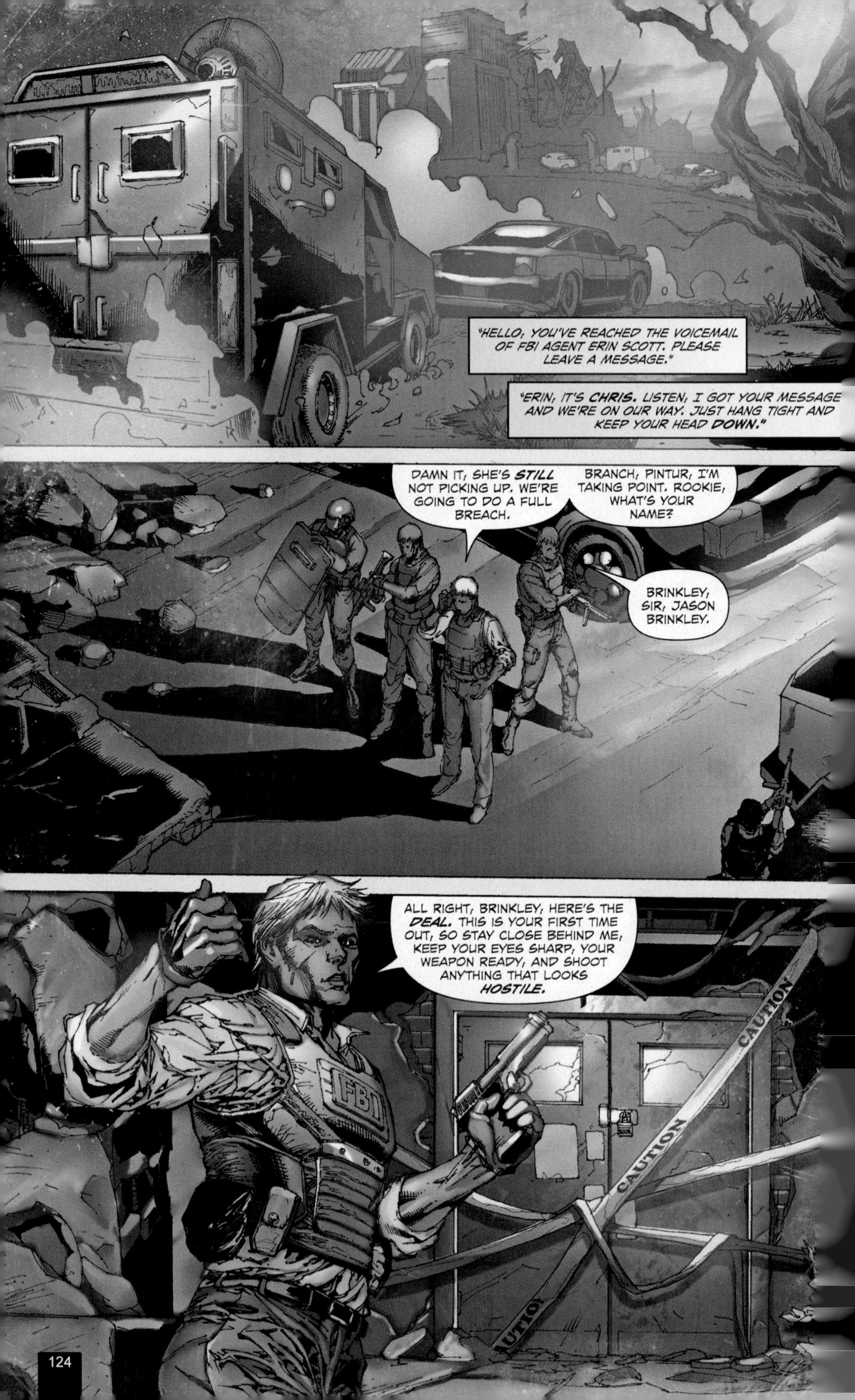
"HELLO, YOU'VE REACHED THE VOICEMAIL OF FBI AGENT ERIN SCOTT. PLEASE LEAVE A MESSAGE."
"ERIN, IT'S CHRIS. LISTEN, I GOT YOUR MESSAGE AND WE'RE ON OUR WAY. JUST HANG TIGHT AND KEEP YOUR HEAD DOWN."
DAMN IT, SHE'S STILL NOT PICKING UP. WE'RE GOING TO DO A FULL BREACH.
BRANCH, PINTUR, I'M TAKING POINT. ROOKIE, WHAT'S YOUR NAME?
BRINKLEY, SIR, JASON BRINKLEY.
ALL RIGHT, BRINKLEY, HERE'S THE DEAL. THIS IS YOUR FIRST TIME OUT, SO STAY CLOSE BEHIND ME, KEEP YOUR EYES SHARP, YOUR WEAPON READY, AND SHOOT ANYTHING THAT LOOKS HOSTILE.
FBI
CAUTION
CAUTION

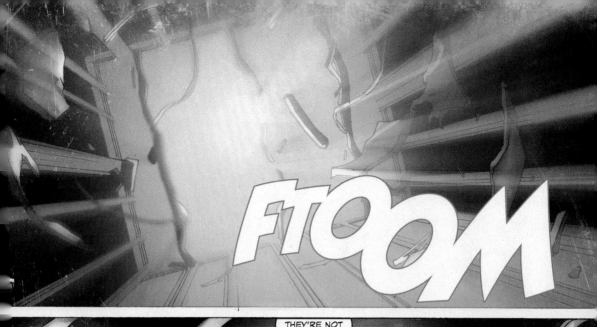

FTOOM

THEY'RE NOT *HUMAN!*

MOW THEM DOWN!

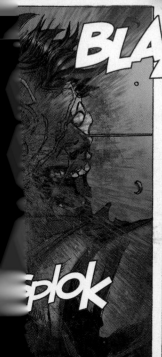

BLAM

splok

BLAM

sklutch

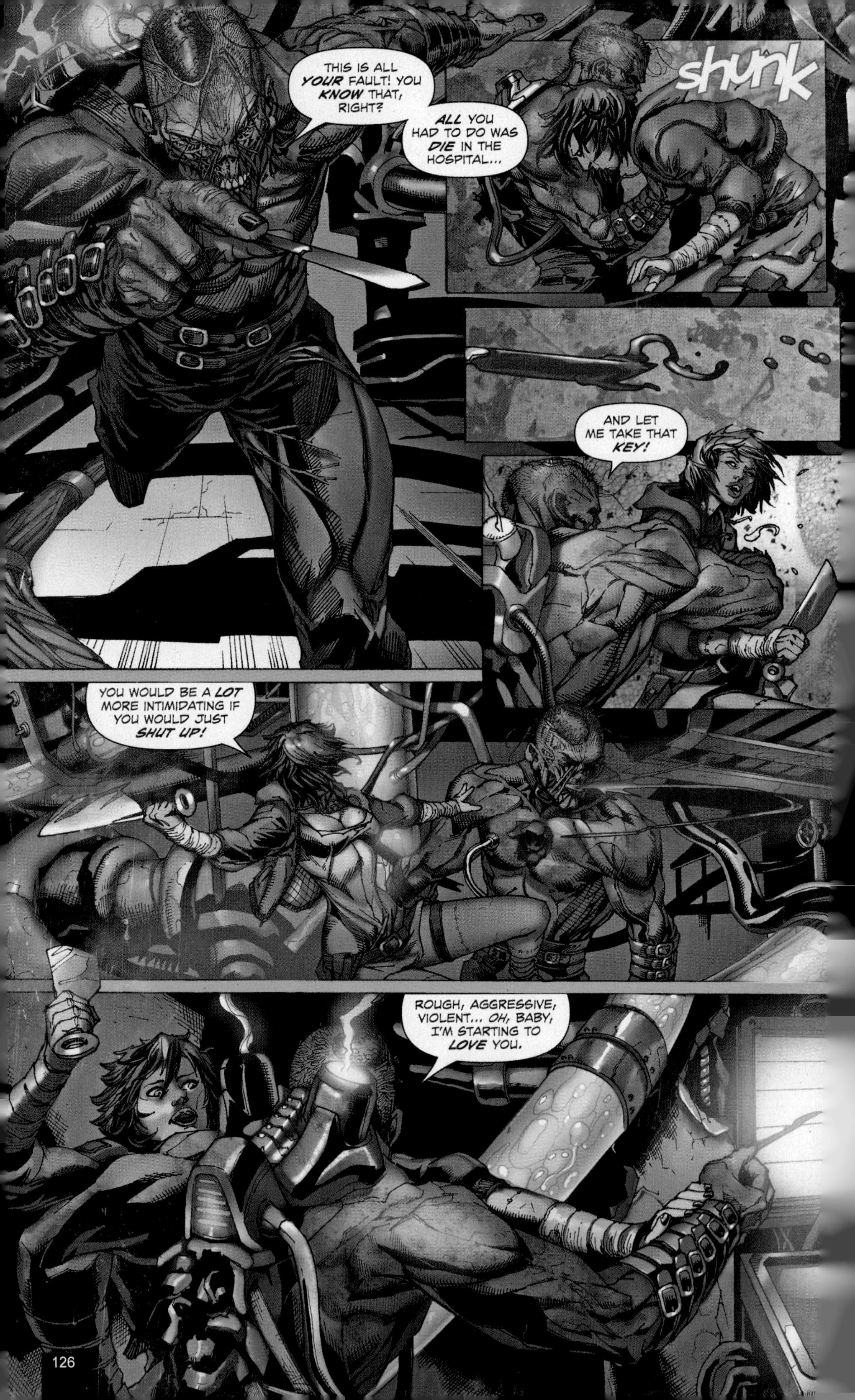
THIS IS ALL YOUR FAULT! YOU KNOW THAT, RIGHT?
ALL YOU HAD TO DO WAS DIE IN THE HOSPITAL...
shunk
AND LET ME TAKE THAT KEY!
YOU WOULD BE A LOT MORE INTIMIDATING IF YOU WOULD JUST SHUT UP!
ROUGH, AGGRESSIVE, VIOLENT... OH, BABY, I'M STARTING TO LOVE YOU.

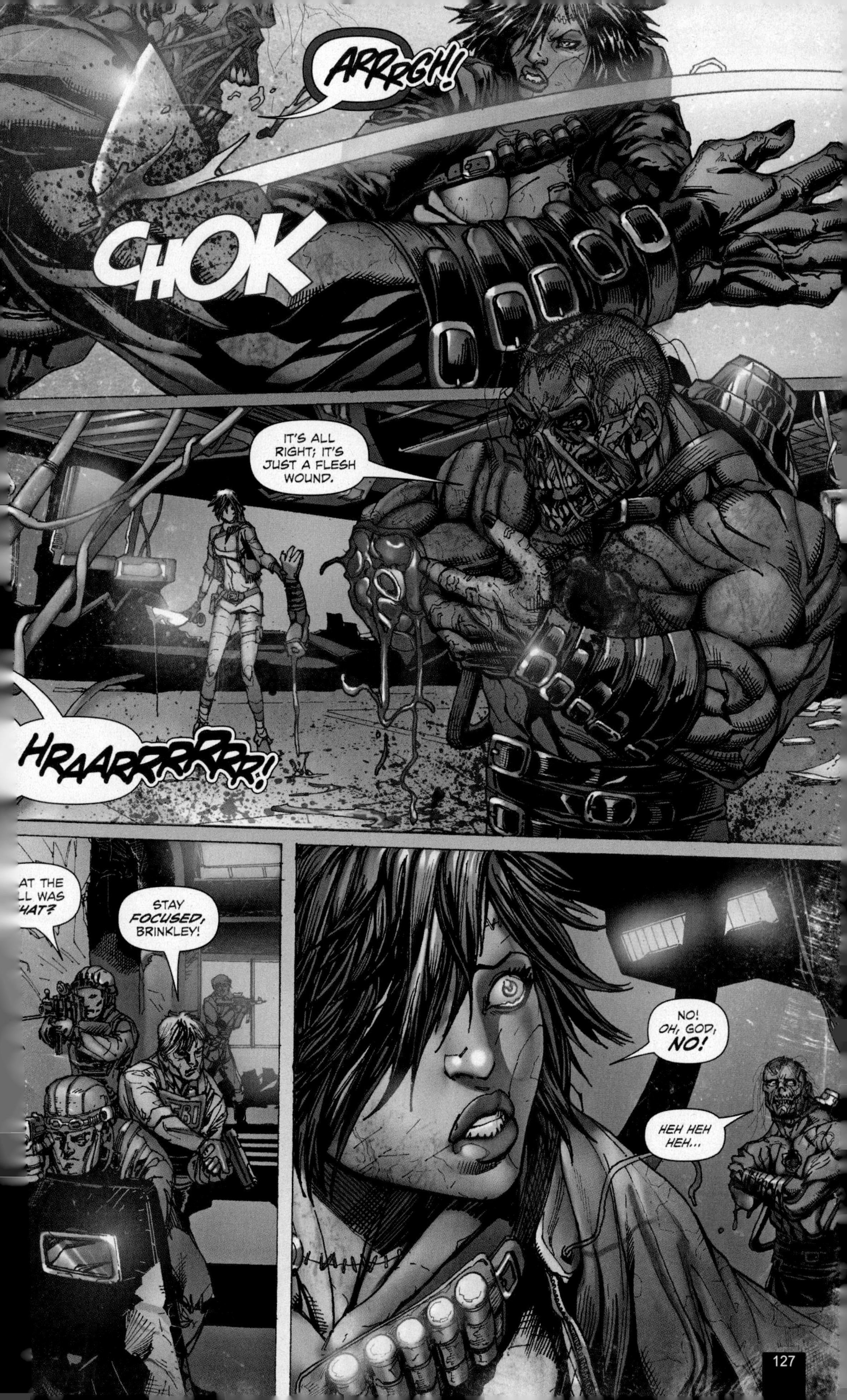

ARRRGH!
CHOK
IT'S ALL RIGHT; IT'S JUST A FLESH WOUND.
HRAARRRRRRR!
AT THE
LL WAS
HAT?
STAY *FOCUSED*, BRINKLEY!
NO! OH, GOD, **NO!**
HEH HEH HEH...

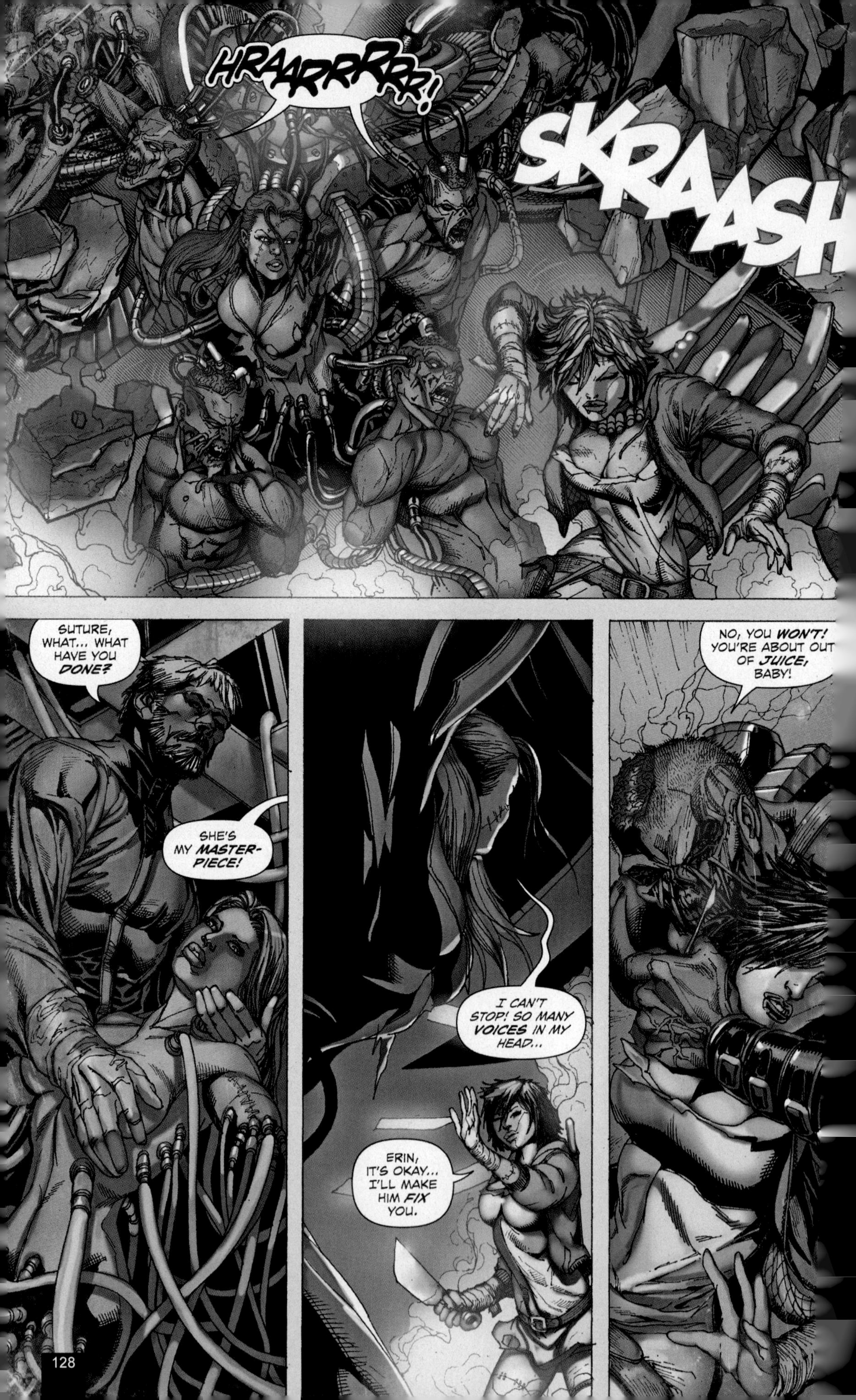
HRAARRRRR!
SKRAASH
SUTURE, WHAT... WHAT HAVE YOU DONE?
SHE'S MY MASTER-PIECE!
I CAN'T STOP! SO MANY VOICES IN MY HEAD...
ERIN, IT'S OKAY... I'LL MAKE HIM FIX YOU.
NO, YOU WON'T! YOU'RE ABOUT OUT OF JUICE, BABY!

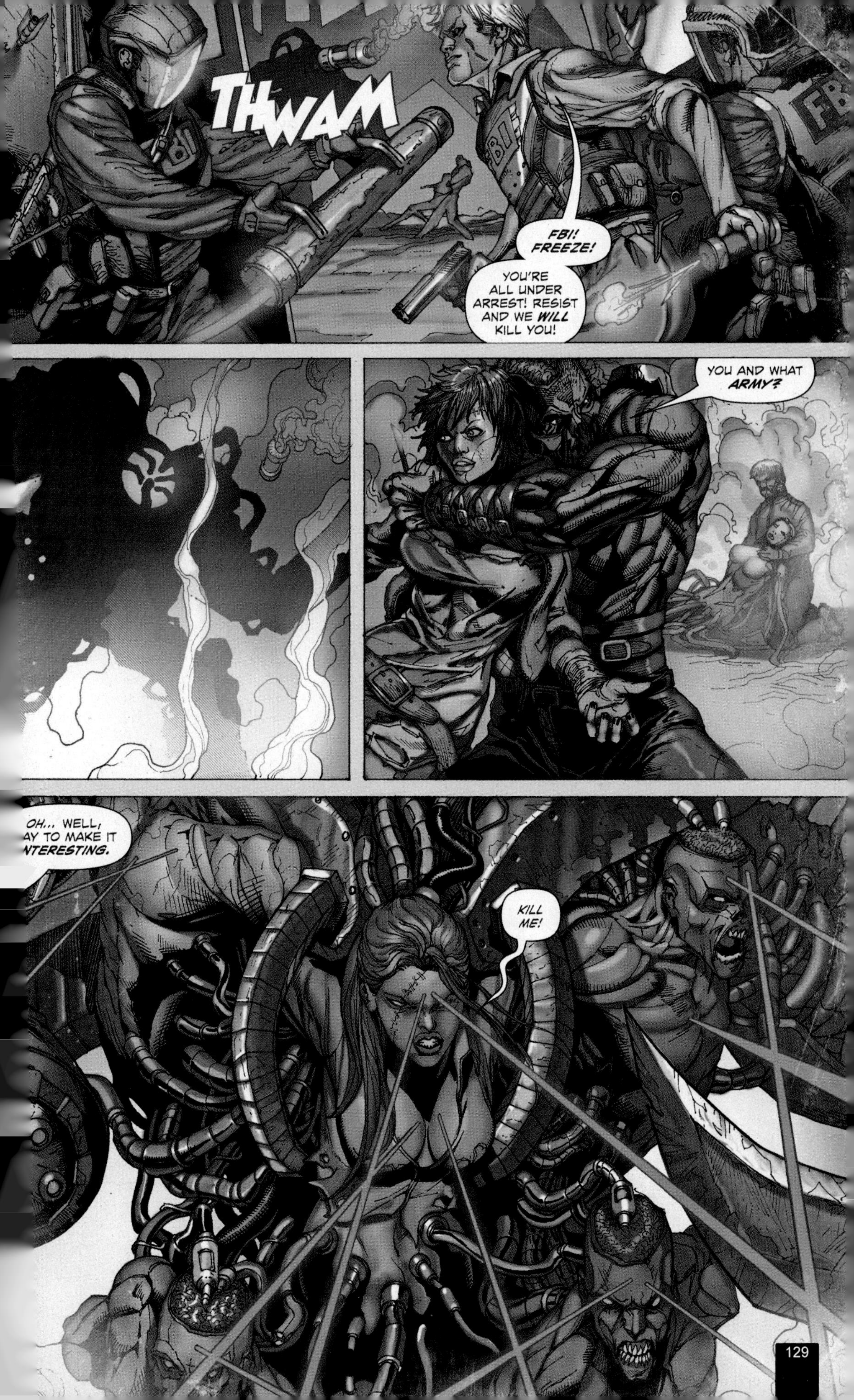
THWAM
FBI! FREEZE!
YOU'RE ALL UNDER ARREST! RESIST AND WE WILL KILL YOU!
YOU AND WHAT ARMY?
OH... WELL, AY TO MAKE IT NTERESTING.
KILL ME!

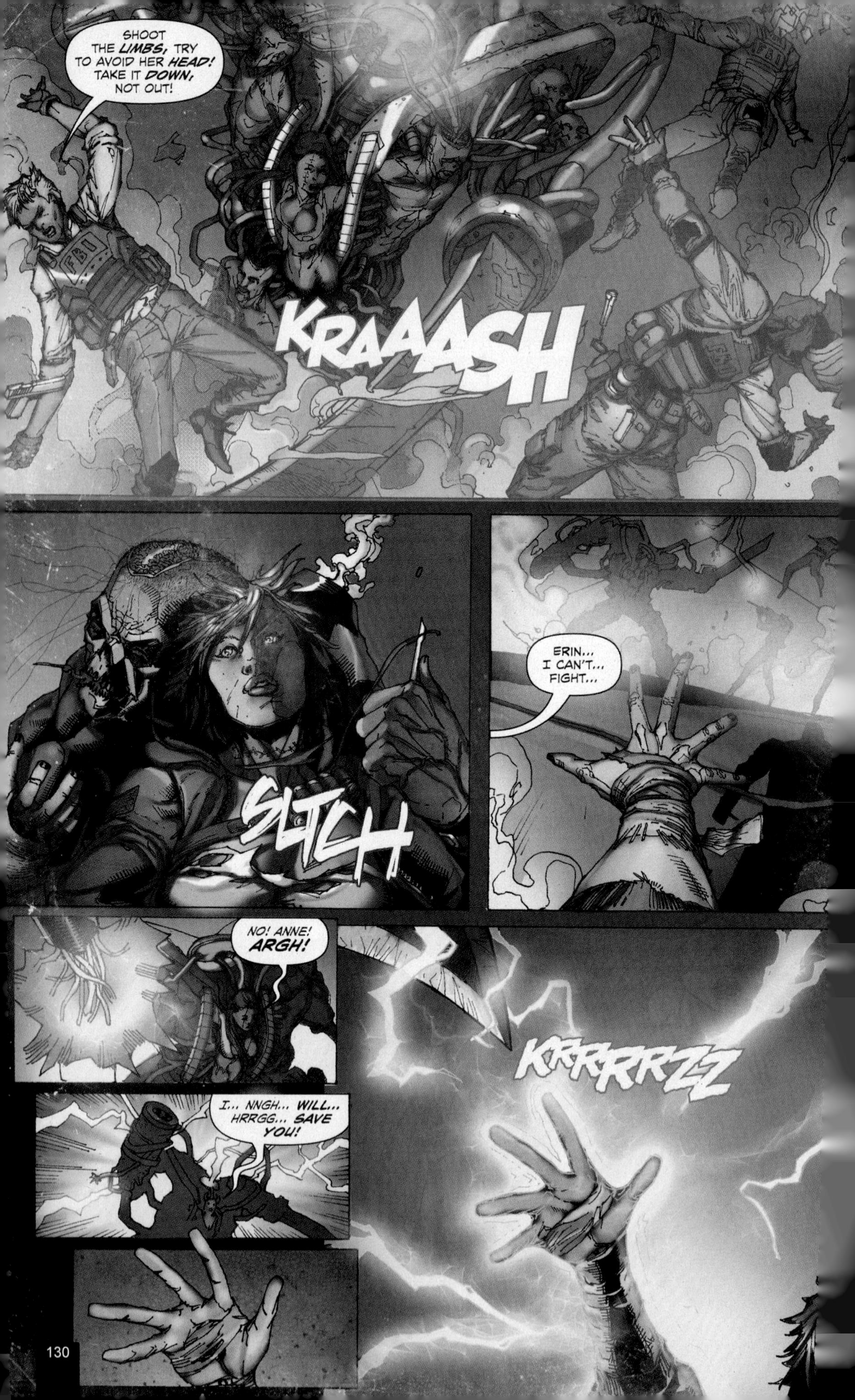
SHOOT THE LIMBS, TRY TO AVOID HER HEAD! TAKE IT DOWN, NOT OUT!
KRAAASH
SLTCH
ERIN... I CAN'T... FIGHT...
NO! ANNE! ARGH!
KRRRRZZ
I... NNGH... WILL... HRRGG... SAVE YOU!

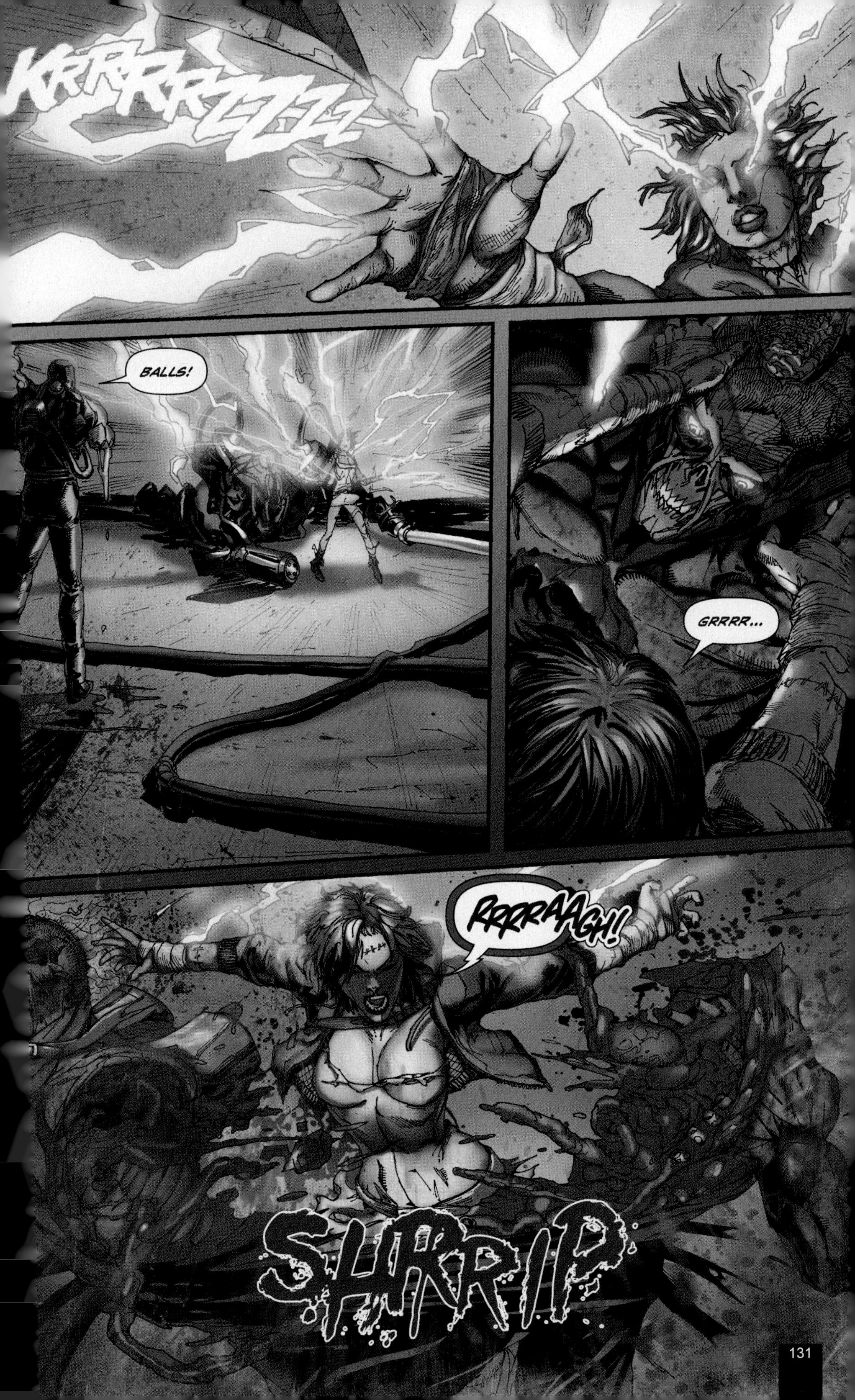
KRRRRZZZZ
BALLS!
GRRRR...
RRRRAAAGH!
SHRRIP

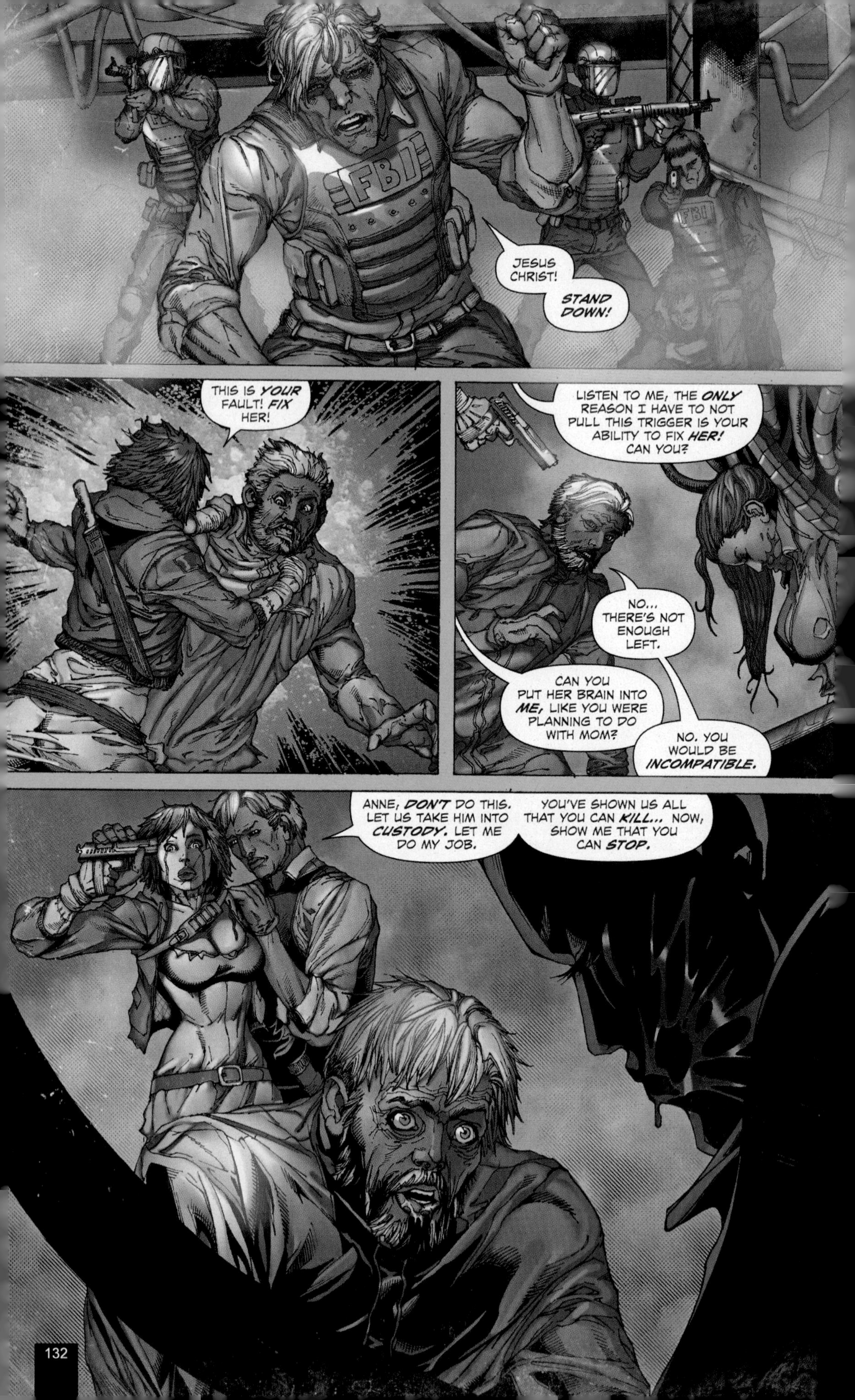

JESUS CHRIST!
STAND DOWN!
THIS IS YOUR FAULT! FIX HER!
LISTEN TO ME, THE ONLY REASON I HAVE TO NOT PULL THIS TRIGGER IS YOUR ABILITY TO FIX HER! CAN YOU?
NO... THERE'S NOT ENOUGH LEFT.
CAN YOU PUT HER BRAIN INTO ME, LIKE YOU WERE PLANNING TO DO WITH MOM?
NO. YOU WOULD BE INCOMPATIBLE.
ANNE, DON'T DO THIS. LET US TAKE HIM INTO CUSTODY. LET ME DO MY JOB.
YOU'VE SHOWN US ALL THAT YOU CAN KILL... NOW, SHOW ME THAT YOU CAN STOP.

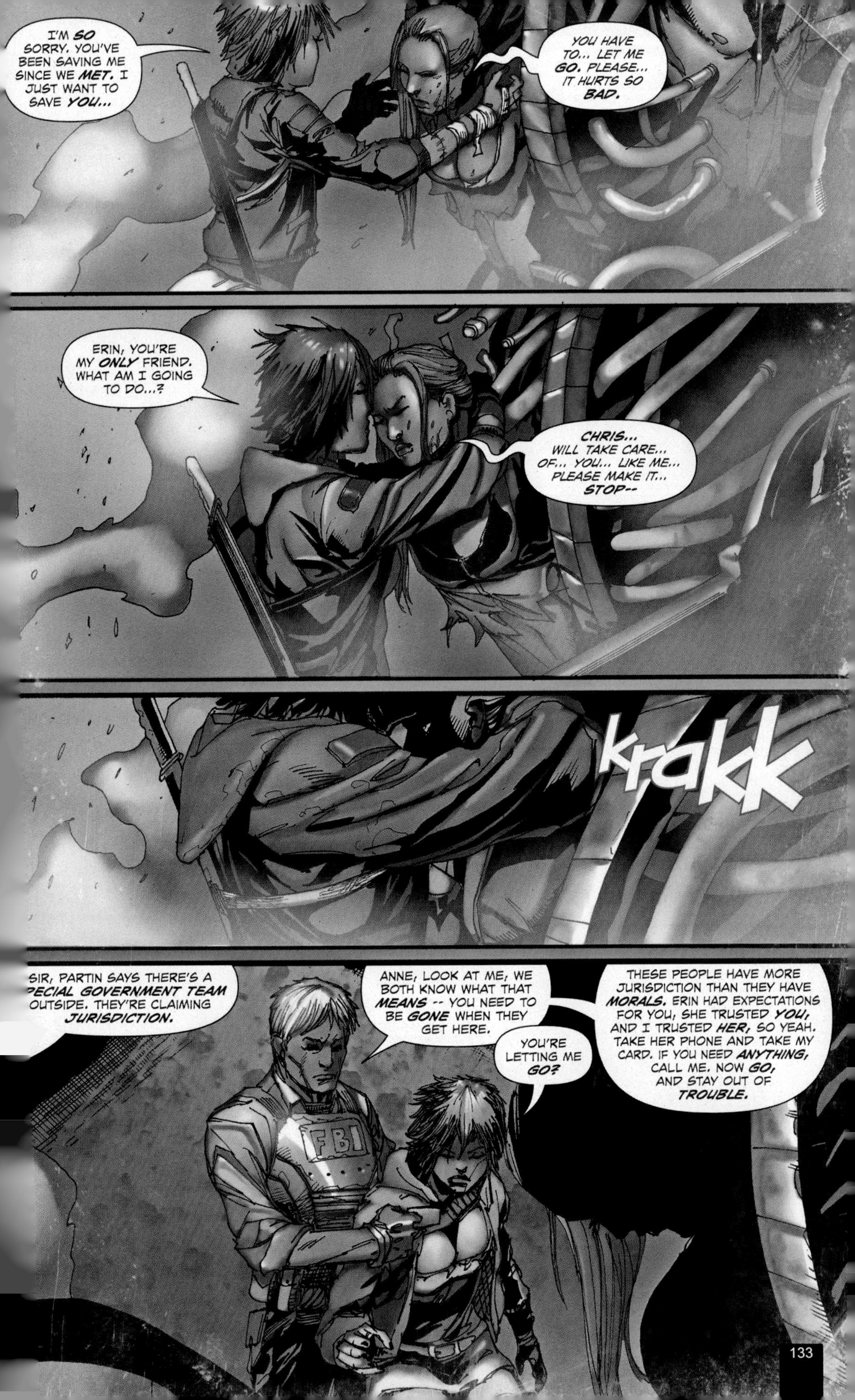
I'M SO SORRY. YOU'VE BEEN SAVING ME SINCE WE MET. I JUST WANT TO SAVE YOU...
YOU HAVE TO... LET ME GO. PLEASE... IT HURTS SO BAD.
ERIN, YOU'RE MY ONLY FRIEND. WHAT AM I GOING TO DO...?
CHRIS... WILL TAKE CARE... OF... YOU... LIKE ME... PLEASE MAKE IT... STOP--
krakk
SIR, PARTIN SAYS THERE'S A SPECIAL GOVERNMENT TEAM OUTSIDE. THEY'RE CLAIMING JURISDICTION.
ANNE, LOOK AT ME, WE BOTH KNOW WHAT THAT MEANS -- YOU NEED TO BE GONE WHEN THEY GET HERE.
YOU'RE LETTING ME GO?
THESE PEOPLE HAVE MORE JURISDICTION THAN THEY HAVE MORALS. ERIN HAD EXPECTATIONS FOR YOU, SHE TRUSTED YOU, AND I TRUSTED HER, SO YEAH. TAKE HER PHONE AND TAKE MY CARD. IF YOU NEED ANYTHING, CALL ME. NOW GO, AND STAY OUT OF TROUBLE.

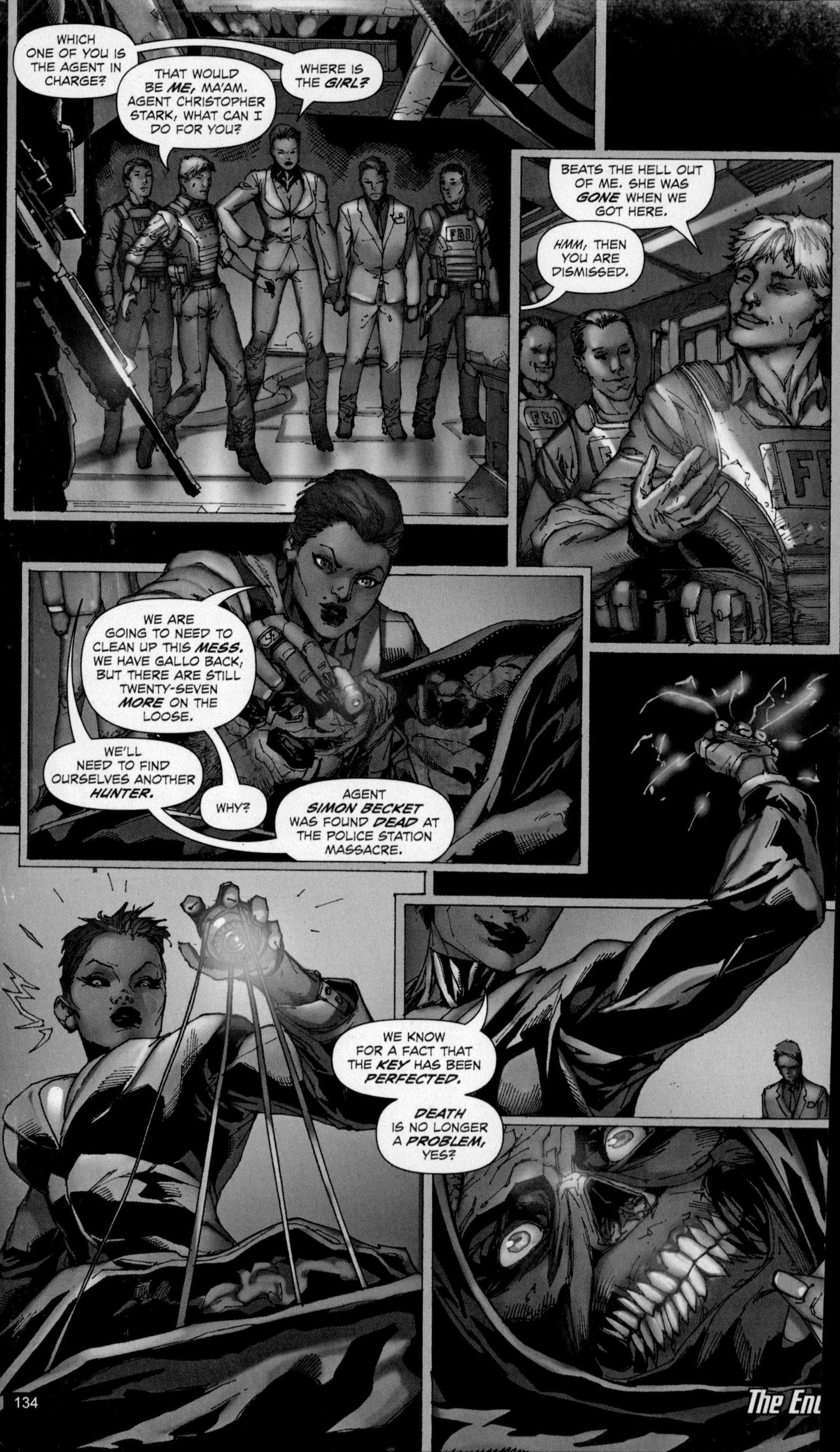

WHICH ONE OF YOU IS THE AGENT IN CHARGE?
THAT WOULD BE *ME,* MA'AM. AGENT CHRISTOPHER STARK, WHAT CAN I DO FOR YOU?
WHERE IS THE *GIRL?*
BEATS THE HELL OUT OF ME. SHE WAS *GONE* WHEN WE GOT HERE.
HMM, THEN YOU ARE DISMISSED.
WE ARE GOING TO NEED TO CLEAN UP THIS *MESS.* WE HAVE GALLO BACK, BUT THERE ARE STILL TWENTY-SEVEN *MORE* ON THE LOOSE.
WE'LL NEED TO FIND OURSELVES ANOTHER *HUNTER.*
WHY?
AGENT *SIMON BECKET* WAS FOUND *DEAD* AT THE POLICE STATION MASSACRE.
WE KNOW FOR A FACT THAT THE *KEY* HAS BEEN *PERFECTED.*
DEATH IS NO LONGER A *PROBLEM,* YES?
The En

SCREWED

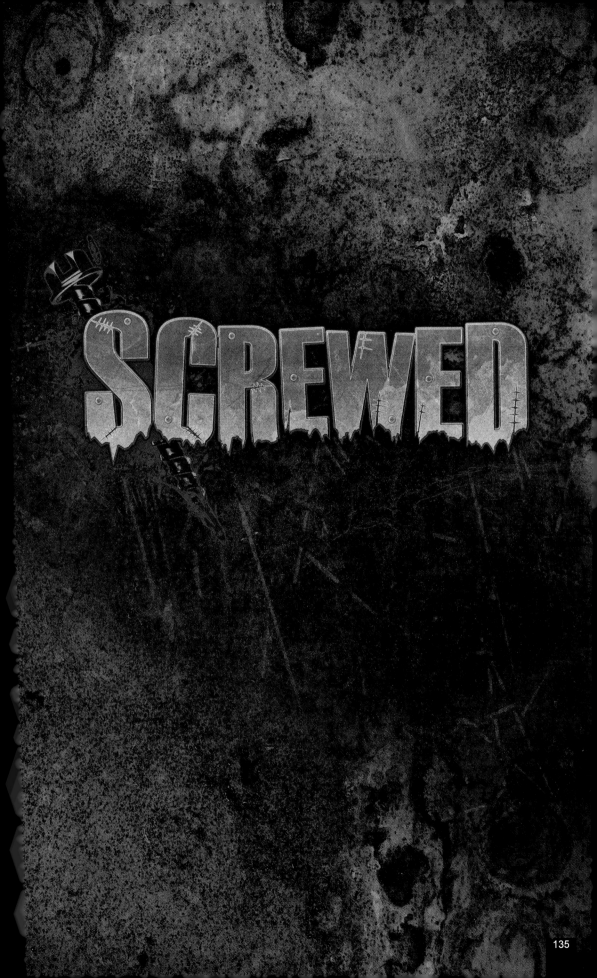

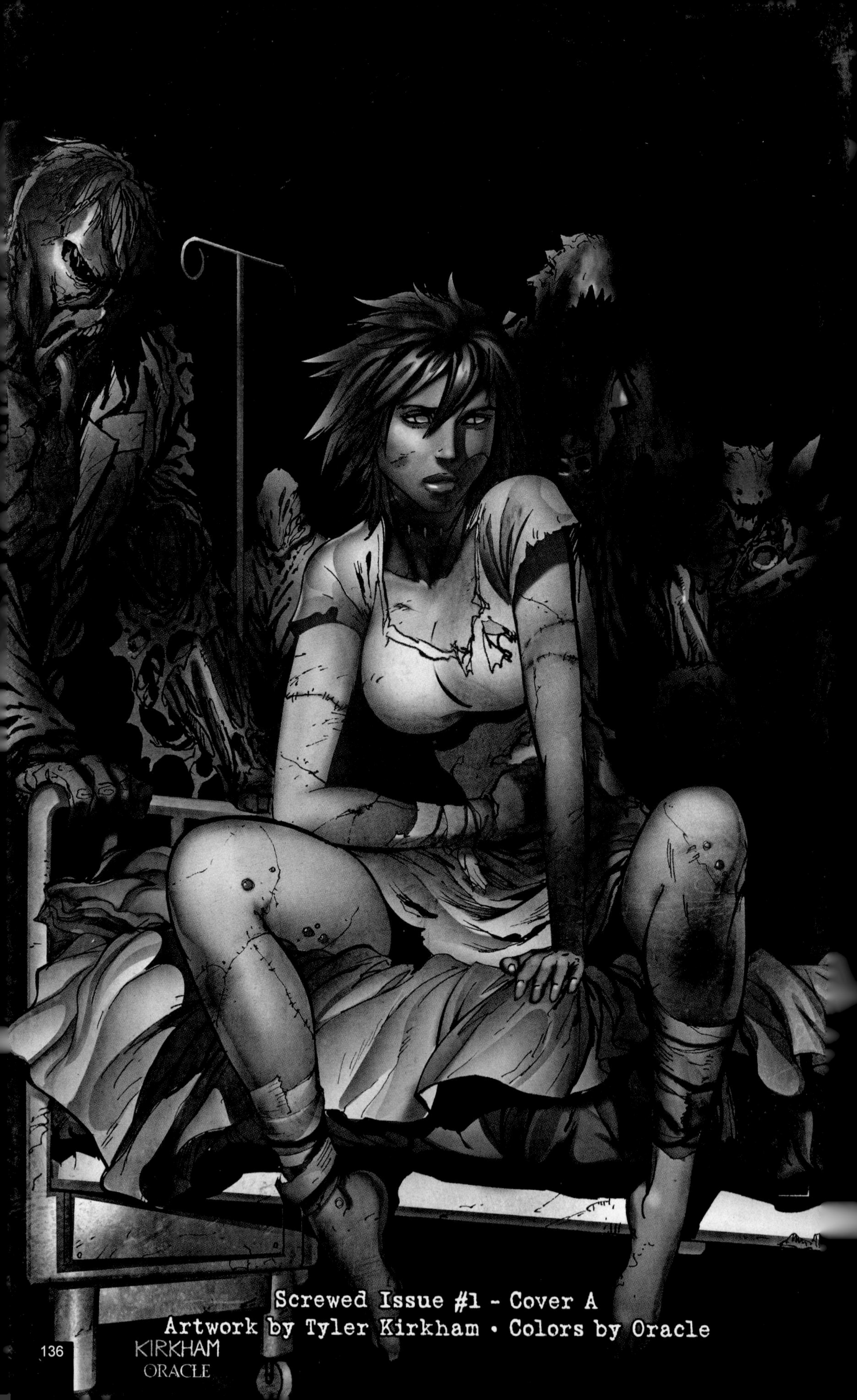
KIRKHAM
ORACLE

Screwed Issue #1 - Cover A
Artwork by Tyler Kirkham • Colors by Oracle

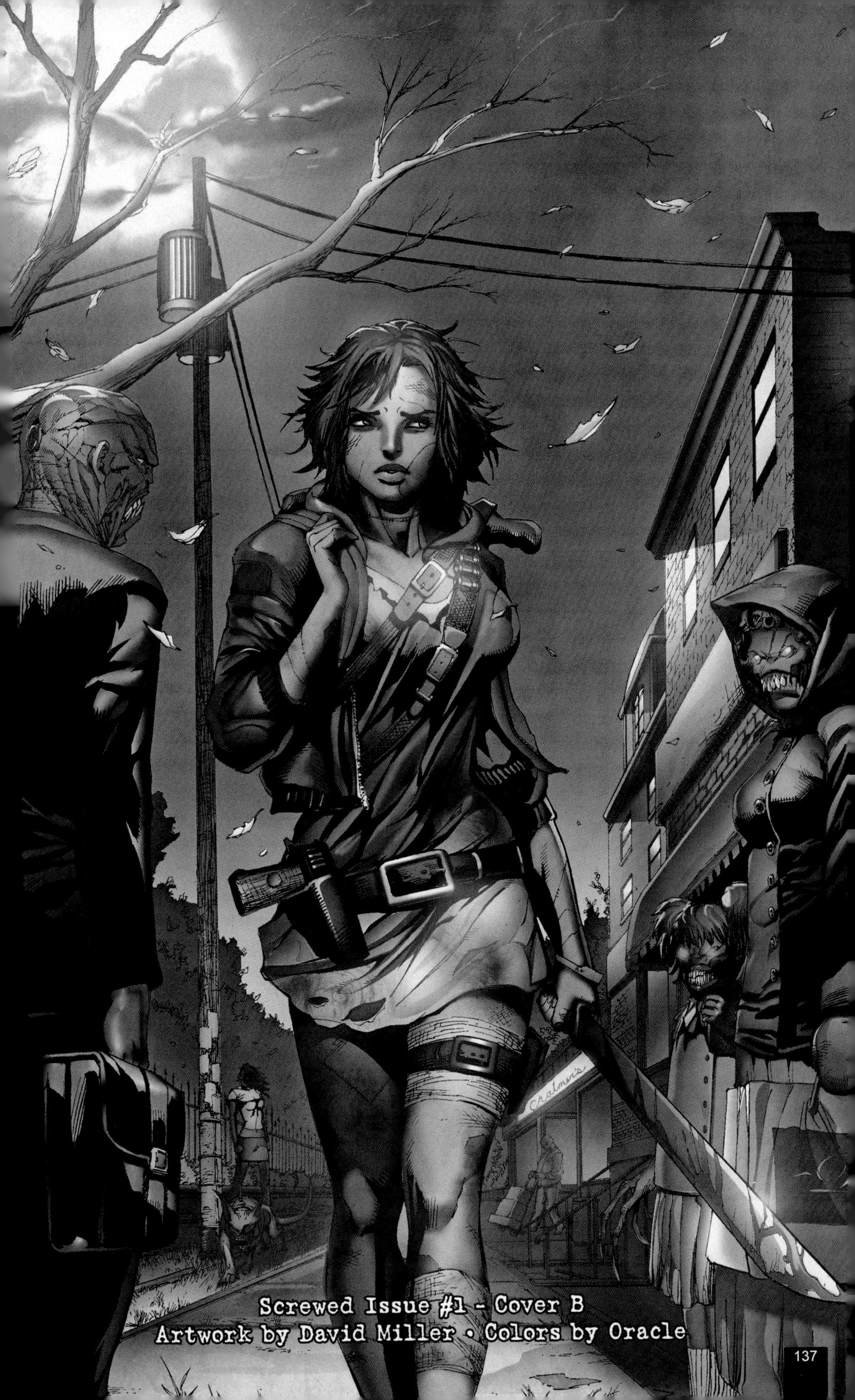

Screwed Issue #1 - Cover B
Artwork by David Miller • Colors by Oracle

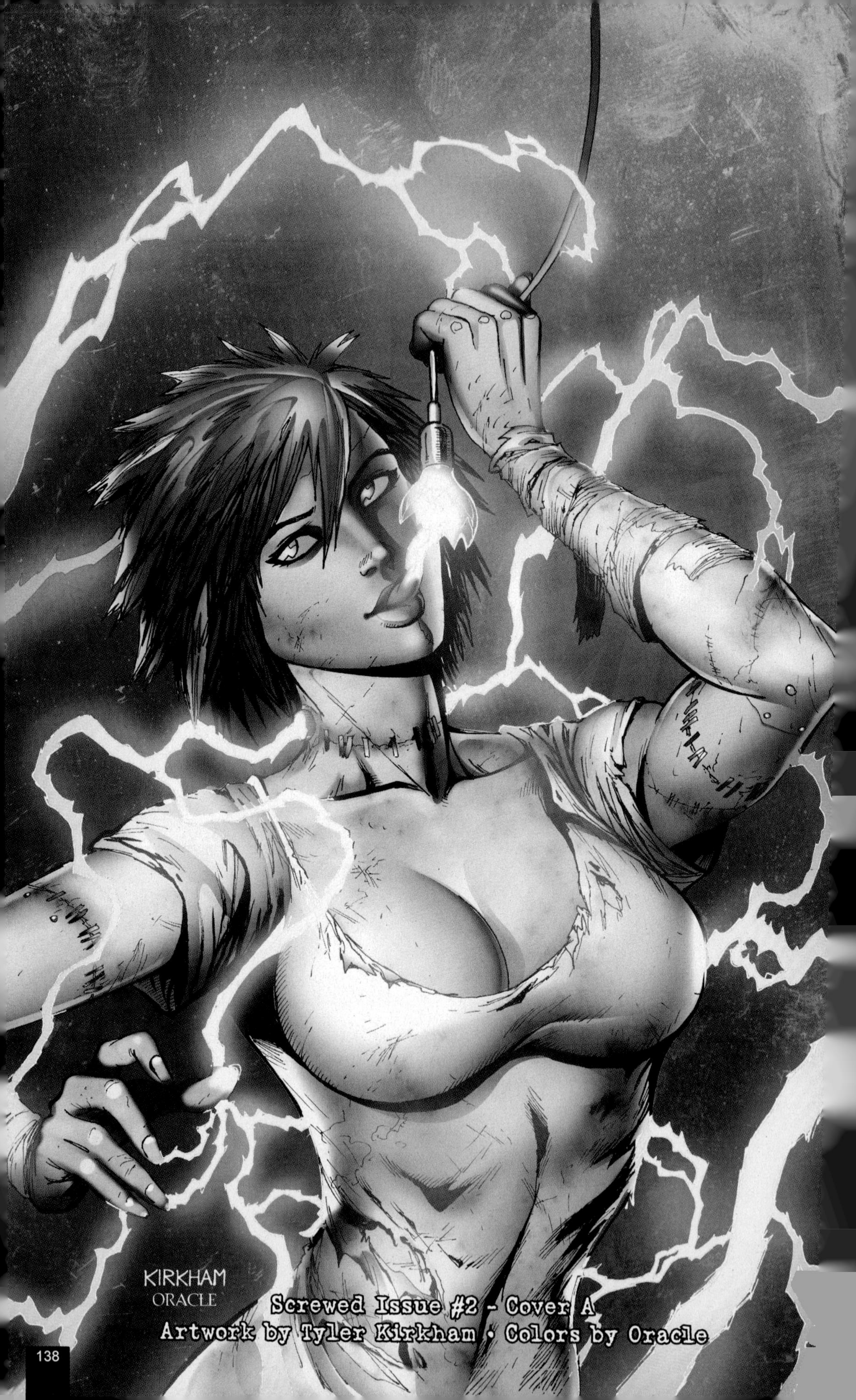
KIRKHAM
ORACLE

Screwed Issue #2 - Cover A
Artwork by Tyler Kirkham • Colors by Oracle

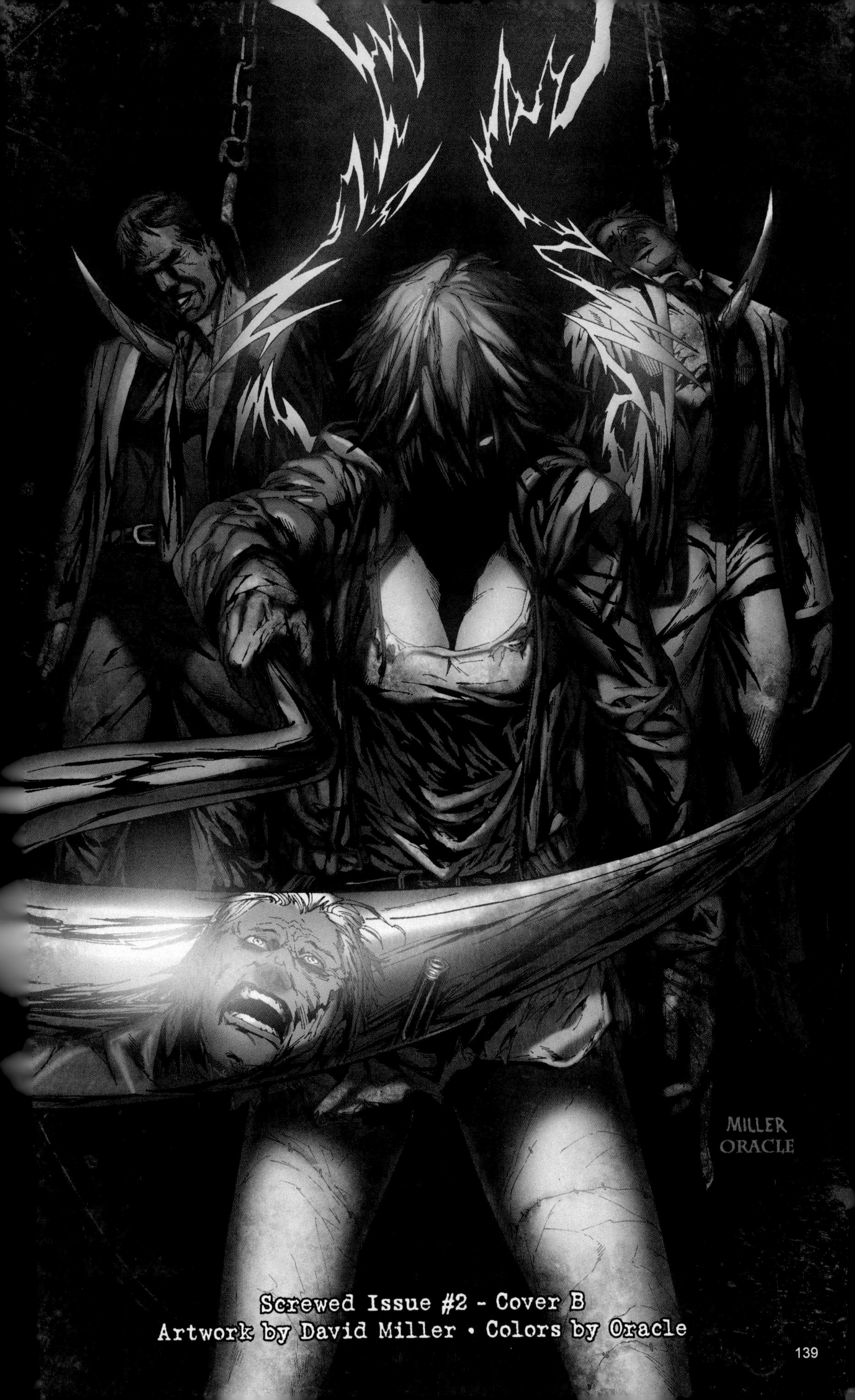
MILLER
ORACLE

Screwed Issue #2 - Cover B
Artwork by David Miller • Colors by Oracle

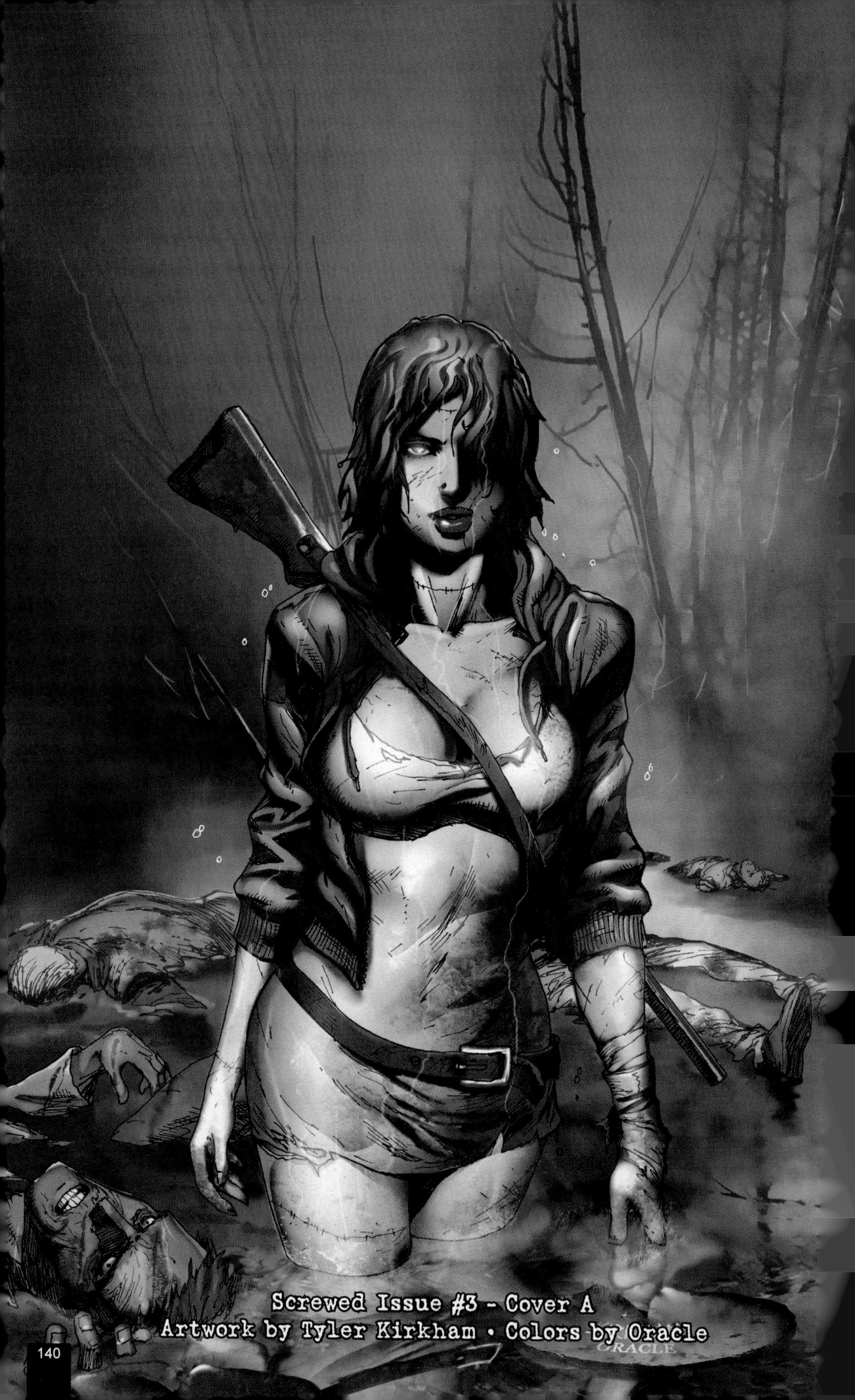
ORACLE

Screwed Issue #3 - Cover A
Artwork by Tyler Kirkham • Colors by Oracle

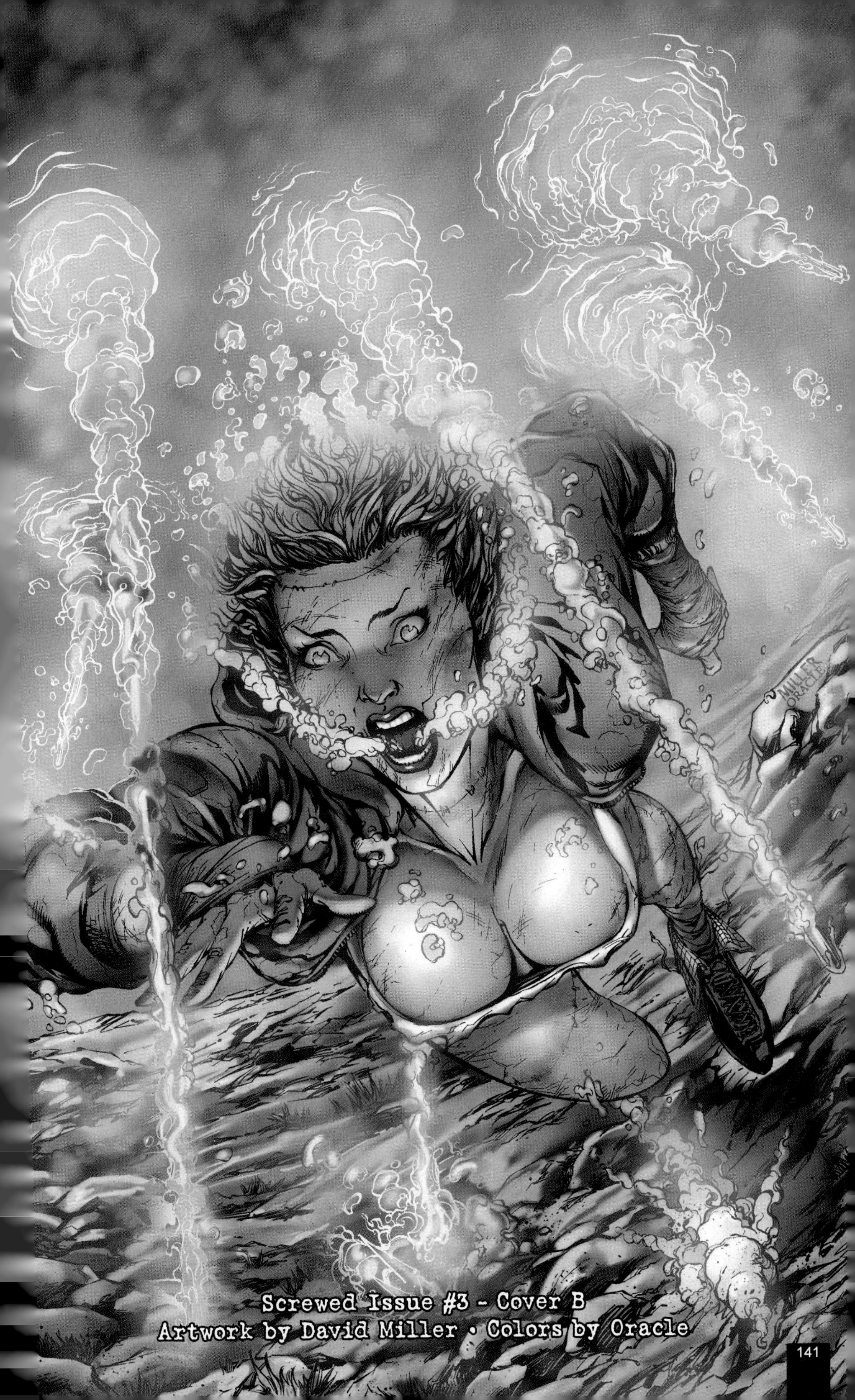
MILLER
ORACLE

Screwed Issue #3 - Cover B
Artwork by David Miller • Colors by Oracle

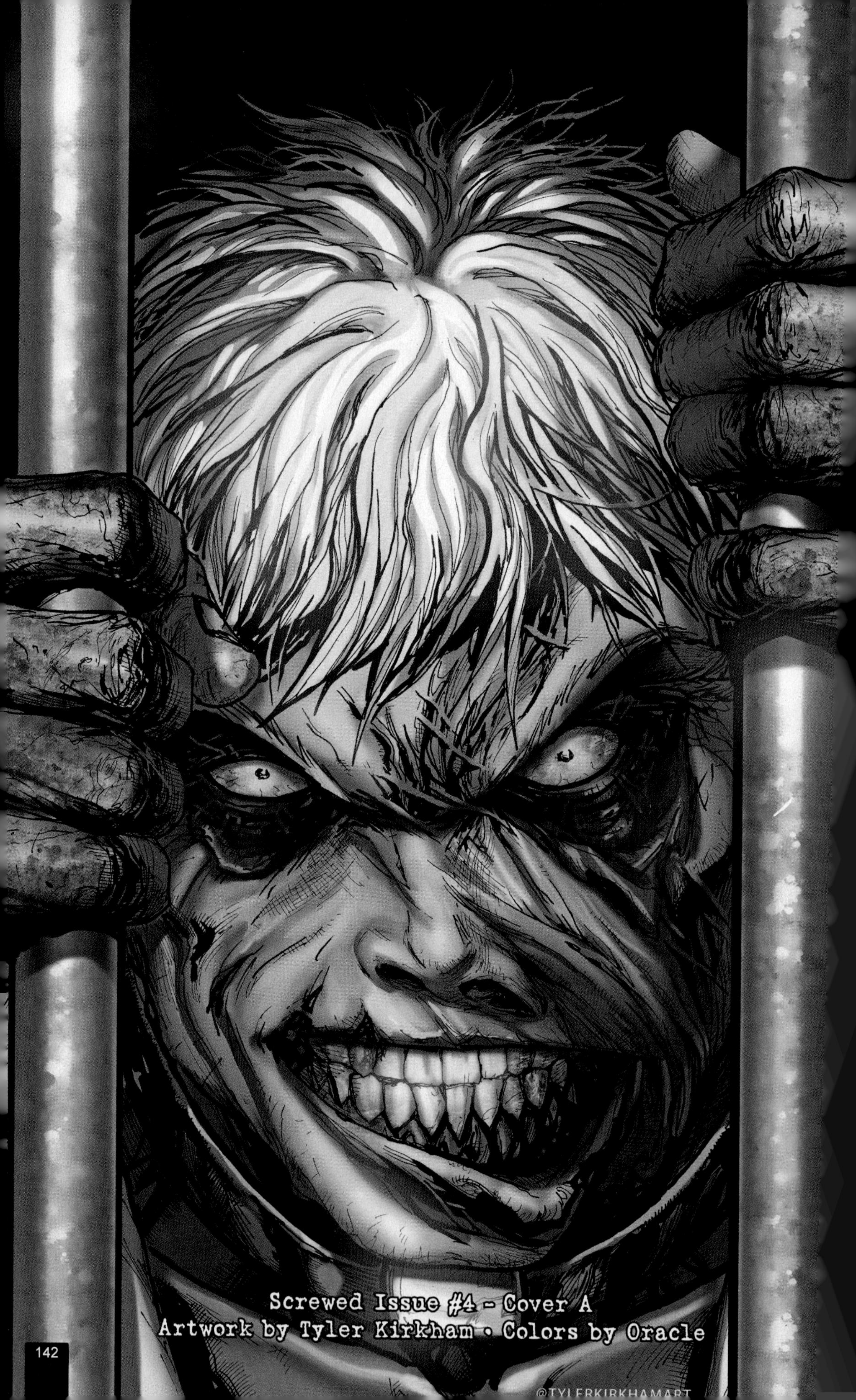

Screwed Issue #4 - Cover A
Artwork by Tyler Kirkham • Colors by Oracle

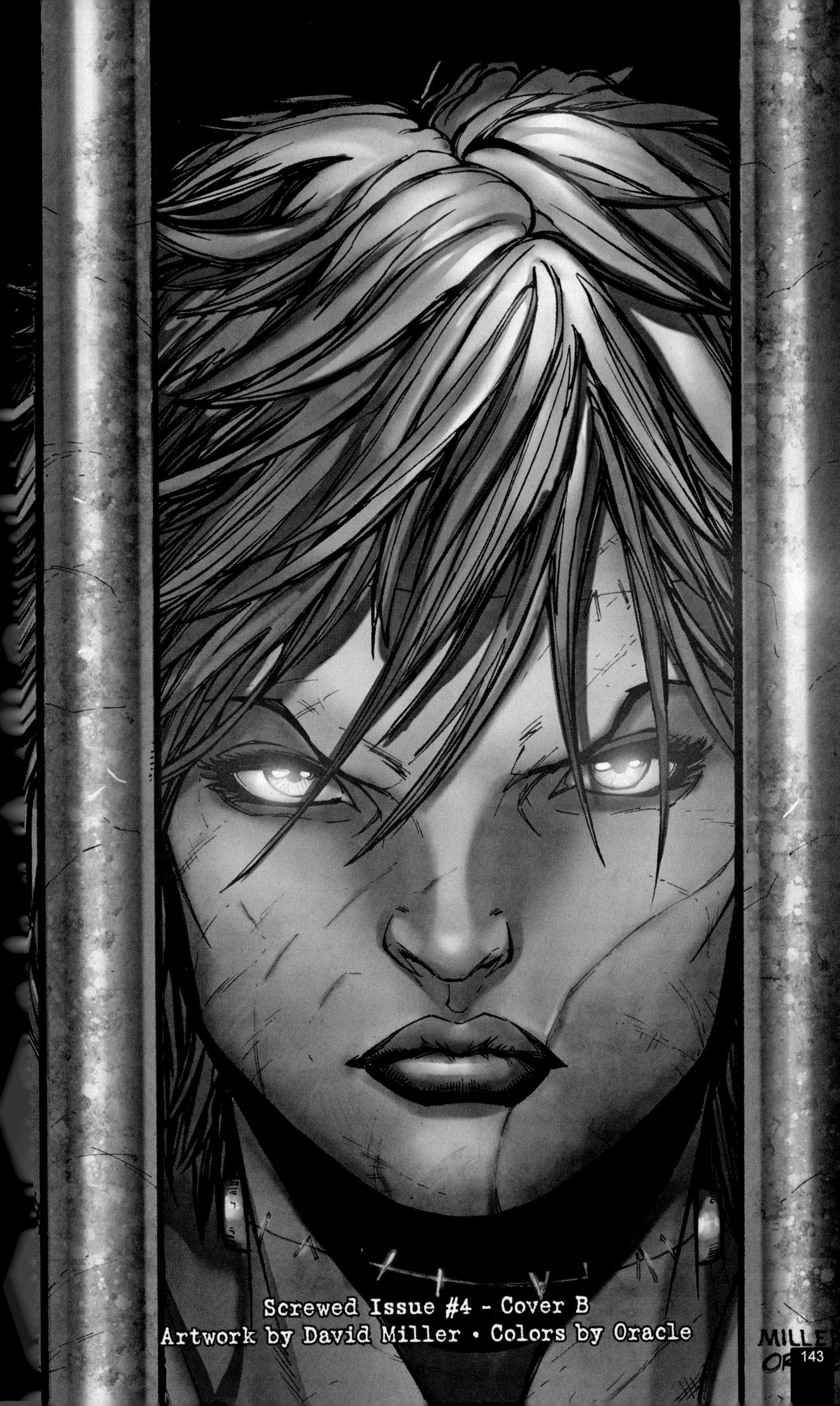
MILLER
Screwed Issue #4 - Cover B
Artwork by David Miller • Colors by Oracle

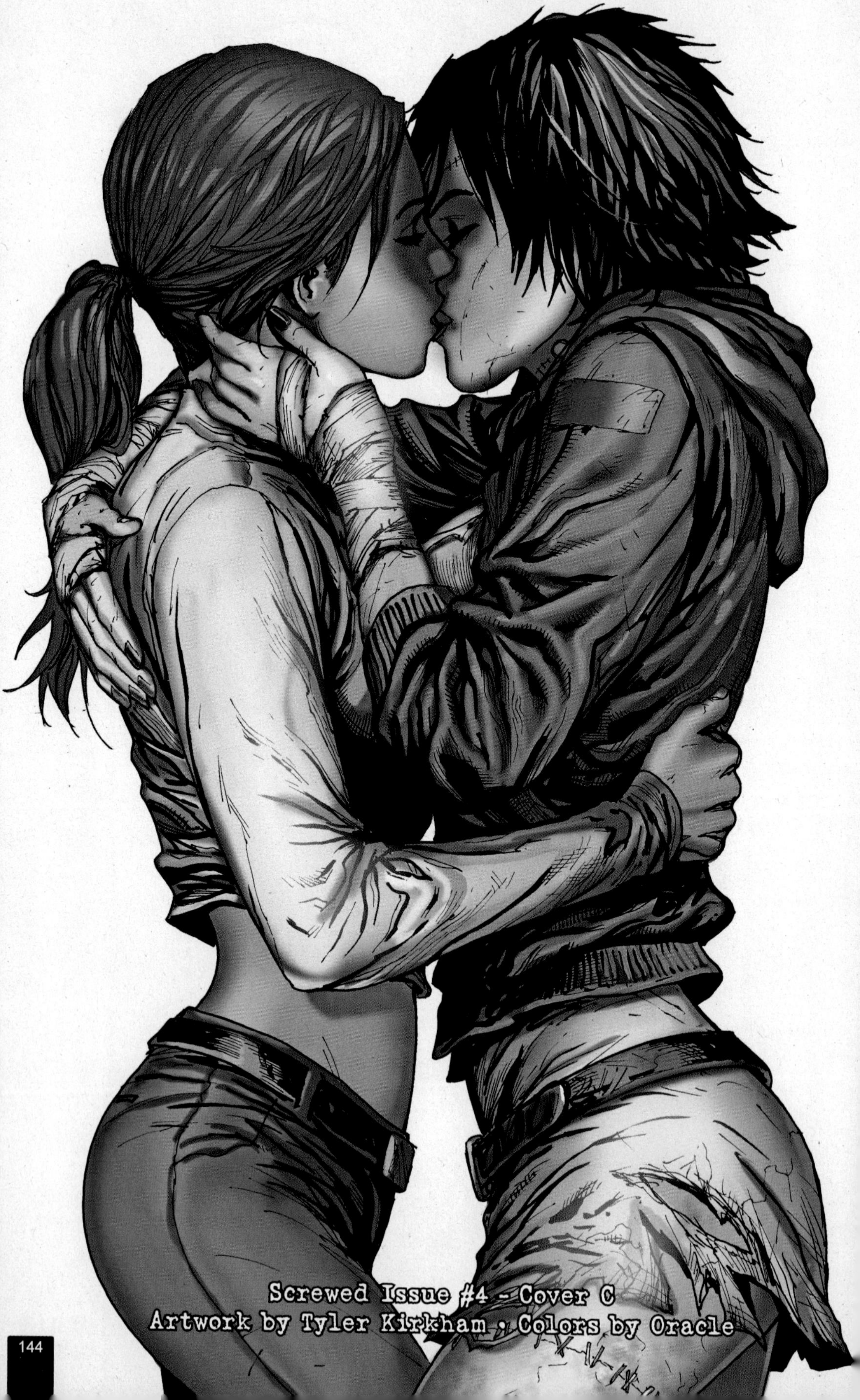

Screwed Issue #4 - Cover C
Artwork by Tyler Kirkham - Colors by Oracle

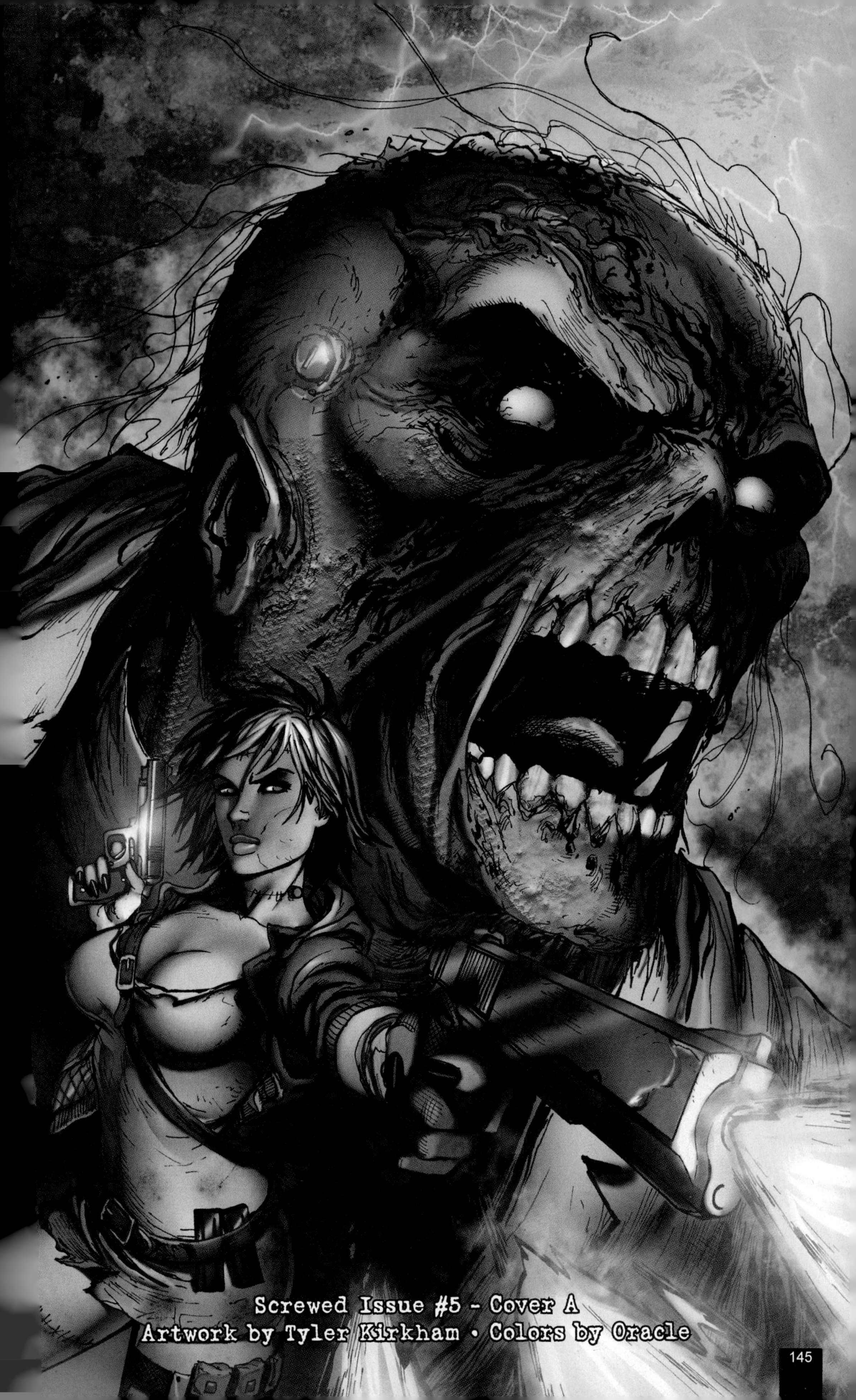

Screwed Issue #5 - Cover A
Artwork by Tyler Kirkham • Colors by Oracle

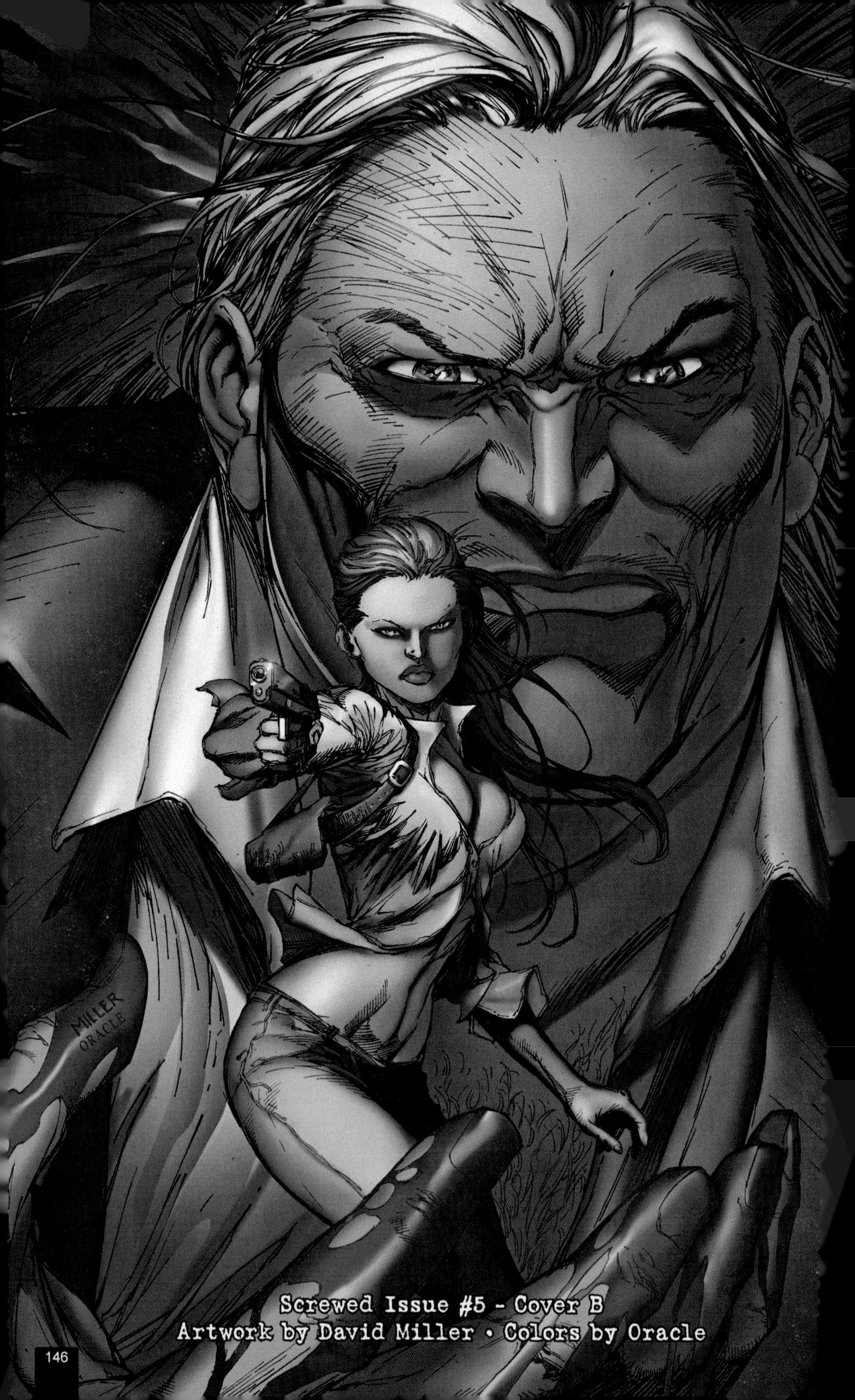
MILLER
ORACLE

Screwed Issue #5 - Cover B
Artwork by David Miller • Colors by Oracle

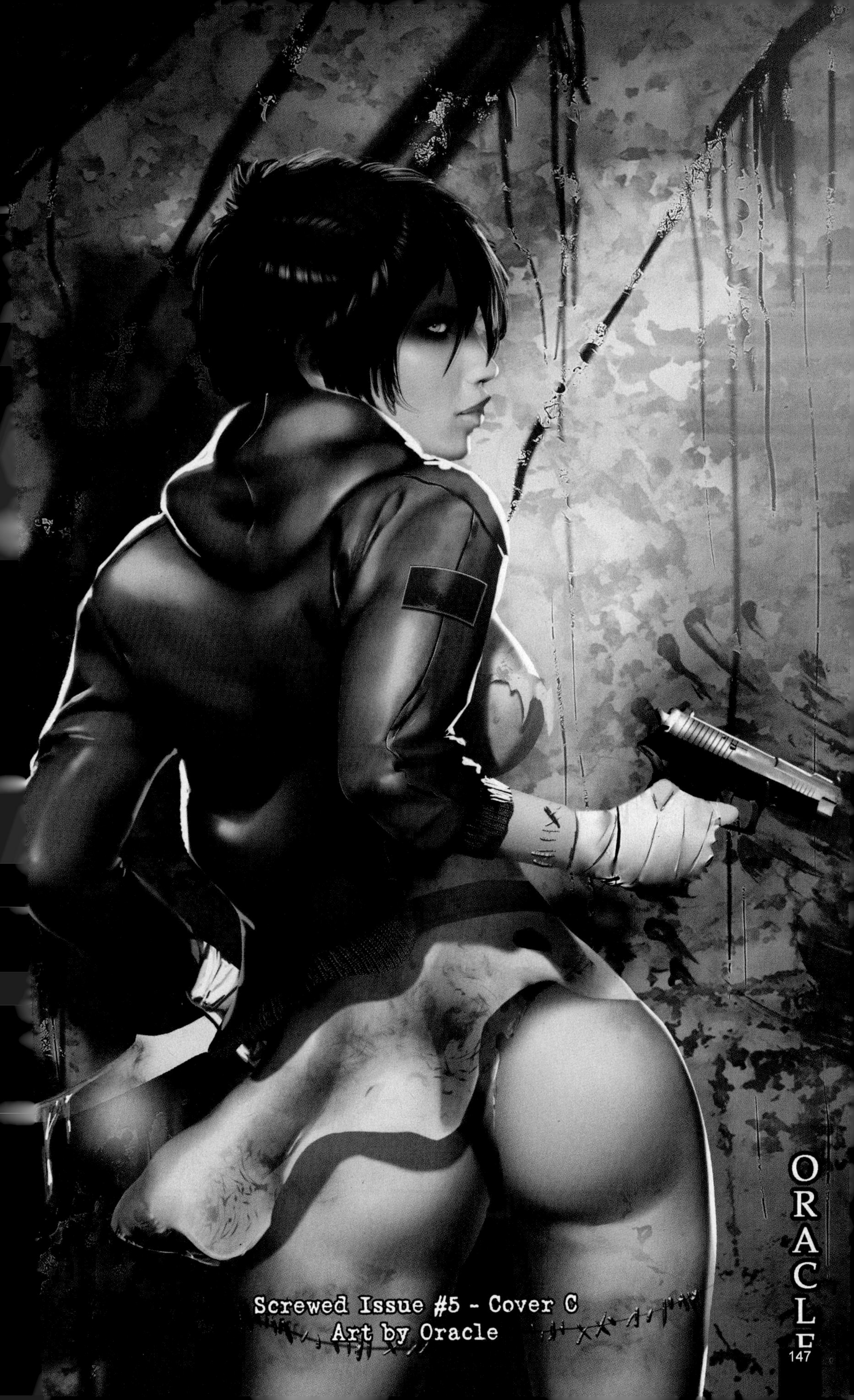
ORACLE

Screwed Issue #5 - Cover C
Art by Oracle

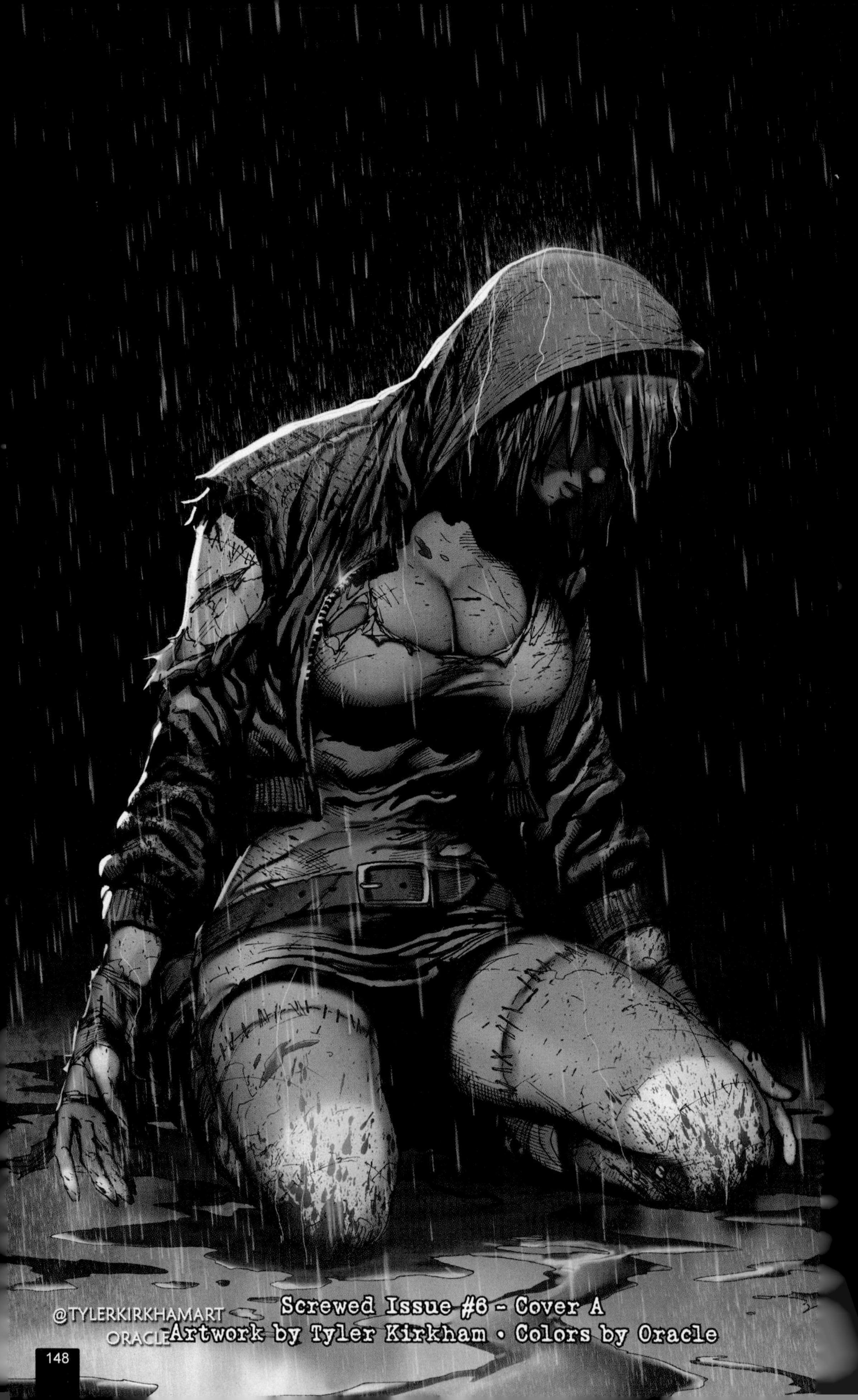
@TYLERKIRKHAMART
ORACLE

Screwed Issue #6 - Cover A
Artwork by Tyler Kirkham • Colors by Oracle

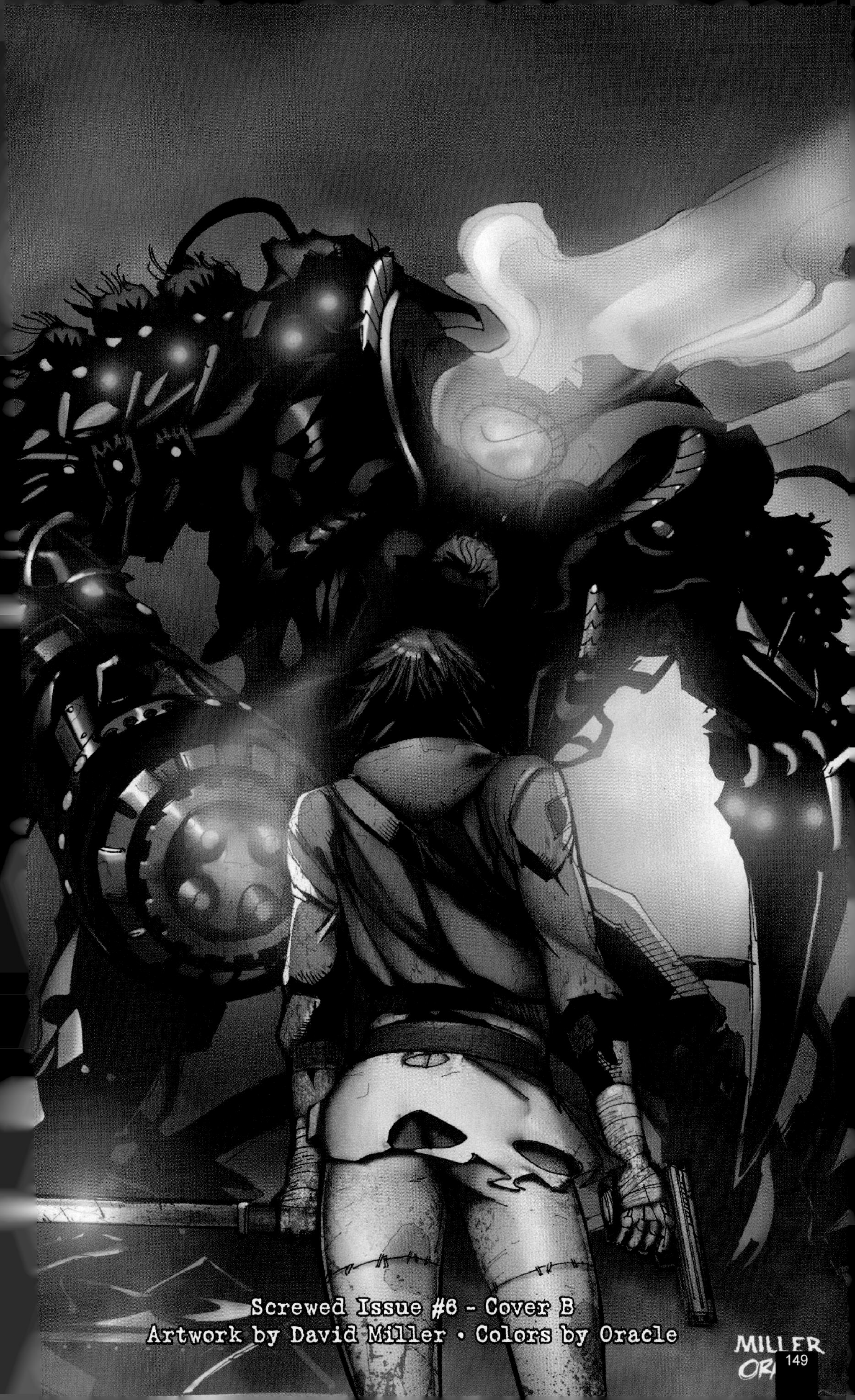
MILLER

Screwed Issue #6 - Cover B
Artwork by David Miller • Colors by Oracle

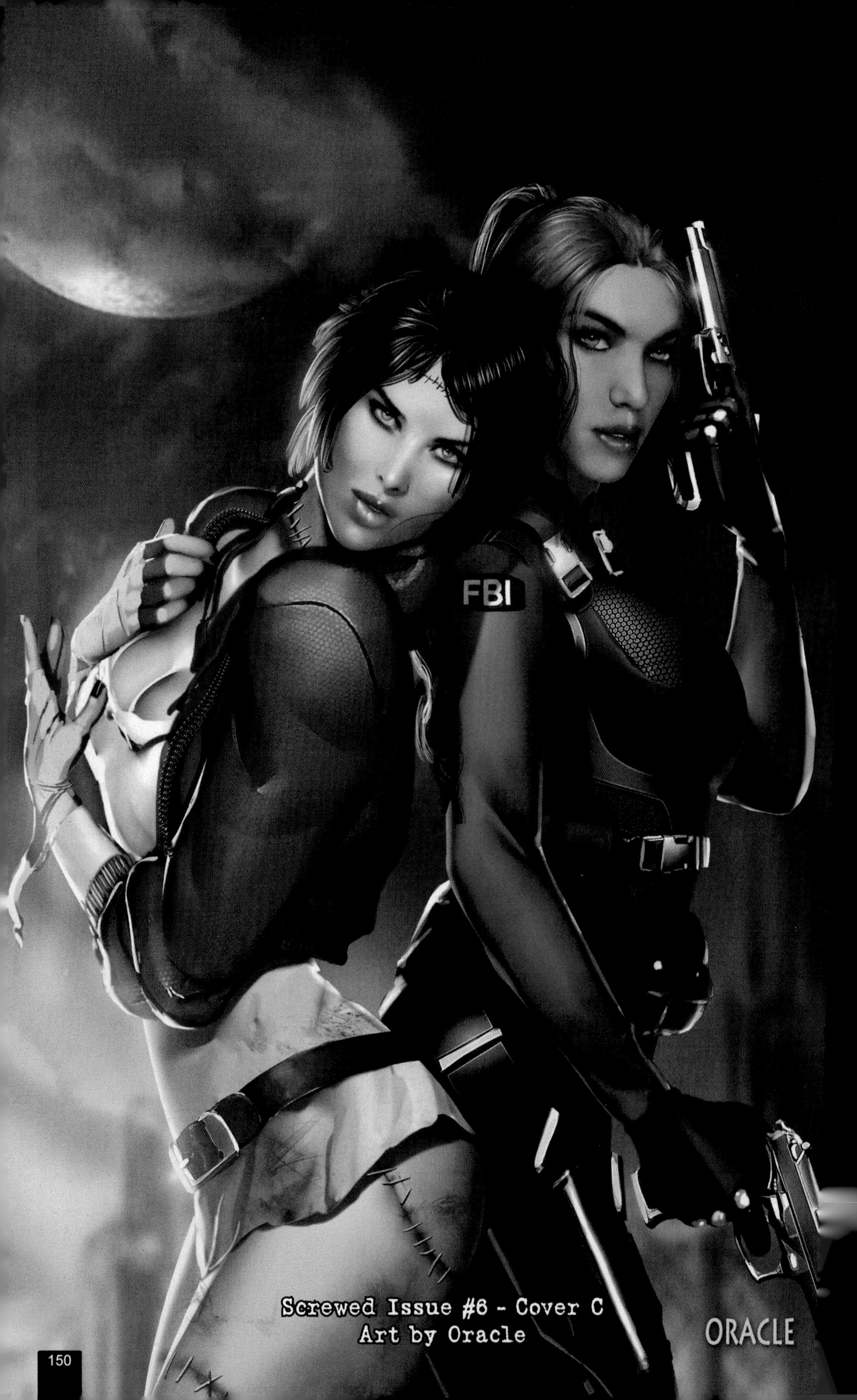
FBI
ORACLE

Screwed Issue #6 - Cover C
Art by Oracle

SCREWED

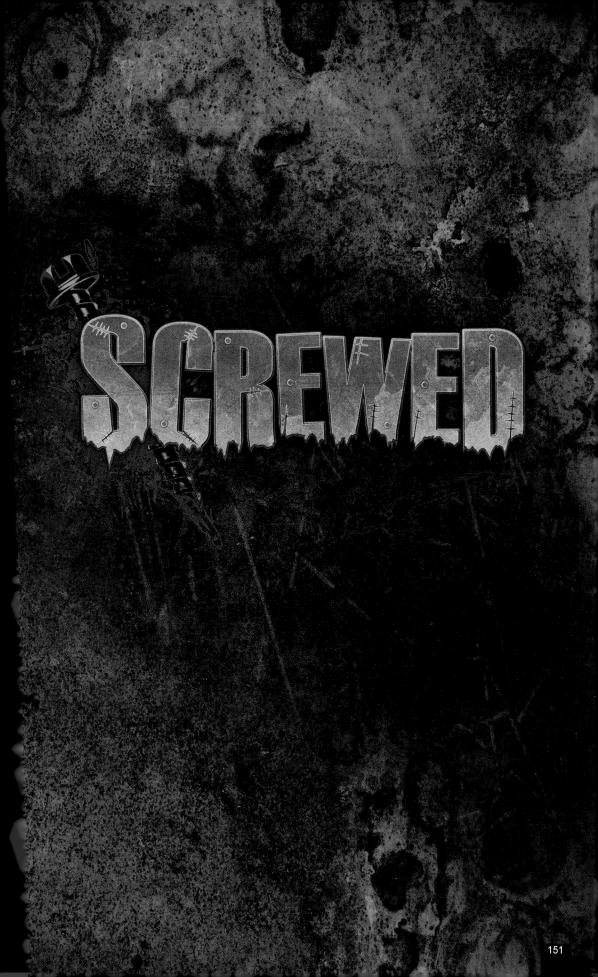

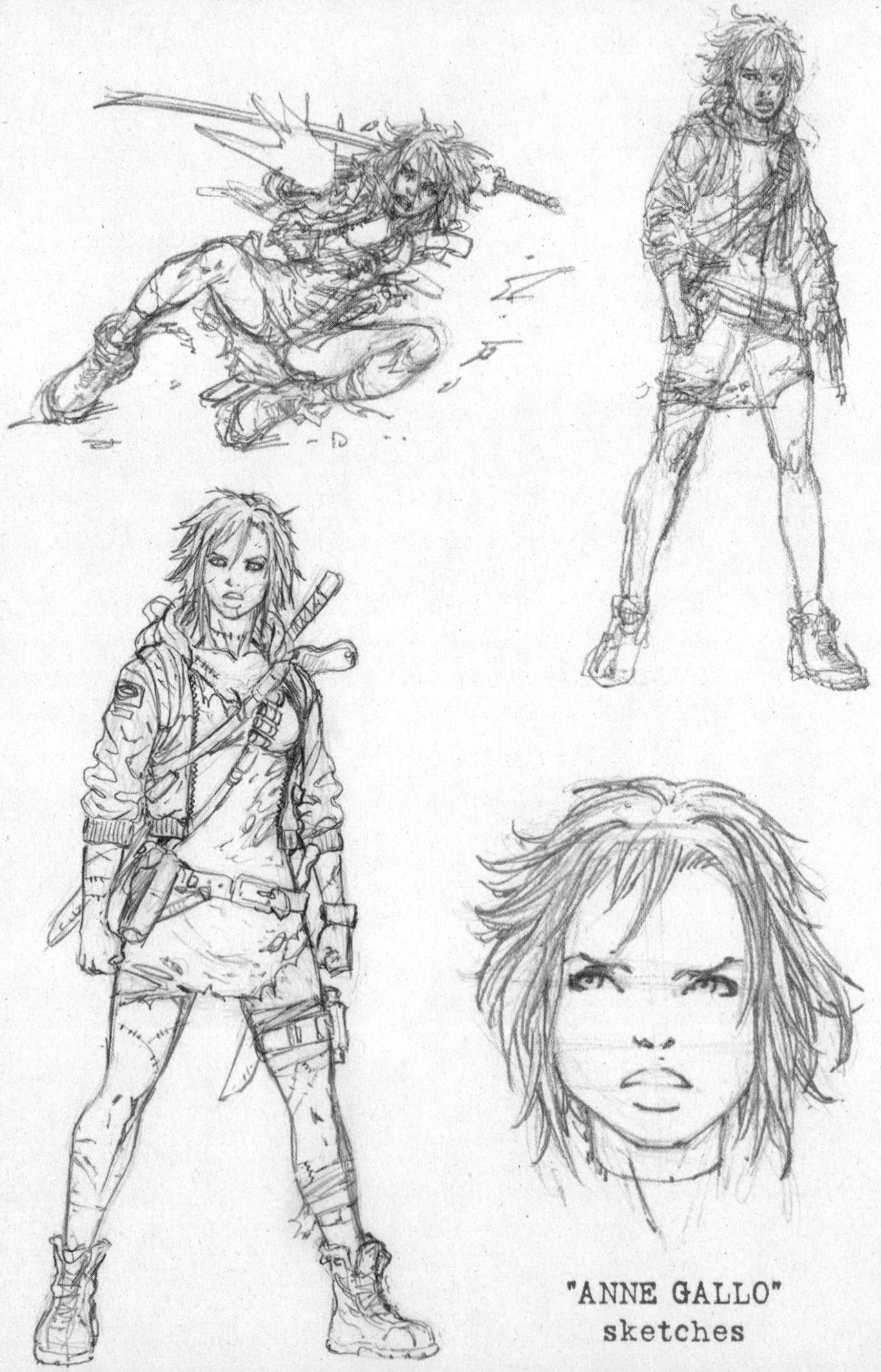

"ANNE GALLO"
sketches

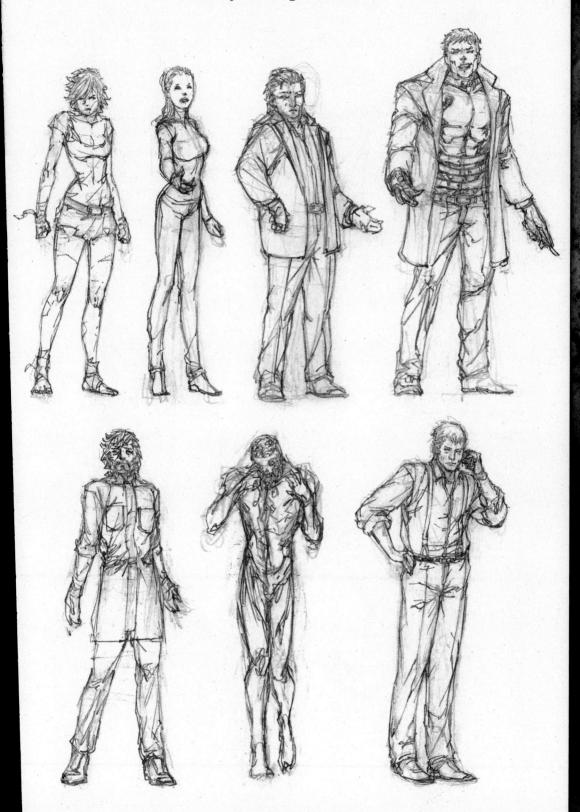

SCREWED
Cast of Characters

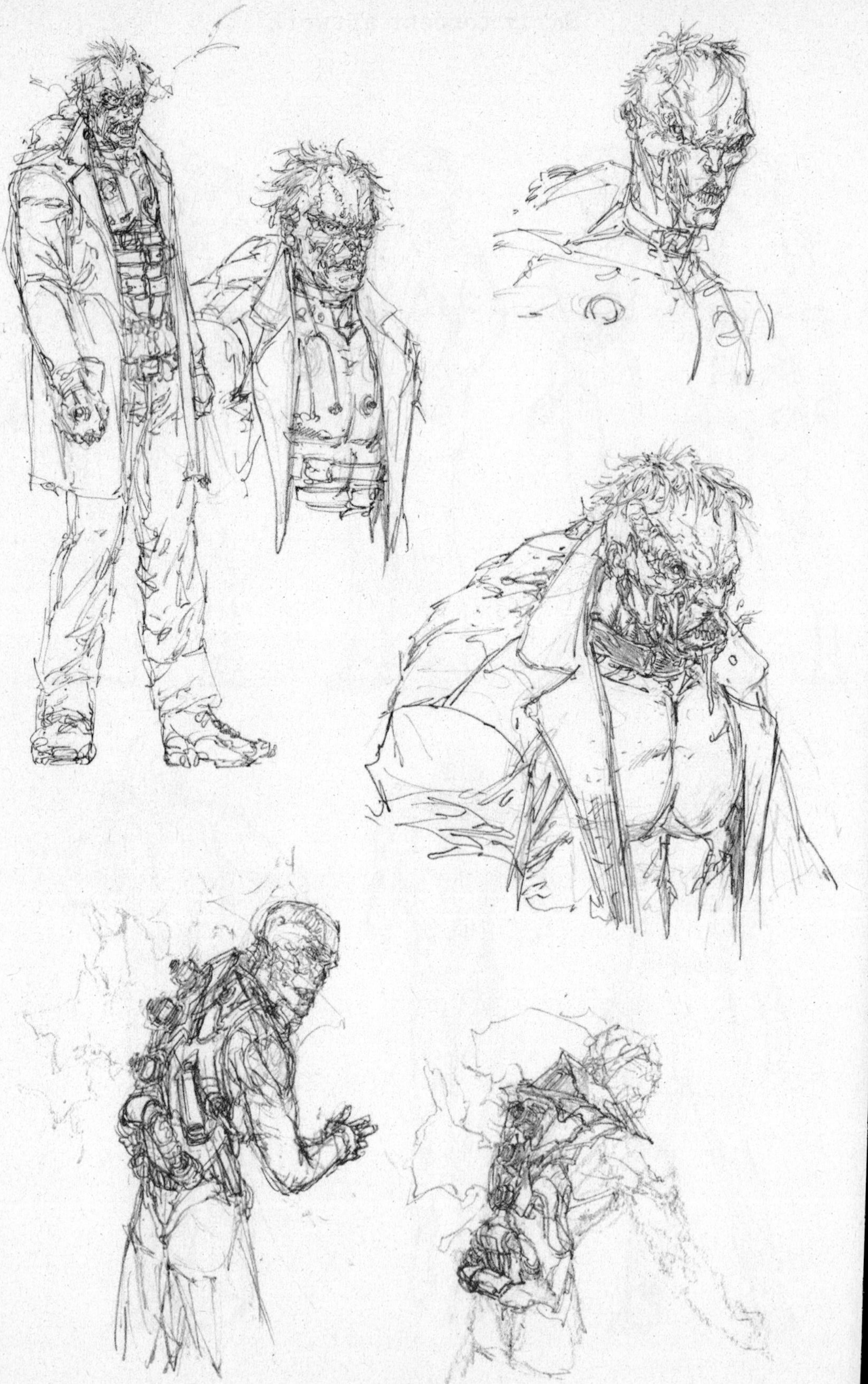

"SUTURE"
concept sketches

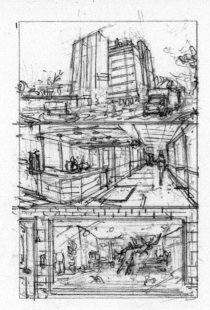

Pencil layouts for
SCREWED Issue #1

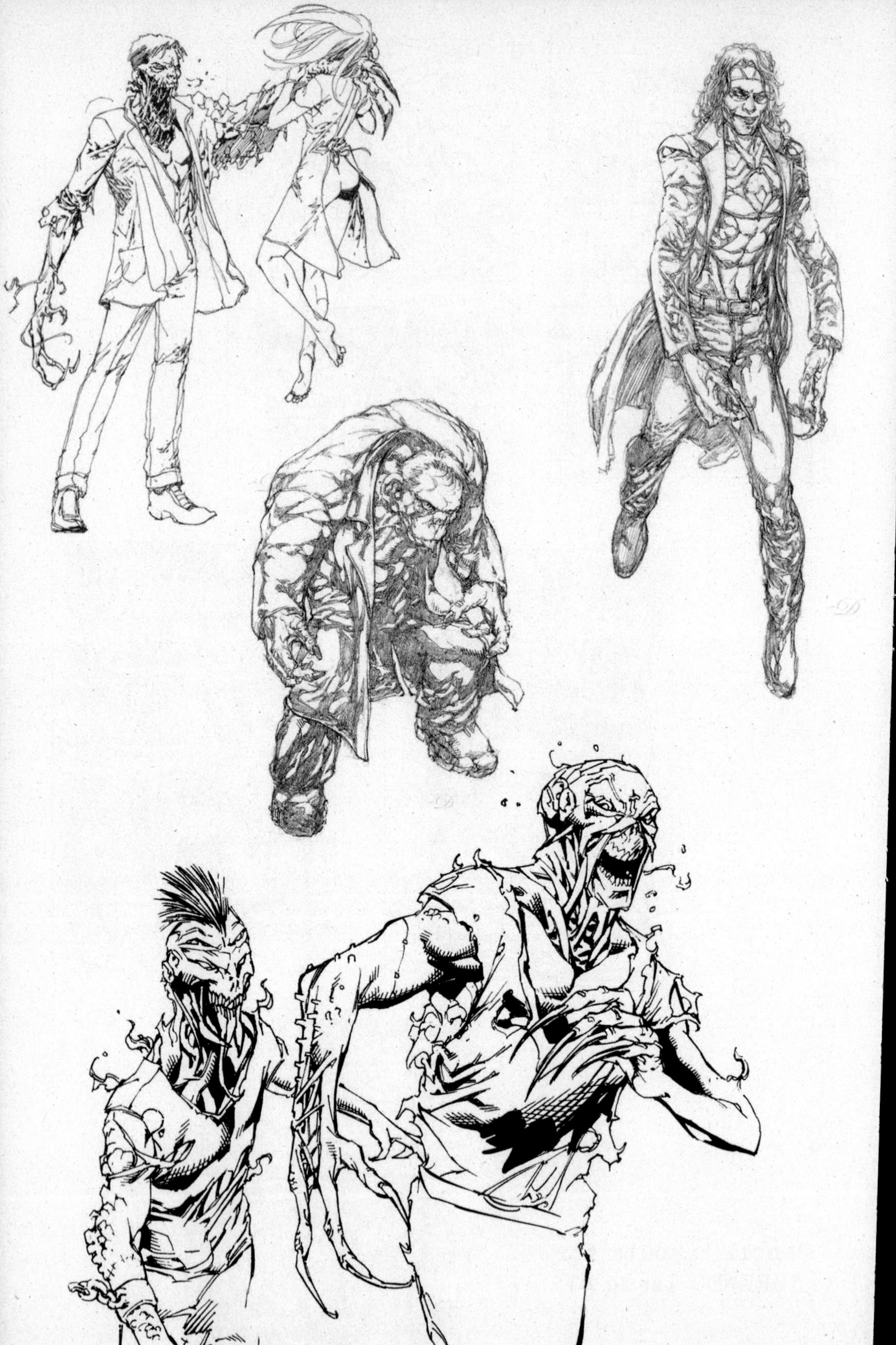

Villain sketches

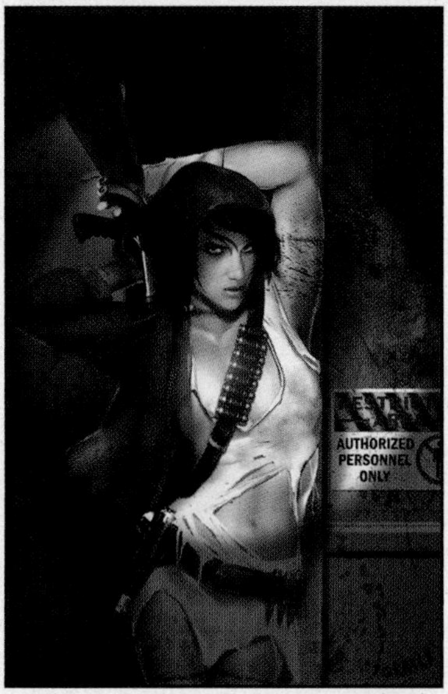
AUTHORIZED
PERSONNEL
ONLY

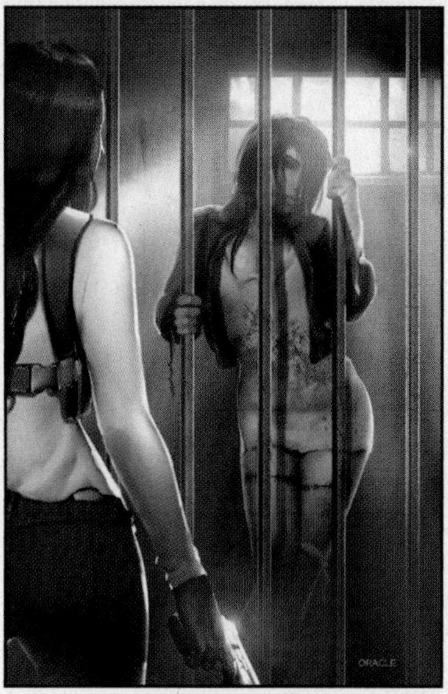
ORACLE

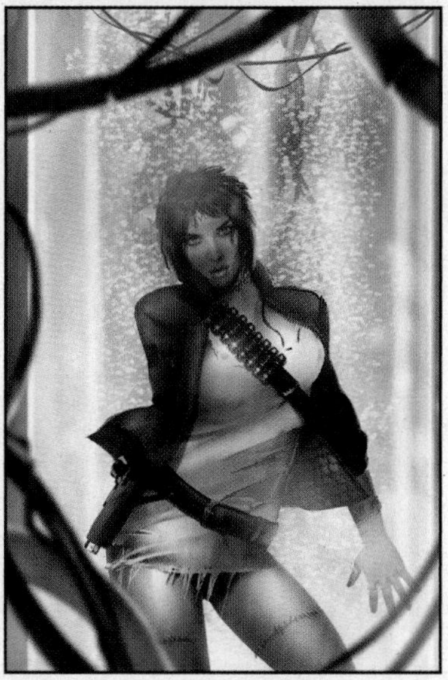

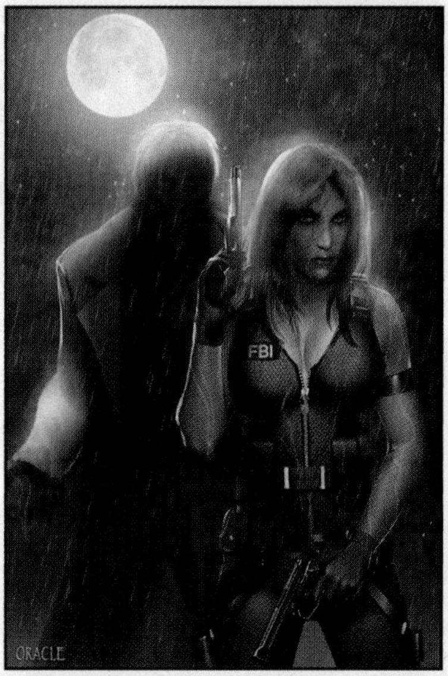
FBI
ORACLE

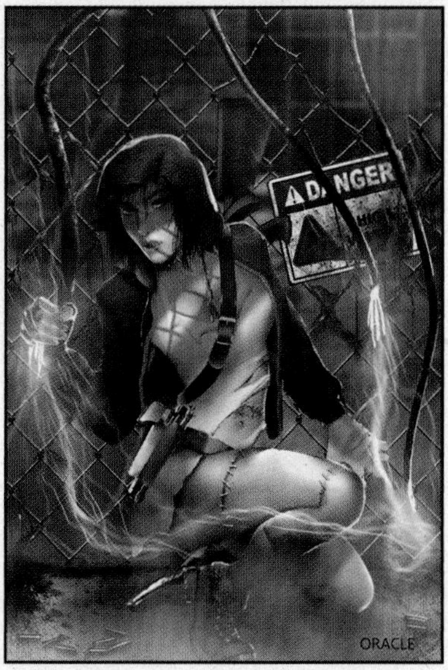
DANGER
ORACLE

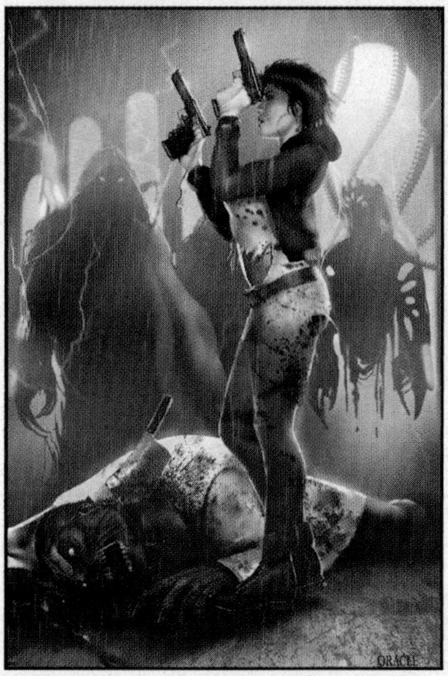
ORACLE

Unused cover designs by series colorist Oracle

SCREWED

PROJECT FRANKENSTEIN

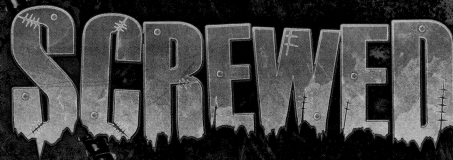